C0-APC-522

Isaiah and the Twelve

Beihefte zur Zeitschrift für die alttestamentliche Wissenschaft

Edited by
John Barton, Reinhard G. Kratz, Nathan MacDonald,
Sara Milstein, and Markus Witte

Volume 527

Richard J. Bautch, Joachim Eck,
Burkard M. Zapff (eds.)

Isaiah
and the Twelve

Parallels, Similarities and Differences

GRADUATE THEOLOGICAL UNION LIBRARY 1962

DE GRUYTER

BS
1116
Z37
V.527

G

ISBN 978-3-11-070573-7
e-ISBN (PDF) 978-3-11-070579-9
e-ISBN (EPUB) 978-3-11-070588-1
ISSN 0934-2575

Library of Congress Control Number: 2020939267

Bibliografische Information der Deutschen Nationalbibliothek
The Deutsche Nationalbibliothek lists this publication in the Deutsche Nationalbibliografie;
detailed bibliografic data are available on the Internet at http://dnb.dnb.de.

© 2020 Walter de Gruyter GmbH, Berlin/Boston
Typesetting: Dörlemann Satz, Lemförde
Printing and binding: CPI books GmbH, Leck

www.degruyter.com

MIX
Papier aus verantwor-
tungsvollen Quellen
FSC
www.fsc.org   FSC® C083411

b17793208

Contents

Introduction

Theological research has repeatedly noted similarities and intersections between the book of the prophet Isaiah and specific passages of Scripture within the Book of the Twelve (the Twelve Minor Prophets), or the Book as a whole. The various attempts to explain these parallels culminated – for the time being – in the suggestion by Odil-Hannes Steck and his student Erich Bosshard-Nepustil that interrelated theological circles carried out one or multiple revisions to Isaiah and the Book of the Twelve, or to particular parts of the same, with the aim of making these corpora more closely analogous in their structure and content. From 31 May to 3 June 2018 and sponsored by the Deutsche Forschungsgemeinschaft (DFG), an international conference held at the Catholic University of Eichstätt-Ingolstadt considered, first, whether particular writings within the Book of the Twelve, or the complete corpus, do indeed share features with Isaiah or parts of it, and second, if this is the case, how we might describe and seek to explain these commonalities. A previous event, held in November 2016 at St. Edward's University (the Catholic University in Austin, Texas), had explored 'Voices of Israel – Isaiah and Micah: Intersections in Judean Prophecy during the Eighth Century BCE' in the context of the relationship between Isaiah and Micah.[1] The conference in Eichstätt sought to expand this specific focus to include the entire Book of the Twelve. Its organisers, in bringing together eminent experts on these Biblical writings from Germany and around the world, hoped to initiate methodological dialogue, countering the tendency occasionally witnessed among Old Testament scholars to talk about one another rather than to one another and providing optimum conditions for illuminating the process of growth and theological depth of the scriptures under study.

Exegesis should not be an end unto itself, but should rather serve to inspire and vivify the way the Church views itself and the life it leads. That life energizes the practice of exegesis and raises new questions to explore, opening up paths to a fresh understanding of Biblical texts. This tenet shines forth clearly in this volume's concluding essay by His Excellency Bishop Rudolph Voderholzer, a specialist in Biblical hermeneutics whose work takes a systematic approach to the subject. Since his *Festvortrag* reflects upon and responds to our exegetical work during our time together, he receives the last word in this volume. We are pro-

---

1 The published main papers of this conference are: Burkard Maria Zapff, "Why is Micah similar to Isaiah?" *ZAW* 129 (2017): 536–554; Richard J. Bautch, "In Vino Veritas? Critiquing Drunkenness and Deceit in Micah and Isaiah," *ZAW* 129 (2017): 555–567; Joachim Eck, "Divine Strategies against Abuse of Power in the Opening of the Book of Isaiah and the Exodus Story. Some Aspects where Micah is not Similar to Isaiah," *ZAW* 130 (2018): 4–25; Todd Hibbard, "To Err is Human, Unless You're a Prophet: Isaiah and Micah on Prophetic Opposition," *ZAW* 130 (2018): 26–39.

https://doi.org/10.1515/9783110705799-001

foundly grateful to him for having taken the time out of his demanding schedule as a diocesan bishop to attend our conference and help build a bridge between exegesis and systematic theology.

In this volume, the chapters progress in line with the two central questions outlined above. In parts one and two, the authors examine the interrelationships between Isaiah and specific writings from the Book of the Twelve. The order of these chapters is chronological, beginning with writings attributed to prophets of the eighth century BCE and their connections to Isaiah, particularly its opening part, and proceeding to texts – or groups of texts – from both corpora which probably date from the period of the exile or thereafter. Along with identifying and seeking to validate similarities and parallels between the various writings, the chapters examine the history of their redaction and revision. After establishing whether a relationship of any kind exists, our authors aim to find potential explanations for their findings, an endeavour in which they apply a range of recent insights on the hermeneutics of the Prophets.

In the volume's opening chapter, **Franz Sedlmeier** takes on the relatively neglected issue of the relationship between Isaiah and the book of Hosea. His findings present a nuanced picture. The indications are that the historical figure of Hosea is unlikely to relate directly to that of Isaiah. Further, the occasionally occurring common themes and the conspicuous parallels between the headings found in Isaiah and in Hosea in terms of the chronology of the prophets' public activity appear to be attributable to later revisions, at least some of which require interpretation in the context of Hosea's incorporation into the Book of the Twelve.

Uwe Becker, the author of chapter two, examines the prophecies about social justice found in the book of Amos as potential sources for the passages in Isaiah that herald social justice. Becker demonstrates that Isaiah's castigation of injustices is not an authentic part of his prophecy, but rather was drawn from both the original text of Amos and from secondary additions. His chapter points to the process of alignment or approximation that took place between various prophetic books of the Bible and their key messages.

James Nogalski, analysing the final verses of Zephaniah, lays bare the numerous parallels they contain to the content and language of Isaiah and suggests that they might point to commonalities in the circles of their authorship. Conversely, contrasts in the parallels highlight the substantial differences in the depiction of Zion in evidence in the two writings.

The chapter by **Burkard M. Zapff** on the relationship between the Book of the Twelve and what is known as Deutero-Isaiah asserts that the Book as a whole both pays virtually no attention to themes at the heart of Deutero-Isaiah and places quotations from it in a new context requiring an altered theological and political setting. In Zapff's view, any distinct intersections between themes in the Book of the Twelve and those in what is termed Trito-Isaiah might point to the revisions to the Book which aligned it more closely with Isaiah in the post-exilic period.

The contribution by **Richard Bautch** centres on the much-discussed, highly intertextual passage Zechariah 11 with its multiplicity of intertextual references, particularly to Isaiah 10:33–34. Bautch succeeds in demonstrating that Isaiah 10:33–34, one of the central passages on which the text draws, creates new possibilities for interpreting Zechariah 11 by effectively serving as a form of bridge for its opening and closing oracles.

The similarities remarked upon repeatedly in more recent research on the Twelve Minor Prophets between the concluding chapter of Zechariah and Isaiah's final section is the subject of **Todd Hibbard**'s essay. The assumption hitherto has been that theologically aligned groups of authors worked on these writings. Hibbard's examination of the texts, by contrast, uncovers within the texts a distinctly different treatment and development of similar theological interests and motifs. Following Hibbard's analysis, there is no straightforward answer to the question of whether later writings of Isaiah had a direct influence on Zechariah 14; topical resemblances between the two texts stand against a striking contrast in these themes' specific treatment.

A different conclusion emerges from **Christopher Hays**' analysis of the relationship between Zephaniah and Isaiah 24–27, often termed the Isaiah Apocalypse, which reveals close interconnections in both language and content. While the conclusions Hays draws from his findings may surprise some, the rationale he presents has a high degree of plausibility: The broad consensus dating a substantial core of Zephaniah to the seventh century BCE justifies, in Hays' view, the attribution of an equivalent date to the rather misleadingly named 'Isaiah Apocalypse', notwithstanding its frequent interpretation as a later text. A further assertion Hays bases on his findings is that those responsible for penning Zephaniah's original version also created the substance of Isaiah 24–27.

Turning from the previous chapters' dominant theme of literary connections and interdependencies between Isaiah and writings from the Twelve Minor Prophets, the authors of the chapters collected in the volume's third part make motifs in both corpora, and responses to them, their principal concern.

In this context, **Joachim Eck** examines the role of Isaiah 5:1–7, the Song of the Unfruitful Vineyard, in the thematic thrust of Isaiah 1–12. His essay then proceeds to explore, via selected examples, the resonance of this motif within Isaiah as a whole and its reprise in Micah; this reappraisal of passages such as Micah 7:1–20 points to the way in which these presuppose knowledge of the Song of the Vineyard on the part of their reader. Thus, light is cast on the creative work by the writers responsible for the latter such passages, which thereby impart their own distinct message.

The motif of the kingship of YHWH is at the core of **Carol Dempsey**'s chapter and of her distinctive approach to the subjects of this volume. Dempsey retraces developments in conceptions of this metaphorical imagery covering a range of associations – from oppression to liberation. She shows that the kingship motif is occasionally susceptible to abuse in the service of human power, yet it carries as well the potential to inspire visions of global leadership for our day.

Archibald van Wieringen analyses the role of the Oracles against the Nations in Isaiah and the Book of the Twelve. Notwithstanding a series of differences, relating not least to the names of the nations addressed, the author concludes that these passages are not so much oracles *against* other nations as documents produced in a context of self-critical reflection undertaken by Israel and Jerusalem.

The motif of the Day of YHWH in both corpora is at the heart of **Hugh Williamson**'s chapter, which delineates three – or four – iterations of the concept. The original concept, widespread among the contemporary populace, regarded the Day of YHWH as YHWH's intervention against Israel's foes. There followed, secondarily, a creative transformation of this notion into a day of judgement upon Israel, and, thirdly, an interpretation linking the Day of YHWH to historical events – to the extent that it was directed against communities such as Babel. Finally, Williamson outlines an eschatological view which cast the Day as one of liberation from all oppression by hostile powers. Williamson's essay illuminates the parallels between the development of the concept in Isaiah and in the Twelve Minor Prophets.

Thus far, the volume's chapters have illustrated a range of methodological approaches to the core question of the relationship between the Book of the Twelve and Isaiah, taking account of both synchronic and diachronic manners of proceeding. Bringing the volume to its conclusion, the *Festvortrag* by the Regensburg-based Bishop **Rudolph Voderholzer** points beyond its horizons towards the matter of what exegesis, done today, means – and has the potential to mean – for and within the life of the Church. Voderholzer succeeds in illuminating the vital importance of referencing the historical context and the literal sense of the Biblical text as the foundations of a faith resting on a historical bedrock. Further, he reminds us of the potential of these texts to direct the attention of their readers and hearers to the salvific action of God, to the necessity of building a life around an ethical compass, and to the hope we are justified in holding. In this context, Voderholzer's contribution urges us to pursue our studies fully informed by the tradition of the fourfold sense of Scripture, whose roots stretch back to the early Church.

The rich diversity of research questions and methodological responses to them manifest in this volume are indicative of great exploration and debate around the interconnections between Isaiah and the Book of the Twelve. A **Synthesis** at the end draws an overall picture of converging insights which can be gained from the different foci and perspectives of the individual contributions. It describes a complex development from prophetic personalities and movements whose theological opinions varied considerably but agreed on the unique significance of YHWH for Israel towards a deeper unity which nonetheless preserved a wide range of valuable points of view. The volume suggests that the theological bridges between Isaiah and the Twelve are highly relevant now and for the foreseeable future. Our hope is that it will provide impetus and inspiration to researchers in this field to redouble their analytical efforts in this direction.

Burkard M. Zapff, Richard Bautch, Joachim Eck

I Analyses Concerning the Relationships between the Book of Isaiah and Books Associated with Pre-exilic Prophets

Franz Sedlmeier
Hosea and Isaiah: Aspects of Convergence and Difference

1 Introduction

It is widely undisputed that the book of Hosea shows a particular affinity with the prophecy of Jeremiah and Ezekiel and with the books named after them. In a similar way this is true for the relationship between Hosea and Deuteronomy and deuteronomic/deuteronomistic (dtn-dtr) literature, whilst in individual cases explanation is needed, where exactly the donor text and where the recipient text can be found.

The results will be far less productive where the relationship between Hosea and the book of Isaiah is concerned. Erich Bosshard-Nepustil has examined the literary connections between Isaiah and the Dodekapropheton with regard to equivalents in terms of content as well as structure in his stimulating dissertation "Receptions of Isaiah 1–39 in the Book of the Twelve Prophets"[1]. He is able to make a number of important observations and concludes: significant keywords would suggest that the editors deliberately correlated the two books.[2] Bosshard-Nepustil tends to give at least partial priority to the book of Isaiah. Quite a number of equivalents suggested by him seem plausible, as do the chronological details at the beginning of the book of Isaiah (Is 1:1) and of the Dodekapropheton (Hos 1:1). However other references remain controversial. The question is whether the structural correspondences between Isaiah and the Dodekapropheton actually have a comparable significance. Aaron Schart comments critically: "In dieser Form kann die Gesamtthese Bosshards deshalb nicht überzeugen, auch wenn er in vielen Einzelheiten interessante Beobachtungen gemacht hat."[3] Therefore, the relation-

---

1 Erich Bosshard-Nepustil, *Rezeptionen von Jesaia 1–39 im Zwölfprophetenbuch. Untersuchungen zur literarischen Verbindung von Prophetenbüchern in babylonischer und persischer Zeit.* OBO 154 (Freiburg/CH: Universitätsverlag Freiburg; Göttingen: Vandenhoeck & Ruprecht 1997).
2 More detailed: Erich Bosshard, "Beobachtungen zum Zwölfprophetenbuch," in BN 40 (1987): 30–62. Bosshard leaves open how the dependency runs, as the literary references are markedly intricate and complex. However he supposes, that the book of Isaiah can be assumed as the donor text in at least one stratum. "Es spricht viel dafür, daß wenigstens eine Schicht der Buchbildung von XII analog zu Jes, wahrscheinlich sogar anhand von Jes gestaltet wurde" (57).
3 Aaron Schart, *Die Entstehung des Zwölfprophetenbuchs. Neubearbeitungen von Amos im Rahmen schriftenübergreifender Redaktionsprozesse.* BZAW 260 (Berlin/New York: Walter de Gruyter 1997), 10.

https://doi.org/10.1515/9783110705799-002

ship between the Dodekapropheton and the book of Isaiah remains a *quaestio disputata et disputanda*. And much remains to be clarified for our meeting.

However, my contribution is not concerned with the relationship between the Book of the Twelve and Isaiah, but with the relationship between Hosea and Isaiah. Bosshard-Nepustil's study shows, that indeed there are significant references, but these are far more modest compared with the other books of the XII.

A significantly greater kinship appears to exist between Amos and Isaiah, even though the exegetic study by Jan Kreuch entitled "Das Amos- und Jesajabuch"[4] leads to a sobering conclusion, when trying to determine the relationship between Amos and Isaiah in more detail. According to his study, the historical prophet Isaiah was not aware of Amos' proclamation. The "common rootedness of both in the YHWH faith and the traditions related thereto" are enough according to Kreuch "to explain a good part of what both prophets have in common.".[5] The "thematic similarities" can be "explained by the comparable social situation with their grievances in Israel and Judah during the 8th century BC. Also, proclamations or reviews on military catastrophes in both books are quite understandable because of the acute threat to both the Northern- and Southern-Kingdom by the Assyrians."[6]

The finding has to be evaluated differently for the relationship between Micah and Isaiah, if Burkard M. Zapff is right that the book of Micah never existed independently. "Es wurde vielmehr als Fortsetzung der Prophetie von Hosea und Amos sowie als Repräsentant zentraler Inhalte der Botschaft Jesajas im Zwölfprophetenbuch verfasst."[7]

An examination of the references between Hosea and Isaiah seems to be less fruitful than in the case of Amos and Micah. Hence the question arises whether this article not ultimately turns out to be negative. But even that would not be

---

4 Jan Kreuch, *Das Amos- und Jesajabuch. Eine exegetische Studie zur Neubestimmung ihres Verhältnisses*. BThSt 149 (Neukirchen-Vlyun: Neukirchener Verlagsgesellschaft 2014).

5 Kreuch, *Amos und Jesaja*, 197: "Schon dieser Umstand der gemeinsamen Verwurzelung im JHWH-Glauben und der mit ihm verbundenen Traditionen reicht meines Erachtens zur Erklärung eines Gutteils der Gemeinsamkeiten beider Propheten aus."

6 See *ibid.*, 197: "Diese thematischen Gemeinsamkeiten lassen sich … durch die vergleichbare soziale Situation mit ihren Missständen in Israel und Juda im 8. Jh. v. Chr. erklären. Und auch die Ankündigungen bzw. Rückblicke auf militärische Katastrophen in beiden Büchern sind wegen der akuten Bedrohung sowohl des Nord- wie des Südreiches durch die Assyrer hinlänglich verständlich." Kreuch, *ibid.*, arrives at the conclusion: "Sowohl also die Traditionen, in denen Amos und Jesaja wurzeln, wie auch die Umstände, unter denen sie lebten, können die Gemeinsamkeiten hinreichend erklären. Eine Beeinflussung Jesajas durch Amos muss nicht angenommen werden." See also the article by Uwe Becker in this volume.

7 Burkard M. Zapff, "Why is Micah similar to Isaiah?" in ZAW 129 (2017/4): 536–554, 554. See also: "Vielmehr wurde das Buch Micha durch Redaktoren einerseits der Prophetie Jesajas und andererseits der Prophetie von Amos und Hosea angenähert" (*ibid.*).

completely an unimportant result. And so, I would like to invite you to search for clues in the following.

2 Isaiah and Hosea: A Confusing Terrain

Since it turns out that a longer period of development has to be estimated both for Isaiah and for Hosea, the questioning in terms of determining the Hosea-Isaiah relationship is complex and not easily ascertainable. Only a few decades ago it was deemed obvious regarding the exegesis of Hosea that this prophet could rank mostly as the donor text for Jeremiah, Ezekiel and the dtn-dtr theologians. The question of dependency is considered far more differentiated in current exegetical literature, so that mutual dependency is to be expected.

Since the historical persons, Hosea and Isaiah were contemporaries and worked in the hostile states of Israel and Judah respectively, one will have to assume that they could not exercise any direct influence on one another in their proclamation. Any influencing may have occurred at the earliest after the fall of the Northern Kingdom and during the course of the working in common on the message of Amos and Hosea by later editors. One can assume that in the process of editing, references can increasingly be built between Hosea's text material, that is already linked with Amos, and what was handed down by Isaiah. This is already evident from the dating in Is 1:1 and Hos 1:1.

3 Aspects of Convergence and Difference between Hosea and Isaiah

3.1 Dating in Hos 1:1 and Is 1:1

Particularly striking are the equivalents between Hos 1:1 and Is 1:1. Both headings mention the same four kings from the Southern Kingdom, namely: Uzziah, Jotham, Ahaz and Hezekiah.

This is what is written in Is 1:1:

חֲזוֹן יְשַׁעְיָהוּ בֶן־אָמוֹץ אֲשֶׁר חָזָה עַל־יְהוּדָה וִירוּשָׁלָ͏ִם
בִּימֵי עֻזִּיָּהוּ יוֹתָם אָחָז יְחִזְקִיָּהוּ מַלְכֵי יְהוּדָה׃

"The vision of Isaiah the son of Amoz, which he saw concerning Judah and Jerusalem in the days of *Uzziah*, *Jotham*, *Ahaz*, and *Hezekiah*, kings of Judah."

The formulation in Hos 1:1 is quite similar:

דְּבַר־יְהוָה ׀ אֲשֶׁר הָיָה אֶל־הוֹשֵׁעַ בֶּן־בְּאֵרִי
בִּימֵי עֻזִּיָּה יוֹתָם אָחָז יְחִזְקִיָּה מַלְכֵי יְהוּדָה
וּבִימֵי יָרָבְעָם בֶּן־יוֹאָשׁ מֶלֶךְ יִשְׂרָאֵל:

"The word of the LORD that came to Hosea, the son of Beeri, in the days of *Uzziah*, *Jotham*, *Ahaz*, and *Hezekiah*, kings of Judah, and in the days of Jeroboam the son of Joash, king of Israel."

The sequence בִּימֵי עֻזִּיָּהוּ יוֹתָם אָחָז יְחִזְקִיָּהוּ מַלְכֵי יְהוּדָה is particularly striking as it only appears here in the entire Old Testament. Not only can the two books of Isaiah and Hosea be correlated with each other by this dating, but also with the Major Prophets who are referred to in the book of Isaiah and with the Minor Prophets referred to in the book of Hosea. This relationship between the greater text corpora is supported by the fact that the heading of Hos 1:1 not only forms a bridge with Is 1:1, but also links the books of the prophets Hosea, Amos, Micah and – to some degree also – Zephaniah with each other.

Thus dates Am 1:1 the activity of the eldest writing prophet:

בִּימֵי ׀ עֻזִּיָּה מֶלֶךְ־יְהוּדָה וּבִימֵי יָרָבְעָם בֶּן־יוֹאָשׁ מֶלֶךְ יִשְׂרָאֵל

"in the days of *Uzziah* king of Judah and in the days of *Jeroboam* the son of Joash, king of Israel".

The prophetic activity of Hosea and that of Amos is paralleled in the time of Uzziah in the Southern Kingdom and of Jeroboam in the Northern Kingdom.

Similar possibilities apply to the relationship between Hosea and Micah. The work of Micah occurred בִּימֵי יוֹתָם אָחָז יְחִזְקִיָּה מַלְכֵי יְהוּדָה "in the days of *Jotham*, *Ahaz*, and *Hezekiah*, kings of Judah". Even though the heading of the book of Zephaniah is arranged according to the so-called דבר-pattern, it refers to a distinctly later period, the time of king Josiah.

Therefore, the dating of Hos 1:1 lets the northern prophet Hosea appear together with the northern prophet Amos and the southern prophet Micah. The timing of Hosea's activity includes the period of Amos and Micah. That among the Northern Kingdom prophets Hosea and Amos the kings of the Southern Kingdom gain a particular significance, can be explained (1) by the fact that the message of both prophets was meant for Jewish listeners in the first place who at best knew the most important northern king Jeroboam II, and were otherwise familiar with the kings of the Southern Kingdom.[8] And (2): by the fact that the message of both Hosea and Amos concerns north and south.

The chronological information is combined with yet another intention to state as described by Aaron Schart: "Demnach sind mindestens zwei Propheten gleichzeitig aufgetreten: Zuerst Hosea zusammen mit Amos, dann Hosea und Micha".[9] Clearly the credibility of the witness of the two prophets should be emphasized by their appearing simultaneously in pairs.[10] The fact that the appearance of Hosea is each time flanked by another prophet, certainly emphasizes his particular importance.

Whether one can go as far as assigning Hosea a key role historically, as Freedman suggests, is highly questionable. "What the heading suggests or implies is that Hosea is the key figure in the group and that his ministry overlapped with all the others, and that he may at some time or other have had contact with them. We may even speculate that he had an important part in the compilation and assembly of the materials that went into the four books."[11]

The systematically structured heading of the books of the prophets Hosea, Amos, Micah and Zephaniah is certainly the work of later editors. Together with Schart and others I assume that the chronological reference of the headings links the mentioned four books of prophets to a "Four Prophet Book" and may well originate from the hands of Deuteronomistic or closely associated circles. Hosea's

---

8 Susanne Rudnig-Zelt, *Hoseastudien. Redaktionskritische Untersuchungen zur Genese des Hoseabuches.* FRLANT 123 (Göttingen: Vandenhoeck & Ruprecht, 2006), 107 interprets this finding differently: "Die Intention des Verfassers von Hos 1,1 war zunächst nicht, das Buch einem Nordreichpropheten zuzuordnen, sondern klarzustellen, daß die Botschaft in Hos Nord und Süd angeht. ... Hätte er das Buch einem Nordreichpropheten zuschreiben wollen, so hätte er nach dem Vorbild der Überschriften für judäische Propheten (z. B. Jes 1,1; Jer 1,1–3; Mi 1,1a; Zeph 1,1) allein nach den Nordreichkönigen datieren müssen." Similarly also Marie-Theres Wacker, *Figurationen des Weiblichen im Hosea-Buch.* HBS 8 (Freiburg: Herder; 1996), 222f. However, Rudnig-Zelt does not take into account enough, that the heading has in view the listeners of the Southern Kingdom, which explains the mention of the southern kings sufficiently. Correct, however, is the statement of Rudnig-Zelt, *Hoseastudien*, 106: "Hinter Hos 1,1 steht die Absicht, einen Propheten Hosea als Zeitgenossen von Amos und Jesaja zu präsentieren."
9 Aaron Schart, *Die Entstehung des Zwölfprophetenbuchs: Neubearbeitungen von Amos im Rahmen schriftenübergreifender Redaktionsprozesse.* BZAW 260 (Berlin: De Gruyter, 1998), 36.
10 See Schart, *Entstehung*, 44: Schart supposes, "dass die Propheten erst in der Zweizahl ihre volle Überzeugungs- und Durchschlagekraft entfalten, weil sie sich in ihrer Verkündigung wechselseitig verstärken".
11 D. N. Freedman, "Headings in the Books of the Eighth-Century Prophets,", in *AUSS* 25 (1987): 9–26, 18. It will have to remain pure speculation, that Hosea had contact with his prophet colleagues or that he was involved in the writing and compilation of the prophetic proclamation.

preceding position could be explained by the fact – here I am following Jörg Jeremias – that Hosea's head position was already a given fact for the editors.[12]

Whilst the Hos 1:1 heading within the Dodekapropheton links the writings of Hosea with Amos, Micah and Zephaniah, the question remains, however, how Hos 1:1 relates to Is 1:1. In both texts Is 1:1b and Hos 1aβ the naming of the four judaic kings matches exactly, apart from the different spelling of the name Uzziah (Is 1:1b: עֻזִּיָּהוּ; Hos 1aβ: עֻזִּיָּה). One can assume that the dating in Isaiah serves as a basis for Hosea. Aaron Schart supposes "daß die Königsdatierung in Jes 1,1 ... den dtr beeinflußten Redaktoren von Hos bereits vorgelegen hat. Träfe dies zu, könnten diese in der Überschrift Hos 1,1 auch Jes 1,1 – kritisch – berücksichtigt haben."[13] Hans Walter Wolff has already pointed out explicitly that in Hos 1:1 it is not the prophet's name in the vanguard (see Am 1:1; Is 1:1; Jer 1:1; Ob 1; Nah 1:1), but the word of YHWH in connection with the Word-event, giving a clear indication that Hos 1:1 delineates a later development.[14]

Consequently, we can assume that Is 1:1 is regarded as the donor text, whilst Hos 1:1 has been developed under the influence of Am 1:1 and Is 1:1. The merit of this heading consists therefore in connecting the book of Hosea and the more

---

12 It still seems to me the most plausible, with Jörg Jeremias, "Die Anfänge des Dodekapropheton: Hosea und Amos," in Jörg Jeremias (Hg.), *Hosea und Amos: Studien zu den Anfängen des Dodekapropheton*. FAT 13 (Tübingen: Mohr 1996), 34–54, to assume, that the book of Hosea at least in parts was created already before the book of Amos and that the latter was under the influence of Hosea from the beginning. The comparison between the two books of prophets shows as likely "daß das Amosbuch später als das Hoseabuch niedergeschrieben wurde, zu einer Zeit, als das Hoseabuch in prophetischen Kreisen Judas schon Autorität gewonnen hatte. Insofern setzt das Dodekapropheton zu Recht mit dem Hoseabuch ein, obwohl Amos geschichtlich früher als Hosea gewirkt hat" (53).
13 A. Schart, *Entstehung*, 349, note 2. Schart does not give further explanation, where the criticism of the dtr theologians lies.
14 See Hans Walter Wolff, *Hosea*. BK.AT XIV/1 (Neukirchen-Vluyn: Neukirchener Verlag ³1976), 5: "Denn in jenen Tagen ist das Jahwewort als das über Israel entscheidende ergangen, das eben darum auch im späteren Juda und noch zur Exilszeit als das gültige Jahwewort zu hören ist. Es ist bewährtes Wort des Herrn der Geschichte. Dieser Sammler hat die Geschichte Israels als eine Geschichte des sich erfüllenden Jahwewortes durchschaut ... Er formuliert darum die Überschrift bewusst anders als sonstige, z.T. sogar ältere Prophetenbuchredaktoren, die den Prophetennamen an die Spitze setzen (Am 1,1; Jes 1,1; Jer 1,1 ...; Ob 1; Na 1,1)."
Also according to Rudnig-Zelt, *Hoseastudien*, 104, Hos 1:1 shows "ein sehr viel höheres Reflexionsniveau als Bucheinleitungen, deren vorexilische Herkunft in der Forschung berechtigterweise erwogen wird." Rudnig-Zelt, *ibid.*, sees such headings, which do not yet even mention Yahweh, in the initial versions of Am 1:1 and Is 1:1. "Während diese Überschriften Jahwe gar nicht erwähnen, stellt Hos 1,1 von vornherein klar, daß Jahwe die folgenden Worte autorisiert ... Dies ist auf eine Weiterentwicklung in der Prophetentheologie zurückzuführen."

extensive text corpus of a "Four Prophet Book" with Isaiah and with the developing text corpus of the Major Prophets. At the same time the older chronological
specifications are being deepened by a prophetic theological reflection and sub-
ordinate to the comprehensive validity of the YHWH word and the Word-event.[15]

3.2 Structural Equivalents in the Arrangement of the Book of Isaiah and the Twelve?

Besides the striking concordance at the start of the Is 1:1 and Hos 1:1 texts,
Erich Bosshard-Nepustil identifies also further equivalents in their continuation "in largely parallel sequence".[16] He thereby refers mainly to the chapters
Is 6.7–8 and Hos 5–9, which correlate to each other as "the prophetic main text
to the Syro-Ephraimite War"[17] and as reflections on the history of the Northern
Kingdom.[18] Furthermore, he quotes the choice of names in Is 8 and Hos 1, which
visualize the activities of the divine judgement as a prophetic action. As the names
of menace in Hos 1 and Is 8 are unique within the Old Testament literature, they
need to be addressed specifically in order to capture the relationship between
both texts more precisely. As to equivalents between Is 8 and Hos 5–9 we have
to critically ask, whether these are sufficiently robust to bear the hypothesis of a
conscious coordination of the two text complexes by the editors.

Erich Bosshard-Nepustil includes not only Hos, but also the books of Am and
Mic in the structural comparison of the text corpora of Is*1–32,14, which exist after
701 B.C. "Es zeigt sich …, daß Hos, Am und Mi in dieser Reihenfolge zusammen
hinsichtlich Makroanlage und wichtigen Einzelpunkten auffallende Parallelen mit
I Jes, wie es u. E. nach 701 v. Chr. vorliegt, … aufweist."[19] Since the three individual
books Hos, Am and Mic[20] are even less solidified in their text continuation than is
Isaiah according to Bosshard-Nepustil, one has to suppose, "daß Hos, Am und Mi
schon nach 701 v. Chr. in Entsprechung zu I Jes (Jes *1–32) formiert waren."[21] Unfor-
tunately the author does not reflect on the newly created formulations within the
three books of the prophets, which could show the intention of the editors.

---

15 Compare in this context also the observations of M. T. Wacker, *Figurationen*, 222–224.
16 E. Bosshard-Nepustil, *Rezeptionen*, 8: "in weitgehend paralleler Abfolge".
17 *Ibid.*: "die prophetischen Haupttexte zum syrisch-ephraimitischen Krieg".
18 See E. Bosshard-Nepustil, *Rezeptionen*, 413.
19 *Ibid.*, 413.
20 The question, whether Mic existed as single book or whether it was conceived as an editing of
the book of Isaiah from the outset, is disputed. According to Zapff an autonomous book of Micah
never existed. Zapff's position contrasts that of A. Schart and the majority of exegetes.
21 Bosshard-Nepustil, *Rezeptionen*, 414.

Bosshard-Nepustil sees the city of Jerusalem, having just escaped the threat of the Assyrians, and being the common geographical location, as one of the pre-suppositions for the rapprochement of the three books of prophets Hos-Am-Mic. And further: "Der im Geschehen von 701 v. Chr. gipfelnde Druck Assurs von außen bewirkt einen Schulterschluss im Innern, was sich auch in einer Vereinheitlichung von Büchern äußern kann."[22] In addition, the third reason for the coming together of the three books of prophets would be the sharpening announcement of judgement against Zion in the face of the Assyrian crisis, as expressed in Is 31:4 and Mic 3:12, and the aligned question of Zion's fate. "Die Frage um Bewahrung oder eben Preisgabe Zions ist – jedenfalls aus der Sicht Jesajas bzw. seiner Tradenten – so zentral, dass sich die Propheten nur una voce darüber äußern (sollen) und zwar speziell auch im Blick auf die Situation des Eintreffens des Gerichts."[23] Finally the end of the activity of the two prophets of the Southern Kingdom, Isaiah and Micah, around 701 may have led to a more pronounced systematic arrangement of the prophets' words and their "books", whereby a dominance of Isaiah's tradition can be assumed according to Bosshard-Nepustil. "Wer bei der Vereinheitlichung die treibende Kraft ist, ist nicht einfach zu sagen, doch wird man am ehesten an (Jesaja bzw.) die Jesaja-Tradenten denken können."[24]

However, the critical question arises as to how far the textual findings of Isaiah and the Twelve can carry Bosshard-Nepustil's hypothesis. Other contributions in the frame of this congress refer to Amos and Micah. My questioning centers on the references between the books of Hosea and Isaiah. It seems to me that the references between these two books simply cannot support the hypothesis that there were conscious equivalences in the structure of the two text corpora created. There are surely significant lexical references between Isaiah and Hosea, which need to be followed up. However, it is hard to prove that one of these two books has served the authors as a text template. Bosshard-Nepustil supposes, that Isaiah should be allotted priority as donor text for a certain stratum in the genesis of the Dodeka-propheton. "Es spricht viel dafür, daß wenigstens eine Schicht der Buchbildung von XII analog zu Jes, wahrscheinlich sogar anhand von Jes gestaltet wurde."[25]

---

22 *Ibid.*, 414.

23 *Ibid.*, 415.

24 *Ibid.*, 415. Bosshard-Nepustil sees in the connection of First Isaiah and Hos-Am-Mic the beginnings of the Dodekapropheton, which at best could be preceded by the two-prophet book Hosea-Amos proposed by Jörg Jeremias: "*es gibt u. E. auch keine Indizien für eine weiter zurück-reichende übergreifende, redaktionelle Annäherung zwischen den Zwölf Propheten und I Jes*" (ibid.).

25 E. Bosshard, "Beobachtungen zum Zwölfprophetenbuch," *Biblische Notizen* 40 (1987): 30–62, 57.

The current location within the books of prophets does not allow to identify structurally comparable functions for the relationship between the chapters Is 1 and Is 7–8 on the one hand and Hos 1 and 5–9 on the other hand,[26] apart from the relationship between Is 1:1 and Hos 1:1, for which a targeted reference has already been established.

The lexical text references between Isaiah and Hosea have to be questioned in terms of their strength on a case by case basis. What about the references between the chapters Is 6.7–8 and Hos 5–9 which reflect the experiences of the Syro-Ephraimite War? The depiction in Is 7 f. embeds the children's names in the wartime events, whereas in Hos the children's names are clearly distinct from these wartime events of ch. 5–9 and – in an later reflection – are positioned at the beginning of the Book of Hosea. A structural reference in the macro-text is not given at all in this respect. The name-assignment is added in the Book of Hosea in a markedly different way than in Isaiah. The name assignment per se will have to be discussed separately.

3.3 Lexical References between Hosea and Isaiah?

What about the lexical references in the description of the wartime events? In the Hos-Am-Mic series of books Bosshard-Nepustil views the following references from their dating after 701 BC between Hosea and Isaiah as given:[27] (1) Hos*5:8 ff. and Is 6.7–8 would refer to the event of the Syro-Ephraimite War, (2) Hos*9:10 ff. and Is*9:7–20 would offer historical reviews referring to the Northern Kingdom Israel. Bosshard-Nepustil refers to Jörg Jeremias[28] and Herbert Donner[29] for the references regarding the Syro-Ephraimite War. For Donner and Jeremias it is not a question of literary dependency of the text corpora and certainly not of a structural equivalent in the texts during the development of the two prophetic books, but solely of the possible historical background of the two narrations. The lexical equivalents are not sufficient to validate strong statements about a literary relationship of dependency between the Isaian and the Hosean text-structure.

---

26 Cf. in this context the legitimate criticism of A. Schart, *Entstehung*, 9–10.
27 See Bosshard-Nepustil, *Rezeptionen*, 413–415
28 See Jörg Jeremias, *Der Prophet Hosea*. ATD 24/1 (Göttingen: Vandenhoeck & Ruprecht, 1983), 17; 78 ff.
29 See Herbert Donner, *Geschichte des Volkes Israel und seiner Nachbarn in Grundzügen 2*. ATD Ergänzungsreihe Band 2 (Göttingen: Vandenhoeck & Ruprecht, 1986), 306 [=⁴2008, 337].

The text references between Hos 1:4 f. and Is 9:13,15 f.[30] both reflect the end of history of the Northern Kingdom. But in Hos 1:4 f this ending is connected with the name of Hosea's son Jezreel and with the blood guilt of Jehu which cause the fall of the Kingdom. In Is 9:13,15 f. the guilt of the persons responsible fits into the image of head (the elder and honored) and tail (the prophet and liar) and states the impiousness of all people. Language, addressees and scenery are too diverse to detect a literary parallel.

At least one common signal word is given between Hos 1:6 with the name of the second child, *Lo Ruchama*, and Is 9:16 through the root *rḥm* which in both texts is part of an announcement of judgement.[31] The name of the daughter לֹא רֻחָמָה corresponds in Is 9:16 to the statement וְאֶת־יְתֹמָיו וְאֶת־אַלְמְנֹתָיו לֹא יְרַחֵם "and he [= the Lord] has no compassion on the fatherless and widows". The negation of God's mercy connects both text passages, whereby in Hos 1:6 the statement is more fundamental and hence clearly dated later.

Hos 5:14 uses the imagery of the lion as a judgement metaphor:

כִּי אָנֹכִי כַשַּׁחַל לְאֶפְרַיִם וְכַכְּפִיר לְבֵית יְהוּדָה אֲנִי אֲנִי אֶטְרֹף וְאֵלֵךְ אֶשָּׂא וְאֵין מַצִּיל׃

> "For I will be like a lion (כַשַּׁחַל) to Ephraim, and like a young lion (וְכַכְּפִיר) to the house of Judah. I, even I, will tear (אֶטְרֹף) and go away; I will carry off, and no one shall rescue (וְאֵין מַצִּיל)."

The image of the robbing lion also emerges in Is 5:29, even though in another diction and in connection with the Assyrian invasion:

שְׁאָגָה לוֹ כַּלָּבִיא וְשָׁאַג כַּכְּפִירִים וְיִנְהֹם וְיֹאחֵז טֶרֶף וְיַפְלִיט וְאֵין מַצִּיל

> "Their roaring is like a lion (כַּלָּבִיא), like young lions (כַּכְּפִירִים) they roar; they growl and seize their prey (טֶרֶף); they carry it off, and none can rescue (וְאֵין מַצִּיל)."

The two texts have three signal words in common: the "young lion" (כְּפִיר), the "prey" (טרף) and the negated rescue (וְאֵין מַצִּיל). It is about a hopeless situation in both texts. Whilst Is 5:29 characterizes the Assyrian aggressors with the lion metaphor, YHWH standing as the actual doer behind the Assyrian aggressor, in Hos 5 YHWH appears himself and quite directly as the attacking lion which means death to Israel.

Finally, Bosshard-Nepustil points to Hos 6:5 and Is 9:7.8a. Both have the motive of the divine word in common, to which a far greater importance is accorded in

---

30 Bosshard-Nepustil, *Rezeptionen*, 413, note 5.
31 *Ibid.*

the book of Isaiah than in Hosea. In the face of the people's refusal to convert, the judgement now takes place in Hos 6:5 through the divine word, revealing itself through the Prophets, the judgement having previously been announced in the lion image (Hos 5:14).

עַל־כֵּ֤ן חָצַ֙בְתִּי֙ בַּנְּבִיאִ֔ים הֲרַגְתִּ֖ים בְּאִמְרֵי־פִ֑י וּמִשְׁפָּטֶ֖יךָ א֥וֹר יֵצֵֽא׃

"Therefore I have hewn [them] by the prophets; I have slain them by the words of my mouth (בְּאִמְרֵי־פִי), and my judgement[32] goes forth as the light."

Is 9:7–8a (8–9a):

דָּבָ֞ר שָׁלַ֤ח אֲדֹנָי֙ בְּיַֽעֲקֹ֔ב וְנָפַ֖ל בְּיִשְׂרָאֵֽל׃ וְיָדְע֤וּ הָעָם֙ כֻּלּ֔וֹ אֶפְרַ֖יִם וְיוֹשֵׁ֣ב שֹׁמְר֑וֹן

"The Lord has sent a word (יְֹנדָ֣א חלָ֣שׁ רבָ֔ד) against Jacob, and it will fall on Israel; and all the people will know, Ephraim and the inhabitants of Samaria".

Both text passages have the motif of the divine word in common. However, again the linguistic realization shows great differences. Since the effective power of divine word is otherwise no issue in the book of Hosea, a later addition may be present here, which may well be influenced by the book of Isaiah, that emphasizes the efficacy of the word besides Is 9:7 and especially in Deutero-Isaiah (see Is 40:8 and 55:10 f.).[33]

The considerations so far show that a structural equivalent concerning the sequence of events in Isaiah and in the Twelve cannot be demonstrated, at least not for Hosea. That the Syro-Ephraimite War and the fall of the Northern Kingdom may well be in the background in the Hosean and Isaian texts and have influence on proclamation of judgement and punishment, does not necessarily mean a literary dependence of the text corpora. Common lexemes and key words between Isaiah and Hosea may well signal references between the two books. It is striking therefore that the dependence appears to show a tendency to go from Isaiah as donor text to Hosea as recipient text.

---

32 The Hebrew text וּמִשְׁפָּטֶיךָ "and your judgement" can probably be explained by incorrect word separations. We read with the ancient textual witnesses LXX, S and T "and my judgement".
33 Roman Vielhauer, *Das Werden des Buches Hosea*. BZAW 349 (Berlin, New York: Walter der Gruyter, 2007), 61 f. sees in Hos 6,5 a later addition, which already looks back on the judgement, announced in the context: "der auf das im Kontext für die Zukunft angekündigte Gericht bereits zurückblickt und mit dem heilvollen Hervorbrechen der Lebensordnung JHWHs eine nunmehr positive Zielbestimmung für das Gericht angibt. Als neue Gerichtswerkzeuge dienen dabei die Propheten und die Worte aus dem Munde Gottes."

3.4 The Names of the Children: Hos 1:2–9 and Is 8:1–4

Bosshard-Nepustil also mentions the striking naming of the children in the context of proclamation of salvation or judgement respectively as the common feature between Isaiah and Hosea. The fact that this particular naming[34] only appears in Is 8 and Hos 1 throughout the entire Old Testament is conspicuous and requires some explanation. Christoph Levin has listed good reasons in his studies entitled "Die Bundesverheißungen im Hoseabuch"[35], outlining Is 8:1–4* as being a donor text for Hos 1:1–4*. The similarities between statements in Is 8:1.3–4 and Hos 1:2b–4abα are astonishing. Both texts open with an introduction: that of naming the addressee ויאמר יהוה אל, the assignment of a mission קח־לך and the execution of the mission. Then gestation and birth are mentioned ותהר ותלד בן and an order for the naming ויאמר יהוה אל ... קרא שמו stating the reasons: כי. The words conclude with a date specification and a threat.

Is 8:1.3b–4:[36]

וַיֹּ֤אמֶר יְהוָה֙ אֵלַ֔י קַח־לְךָ֖ גִּלָּי֣וֹן גָּד֑וֹל
וּכְתֹ֤ב עָלָיו֙ בְּחֶ֣רֶט אֱנ֔וֹשׁ לְמַהֵ֥ר שָׁלָ֖ל חָ֥שׁ בַּֽז׃

וָאֶקְרַב֙ אֶל־הַנְּבִיאָ֔ה וַתַּ֖הַר וַתֵּ֣לֶד בֵּ֑ן
וַיֹּ֤אמֶר יְהוָה֙ אֵלַ֔י קְרָ֣א שְׁמ֔וֹ מַהֵ֥ר שָׁלָ֖ל חָ֥שׁ בַּֽז׃
כִּ֗י בְּטֶ֙רֶם֙ יֵדַ֣ע הַנַּ֔עַר קְרֹ֖א אָבִ֣י וְאִמִּ֑י | יִשָּׂ֣א ׀ אֶת־חֵ֣יל
דַּמֶּ֗שֶׂק וְאֵת֙ שְׁלַ֣ל שֹׁמְר֔וֹן לִפְנֵ֖י מֶ֥לֶךְ אַשּֽׁוּר׃ ס

Hos 1:2b–4abα

וַיֹּ֨אמֶר יְהוָ֜ה אֶל־הוֹשֵׁ֗עַ
לֵ֣ךְ קַח־לְךָ֞ אֵ֤שֶׁת זְנוּנִים֙ וְיַלְדֵ֣י זְנוּנִ֔ים
כִּֽי־זָנֹ֤ה תִזְנֶה֙ הָאָ֔רֶץ מֵאַחֲרֵ֖י יְהוָֽה׃

וַיֵּ֙לֶךְ֙ וַיִּקַּ֔ח אֶת־גֹּ֖מֶר בַּת־דִּבְלָ֑יִם וַתַּ֥הַר וַתֵּֽלֶד־ל֖וֹ בֵּֽן׃
וַיֹּ֤אמֶר יְהוָה֙ אֵלָ֔יו קְרָ֥א שְׁמ֖וֹ יִזְרְעֶ֑אל
כִּי־ע֣וֹד מְעַ֗ט וּפָקַדְתִּ֞י אֶת־דְּמֵ֤י יִזְרְעֶאל֙ עַל־בֵּ֣ית יֵה֔וּא

Then the LORD said to me, "Take a large tablet and write on it in common characters, 'Belonging to Maher-shalal-hashbaz.'"	The LORD said to Hosea, "Go, take to yourself a wife of whoredom and have children of whoredom, for the land commits great whoredom by forsaking the LORD."
And I went to the prophetess, and she conceived and bore a son. Then the LORD said to me, "Call his name Maher-shalal-hashbaz; for before the boy knows how to cry 'My father' or 'My mother,' the wealth of Damascus and the spoil of Samaria will be carried away before the king of Assyria."	So he went and took Gomer, the daughter of Diblaim, and she conceived and bore him a son. And the LORD said to him, "Call his name Jezreel, for in just a little while I will punish the house of Jehu for the blood of Jezreel,"

---

34 Bosshard-Nepustil, *Rezeptionen*, 467: "Drohnamengebung als prophetisches Zeichen" (see also *ibid.*, 8, 413).

35 Christoph Levin, *Die Verheißung des neuen Bundes in ihrem theologiegeschichtlichen Zusammenhang ausgelegt*. FRLANT 137 (Göttingen: Vandenhoeck & Ruprecht, 1987), 235–245.

36 V. 2 involving witnesses probably represents a later amendment.

It is precisely the striking similarities between the two texts that, at the same time, make the differences all the more obvious. The first-person view (Ich-Bericht) in Isaiah 8 announces a concretely foreseeable foreign political event in view of the Syro-Ephraimite War of 733 B.C., which means misfortune for both aggressors – Israel and Aram –, whereas for the Southern Kingdom it means hope and salvation. Thus, it is a word of salvation for Judah. However, the third-person view (Er-Bericht) in Hos 1 threatens the own royal family (V. 4 f.) and the own people with calamity (V. 6) and revokes God's covenant with his people (V. 8–9). Therefore, Hos 1:2 ff is word of punishment.

Now C. Levin has suggested interpreting the so-called Hosea-word Hos 1:2b–4 as a replica ("Nachbildung") of Is 8 that came into being in the Southern Kingdom. "In diesem Falle nämlich stammte die Prophetie gegen Israel nicht aus Israel, sondern aus Judah."[37] Against the background of the Syro-Ephraimite War, in which the troops of the Northern Kingdom marched against Judah, this meant according to Levin: "Damals war das Unmögliche geschehen: Der eine Jahwe hatte sich gespalten und sich angeschickt, als Jahwe, der Gott Israels, in den Krieg zu ziehen gegen Jahwe, den Gott Judas. Man versteht unmittelbar, wie in dieser Lage ein Judäer Jahwe das Wort in den Mund legen konnte: ,Ihr seid nicht mein Volk, und ich bin nicht euer Gott!'"[38]

Yet it is more likely that Hos 1 already presupposes the fall of the Northern Kingdom.[39] The author sees the reason for the fall of the Northern Kingdom as forsaking YHWH and in following other gods. When Hos 1:2b formulates כִּי־זָנֹה תִזְנֶה הָאָרֶץ מֵאַחֲרֵי יְהוָה, he speaks of committing whoredom going away from following YHWH, the closeness to deuteronomic-deuteronomistic language is unmistakable.[40] Roman Vielhauer has pointed out, that the references between Hos 1:4 with its radical criticism of the kingship and 2 Kings 9 f are revealing, in that in both Hos 1 and 2 Kings 9 f worshipping alien gods is cited as the central charge. However, whilst in the deuteronomistic historical reflection in 2 Kings 9 f Jehu receives as the only king from the house of Omri a positive appraisal for fighting the Baal cult,

---

37 Levin, *Verheißung*, 238: "In this case, namely the prophecy against Israel did not originate in Israel, but in Judah".

38 *Ibid.*, 238 f.: "At that time the impossible had happened, namely the one Yahweh had split and set out as Yahweh, the God of Israel going to war against Yahweh, the God of Judah. It is immediately understandable how a Judean in this situation could put the word in Yahweh's mouth: 'you are not my people, and I am not your God!'".

39 Similarly Jeremias, *Der Prophet Hosea*, 29 f.: "Da die Erwähnung der Dynastie Jehus in V. 4b nicht zwingend auf Hoseas Frühzeit weist …, ist Kap. 1 mit hoher Wahrscheinlichkeit von einem Vertrauten Hoseas im letzten Jahrzehnt des Nordreichs oder aber – wahrscheinlicher noch – unmittelbar nach dessen Fall im Rückblick verfaßt worden."

40 In more detail Vielhauer, *Das Werden des Buches Hosea*, 138–141.

in Hos 1 he undergoes radical criticism, his blood shed even appears to be the reason for the fall of kingship in Israel.[41] If Hos 1:4 at the same time corrects the deuteronomistic historical reflection with his radical criticism of Jehu's religious policy, as Vielhauer assumes, it would be an indication for the late or post-exilic origin of Hos 1:4. For this view, however, the literary references between Hos 1 and 2 Kings 9 f are too weak.[42]

In any case, with regard to Hosea and Isaiah, it seems to be obvious that Is 8 must be considered as donor text for the later Hoseanic reflection.

3.5 Theological Turning Points in Hosea and Isaiah

The striking references between Is 8:1–4* and Hos 1 show how Hos 1 can clearly be dated later and how, probably influenced by Deuteronomistic theology, he speaks during or after the exile, whilst the donor text Is 8,1–4* is probably conveying Isaian thoughts from the time of the Syro-Ephraimite War. Is 7:3–9a*[43] and Is 17:1–3*[44] should also be quoted in this context. We are dealing with words of

---

41 The blood guilt of the house of Jehu, which causes the fall of the kingship in Israel illustrates and at the same time explains the basic reproach in Hos 4:2, according to which the blood guilt infects and corrupts the living together in Israel: וְדָמִים בְּדָמִים נָגָעוּ "and bloodshed follows bloodshed".

42 Cf., however, the view of Vielhauer, *Das Werden des Buches Hosea*, 141: "Hos 1 reflektiert den Untergang des Nordreiches in den Bahnen deuteronomistischer Geschichtstheologie, geht aber insofern einen Schritt weiter, als mit Jehu der einzige Nordreichkönig, der im Königebuch eine positive Bewertung erfährt, auch noch disqualifiziert wird. Die Beschränkung des Entzugs göttlichen Erbarmens auf das Nordreich rückt Hos 1 zudem in eine gewisse Nähe zur Chronik."

43 Is 7:3–9a: [3] And the LORD said to Isaiah, "Go out to meet Ahaz, you and Shear-jashub your son, at the end of the conduit of the upper pool on the highway to the Washer's Field. [4] And say to him, 'Be careful, be quiet, do not fear, and do not let your heart be faint because of these two smoldering stumps of firebrands, at the fierce anger of Rezin and Syria and the son of Remaliah. [5] Because Syria, with Ephraim and the son of Remaliah, has devised evil against you, saying, [6] "Let us go up against Judah and terrify it, and let us conquer it for ourselves, and set up the son of Tabeel as king in the midst of it," [7] thus says the Lord GOD: "'It shall not stand, and it shall not come to pass. [8] For the head of Syria is Damascus, and the head of Damascus is Rezin. (Within sixty-five years Ephraim will be broken to pieces so that it will no longer be a people.) [9] "'And the head of Ephraim is Samaria, and the head of Samaria is the son of Remaliah.'"

44 Is 17:1–3*: An oracle concerning Damascus. Behold, Damascus will cease to be a city and will become a heap of ruins. [2] The cities of Aroer are deserted; they will be for flocks, which will lie down, and none will make them afraid. [3] The fortress will disappear from Ephraim, and the kingdom from Damascus; and the remnant of Syria will be like the glory of the children of Israel, declares the LORD of hosts.

salvation for Judah and the announcements of the judgement against Judah's enemies, namely Aram and Ephraim. Clearly Isaiah is qualified as prophet of salvation, who strengthens the Kingdom of Judah stabilizing the political system, by announcing salvation for his own people and uttering words of judgement against the aggressors. The question arises here, as to whether Isaiah was exclusively prophet of salvation and the words of judgement are to be determined as subsequent *vaticinia ex eventu.*

In his contribution "Vom Heil zum Gericht. Die Selbstinterpretation Jesajas in der Denkschrift"[45] Hermann-Josef Stipp clarified that the process of Isaiah's transformation from prophet of salvation to prophet of judgement was not a subsequent reinterpretation, but something which occurs within Isaiah's annunciation. Isaiah had proclaimed doom against the aggressors in the context of the Syro-Ephraimite War and asked for trust in Zion's God at the same time. Ahas had undermined this condition and had turned to Assur for military help. The ensuing message of judgement of Isaiah went almost unheard, "weil er gewissermaßen seinem eigenen Erfolg zum Opfer fiel, da er ja den glücklichen Ausgang für Juda selbst vorhergesagt hatte. Die Tiefe seiner Glaubwürdigkeitskrise ist an dem Umstand zu ermessen, dass man seinen Protesten seine eigenen, vom Lauf der Geschichte bestätigten Prophezeiungen entgegenhalten konnte."[46] Therefore Isaiah revised the original oracle of salvation for the king in Is 7:4d-9b, combining it with conditional words of judgement in the case of lack of trust. Thus, the prophecy of Immanuel also acquires its own ambivalence of salvation and doom.[47] It can be assumed that originally Isaiah's prophecy of salvation took on great significance. The change from proclamation of salvation to proclamation

---

45 Hermann-Josef Stipp, "Vom Heil zum Gericht. Die Selbstinterpretation Jesajas in der Denkschrift," in: F. Sedlmeier (Hg.), *Gottes Weg suchend. Beiträge zum Verständnis der Bibel und ihrer Botschaft.* FS Rudolf Mosis (Würzburg: Echter, 2003): 323–354.
46 Stipp, "Vom Gericht zum Heil", 347: "The Prophet's message of judgement went almost unheard, because he somehow fell victim to his own success, as he himself had foretold the happy ending for Judah. The depth of his credibility-crisis can be measured by the fact that his protests could be countered by his own prophecies which were confirmed by history."
47 *Ibid.,* 350 f.: "Nach der Bewahrheitung seiner Heilsansagen sah sich Jesaja genötigt, einem kapitalen Missverständnis seiner Prophetie entgegenzutreten, das deren zionstheologischen Bezugsrahmen glaubte ignorieren zu können – eine fatale Verkennung der Lage, die Juda unweigerlich ins Verderben stürzen würde. Wie die Art der Fusion von Heil und Gericht in der Denkschrift noch durchblicken lässt, hatte Jesaja die Heilsalternative derart hevorgekehrt, dass er als reiner Heilsprophet wahrgenommen wurde. Der Missbrauch seiner Prophetie zwang ihn schließlich, die Gewichte zurechtzurücken, was auf die Notwendigkeit hinauslief, seine eigene Frühzeitverkündigung unwirksam zu machen. Vor allem musste er dem Eindruck des Selbstwiderspruchs wehren, indem er darlegte, dass seine damalige Prophetie in Wahrheit schon die jetzige war."

of doom is not explained by "unterschiedlichen Adressatenkreisen" ("different target groups")[48] or by "sekundäre[r] Umpolung eines reinen Heilspropheten" ("the secondary pole reversal of a pure salvation-prophet").[49] Much rather we find mirrored "ein Nacheinander in Jesajas eigener Biographie. ... Es waren ernüchternde Erfahrungen mit seiner Heilsprophetie, die ihn bewogen, die schon immer latente Unheilsalternative schließlich ganz in den Vordergrund zu rücken. Insofern bezeugt die Denkschrift indirekt die Bekehrung Jesajas vom Heilspropheten zum Künder des Gerichts."[50]

Therefore, the transformation from prophet of salvation to prophet of judgement has to be viewed as an evolutionary process in Isaiah's prophetic efficaciousness.

Similarly, Jan Christian Gertz does not interpret the emergence of the radical prophecy of doom in Amos as *vaticinium ex eventu*, but as an expression of prophetic intuition in a crisis filled time.[51] "Amos' No" is not merely an interpretament after suffering catastrophe, nor merely an adaptation of the prophetic word to the normative power of the facts, but rather an expression of a genuine religious experience, which of course, owed its assertion to the facts that confirmed it.[52]

A very similar question arises for Hosea now. The book of Hosea presents the prophet consistently as prophet of doom and salvation, whereby the path from disaster to salvation is crossed several times. Most of the words of salvation originate with certainty from latter, partly from exilic or post-exilic times. The words

---

48 Different target groups are supposed by Stuart A. Irvine, *Isaiah, Ahaz, and the Syro-Ephraimic crisis*. SBDL.DS 123 (Atlanta; GA, 1990) und J. Barthel, *Prophetenwort und Geschichte. Die Jesaja-überlieferung in Jes 6–8 und 28–31.* FAT 19 (Tübingen: Mohr Siebeck, 1997), 43–56.

49 A secondary pole reversal of a pure prophet of salvation is found in Ulrich Becker, *Jesaja – von der Botschaft zum Buch*. FRLANT 178 (Göttingen: Vandenhoeck & Ruprecht, 1996) and Ernst Axel Knauf, "Vom Prophetinnenwort zum Prophetenbuch: Jes 8,3f. im Kontext von Jes 6,1–8,16," in Lectio difficilior (Internet) 2/2000 (no pages).

50 Stipp, "Vom Gericht zum Heil", 353–354. Also J. Høgenhaven, *Gott und Volk bei Jesaja. Eine Untersuchung zur biblischen Theologie.* AThD 24 (Leiden u. a.: 1988), 94 depicts similarly the concept of succession in the biography, represented by Stipp. The combination of conflicting statements for Høgenhaven must be assigned to later editors, according to Stipp this is Isaiah's original work.

51 Jan Christian Gertz, "Die unbedingte Gerichtsankündigung des Amos," in: Franz Sedlmeier (Hg.), *Gottes Weg suchend. Beiträge zum Verständnis der Bibel und ihrer Botschaft.* FS Rudolf Mosis (Würzburg: Echter, 2003): 153–170.

52 Gertz, "Gerichtsankündigung", 170: "Die religiöse Idee bleibt unableitbar. Sie geht dem äußeren Anlass voraus. Ihre historische Durchsetzung verdankt sie jedoch der faktischen Lage. Die religiöse Idee konnte nur wirksam werden, weil sie sich in der geschichtlichen Erfahrung bewährte und als das geeignete Mittel zur Bewältigung der Katastrophe erwies."

of judgement also partly presume the fall of the Northern Kingdom and partly the Babylonian exile.

Roman Vielhauer sees the oldest material of Hosea in Hos 5–9, whereby he surmises the oral announcement of the prophet behind Hos 5:8–11;[53] 6:7–9*;[54] 7:5f[55] and 7:8b–9[56]. These list concrete offences such as murder, theft, breach of contract, committed in cities like Adam or Gilead or by particular groups like the priesthood or the royal house. But: "Eine grundsätzliche Kritik am politischen und religiösen Status quo des Nordreiches ist damit nicht verbunden."[57]

Behind Hos 5:8–11 Vielhauer suspects border disputes between Ephraim and Judah, perhaps in connection with the Syro-Ephraimite War, whereby the use of foreign oracles directed against the other's salvation for one's own party is claimed. It is not clear from which perspective the text is speaking.

Hos 5:9a.11a could come from the Judean point of view: 9a: אֶפְרַיִם לְשַׁמָּה תִהְיֶה בְּיוֹם תּוֹכֵחָה "Ephraim shall become a desolation in the day of punishment." 11a: עָשׁוּק אֶפְרַיִם רְצוּץ מִשְׁפָּט "Ephraim is oppressed, crushed in judgement," while v. 10 could be phrased from the point of view of the North: הָיוּ שָׂרֵי יְהוּדָה כְּמַסִּיגֵי גְּבוּל עֲלֵיהֶם אֶשְׁפּוֹךְ כַּמַּיִם עֶבְרָתִי: "The princes of Judah have become like those who move the landmark; upon them I will pour out my wrath like water." V. 8 could be understood as an invitation, to defend their own country Ephraim: תִּקְעוּ שׁוֹפָר בַּגִּבְעָה חֲצֹצְרָה בָּרָמָה הָרִיעוּ בֵּית אָוֶן אַחֲרֶיךָ בִּנְיָמִין: "Blow the horn in Gibeah, the trumpet in Ramah. Sound the alarm at Beth-aven; we follow you, O Benjamin!"

The statements in Hosea's text cannot be unambiguously assigned. However, it is paramount – according to Vielhauer – "daß das erwartete Unheil in diesen Sprüchen nicht als Strafe Gottes interpretiert ist, JHWH vielmehr als Staats- und Dynastiegott Partei für das jeweils eigene Staatswesen in Juda bzw. Ephraim

---

53 Hos 5:8–11: [8] Blow the horn in Gibeah, the trumpet in Ramah. Sound the alarm at Beth-aven; we follow you, O Benjamin! [9] Ephraim shall become a desolation in the day of punishment; among the tribes of Israel I make known what is sure. [10] The princes of Judah have become like those who move the landmark; upon them I will pour out my wrath like water. [11] Ephraim is oppressed, crushed in judgement, because he was determined to go after filth.

54 Hos 6:7–9*: [7] But like Adam they transgressed the covenant; there they dealt faithlessly with me. [8] Gilead is a city of evildoers, tracked with blood. [9] As robbers lie in wait for a man, so the priests band together; they murder on the way to Shechem; they commit villainy.

55 Hos 7:5f: [5] On the day of our king, the princes became sick with the heat of wine; he stretched out his hand with mockers. [6] For with hearts like an oven they approach their intrigue; all night their anger smolders; in the morning it blazes like a flaming fire.

56 Hos 7:8b–9: Ephraim is a cake not turned. [9] Strangers devour his strength, and he knows it not; gray hairs are sprinkled upon him, and he knows it not.

57 Vielhauer, *Das Werden des Buches Hosea*, 113.

ergreift. Gott und Staat bilden eine natürliche Einheit."[58] Thus, however, the proclamation of Hosea fits "problemlos in die konventionelle Heils- und Mahn-prophetie des Alten Orients."[59] According to Vielhauer the turnaround from prophecy of salvation to a radical prophecy of doom occurs after the fall of the Northern Kingdom within the scope of the first editing of the Book of Hosea. "Diese außerordentliche Wende läßt sich erst damit erklären, daß die Verfasser der hose-anischen Grundschicht den durch Assur gewirkten Untergang des Nordreiches 723/720 v. Chr. bereits erlebt haben. … In der Grundschicht des Hoseabuches läßt sich der Übergang von konventioneller Heils- und Mahnprophetie zur unbe-dingten Gerichtsankündigung im Übergang vom Wort zur Schrift nachvollziehen. Beides, die unbedingte Gerichtsprophetie wie auch die auf Tradierung angelegte Schriftprophetie, hängt ursächlich zusammen und nimmt seinen Ausgang in der theologischen Reflexion über die staatliche Katastrophe des Nordreiches."[60]

According to Vielhauers studies the radical message of doom is voiced only after the fall of the Northern Kingdom. Ultimately, it is nothing more than an interpretive representation of the status quo and is exhausted in confirming the normative power of the factual. This catching interpretation, however, seems to me to trivialise the crimes committed in Hos 5:8–11; 6:7–9*; 7:5 f and 7:8b–9. These serious offences affect the substance of the life of the people of God in so far as they invalidate a life according to the Torah. This is more than a trivial offence. The seriousness of the offences amongst the people of God in connection with an irresponsible policy of alliance and increasing pressure by the New Assyrians had to give an idea of the possibility of the fall to the alert prophetic spirit.[61]

As with Amos and Isaiah, the radical change to the prophet of doom in Hosea is not merely a retrospective confirmation of historical facts, but an insight gained from the inner state of Israel and the political climate. Hosea becomes a prophet of doom even before the fall of the Northern Empire, which corresponds to Isaiah and Amos. The fact that his view of doom was able to prevail is because the pre-viously announced judgement has actually arrived and has confirmed his proc-lamation.

---

58 *Ibid.*, 114.
59 *Ibid.*, 114.
60 *Ibid.*, 117. Vielhauer sees a similar development in Amos (Am 3–6) and in Isaiah (Is 6–8*). But see the deviating positioning by Stipp (to Is 6–8*) and by Gertz (to Am 1–2; 7–9). See also the previous considerations.
61 In this respect, Henrik Pfeiffer, *Das Heiligtum von Bethel im Spiegel des Hoseabuches*. FRLANT 183 (Göttingen: Vandenhoeck & Ruprecht, 1999), 225 is quite right if he sees in the Assyrian dan-ger a reason that influences Hosea's radical "no".

3.6 Further References between Isaiah and Hosea

There are further contact points between Isaiah and Hosea, which are not developed here in detail, but only briefly mentioned.

3.6.1 Trust in Military Power

The trust in military power is broadly unfolded in the Book of Isaiah, as in Is 2:7 f;[62] 17:8;[63] 30:16;[64] 31:1–3,[65] 37:19,[66] often in connection with the expression "work of hands". In Hosea too, pertinent statements emerge (Hos 10:13b[67] and Hos 14:2–4[68]), however, for Hosea these are only a marginal topic, which owes

---

62 The references between the book of Hosea and Deutero- and Trito-Isaiah are not specifically dealt with, as this would go beyond the scope of the work.
Is 2:7–8: ⁷ Their land is filled with silver and gold, and there is no end to their treasures; their land is filled with horses, and there is no end to their chariots. ⁸ Their land is filled with idols; they bow down to the work of their hands, to what their own fingers have made.
63 Is 17:8: ⁸ He will not look to the altars, the work of his hands, and he will not look on what his own fingers have made, either the Asherim or the altars of incense.
64 Is 30:16: ¹⁵ For thus said the Lord GOD, the Holy One of Israel, "In returning and rest you shall be saved; in quietness and in trust shall be your strength." But you were unwilling, ¹⁶ and you said, "No! We will flee upon horses"; therefore you shall flee away; and, "We will ride upon swift steeds"; therefore your pursuers shall be swift.
65 Is 31:1–3: ¹ Woe to those who go down to Egypt for help and rely on horses, who trust in chariots because they are many and in horsemen because they are very strong, but do not look to the Holy One of Israel or consult the LORD! ² And yet he is wise and brings disaster; he does not call back his words, but will arise against the house of the evildoers and against the helpers of those who work iniquity. ³ The Egyptians are human, and not God, and their horses are flesh, and not spirit. When the LORD stretches out his hand, the helper will stumble, and he who is helped will fall, and they will all perish together.
66 Is 37:19: ¹⁸ Truly, O LORD, the kings of Assyria have laid waste all the nations and their lands, ¹⁹ and have cast their gods into the fire. For they were no gods, but the work of human's hands, wood and stone. Therefore they were destroyed.
67 Hos 10:13b: כִּי־בָטַחְתָּ בְדַרְכְּךָ בְּרֹב גִּבּוֹרֶיךָ "Because you have trusted in your own way and in the multitude of your warriors".
68 Hos 14:2–4: ² Take with you words and return to the LORD; say to him, "Take away all iniquity; accept what is good, and we will pay with bulls the vows of our lips. ³ אַשּׁוּר ׀ לֹא יוֹשִׁיעֵנוּ עַל־סוּס לֹא Assyria shall not save us; we will not ride on horses; וְלֹא־נֹאמַר עוֹד אֱלֹהֵינוּ לְמַעֲשֵׂה יָדֵינוּ and we will say no more, 'Our God,' to the work of our hands. In you the orphan finds mercy." ⁴ I will heal their apostasy; I will love them freely, for my anger has turned from them.

itself to the ideas of Isaiah. Wellhausen had already noted: "Verstehn kann das nur, wer Isa. 30 kennt."[69]

Further Hoseanic references regarding trust in military power can be found in Hos 1:7[70] and 8:14.[71] Here Hosea probably depends on Isaiah and on deuteronomic-deuteronomistic literature. Also A. Schart points to Isaiah's influence on Hosea: "Interessant ist, daß Hos 1,7; 8,14 sich mit Hos 14,2–4 darin berühren, dass sie mit dem Hinweis auf das fehlgeleitete Vertrauen auf militärische Macht ein typisches Jesajathema aufgenommen haben (vgl. Jes 2,7–8)."[72]

Since the posterior text Hos 14:2–4 with its late deuteronomistic theology of conversion might also presuppose Joel 2:12,[73] Hos 14:2–4 could link the book of Hosea with the Dodekapropheton and at the same time the Dodekapropheton with the book of Isaiah.

3.6.2 YHWH's Plan

The motive of the plan of YHWH emerges in Hos 10:6b: "Just so, the calf itself will be carried off to Assyria, a gift for the great king. Ephraim brings shame upon himself, and Israel is ashamed because of his plan (מֵעֲצָתוֹ)."

גַּם־אוֹתוֹ לְאַשּׁוּר יוּבָל מִנְחָה לְמֶלֶךְ יָרֵב בָּשְׁנָה אֶפְרַיִם יִקָּח וְיֵבוֹשׁ יִשְׂרָאֵל מֵעֲצָתוֹ:

The motive of עצה ("plan") in connection with בוש ("to be put to shame") uses Isaian wording, cf. Is 30:1–5. In Hos 10:6b there might be a later gloss.

3.6.3 Cult Polemic Texts

Within the cult polemic Isaiah and Hosea are standing close together. The polemic in Is 1:10–15 and Is 1:16f (cf. also Am 5:21–27) and the cult polemic statements in Hos 4:1–9:9* show a number of similarities.[74] YHWH is split in two in as much

---

69 Julius Wellhausen, 133, quoted after Vielhauer, *Das Werden des Buches Hosea*, 194, note 33.
70 Hos 1:7: ⁷ But I will have mercy on the house of Judah, and I will save them by the LORD their God. I will not save them by bow or by sword or by war or by horses or by horsemen.
71 Hos 8:14: ¹⁴ For Israel has forgotten his Maker and built palaces, and Judah has multiplied fortified cities; so I will send a fire upon his cities, and it shall devour her strongholds.
72 A. Schart, *Entstehung*, 170.
73 Joel 2:12: "Yet even now," declares the LORD, "return to me with all your heart, with fasting, with weeping, and with mourning."
74 It's about the following texts (see Vielhauer, *Das Werden des Buches Hosea*, 120): Hos 4:1–2,4–10*,11–14*; 5:6–7; 5:15–6:6*; 7:13–16; 8:1–3*; 8:11f; 9:3,9*.

as an alternative is entered in YHWH. YHWH stands on the one hand quite traditionally as a stabilizing factor in the service of a cult confirming the policy, on the other hand – so the position of Hosea or the Hosea-tradents – he insists on the observance of the Torah, which stands in opposition to cult and politics in the time of Hosea. The fall of the Northern Kingdom shows the problematics of the connection of politics, cult and YHWH. By contrast the old alliance "state-religion-national God" seems to continue to work in the Southern Kingdom of Judah. Thus an interior contradiction evolved in YHWH himself, as Vielhauer explains: "der wahre JHWH, der jenseits der staatlichen Institutionen auf seiten Assurs gegen sein Volk auftrat, wurde von einem trügerisch-machtlosen JHWH unterschieden, den man in Juda als Garant der staatlichen Institutionen wirksam sah."[75]

A literary dependence between Isaiah and Hosea cannot be proven here. But there is a theological-historical proximity between the Isaian and Hosean cult polemics. Therefore, the similarities between Isaiah and Hosea can be better explained by the history of tradition.

4 Summary

(1) An immediate relationship between the historical figures Hosea and Isaiah can hardly be assumed. Both operate approximately simultaneously but are integrated into completely different contexts. Contact points between Hosea and Isaiah arise above all in the editorial reworking of both prophets' books. It must have been the concern of the Hosean tradents to connect the book of Hosea not only with the message of Amos, but also with that of Isaiah.

(2) Oldest texts from Isaiah and Hosea refer to the realm of cult polemics. However, the equivalents in the statements of both prophets do not stem from a literary dependency but can be explained in the history of tradition.

(3) A radical theological turn from salvation to judgement is found in the proclamation of Isaiah and Hosea alike. This concentration on the prophecy of judgement is already unfolding in the workings of these prophets themselves. It cannot be ascribed exclusively as a later pole reversal of the editorial work of the revisers. However, the fact that the historical events have confirmed their proclamation explains the success and the special esteem of the proclamation of Isaiah and Hosea (as well as Amos).

---

75 Vielhauer, *Das Werden des Buches Hosea*, 124 ("The true YHWH appearing beyond state institutions on Assurs side against his people was distinguished from a deceptively powerless YHWH, who was seen to be effective in Judah as the guarantor of state institutions.")

(4) The heading Hos 1,1 connects Hosea's message on the one hand with that of Amos and Micah, formally also with Zephaniah's, i.e. the emerging corpus of the Dodekapropheton, but on the other hand also with the book of Isaiah. In this respect, the Hosean writing has a key role: It links the Minor Prophets with the Major Prophets.

(5) That the structure of the book of Isaiah and the Dodekapropheton are supposed to have structural equivalents cannot be confirmed, at least for the text corpus of the book of Hosea. Bosshard-Nepustil's hypothesis that one or more editors would have created a parallel sequence of events between Isaiah and Hosea or Dodekapropheton is rather unlikely.

(6) The striking equivalents between the children's names in Is 8:1–4 and Hos 1:2–9 speak for a dependence of Hosea on Isaiah. See the studies of Christoph Levin.

(7) Other thematic references between Isaiah and Hosea – such as the topic of YHWH's plan and of trust in military power – show Hosea's dependence upon Isaiah's texts.

(8) Since the book of Hosea evidently has a key function in linking the Dodekapropheton with Isaiah, the question of "convergence and difference" between Isaiah and Hosea must be combined with a question of further study: namely the literary and motif-based integration of Hosea into the Dodekapropheton.

Bibliography

Barthel, Jörg, *Prophetenwort und Geschichte: Die Jesajaüberlieferung in Jes 6–8 und 28–31*, FAT 19 (Tübingen: Mohr Siebeck, 1997).

Becker, Ulrich, *Jesaja – von der Botschaft zum Buch*, FRLANT 178 (Göttingen: Vandenhoeck & Ruprecht, 1996).

Erich Bosshard, "Beobachtungen zum Zwölfprophetenbuch," *BN* 40 (1987): 30–62.

Bosshard-Nepustil, Erich, *Rezeptionen von Jesaia 1–39 im Zwölfprophetenbuch: Untersuchungen zur literarischen Verbindung von Prophetenbüchern in babylonischer und persischer Zeit*, OBO 154 (Fribourg: Universitätsverlag Freiburg, 1997).

Donner, Herbert, *Geschichte des Volkes Israel und seiner Nachbarn in Grundzügen 2*, ATD Ergänzungsreihe Band 2 (Göttingen: Vandenhoeck & Ruprecht, 1986).

Freedmann, D. N., *"Headings in the Books of the Eighth-Century Prophet,"*, AUSS 25 (1987): 9–26.

Gertz, Jan Christian, "Die unbedingte Gerichtsankündigung des Amos," in *Gottes Weg suchend: Beiträge zum Verständnis der Bibel und ihrer Botschaft*, ed. Franz Sedlmeier, FS Rudolf Mosis (Würzburg: Echter, 2003): 153–170.

Høgenhaven, Jesper, *Gott und Volk bei Jesaja: Eine Untersuchung zur biblischen Theologie*, AThD 24 (Leiden: Brill, 1988).

Irvine, Stuart A., *Isaiah, Ahaz, and the Syro-Ephraimitic Crisis*, SBDL.DS 123 (Atlanta, GA: Scholars Press, 1990).

Jeremias, Jörg, *Der Prophet Hosea*, ATD 24/1 (Göttingen: Vandenhoeck & Ruprecht, 1983).

Jeremias, Jörg, "Die Anfänge des Dodekapropheton: Hosea und Amos," in *Hosea und Amos: Studien zu den Anfängen des Dodekapropheton*, ed. Jörg Jeremias, FAT 13 (Tübingen: Mohr, 1996): 34–54.

Knauf, Ernst Axel, "Vom Prophetinnenwort zum Prophetenbuch: Jes 8,3 f. im Kontext von Jes 6,1–8,16," *Lectio difficilior* 2 (2000): n.p. <http://www.lectio.unibe.ch/00_2/v.htm> [accessed 9 April 2019].

Kreuch, Jan, *Das Amos- und Jesajabuch: Eine exegetische Studie zur Neubestimmung ihres Verhältnisses*, BThSt 149 (Neukirchen-Vlyun: Neukirchener Verlagsgesellschaft, 2014).

Levin, Christoph, *Die Verheißung des neuen Bundes in ihrem theologiegeschichtlichen Zusammenhang ausgelegt*, FRLANT 137 (Göttingen: Vandenhoeck & Ruprecht, 1987).

Pfeiffer, Henrik, *Das Heiligtum von Bethel im Spiegel des Hoseabuches*. FRLANT 183 (Göttingen: Vandenhoeck & Ruprecht, 1999).

Rudnig-Zelt, Susanne, *Hoseastudien: Redaktionskritische Untersuchungen zur Genese des Hoseabuches*, FRLANT 123 (Göttingen: Vandenhoeck & Ruprecht, 2006).

Schart, Aaron, *Die Entstehung des Zwölfprophetenbuchs: Neubearbeitungen von Amos im Rahmen schrif-tenübergreifender Redaktionsprozesse*, BZAW 260 (Berlin: de Gruyter, 1997).

Stipp, Hermann-Josef, "Vom Heil zum Gericht: Die Selbstinterpretation Jesajas in der Denkschrift," in *Gottes Weg suchend: Beiträge zum Verständnis der Bibel und ihrer Botschaft*, ed. Franz Sedlmeier, FS Rudolf Mosis (Würzburg: Echter, 2003): 323–354.

Vielhauer, Roman, *Das Werden des Buches Hosea*, BZAW 349 (Berlin: de Gruyter, 2007).

Wacker, Marie-Theres, *Figurationen des Weiblichen im Hosea-Buch*, HBS 8 (Freiburg: Herder, 1996).

Wolff, Hans Walter, *Hosea*, BK.AT XIV/1 (Neukirchen-Vluyn: Neukirchener Verlag, 1976).

Zapff, Burkard M., "Why is Micah similar to Isaiah?" in *ZAW* 129 (2017): 536–554.

Uwe Becker
Sozialkritik in Jes 1–39 und im Amos-Buch

Wer sich heutzutage mit Amos und Jesaja 1–39 und mit ihrem Verhältnis zueinander beschäftigt, sticht in gleich zwei Wespennester der Forschung. Weder in
der Amos- noch in der Jesajaforschung gibt es so etwas wie einen tragfähigen
Konsens, auf dem man aufbauen könnte. Vor allem die Fragen nach Umfang
und Charakter der ursprünglichen Verkündigung der Propheten und – darauf
aufbauend – nach der Entstehung der Bücher werden heute unterschiedlicher
denn je beantwortet. Auch die Texte zur Sozialkritik im engeren Sinne sind von
der divergierenden Forschungslage betroffen: Gehören sie im Wesentlichen der
ursprünglichen, „authentischen" Verkündigung der Propheten an? Oder spiegelt
sich in ihnen das Selbstverständnis späterer, nachprophetischer Kreise wider?
Die These, die im Folgenden begründet werden soll, lautet: Die Sozialkritik in
Jes 1–39 ist literarisch vom Amos-Buch abhängig. Sie ist kein genuin „jesajanisches" Thema, vielmehr erst im Verlaufe der Buchwerdung zu einem solchen geworden.

1 Einführung

Immer noch steht die Sozialkritik der Propheten – insbesondere eines Amos
oder Jesaja – hoch im Kurs. Beispielhaft kann auf zwei deutschsprachige Studien
hingewiesen werden, die noch nicht allzu alt sind und als repräsentativ gelten
können: 1992 erschien die bei Frank Crüsemann gearbeitete Betheler Dissertation
des Brasilianers Haroldo Reimer mit dem Titel *Richtet auf das Recht! Studien zur
Botschaft des Amos*[1], in der – inspiriert von der Befreiungstheologie – die konkrete Gesellschaftskritik des Amos in den Blick genommen und ein farbenpräch-
tiges Bild seiner Verkündigung gezeichnet wird. Amos habe, so die These der
Arbeit, nicht etwa das Volksganze angeredet, wie man (zumal in weiten Teilen der
damaligen protestantischen Bibelwissenschaft) dachte, vielmehr war seine Verkündigung *„sozial- und schichtenspezifisch"*[2] ausgerichtet, betraf also konkrete
Missstände einzelner Menschen und Gruppen.

---

1 Haroldo Reimer, *Richtet auf das Recht! Studien zur Botschaft des Amos*, SBS 149 (Stuttgart: Verlag Katholisches Bibelwerk, 1992).
2 *Ibid.*, 229.

https://doi.org/10.1515/9783110705799-003

Das Gegenstück zum Jesajabuch, ebenfalls aus der Feder eines Brasilianers, erschien 1994. Es handelt sich um eine bereits 1986 abgeschlossene, von Jörg Jeremias betreute Dissertation von Renatus Porath *Die Sozialkritik im Jesajabuch*[3]. Stärker noch als Reimer bemüht er sich um eine redaktionsgeschichtliche Analyse der einschlägigen jesajanischen Texte, aber auch er gelangt zu klaren sozialgeschichtlichen Verortungen: Am Anfang standen mündlich ergangene Worte gegen bestimmte Gruppen in Juda (3,14 f.; 3,16 f.24; 10,1–3; 5,8); erst die redaktionelle Zusammenstellung der Worte machte aus ihnen einen Schuldaufweis gegen *ganz* Juda. Sowohl Reimer als auch Porath legen die sozialkritischen Worte des Amos und des Jesaja ohne Bezug zueinander als Widerspiegelung einer sozio-ökonomisch prekären Lage im Land (in Israel wie in Juda) aus.

Etwa zur selben Zeit gab es freilich auch andere Arbeiten, die methodisch differenzierter ansetzten. Als Beispiel sei die 1989 erschienene, von Frank-Lothar Hossfeld betreute, Bonner Dissertation zum Amosbuch von Gunther Fleischer genannt. Sie trägt den ebenso schönen wie schlagwortartigen Titel *Von Menschenverkäufern, Baschankühen und Rechtsverkehrern*[4]. Fleischer beginnt seine Studie mit einem Stoßseufzer: „Schon wieder eine Arbeit zum Amosbuch und seiner Sozialkritik!"[5] Er sieht die Defizite bisheriger Arbeiten zur Sozialkritik darin, dass sich diese vornehmlich auf die Propheten im allgemeinen bezögen, also eine Anthologie der sozialkritischen Texte böten, um daraus eine gesellschaftliche Krisenzeit zu rekonstruieren, anstatt sich dem spezifischen Profil der einzelnen Propheten zuzuwenden. Tatsächlich gibt es, so Fleischer, „kein zweites Prophetenbuch, in dem die Sozialkritik eine vergleichbar dominante Rolle spielt"[6], wie Amos. Im Unterschied zu vielen eher flächig vorgehenden Arbeiten sieht Fleischer seine Aufgabe darin, die sozialkritischen Texte des Amos-Buches redaktionsgeschichtlich zu analysieren und zu verorten, um sie dann in einen sozialgeschichtlichen Hintergrund einordnen zu können. In diesem methodischen Ansatz bei der Redaktionsgeschichte liegt die Stärke der Studie.

Hinter die Einsicht in das redaktionelle Wachstum der Prophetenbücher sollte man nicht mehr zurückkehren. Das persönlichkeitsorientierte Prophetenbild, das viele Studien zur Sozialgeschichte begleitet – der Prophet als vollmächtiger Künder des Gotteswillens –, entspricht dem Bild des Buches, der *presentation*

---

3 Renatus Porath, *Die Sozialkritik im Jesajabuch. Redaktionsgeschichtliche Analyse*, EHS.T 503 (Frankfurt a.M. u. a.: Peter Lang, 1994).

4 Gunther Fleischer, *Von Menschenverkäufern, Baschankühen und Rechtsverkehrern. Die Sozialkritik des Amosbuches in historisch-kritischer, sozialgeschichtlicher und archäologischer Perspektive*, BBB 74 (Frankfurt a.M.: Athenäum, 1989).

5 *Ibid.*, 1.

6 *Ibid.*, 8 f.

of a prophet, aber nicht der Historie. Ein weiterer Aspekt kommt hinzu: Im Amos-Buch wird man keineswegs nur mit einer „klassischen" Kritik an sozialen Missständen konfrontiert, sondern auch mit Texten, die man unter der Überschrift „Armenfrömmigkeit" fassen kann. Hinter diesem Begriff steht nicht primär eine sozioökonomisch beschreibbare Armut, sondern eher eine „geistliche" Armutshaltung, die vornehmlich *religiöse* Motive – oder besser: eine bestimmte religiöse Haltung – zum Hintergrund hat.[7] Dieses Phänomen ist aber, wie vor allem Christoph Levin gezeigt hat, auch schon im Amos-Buch sichtbar und gehört dort, wie sich zeigen wird, nicht zum literarischen Kernbestand.[8]

Im Hinblick auf die sozialkritische Rekonstruktion ist der folgende, beliebte Zirkelschluss methodisch problematisch: Der sozialgeschichtliche Hintergrund wird in der Regel aufgrund der prophetischen Texte rekonstruiert, die wiederum von diesem Hintergrund her interpretiert werden. So ist etwa für Rainer Kessler in seiner Studie zu *Staat und Gesellschaft im vorexilischen Juda*[9] „die Frage nach den sog. *ipsissima verba* des Propheten [...] insofern belanglos, als es für die sozialgeschichtliche Auswertung nicht auf den Namen des Autors ankommt, sondern nur darauf, ob das, was dasteht, aussagekräftig ist."[10] Und das gilt dann auch für den Schülerkreis des Propheten. Verständlich ist deshalb, dass Kessler einer „generellen Datierung der prophetischen Sozialkritik in nachexilische Zeit"[11] sehr reserviert gegenübersteht.

„[Der] methodische Fehler bei einer generellen Spätdatierung liegt u. a. nämlich darin, daß die für die gesamte israelitische Antike gleiche soziale Grundkonstellation, die – kurz gesagt – im Widerspruch zwischen Gläubiger und Schuldner besteht, zum Ausgangspunkt der Datierung gemacht wird."[12]

Kessler verweist etwa auf die Nähe mancher Jesaja-Texte zu Neh 5.

---

7 Das Phänomen spielt auch in der neueren Psalmenforschung eine große Rolle, vgl. etwa Johannes Bremer, „The Theology of the Poor in the Psalter," in *The Psalter as Witness. Theology, Poetry, and Genre*, Hg. W. Dennis Tucker und William H. Bellinger (Waco, TX: Baylor University Press, 2017): 101–116. Darüber hinaus ders., *Wo Gott sich auf die Armen einlässt. Der sozio-ökonomische Hintergrund der achämenidischen Provinz Yəhūd und seine Implikationen für die Armentheologie des Psalters*, BBB 174 (Göttingen: V&R unipress, 2016).
8 Christoph Levin, „Das Amosbuch der Anawim [1997]," in *Fortschreibungen. Gesammelte Studien zum Alten Testament*, BZAW 316 (Berlin-New York: Walter de Gruyter, 2003): 265–290.
9 Rainer Kessler, *Staat und Gesellschaft im vorexilischen Juda. Vom 8. Jahrhundert bis zum Exil*, VTS 47 (Leiden: E. J. Brill, 1992).
10 *Ibid.*, 22.
11 *Ibid.*, 23 mit Verweis auf Otto Kaisers Jesajakommentar.; vgl. etwa Otto Kaiser, *Das Buch des Propheten Jesaja. Kapitel 1–12*, ATD 17 (Göttingen: Vandenhoeck & Ruprecht, ⁵1981).
12 Kessler, *Staat*, 23.

In den folgenden Überlegungen soll der Fokus nicht auf die (rekonstruierte) sozialgeschichtliche Lage in Israel und Juda des 8. Jahrhunderts gelegt werden, sondern auf die vermuteten Bezüge zwischen Amos und dem protojesajanischen Bestand in Jes 1–39.

2 Das Verhältnis von Amos und Jesaja: ein Blick in die Forschungsgeschichte

Es unterliegt keinem Zweifel: Die Bücher Amos und Jesaja berühren sich in keinem Bereich so sehr wie in der prophetischen „Sozialkritik". Die einfachste Erklärung für diesen Befund liegt in der Annahme, die gesellschaftlichen Verhältnisse im 8. Jahrhundert seien vergleichbar gewesen und hätten ähnliche prophetische Anklagen provoziert. Denn die primäre Aufgabe der Propheten sei es nach Ansicht vieler Ausleger, die Mächtigen zur Räson zu rufen, Ungerechtigkeit anzuprangern und für gerechte Verhältnisse einzutreten. Der Prophet tritt damit primär als Gesellschaftskritiker in Erscheinung. Mit den Worten der Ethik des Alten Testaments aus der Feder Rainer Kesslers: „Mit dem *Binom ‚Recht und Gerechtigkeit'* wird eine *zentrale Kategorie der prophetischen Ethik* formuliert."[13] Dieser „Gesellschaftskritiker" aber steht in direkter Gegnerschaft zum König und zur etablierten Kaste der Propheten. So führt Rainer Albertz in seiner Religionsgeschichte Israels, die sich im Kern als eine Sozialgeschichte darstellt, unter der Überschrift „Die prophetische Total-Opposition" folgendes über den Propheten Amos und seine Kollegen im 8. Jahrhundert aus:

„Die Männer, die sich in dem Zeitraum von ca. 760–700 von Gott getrieben sahen, in bis dahin unbekannt radikaler Weise zu den krisenhaften Entwicklungen dieser Epoche Stellung zu nehmen, gehören alle zum Typ des institutionell ungebundenen Einzelpropheten. Amos, der aus Thekoa im Südreich stammte, aber im Nordreich wahrscheinlich nur relativ kurze Zeit um 760 als Prophet auftrat, war eigentlich Landwirt und wehrte sich energisch dagegen, mit den berufsmäßigen Propheten (*nābī'*) bzw. Prophetengenossen (*ben-nābī'*) in einen Topf geworfen zu werden (Am 7,14). Jesaja, dessen prophetische Wirksamkeit im Südreich sich über einen Zeitraum von ca. 40 Jahren hinzog (739–701), entstammte einer einflußreichen Aristokratenfamilie Jerusalems. [...] Diese Propheten [unter Einschluss Michas] waren somit finanziell unabhängig; sie gehörten

---

13 Rainer Kessler, *Der Weg zum Leben. Ethik des Alten Testaments* (Gütersloh: Gütersloher Verlagshaus, 2017), 363.

eher begüterten Schichten, ja, sogar im Fall Jesajas eindeutig der Oberschicht an."[14]

Mit diesen Sätzen zeichnet Albertz das klassische Bild der Prophetie des 8. Jahrhunderts als Teil einer in Distanz zum königlichen Hof stehenden und im Kern sozialkritisch orientierten Oppositionsbewegung. Und doch hat dieses Bild seine eigentümlichen, ja erstaunlichen Züge: Denn wie ist es zu erklären, dass sich die Propheten gerade *wegen* ihrer finanziellen Unabhängigkeit und ihrer Zugehörigkeit zur Oberschicht so radikal um die Armen und Entrechteten kümmern konnten? Albertz macht aus der Erklärungsnot eine Tugend. Denn es macht „die Stärke ihrer [der Propheten] religiösen Motivation deutlich, wie sehr sie sich von den Interessen und Ansichten ihrer Schichten trennen konnten."[15]

Die Beurteilung der Sozialkritik bei Amos und Jesaja hängt, wie die Erklärungen von Albertz hinreichend zeigen, aufs engste mit einer bestimmten Sicht des Propheten und auch *gegenwärtiger* Vorstellungen von sozialer Gerechtigkeit zusammen. Bei Albertz und vielen anderen ist es der von Gott in Anspruch genommene, unabhängige Geist, der den Mächtigen entgegentritt und sich durch „eine bewußt einseitige Parteinahme"[16] mit den Armen solidarisiert und mit „‚Recht und Gerechtigkeit' [...] [die] Grundwerte der vorstaatlichen israelitischen Gesellschaft"[17] wieder zur Geltung bringen möchte. Aber sind damit die erstaunlichen Ähnlichkeiten zwischen Amos und Jesaja hinreichend erklärt? Drei wichtige Studien sind dieser Frage nachgegangen und schlagen eine *literarische* Lösung vor.

2.1 Jesaja kannte die Verkündigung des Amos (Reinhard Fey, 1963)

Eine außerordentlich fein ausgearbeitete These steht hinter der Monographie von Reinhard Fey aus dem Jahr 1963.[18] Er zieht aus einem detaillierten Vergleich der sozialkritischen Worte der beiden Propheten den eindeutigen Schluss, Jesaja habe die sozialkritischen Worte des Amos gekannt und zitiere sie aus dem Gedächtnis, ohne eine *literarische* Abhängigkeit *a limine* auszuschließen. Die Parallelen, die Fey auswertet, seien um der Übersicht willen wie folgt zusammengestellt:

---

14 Rainer Albertz, *Religionsgeschichte Israels in alttestamentlicher Zeit. Band 1: Von den Anfängen bis zum Ende der Königszeit*, GAT 8/1 (Göttingen: Vandenhoeck & Ruprecht, 1992), 255 f.
15 *Ibid.*, 256.
16 *Ibid.*, 258.
17 *Ibid.*, 259.
18 Reinhard Fey, *Amos und Jesaja. Abhängigkeit und Eigenständigkeit des Jesaja*, WMANT 12 (Neukirchen-Vluyn: Neukirchener Verlag, 1963).

Amos	Jesaja
5,7.10.12b	5,20.23
5,11–12	5,8–10
6,1–7	5,11–13
(Amos insgesamt)	3,13–15
(Amos insgesamt)	1,21–26
4,4–5; 5,4–6.14–15; 5.21–25 (Kultpolemik, Recht)	1,10–17
4,1–3; 5,18–20 (Hochmut)	2,6–19*
6,8–11	3,1–9
4,6–12	9,7–20

So entnimmt er dem Vergleich von Am 6,1–7 und Jes 5,11–13, dass Jesaja seine Vorlage nicht einfach zitiert, sondern nach bestimmten Regeln verändert und angepasst habe: „Jesaja beschränkt sich in der Auswahl, aber steigert die Eindringlichkeit übernommener Gedanken. Das erreicht er durch Entfaltung und Zuspitzung der einzelnen Motive. Das Ergebnis ist die gegenüber Amos erhöhte theologische Deutlichkeit."[19]

Die gründliche Arbeit Feys zeichnet sich durch einen detaillierten Vergleich aller relevanten Texte aus. Sie unternimmt damit erstmals – und vor dem Hintergrund der zeitgenössischen Prophetenforschung durchaus innovativ! – den Versuch, die *literarischen Bezüge* auszuwerten. Der Arbeit ist merkwürdigerweise (oder: verständlicherweise) keine nachhaltige Wirkung beschieden gewesen, weil sie ihrer Zeit in gewisser Weise voraus war.

2.2 Jesaja kannte das (frühe) Amos-Buch (Erhard Blum 1994)

In einem 1994 erschienenen Aufsatz mit dem Titel „Jesaja und der דבר des Amos" möchte Erhard Blum in Abgrenzung zu Reinhard Fey die These begründen, dass der Prophet Jesaja „nicht nur einzelne Amosworte, sondern Texte eines nicht lange davor im Nordreich erstellten Amosbuches kannte und daran anknüpfend, möglicherweise auch durch die Aktualisierung der Amostradition angestoßen, sich seinerseits als Gerichtsprophet an Israel wandte."[20]

Dieser Bezug ist vor allem im Kehrversgedicht 9,7–20 sichtbar (Blum zählt 5,25 als Rest einer ersten Strophe und 10,1–4 als fünfte und letzte Strophe hinzu).

---

19 *Ibid.*, 20.
20 Erhard Blum, „Jesaja und der דבר des Amos. Unzeitgemäße Überlegungen zu Jes 5,25; 9,7–20; 10,1–4," *DBAT* 28 (1992/93) (1994): 75–95, 76.

Datiert wird das Gedicht aufgrund seiner zeitgeschichtlichen Anspielungen recht genau auf die Jahre zwischen 733 und 722.[21]

„Für *Jesaja* ist an diesem Text [d. h. dem Kehrversgedicht] abzulesen, daß der Jerusalemer sich selbst in einer unmittelbaren prophetischen Kontinuität zu dem in der Vergangenheit im Norden wirkenden Amos sah: In dessen Nachfolge und erinnernder Bekräftigung wendet er sich seinerseits an das Nordreich."[22]

Jesaja macht sich also die Amos-Worte zu eigen. Besonders anschaulich wird dieser Zusammenhang, wie man immer schon beobachtet hat, an der Amos-Fassung des Kehrversgedichtes in Am 4,6–13. Hier geht Blum von einer klar erkennbaren „intertextuellen Abhängigkeit"[23] aus: Jesaja hat nicht – ganz allgemein – die Verkündigung des Amos gekannt (so R. Fey), sondern bei der Konzipierung seines Buches auf das vorliegende Amos-Buch *literarisch* zurückgegriffen. Es versteht sich von selbst, dass dieses Konzept nur bei einer extremen Frühdatierung der Bücher (!) Amos und Jesaja aufgeht.

Blum trifft im Blick auf das Verhältnis von Jes 9,7–20 und Am 4,6–13 einige grundlegende Feststellungen: Auf der einen Seite ist es für ihn unstrittig, dass das jesajanische Gedicht von Am 4 abhängig ist und nicht umgekehrt. Auf der anderen Seite bestätigt er die mehrfach (u. a. von Hans Walter Wolff[24]) begründete Einsicht, Am 4 sei seinerseits Teil einer Fortschreibung der älteren Amos-Tradition.[25] Kann die These der literarischen Abhängigkeit dennoch aufrechterhalten werden? Nach Blum ist das möglich, weil er Am 4 als eine *ganz frühe* Fortschreibung der Amos-Tradition betrachtet, die noch vor 722 erfolgt sein müsse. Deshalb kann er zu dem Schluss kommen, „daß Jesaja sich in seinem Strophengedicht ... 5,25; *9,7–20; 10,1–4a an Texten eines ‚Amosbuches' orientierte, das allenfalls wenige Jahre zuvor in Rest-Israel von Amos-Schülern erstellt worden war."[26]

Die *Beobachtungen* Blums sind gewichtig, seine *Auswertung* indes gibt Anlass zu kritischen Fragen. Sie richten sich insbesondere gegen die – überaus gezwungene – Frühdatierung der Amos- und Jesaja-Texte, die einer näheren Überprüfung nicht standhält. Für Blum ist nach wie vor die vermutete historische Situation *hinter* dem Text der Schlüssel zum Verständnis der Prophetenworte – ein Zugang, der angesichts der neueren redaktionsgeschichtlichen Erforschung der Rechtfertigung bedarf. Denn die Auslegungsbasis der prophetischen Bücher können nicht

---

21 *Ibid.*, 81.

22 *Ibid.*, 83.

23 *Ibid.*, 84.

24 Hans Walter Wolff, *Dodekapropheton. 2. Joel und Amos*, BKAT XIV/2 (Neukirchen-Vluyn: Neukirchener Verlag, ³1985), 250–258.

25 Blum, „Jesaja und der דבר des Amos": 84–88.

26 *Ibid.*, 88.

die vermuteten historischen Situationen *hinter* den Texten (das entspräche dem alten Paradigma der Prophetenforschung) sein, sondern nur die Texte selbst in ihrem literarischen Beziehungsgefüge.

2.3 Keine Bezugnahmen auf Amos (Jan Kreuch 2014)

Die kleine Studie von Jan Kreuch aus dem Jahr 2014 – sie entstand im Anschluss an seine Dissertation zu Jes 28–31[27] – setzt sich gleich zu Beginn mit „Anfragen an das traditionelle Am-Bild" auseinander, wie er es bei Uwe Becker, Reinhard G. Kratz und Oswald Loretz findet.[28] Es geht bei den genannten Autoren um den Versuch, die Verkündigung des historischen Amos auf der Basis redaktionsge-schichtlicher Entscheidungen als eine im wesentlichen hofnahe Heilsprophetie zu klassifizieren.[29] Kreuch lehnt dieses Vorhaben entschieden ab und verwahrt sich auch gegen eine allzu rasche Auswertung intertextueller Bezüge zwischen Amos und Jesaja. Im Mittelpunkt seiner Untersuchung steht vielmehr eine *separate* Untersuchung und vor allem Datierung der Einzeltexte. An eine Übersetzung des jeweiligen Amos- und Jesaja-Textes schließt sich stets ein Datierungsvorschlag und die „Bestimmung des Verhältnisses der Texte" an. Das Ergebnis ist eindeutig: „Nur im Falle der Überschriften der beiden Bücher (Am 1,1 und Jes 1,1) und von Am 9,11.14 f und Jes 1,7 f; 58,11 f scheint mir die Indizienlage auszureichen, um eine Bezugnahme zwischen den Texten zu vermuten."[30] Für ihn ist damit auch die These Reinhard Feys falsifiziert worden. Für den historischen Jesaja, dem Kreuch einen großen und maximalen Bestand an Worten zuweist, sieht er noch keinerlei literarische Bezugnahmen auf Amos; dies ändere sich erst ab der exilischen Zeit (vgl. Jes 2; 13; 24–27 u. a.). Die großen Gemeinsamkeiten zwischen der Verkündi-gung (!) der Propheten Amos und Jesaja, die es zweifellos gebe, erklärt er mit dem gemeinsamen Jahweglauben, in dem die Propheten verwurzelt sind; als Beispiel nennt er etwa die alt-israelitischen Rechtstraditionen.

So sehr die Studie auf Schwächen und vielleicht auch gelegentlich allzu rasche literarische Auswertungen „intertextueller" Bezüge hinweist, so dürfte sie die Parallelen doch zu Unrecht herunterspielen. So wird bei Am 5,11–12a und

---

27 Jan Kreuch, *Unheil und Heil bei Jesaja. Studien zur Entstehung des Assur-Zyklus Jesaja 28–31*, WMANT 130 (Neukirchen-Vluyn: Neukirchener Verlag, 2011).
28 Ders., *Das Amos- und Jesajabuch. Eine exegetische Studie zur Neubestimmung ihres Verhält-nisses*, BThSt 149 (Neukirchen-Vluyn: Neukirchener Verlag, 2014), 8–27.
29 Vgl. zur Problematik Uwe Becker, „Jesaja, Jeremia und die Anfänge der Unheilsprophetie in Juda," *HeBAI* 6/1 (2017): 79–100.
30 Kreuch, *Amos- und Jesajabuch*, 189.

Jes 5,8–10 ein literarischer Einfluss für ganz unwahrscheinlich erklärt, „zumal sich die gemeinsame Thematik aus einer vergleichbaren historischen und sozialen Situation in Israel und Juda im 8. Jh. v. Chr. erklären lässt."[31] Hier wird also wieder mit einem gemeinsamen sozioökonomischen Hintergrund argumentiert (vgl. die eingangs zitierten Voten von Rainer Albertz und Rainer Kessler). Die Studie von Jan Kreuch stellt deshalb einen deutlichen Rückschritt hinter die 50 Jahre zuvor erschienene Studie Reinhard Feys dar. Sie ist im Grunde apologetisch angelegt; sie wendet sich v. a. gegen ein neues Prophetenbild, das den Propheten keineswegs *a limine* für einen Oppositionellen hält, sondern ihn – zunächst – in eine Nähe zum Hof und zum Königtum rückt. Es ist interessant und bezeichnend zugleich, dass Blums gute Beobachtungen und Argumente für eine *literarische* Bezugnahme Jesajas auf eine frühe Amos-Schrift fast gar nicht zur Sprache kommen.

Die drei Beispiele aus der jüngeren und älteren Forschungsgeschichte zeigen anschaulich, dass man die zweifellos vorhandenen *substantiellen* Bezüge zwischen Amos und Jes 1–39 – zumal in der Sozialkritik – auf unterschiedliche Weise deuten und erklären kann. Dabei hängen die Unterschiede nicht nur mit einem bestimmten Prophetenbild zusammen (der Prophet wird gern als ein mehr oder weniger radikaler Gesellschaftskritiker betrachtet), sondern vor allem mit differierenden Auffassungen von der Entstehung der Prophetenbücher. So sollen einer eigenen Erklärung der Gemeinsamkeiten zwischen Amos und Jes 1–39 zunächst stichwortartig einige Überlegungen zur Entstehung des Amos-Buches und der Verkündigung des Propheten vorangestellt werden. Denn an der Frage, wie man sich die Entstehung der Prophetenbücher und die Verkündigung der „historischen" Propheten vorstellt, entscheidet sich beinahe alles.

3 Das Amos-Buch und seine Entstehung in groben Zügen

1) Ursprünglich war Amos ein Prophet des Nordreiches, der auch aus dem Nordreich stammte. Die Überschrift in Am 1,1 ist in ihrer jetzigen Gestalt nicht alt; sie spiegelt in gewisser Weise das Buchwachstum wider:

Die Worte des Amos,
der zu den Schafzüchtern gehörte, *aus Tekoa,*
die er über Israel schaute in den Tagen Usijas, des Königs von Juda,
und in den Tagen Jerobeams, des Sohnes Joaschs, des Königs von Israel,
zwei Jahre vor dem Erdbeben.

---

31 Kreuch, *Amos- und Jesajabuch,* 110.

Im Kern dürfte die Überschrift gelautet haben: „Die Worte des Amos". Sie fügen sich gut zur ältesten Spruchüberlieferung, die man im Mittelteil des Buches, in Am 3–6, findet. Die beiden nachfolgenden Relativsätze spiegeln bereits das Bemühen wider, später zugewachsene Buchteile in die Überschrift zu integrieren. So entnahm der Ergänzer des ersten Relativsatzes „der zu den Schafzüchtern gehörte" die Berufsangabe des Propheten aus dem Buch selbst, wie die Prophetengeschichte Am 7,10–17 zeigt (die Herkunftsangabe „aus Tekoa" ist wiederum später zugefügt). Dass es sich bei dieser Szene am Altar von Bet-El nicht um eine authentische biographische Überlieferung, sondern eine späte „Inszenierung" handelt, ist inzwischen allgemein anerkannt,[32] auch wenn man hier und da noch an der prinzipiellen Historizität der Episode festhalten möchte.[33] Der zweite Relativsatz „die er über Israel schaute ..." dürfte bereits die Visionen in Am 7–9 im Blick haben, die dem Kern des Buches als Interpretament – wie auch die Völkerworte in Am 1–2 – nachträglich zugewachsen sind und den ältesten Kern des Buches rahmen.[34] Ob die Angabe „zwei Jahre vor dem Erdbeben" einer authentischen Überlieferung entspringt, die zum ältesten Kern der Überschrift gehört, kann man vermuten,[35] ist aber nicht beweisbar.

2) Die Lokalisierung der Heimat des Amos in *Tekoa* (Südreich) könnte einem späteren Interesse entsprungen sein: Amos soll als Prophet des *Südreiches* präsentiert werden, der auch im Norden aufgetreten ist. Damit wird zugleich ein Gesamtbewusstsein Israel-Juda hergestellt. Schon die Sprüche gegen den Zion (vgl. 6,1) machen dieses Interesse deutlich, vor allem aber 1,2: Der Gott des Amos „brüllt vom Zion her". Dass man Amos mit einem landjudäischen Ort in Verbindung brachte, könnte mit der zionskritischen Auslegung und Rezeption seiner Worte zusammenhängen. Er wird damit als ein Außenseiter im wörtlichen Sinne präsentiert. Immerhin hat man in der Nachfolge rabbinischer Auslegung ge-

---

32 Vgl. z. B. Helmut Utzschneider, „Die Amazjaerzählung (Am 7,10–17) zwischen Literatur und Historie," *BN* 41 (1988): 76–101; Hugh G. M. Williamson, "The Prophet and the Plumb-Line: A Redaction-Critical Study of Amos 7 [1990]," in *"The Place is Too Small for Us". The Israelite Prophets in Recent Scholarship*, Hg. Robert P. Gordon, Sources for Biblical and Theological Study 5 (Winona Lake, IN: Eisenbrauns, 1995): 453–477.

33 Vgl. trotz der Einsicht in den redaktionellen und späten Charakter der Amazja-Erzählung Jörg Jeremias, *Der Prophet Amos*, ATD 24/2 (Göttingen: Vandenhoeck & Ruprecht, 1995), 105–112. Ähnlich Ludwig Schmidt, „Die Amazja-Erzählung (Am 7,10–17) und der historische Amos," *ZAW* 119 (2007): 221–235, und Peter Riede, *Vom Erbarmen zum Gericht. Die Visionen des Amosbuches (Am 7–9*) und ihr literatur- und traditionsgeschichtlicher Zusammenhang*, WMANT 120 (Neukirchen-Vluyn: Neukirchener Verlag, 2008), der eine alte Reminiszenz hinter der Episode vermutet.

34 Vgl. zum literarhistorischen Ort der Visionen Uwe Becker, „Der Prophet als Fürbitter. Zum literarhistorischen Ort der Amos-Visionen," *VT* 51/2 (2001): 141–165.

35 Vgl. etwa Jeremias, *Amos*, 1–3.

legentlich ein *nordisraelitisches* Tekoa angenommen, um den eigentümlichen Befund des Buches mit der historischen Plausibilität in Einklang zu bringen.[36] Der „historische Amos" dürfte also eine Gestalt Nordreiches gewesen sein, die erst *post mortem* und aus theologischen Gründen in den Süden gewandert ist. Die Episode Am 7,10–17 setzt diesen Vorgang bereits voraus.

3) Ein Problem stellt die zeitgeschichtliche Einordnung des Amos in die Zeit Jerobeams II. (um 760) dar. Diese Einordnung beruht *allein* auf der (späten) Überschrift und den Angaben in der Amazja-Erzählung 7,10–17. Hier liegt möglicherweise, wie Christoph Levin gezeigt hat, eine gleichsam schriftgelehrte Verwechslung von Jerobeam I. und Jerobeam II. vor;[37] ein Zusammenhang mit 1Kön 13 liegt auf der Hand. Stattdessen legt sich, da einzig die Angaben des Buches selbst als Quelle übrigbleiben, eine Einordnung in die 2. Hälfte des 8. Jahrhunderts, also in die Zeit des syrisch-efraimitischen Krieges, nahe.[38] Erst hier, also in der realen Assyrergefahr, ist ein plausibler Hintergrund für die älteren (auch „sozialkritischen") Amos-Worte gegeben.

4) Darauf weist auch der älteste Teil des Buches in Am 3–6 hin: Er gehört im Kern in das Nordreich. Die Worte, die sich explizit gegen das Südreich richten (so etwa 6,1), verdanken sich späterer redaktioneller Übertragung. Über die Frage, welche Worte man auf den „historischen" Amos zurückführen kann, herrscht naturgemäß keine Einigkeit in der Forschung. Schließt man sich, wie es hier geschieht, grundsätzlich und weitgehend den Analysen von Reinhard G. Kratz an,[39] so lassen sich durch ein Subtraktionsverfahren die ältesten Amos-Worte einigermaßen zuverlässig herauslösen. Es handelt sich vor allem um Bildworte (z. B. 3,12abα), Wehrufe bzw. Partizipien (z. B. 3,12bβ; 4,1; 5,7.18+20) und Anklagen (z. B. 3,15).[40]

---

36 Vgl. etwa Klaus Koch, *Die Profeten I. Assyrische Zeit*, UB 280 (Stuttgart: Kohlhammer, ³1995), 114; dagegen Jeremias, *Amos*, 3.
37 Vgl. etwa Christoph Levin, „Amos und Jerobeam I. [1995]," in *Fortschreibungen. Gesammelte Studien zum Alten Testament*, BZAW 316 (Berlin-New York: Walter de Gruyter, 2003): 256–264.
38 Es hat ja schon immer erstaunt, dass gerade in der (vorgeblich) prosperierenden Zeit Jerobeams II. eine derart scharfe Sozialkritik ihren Ort haben sollte.
39 Reinhard G. Kratz, „Die Worte des Amos von Tekoa [2003]," in *Prophetenstudien. Kleine Schriften II*, FAT 74 (Tübingen: Mohr Siebeck, 2011): 310–343, vgl. insbesondere auf S. 328 die Übersicht über den ältesten Bestand, den Kratz in Am 3,12.15; 4,1–3; 5,2.3.7.10–12.16–17.18–20; 6,1.3–6a.7.12.13–14 vermutet.
40 Vgl. *ibid.*, 329–331.

4 Sozialkritische Texte im Amos-Buch

In der Sozialkritik scheint das Kernanliegen des „historischen" Amos zu liegen. Ein genauerer Blick auf die betreffenden Texte zeigt jedoch: Die Sache ist weitaus komplizierter. Gewiss kann man – wie etwa Jörg Jeremias – die sozialkritischen Worte als eine planvoll komponierte Aneinanderreihung ehedem selbständiger Amos-Worte lesen. Gegen diesen Zugang spricht freilich die einfache Beobachtung, dass die meisten der betreffenden „Logien" doch enger miteinander verbunden sind, als es die Sammlungshypothese erklären kann. So legt sich – mit Christoph Levin – eine Fortschreibungshypothese nahe, die ein sukzessives Textwachstum annimmt. Dabei zeigt sich: Die sozialkritischen Texte bei Amos haben selbst eine längere Geschichte, die beim Propheten Amos eingesetzt hat, aber zeitlich weit über ihn hinausgeht. Zwei Beispiele mögen genügen.

4.1 Am 4,1–2

> ^{1} *Hört [m.] dieses Wort,*
> [ihr] **Baschankühe [f.] auf dem Berge Samarias,**
> *die die Geringen (דלים) bedrücken, die Armen (אביונים) zerbrechen,*
> **die zu ihren Herren sagen: Bringt her, daß wir saufen!**
> ^{2} *Geschworen hat der Herr Jhwh bei seiner Heiligkeit,*
> *denn siehe, es kommen Tage über euch [2.m.pl.],*
> *da bringt man euch fort mit Stacheln*
> *und euren Übermut mit Fischhaken.*

Dieses kleine Wort enthält eine Reihe von Merkwürdigkeiten, die sich am besten erklären lassen, wenn man von einer Grundlage ausgeht, die nachträglich erweitert und in einen neuen Kontext gestellt worden ist.[41] Die Redeeinleitung „Hört dieses Wort" (mit maskuliner Anrede) fügt sich nur schlecht zu den angeredeten Baschankühen (im Feminin). Fraglich ist vor allem, ob der Vorwurf an die „Baschankühe" tatsächlich die Bedrückung der Geringen und Armen war. Denn der Versteil „verläßt" nicht nur „zu früh das Bild"[42], sondern trägt zwei Schlüsselbegriffe ein, die sich gewöhnlich auf eine bestimmte (eschatologische) Armenfrömmigkeit beziehen, wie man sie anderwärts im Amosbuch, aber auch im Psalter findet. Schließlich gehört die Gerichtsankündigung in V.2 kaum zum Grundbestand; sie wird mit einer vorgeprägten Formel „siehe, es kommen Tage ..." ein-

---

41 Vgl. die Analyse von Levin, „Anawim": 279–281.
42 *Ibid.*, 280.

geleitet (siehe Jer 16,14; 31,27.31), aber anders als in den Referenzstellen auf ein unheilvolles Geschehen bezogen. Es geht hier um eine totale Katastrophe.

4.2 Am 5,7–13

[7] **[Wehe denen,] die in Wermut verkehren das Recht**
und die Gerechtigkeit zu Boden werfen!
[8] Der die Pleiaden und den Orion schuf,
der die Dunkelheit zum Morgen wandelt [...]
[10] Sie hassen den, der im Tor [richtig] entscheidet,
und wer untadelig redet, den verachten sie.
[11] Darum, weil ihr dem Geringen (דל) Pachtzins (?) auferlegt
und Abgaben von Getreide von ihm nehmt:
Häuser aus Quadersteinen habt ihr gebaut
und werdet nicht darin wohnen.
Prächtige Weinberge habt ihr gepflanzt
und werdet ihren Wein nicht trinken.
[12a] Denn ich weiß, daß eure Verfehlungen zahlreich sind
und eure Sünden gewaltig.
[12b] *Die den Gerechten (צדיק) bedrängen, Bestechung nehmen,*
und die Armen (אביונים) im Tor abweisen.

Auch hier liegt eine vielfach geschichtete Wortfolge vor.[43] An ihrem Anfang stand ein Partizip, das ein wenig in der Luft hängt und vielleicht einmal als Weheruf gestaltet war. Der Preis des Schöpfergottes in V.8 f. erweist sich ebenso als Nachtrag[44] wie die V.11–12a: Der unvermittelte Wechsel der Anrede, die zudem als Gottesrede gedacht ist (vgl. das „denn ich weiß" in 12a), ist kaum (wie Jörg Jeremias annimmt) mit der emotionalen „Entrüstung des Propheten" zu erklären, „der von der Unrechtsschilderung (V.10) zur Anrede an die Schuldigen übergeht"[45], sondern mit nüchterner literarischer Fortführung.

Aber auch schon V.10 stellt keine ursprüngliche Fortsetzung von V.7 dar: Es fällt nicht nur (formal) der Wechsel vom Partizip ins finite Verb ins Auge, sondern (inhaltlich) eine gewichtige Akzentverschiebung: V.7 klagt allgemein die Verkehrung des Rechts an, V.10 spezifiziert: Selbst diejenigen, die im Tor für ein gerechtes Urteil eintreten, werden verachtet.

Von besonderem Interesse ist nun V.12b. Wie schon in Am 4,1–2 ist hier eine redaktionelle Hand sichtbar, der weniger an den konkreten Vorwürfen der

---

43 Vgl. *ibid.*, 281–284.
44 Vgl. Jeremias, *Amos*, 60, 68–69.
45 *Ibid.*, 69.

Missachtung und Verkehrung des Rechts liegt als vielmehr an der Bedrängung des „Armen" (אביון), der mit dem „Gerechten" (צדיק) gleichgesetzt wird. Mit den Worten Christoph Levins: „Wieder sind die Armen als die Gerechten verstanden und ist Gerechtigkeit durch Armut (nicht zuerst durch gerechtes Handeln) definiert."[46] So gehört auch dieser Vers Am 5,12b zu einer späten Armenfrömmigkeit, wie wir sie nicht zuletzt im Psalter wiederfinden.

4.3 Ergebnis

Damit ergibt sich für das Amos-Buch ein klares Bild: Die Worte, die von der Bedrückung des „Armen" sprechen, gehören nicht zum ältesten Kern des Buches, sondern spiegeln eine spezifische Frömmigkeit wider, die man – ganz grob gesagt – in der nachexilischen Zeit verorten muss. Es gibt also nicht *die* Sozialkritik des Amosbuches und schon gar nicht die Sozialkritik des Propheten Amos. Er selbst scheint sich im Wesentlichen auf die Kritik an einem allzu üppigen Lebenswandel der samarischen Oberschicht (vgl. die Baschankühe) und die Verkehrung des Rechts konzentriert zu haben.

5 Sozialkritische Texte in Jes 1–39

Ein Blick auf die sozialkritischen Texte in Jes 1–39 ergibt ein anderes Bild. Hier hat man es weniger mit fragmentierten Einzelworten als vielmehr mit relativ geschlossenen literarischen Einheiten zu tun. Neben Jes 3 kommen als wichtigste Texte die Weherufe in Jes 5,8–24 sowie und 10,1–4 in Betracht.

5.1 Die Weherufe (Jes 5,8–24)

Die Weherufe werden gern – mit dem einleitenden Weinberglied Jes 5,1–7 – der sozialkritischen Frühzeit des Propheten zugeschrieben. Diese Einordnung beruht indes nicht auf Hinweisen im Text, sondern auf einem allgemeinen Bild von der Verkündigung des Propheten Jesaja, die man traditionell in 4 oder 5 Epochen aufteilt. Es gibt jedoch Hinweise darauf, dass diese Texte literarisch vom Amos-Buch

---

46 Levin, „Anawim": 283.

abhängig sind, also keine eigenständigen „Jesaja-Themen" darstellen.[47] So zeigt schon ein flüchtiger Blick auf die Weheruf-Reihe, dass die „sozialkritischen" Worte des Jesaja keineswegs so originell und konkret sind, wie man ihnen gewöhnlich unterstellt. Sie wirken abstrakt und könnten sich auf beinahe jede Epoche in der Geschichte Israels beziehen. Wer ihnen Informationen über die soziale Lage im 8. Jahrhundert entnehmen will, ist auf viel Phantasie – oder Allgemeinplätze – angewiesen.

Im Vergleich mit Worten des Amos (Micha muss an dieser Stelle ausgeklammert werden) wirken die Jesaja-Worte wie eine Verkündigung aus zweiter Hand: Ein mündlicher „Sitz im Leben" legt sich nicht unmittelbar nahe. Als weit fruchtbarer erweist sich hingegen die Frage nach dem „Sitz in der Literatur": Die Weheruf-Reihe weist nicht nur Bezüge zu Amos auf, sondern ist auch im Jesajabuch mit anderen Kapiteln eng vernetzt. Ins Auge fallen vor allem Berührungen mit Jes 6 (s. u.). Sollten diese Bezüge einem bewussten Kompositionswillen entspringen? Die Analyse scheint in diese Richtung zu weisen.

Der *erste Weheruf (V.8–10)* wirkt gegenüber seinen engsten Parallelen Am 5,11 und Mi 2,1 f. auffällig blass. Dieser Umstand schlägt sich in unterschiedlichen sozialgeschichtlichen Einordnungen nieder. Einerseits meint man zu wissen, dass sich der Weheruf gegen eine Praxis wendet, den Haus- und Grundbesitz auf Kosten ärmerer Bevölkerungsschichten völlig unangemessen zu vergrößern. Man spricht mit Vorliebe von Großgrundbesitzern und ihrer Latifundienwirtschaft.[48] Andererseits muss konzediert werden: „Es steht nichts von Habsucht im Text"[49]. Hängt diese Unklarheit mit der vorausgesetzten mündlichen Verkündigung zusammen, deren Hintergrund eben nicht mehr bekannt ist? Oder hat sie andere Gründe?

Die Formulierung des Weherufs scheint in einer geradezu „sarkastischen Übertreibung"[50] auf eine gänzliche (!) Verdrängung der Armen aus dem Lande hinzudeuten. Dabei fällt die nicht zuletzt aus metrischen Gründen auffällige Wendung וְהוּשַׁבְתֶּם לְבַדְּכֶם („und ihr allein siedelt") heraus; sie stellt eine Glosse dar.[51] Der

---

47 Vgl. die eingehende Analyse in Uwe Becker, *Jesaja – von der Botschaft zum Buch*, FRLANT 178 (Göttingen: Vandenhoeck & Ruprecht, 1997), 134–145.

48 Vgl. bes. Kessler, *Staat*, 33–37, der zwar den Begriff „Latifundienwirtschaft" vermeidet, aber analoge Vorgänge aus Jes 5,8 ableitet.

49 Hans Bardtke, „Die Latifundien in Juda während der zweiten Hälfte des achten Jahrhunderts v. Chr. (Zum Verständnis von Jes 5,8–10)," in *Hommages à André Dupont-Sommer*, Hg. André Dupont-Sommer (Paris: Librairie d'Amérique et d'Orient Adrien-Maisonneuve, 1971): 235–254, 236.

50 *Ibid.*

51 Vgl. zum Problem Hugh G. M. Williamson, *A Critical and Exegetical Commentary of Isaiah 1–27. Volume 1: Commentary on Isaiah 1–5*, ICC (London: T & T Clark, 2006), 347, der sich der These, es handle sich um eine Glosse, aber nicht anschließen möchte.

verbleibende Bestand ergibt einen guten Sinn, der das ursprünglich Gemeinte ausdrückt: „bis kein Platz mehr da ist inmitten des Landes". Die Anhäufung von Haus- und Grundbesitz kommt an ihr Ende, wenn das Land gewissermaßen *verbraucht* ist und nichts mehr hergibt. In dichterischer Übertreibung stellt der Weheruf die letzte Konsequenz der kritisierten Praxis vor Augen. Entsprechend kündigt das Drohwort V.9 f. an, Jahwe werde die prächtigen *Häuser* (vgl. V.8aα) zerstören und ihre Bewohner wegführen sowie die *Felder* (vgl. V.8aβ) unfruchtbar lassen. Die kleine Glosse in V.8b[52] versucht nun, der bewusst allgemein gehaltenen Anklage einen konkreteren Zug zu verleihen. Dabei entstellt sie den ursprünglichen Sinn merkwürdig: Das Treiben der raffgierigen Grundbesitzer geht so weit, dass sie am Ende allein sind im Lande.

Die Einleitung des Drohwortes in V.9a ist ungewöhnlich und in der Weheruf-Reihe singulär: „In meinen Ohren [ist] Jahwe Zebaot". Mit dem prophetischen „Ich" ist natürlich „Jesaja" selbst gemeint: Was den Übeltätern widerfährt, wird vorläufig nur dem Propheten offenbar. Die 1. Person des Propheten begegnet erst wieder in c.6.[53] Ist in 5,9a ein verhaltener Vorblick auf die „eigentliche" Berufung des Propheten angedeutet? Immerhin ähnelt die Gerichtsbotschaft von 5,9b auffällig der von 6,11 (vgl. בתים „Häuser", מאין יושב „ohne Bewohner", שמה „Wüste"), so dass sich ein *literarischer* Bezug nahelegt. So hat man der großen *Vision* von c.6 mit Bedacht eine kleine vorbereitende *Audition* vorangestellt, damit der kausale Zusammenhang zwischen den Weherufen und der Verstockungsbotschaft von c.6 deutlicher hervortritt: Was dem Propheten in Jes 6 in einer analogielosen Radikalität zugemutet wird, Verstockung und Unverständnis *zu bewirken*, versuchen die Wehe-Worte am Verhalten des Volkes im Einzelnen aufzuweisen und zu begründen: Die Verstockungsbotschaft wirkt so *einsichtiger* und *nachvollziehbarer*. Dies bedeutet: Jes 5,9 bereitet die Berufungsszene *literarisch* vor, ist also später anzusetzen als Jes 6.

Auf literarischer Abhängigkeit beruhen offenbar auch mancherlei Bezüge zur Amos-Überlieferung. So könnte das Drohwort 5,9b–10 – wie schon der Weheruf 5,8! – aus Am 5,11 entwickelt sein. Dort wird der Führungsschicht ihre anspruchsvolle und auf Genussstreben ausgerichtete Lebensweise vorgeworfen, die sich u. a. im Errichten prächtiger Häuser und im Anlegen üppiger Weinberge (vgl. Jes 5,1 f.!) manifestiert. Aber diese Clique wird ihre Güter nicht genießen können. Jes 5,9b–10 verschärft: Die Häuser werden zerstört, ihre Bewohner weggeschafft

---

[52] Sie ist am ehesten mit Jes 44,26 zu vergleichen: „Du (= Jerusalem) wirst wieder bewohnt sein (תושב)." Es gibt nur diese beiden Belege der Wurzel im *hof*.
[53] Vgl. aber „mein Volk" in 5,13. Hier ist unklar, ob der Prophet spricht oder Jahwe.

(vgl. מֵאֵין יוֹשֵׁב „ohne Bewohner")[54], die Weinberge bringen keinen Ertrag mehr.[55] Dabei könnte V.10 auch von Am 5,3 angeregt sein.

Jes 5,8–10 greift also vorgegebene Anklagen auf und benutzt sie zur Begründung der radikalen Verstockungsbotschaft von Jes 6. Insofern hat die These, in V.9 f. liege eine spätere, aus der Perspektive des Exils formulierte Erweiterung des reinen, auf Jesaja selbst zurückgehenden Weherufes von V.8 vor,[56] nicht viel für sich. Eine solche Trennung wäre nur dann einsichtig, wenn man V.8 für den Propheten „retten" könnte; in diesem Fall müssten V.9 f. später sein. Nun lässt sich V.8 aber nicht nur gut als Anleihe aus Am 5,11 (und Mi 2,1 f.) verstehen, was jesajanische Herkunft unwahrscheinlich macht, sondern bildet mit V.9 f. ein sinnvolles Ganzes: Die Raffgierigen nehmen – so V.8 in hyperbolischer Redeweise – das Gericht, nämlich die Deportation, durch ihr Verhalten selbst vorweg.

Wie am Beispiel des ersten jesajanischen Weherufs gezeigt werden konnte, liegt offenbar eine literarische Abhängigkeit von der Berufungsvision Jes 6 vor. Tatsächlich lassen sich weitere terminologische Berührungen zwischen der Weheruf-Reihe und der Berufungsvision feststellen, die in ihrer großen Zahl eine gewisse Signifikanz aufweisen:

Jes 5,8	בְּקֶרֶב הָאָרֶץ	Jes 6,12
5,9a	„Jahwe Zebaot"	6,3 (auch 5,24b)
	בְּאָזְנָי	vgl. die Ich-Rede in c.6 (auch 5,1–6.13); „Ohr" 6,10.
5,9b	בָּתִּים	6,11
	מֵאֵין יוֹשֵׁב	6,11
	שַׁמָּה	6,11 (שְׁמָמָה)
5,12b	ראה	6,9
5,13a	Deportation (גלה)	vgl. 6,11b
	keine דַּעַת	6,9b (ידע)
5,18	חַטָּאָה/עָוֹן	6,7b (vgl. 1,4a)
5,19	ידע/ראה	6,9bβ
	קָדוֹשׁ	6,3 (vgl. 1,4b; 5,24b u. a.)

Die Ähnlichkeiten werden in aller Regel mit der Einheit der jesajanischen Verkündigung begründet: Die Weherufe enthalten die Frühzeitverkündigung, der

---

54 Möglicherweise ist hier an eine Deportation gedacht, vgl. Jes 6,9; Jer 4,7; 26,9; 33,10; 34,22; 44,22; 46,19; 51,29.37; Zef 2,5; 3,6; vgl. מִבְּלִי יוֹשֵׁב „ohne Bewohner" Jer 2,15; 9,10.
55 Vom Ende der „vielen Häuser" spricht auch das Drohwort Am 3,15; nur an diesen beiden Stellen ist die Verbindung belegt! Im Übrigen scheinen hier die sogenannten „Vergeblichkeitsflüche" durch (vgl. Lev 26,20; Dtn 28,30.32.39.41; Jes 65,21 ff.; Hag 1,6). Hier liegt also weniger eine konkrete Tatfolge vor als vielmehr eine grundsätzliche Aussage über die fundamentale göttliche Strafe, die in der Entziehung der Lebensbasis selbst besteht.
56 Vgl. Kaiser, *Jesaja*, 100.

natürlich die Berufung (obwohl erst später in der Denkschrift platziert!) vorausgegangen sein müsse. Diese *biographische* Interpretation setzt die Authentizität der Jesaja-Worte voraus, die, wie am Beispiel von Jes 5,8–10 gezeigt wurde, nicht mehr vorausgesetzt werden kann. Als Alternative bietet sich eine *literarische* Erklärung der frappanten Parallelen an. Tatsächlich ist Jes 6 ohne die Weherufe 5,8 ff. verständlich, diese hingegen sind kaum ohne Kenntnis von Jes 6 verfasst worden.

Eine allgemeine Erwägung zum Charakter der prophetischen Verkündigung sei angeschlossen. Denn es fällt auf, dass uns im Jes-Buch eigentümlicherweise sonst keine Sozialkritik überliefert ist. Sie ist, so die hier vorausgesetzte These, im Gefolge einer unheilstheologischen *relecture*[57] der (zunächst für Juda heilvollen) Jesaja-Worte (vgl. 6,9+11; 8,6–8a*; 8,17) aus dem Am-Buch „importiert" worden, um auch dem großen Propheten ein sozialkritisches Anliegen zu unterstellen und seine Gerichtsansage (6,9–11) mit der Missachtung des Rechts zu untermauern.

Hierin spiegelt sich ein allgemeines Phänomen in der Redaktionsgeschichte der Prophetenbücher wider, nämlich eine gegenseitige thematische Beeinflussung. Prophetenbücher bewegen sich im Verlaufe ihrer Tradierung aufeinander zu, indem sie Themen, manchmal auch einzelne Worte anderer Bücher aufnehmen und eigenständig umprägen. Bei den Büchern Amos und Hosea ist dies offenkundig.[58] Es ist kein Wunder, dass von einem solchen Vorgang auch das Jes-Buch (und zwar in seiner umfassenden Gestalt Jes 1–66) erfasst wurde, dessen thematisches „Epizentrum" – bei aller Komplexität – der *Zion* geworden ist: Als das Buch von der *Gefährdung und Bewahrung des Zion*, zu dem es sich im Verlaufe seiner Entstehungsgeschichte mit immer deutlicheren Konturen entwickelt hat, zog es wie ein Magnet fremden Stoff an. Am Ende steht eine literarische Jesaja-Gestalt, die „presentation of a prophet", die nicht mit dem „historischen Jesaja" verwechselt werden darf.

5.2 Jes 10,1–4

Einige wenige Bemerkungen sollen für den Weheruf in 10,1–4 genügen. Wie jüngst noch einmal Hugh G. M. Williamson zeigen konnte,[59] hat dieser Weheruf mit 5,8–24 nichts zu tun. Es handelt sich vielmehr um einen späten Nachtrag zum

---

57 Vgl. zusammenfassend den schon genannten Beitrag Becker, „Unheilsprophetie".
58 Eindrückliche Beispiele hat Jörg Jeremias zusammengetragen: Jörg Jeremias, *Hosea und Amos. Studien zu den Anfängen des Dodekapropheton*, FAT 13 (Tübingen: J.C.B. Mohr, 1996).
59 Hugh G. M. Williamson, *A Critical and Exegetical Commentary on Isaiah 1–27 in three Volumes. Volume 2: Commentary on Isaiah 6–12*, ICC (London/New York, NY: Bloomsbury T&T Clark, 2018), 457–479.

Kehrversgedicht von der ausgestreckten Hand Jhwhs im Stile der Weheruf-Reihe von 5,8–24.[60]

Auch dieser Weheruf gibt keine Auskunft über die sozialgeschichtliche Lage zur Zeit des Propheten Jesaja. Man könnte allenfalls erwägen, ob die dort beschriebene Situation auf spätere Epochen zu beziehen wäre. Freilich ist der Weheruf so allgemein formuliert, dass er kaum Rückschlüsse auf den zeitlichen Hintergrund zulässt. Er ähnelt den bereits besprochenen Amos-Worten, die im Geist der Armenfrömmigkeit gehalten sind. Die Begriffe „Geringe" (דלים) und „die Elenden meines Volkes" (עניי עמי) sprechen für sich. Eine direkt literarische Abhängigkeit von Amos wird man hier kaum beweisen können; sie ist aber durchaus möglich.

6 Resümee

Das Ergebnis der Untersuchung lässt sich in einem Satz zusammenfassen: Die sozialkritischen Texte in Jes 1–39 beruhen *literarisch* auf dem Amos-*Buch*; sie beziehen sich nicht allein auf die ältesten Amos-Worte, sondern bereits auf deren Fortschreibungen. Damit erweist sich das Thema Sozialkritik als kein genuin jesajanisches Thema; es ist aus dem Amos-Buch gleichsam importiert worden. Dass dieses Phänomen der schriftgelehrten Anreicherung von Prophetenbüchern keinen Einzelfall, sondern den Normalfall widerspiegelt, lässt sich auch anderwärts beobachten. Nicht eine (vermutete) gemeinsame historische Situation hat zu Ähnlichkeiten in den Prophetenbüchern geführt, sondern bewusste literarische Gestaltung. Was hier für Amos und Jesaja festgestellt werden konnte, lässt sich mühelos auch über Micha und Jesaja feststellen:

> „Micah is similar to Isaiah not because he referred to a similar situation as a contemporary and/or as a disciple of Isaiah or because he walked in the footsteps of his older contemporary, but because he was deliberately stylized as a younger contemporary of Isaiah by the authors and editors of the book, or more specifically: he is supposed to be a kind of representative of Isaiah in the arising Book of the Twelve."[61]

In diesem Fall ist Jesaja der nehmende Teil, aber das prophetenhermeneutische Phänomen ist hier wie dort dasselbe.

---

60 Vgl. Becker, *Jesaja*, 155–159.
61 Burkard M. Zapff, „Why is Micah similar to Isaiah?," *ZAW* 129 (2017): 536–554, 551.

Literaturverzeichnis

Albertz, Rainer, *Religionsgeschichte Israels in alttestamentlicher Zeit. Band 1: Von den Anfängen bis zum Ende der Königszeit*, GAT 8/1 (Göttingen: Vandenhoeck & Ruprecht, 1992).

Bardtke, Hans, „Die Latifundien in Juda während der zweiten Hälfte des achten Jahrhunderts v. Chr. (Zum Verständnis von Jes 5,8–10)," in *Hommages à André Dupont-Sommer*, Hg. André Dupont-Sommer (Paris: Librairie d'Amérique et d'Orient Adrien-Maisonneuve, 1971): 235–254.

Becker, Uwe, *Jesaja – von der Botschaft zum Buch*, FRLANT 178 (Göttingen: Vandenhoeck & Ruprecht, 1997).

Becker, Uwe, „Der Prophet als Fürbitter. Zum literarhistorischen Ort der Amos-Visionen," *VT* 51/2 (2001): 141–165.

Becker, Uwe, „Jesaja, Jeremia und die Anfänge der Unheilsprophetie in Juda," *HeBAI* 6/1 (2017): 79–100.

Blum, Erhard, „Jesaja und der דבר des Amos. Unzeitgemäße Überlegungen zu Jes 5,25; 9,7–20; 10,1–4," *DBAT* 28 (1992/93) (1994): 75–95.

Bremer, Johannes, *Wo Gott sich auf die Armen einlässt. Der sozio-ökonomische Hintergrund der achämenidischen Provinz Yəhūd und seine Implikationen für die Armentheologie des Psalters*, BBB 174 (Göttingen: V&R Unipress, 2016).

Bremer, Johannes, „The Theology of the Poor in the Psalter," in *The Psalter as Witness. Theology, Poetry, and Genre*, Hg. W. Dennis Tucker und William H. Bellinger (Waco, TX: Baylor University Press, 2017): 101–116.

Fey, Reinhard, *Amos und Jesaja. Abhängigkeit und Eigenständigkeit des Jesaja*, WMANT 12 (Neukirchen-Vluyn: Neukirchener Verlag, 1963).

Fleischer, Gunther, *Von Menschenverkäufern, Baschankühen und Rechtsverkehrern. Die Sozialkritik des Amosbuches in historisch-kritischer, sozialgeschichtlicher und archäologischer Perspektive*, BBB 74 (Frankfurt a.M.: Athenäum, 1989).

Jeremias, Jörg, *Der Prophet Amos*, ATD 24/2 (Göttingen: Vandenhoeck & Ruprecht, 1995).

Jeremias, Jörg, *Hosea und Amos. Studien zu den Anfängen des Dodekapropheton*, FAT 13 (Tübingen: J.C.B. Mohr, 1996).

Kaiser, Otto, *Das Buch des Propheten Jesaja. Kapitel 1–12*, ATD 17 (Göttingen: Vandenhoeck & Ruprecht, ⁵1981).

Kessler, Rainer, *Staat und Gesellschaft im vorexilischen Juda. Vom 8. Jahrhundert bis zum Exil*, VTS 47 (Leiden: E. J. Brill, 1992).

Kessler, Rainer, *Der Weg zum Leben. Ethik des Alten Testaments* (Gütersloh: Gütersloher Verlagshaus, 2017).

Koch, Klaus, *Die Profeten I. Assyrische Zeit*, Bd. 280, *Urban Taschenbücher* (Stuttgart: Kohlhammer, ³1995).

Kratz, Reinhard G., „Die Worte des Amos von Tekoa [2003]," in *Prophetenstudien. Kleine Schriften II*, FAT 74 (Tübingen: Mohr Siebeck, 2011): 310–343.

Kreuch, Jan, *Unheil und Heil bei Jesaja. Studien zur Entstehung des Assur-Zyklus Jesaja 28–31*, WMANT 130 (Neukirchen-Vluyn: Neukirchener Verlag, 2011).

Kreuch, Jan, *Das Amos- und Jesajabuch. Eine exegetische Studie zur Neubestimmung ihres Verhältnisses*, BThSt 149 (Neukirchen-Vluyn: Neukirchener Verlag, 2014).

Levin, Christoph, „Amos und Jerobeam I. [1995]," in *Fortschreibungen. Gesammelte Studien zum Alten Testament*, BZAW 316 (Berlin-New York: Walter de Gruyter, 2003): 256–264.

Levin, Christoph, „Das Amosbuch der Anawim [1997]," in *Fortschreibungen. Gesammelte Studien zum Alten Testament*, BZAW 316 (Berlin-New York: Walter de Gruyter, 2003): 265–290.

Levin, Christoph, „The Poor in the Old Testament. Some Observations [2001]," in *Fortschreibungen. Gesammelte Studien Zum Alten Testament*, BZAW 316 (Berlin-New York: Walter de Gruyter, 2003): 322–338.

Porath, Renatus, *Die Sozialkritik im Jesajabuch. Redaktionsgeschichtliche Analyse*, EHS.T 503 (Frankfurt a.M. u. a.: Peter Lang, 1994).

Reimer, Haroldo, *Richtet auf das Recht! Studien zur Botschaft des Amos*, SBS 149 (Stuttgart: Verlag Katholisches Bibelwerk, 1992).

Riede, Peter, *Vom Erbarmen zum Gericht. Die Visionen des Amosbuches (Am 7–9*) und ihr literatur- und traditionsgeschichtlicher Zusammenhang*, WMANT 120 (Neukirchen-Vluyn: Neukirchener Verlag, 2008).

Schmidt, Ludwig, „Die Amazja-Erzählung (Am 7,10–17) und der historische Amos," *ZAW* 119 (2007): 221–235.

Utzschneider, Helmut, „Die Amazjaerzählung (Am 7,10–17) zwischen Literatur und Historie," *BN* 41 (1988): 76–101.

Williamson, Hugh G. M., „The Prophet and the Plumb-Line: A Redaction-Critical Study of Amos 7 [1990]," in *"The Place is Too Small for Us." The Israelite Prophets in Recent Scholarship*, Hg. Robert P. Gordon, Sources for Biblical and Theological Study 5, (Winona Lake, IN: Eisenbrauns, 1995): 453–477.

Williamson, Hugh G. M., *A Critical and Exegetical Commentary on Isaiah 1–27. Volume 1: Commentary on Isaiah 1–5*, ICC (London: T & T Clark, 2006).

Williamson, Hugh G. M., *A Critical and Exegetical Commentary on Isaiah 1–27 in three Volumes. Volume 2: Commentary on Isaiah 6–12*, ICC (London/New York, NY: Bloomsbury T&T Clark, 2018).

Wolff, Hans Walter, *Dodekapropheton. 2. Joel und Amos*, BKAT XIV/2 (Neukirchen-Vluyn: Neukirchener Verlag, ³1985).

Zapff, Burkard M., „Why is Micah similar to Isaiah?," *ZAW* 129 (2017): 536–554.

James Nogalski
The Role of Lady Zion in the Concluding Section of Zephaniah and Isaiah 40–66

Prolegomena

I was asked to consider the relationship between the concluding section of Zeph 3 and its relationship to Isaiah. As it turns out, this task is fraught with at least two major preliminary difficulties: how do we define "relationship" and what is the "concluding section" of Zephaniah? In the context of a relatively short paper, I cannot begin to solve either of these questions to everyone's satisfaction, but I must set some parameters regarding what I will and will not attempt. Let me begin by dealing with these two prolegomena as a way of being transparent about these decisions before I turn to the comparative task. First, I will admit to a major assumption that, in fact, a relationship does exist between Isaiah and Zeph 3, and second, I will explain why I have chosen to limit my analysis to Zeph 3:11–20 as the final (albeit composite) section of Zephaniah.

Regarding the question of a relationship, occasional references appear in secondary literature with some regularity that claim (usually in passing) some kind of relationship between Zeph 3 and Isaiah. The links between Isaiah and Zeph 3 suggested by scholars vary widely in terms of their location, function, and significance. Consider the following list of Isaiah texts based upon a sampling of recent scholarship on Isaiah and Zephaniah. Scholars have claimed that more than half of the 66 chapters in Isaiah share some kind of lexical conceptual, literary, or redactional link with Zeph 3.

https://doi.org/10.1515/9783110705799-004

Isa (scholars)[1]	Isa (scholars)
3 (Berges, King, Roberts)	40 (Roberts, Tuell)
5–11 (Ahn, Blenkinsopp, Ginsberg, Roberts, Ryoo)	41 (Roberts)
	42 (Dietrich)
6 (Gärtner)	43 (Blenkinsopp)
8 (Sweeney	44 (Berlin, Curtis, Dietrich, Holladay)
11 (King, O'Brien, Sadler, Sweeney)	49–54 (Sweeney)
12 (Ahn, Berges, Boda, Dietrich, Roberts)	49 (Gärtner)
13 (Bosshard, Blenkinsopp, Dietrich)	52 (Roberts, Low)
14 (Blenkinsopp, Hadjiev)	54 (Berlin, Boda, Dietrich, Holladay, Roberts)
16 (Dietrich, Low, Ryoo)	
17 (Berges)	56 (Blenkinsopp, Tuell)
18–19 (Blenkinsopp, Bosshard, Berges, Ryoo, Sadler, Steck, Sweeney)	57 (Tuell)
	59 (Ryoo)

---

1 Sources include the following: John J. Ahn, "Zephaniah, a Disciple of Isaiah?" in *Thus Says the Lord: Essays on the Former and Latter Prophets in Honor of Robert R. Wilson*, eds. John J. Ahn and Stephen L. Cook, LHBOTS 502 (London: T&T Clark, 2010): 292–307; Rainer Albertz, "Exile as Purification: Reconstructing the Book of the Four (Hosea, Amos, Micah, Zephaniah)," *SBLSP* 41 (2002): 213–233; Ulrich Berges, *The Book of Isaiah: Its Composition and Final Form*, trans. Millard C. Lind, HBM 46, (Sheffield: Sheffield Phoenix, 2012), 120; 146; 282; 430; Adele Berlin, *Zephaniah*, AB 25A (New York: Doubleday, 1994), 142–148; Joseph Blenkinsopp, *Isaiah 1–39*, Anchor Bible 19 (New Haven: Yale University Press, 2000), 304; 311; Joseph Blenkinsopp, *Isaiah 56–66*, AB 19B (New Haven: Yale University Press, 2000), 140; Erich Bosshard, "Beobachtungen zum Zwolf-prophetenbuch," *BN* 40 (1987): 34; 53; 54; Walter Dietrich, *Nahum Habakkuk Zephaniah*, IECOT (Stuttgart: Kohlhammer, 2016), 191–192; 242; 247; 250–251; Judith Gärtner, "Jerusalem — City of God for Israel and for the Nations in Zeph 3:8, 9–10, 11–13," in *Perspectives on the Formation of the Book of the Twelve: Methodological Foundations, Reactional Processes, Historical Insights*, eds. Rainer Albertz, James D. Nogalski, and Jakob Wöhrle, BZAW 433 (Berlin: de Gruyter, 2012): 276; 280; H. L. Ginsberg, "Some Emendations in Isaiah," *JBL* 69 (1950): 51–60; Tchavdar S. Hadjiev, "Zephaniah and the 'Book of the Twelve' Hypothesis," in *Prophecy and Prophets in Ancient Israel: Proceedings of the Oxford Old Testament Seminar*, ed. John Day (London: T&T Clark, 2010): 331; Greg A. King, "The Message of Zephaniah: An Urgent Echo," *Andrews University Seminary Studies* 32 (1996): 217; Maggie Low, *Mother Zion in Deutero-Isaiah: A Metaphor for Zion Theology* (New York: Lang, 2013), 51; 56; Julia O'Brien, *Nahum Habakkuk Zephaniah Haggai Zechariah Malachi*, Abingdon Old Testament Commentaries (Nashville: Abingdon, 2004), 128–129; J. J. M. Roberts, *Nahum, Habakkuk, and Zephaniah*, Old Testament Library (Louisville: Westminster John Knox, 1990), 211–214; 222–223; Daniel Hojoon Ryoo, *Zephaniah's Oracles Against the Nations: A Synchronic and Diachronic Study of Zephaniah 2:1–3:8*, BibInt 13 (Leiden: Brill, 1995), 260; 276–277; 279; 321; William L. Holladay, "Reading Zephaniah with a Concordance: Suggestions for a Redaction History," *JBL* 120 (2001): 683–684; Rodney Steven Sadler, *Can a Cushite Change His Skin? An Examination of Race, Ethnicity, and Othering in the Hebrew Bible*, LHBOTS 425 (London: T&T Clark, 2005), 73; 75–76; Odil Hannes Steck, "Zu Zef 3:9–10," *BZ* 34 (1990): 90–95; Marvin A. Sweeney, *Zephaniah: A Commentary*, Hermeneia (Minneapolis: Augsburg Fortress, 2003), 177–178; 200–201; Steven Tuell, *Reading Nahum—Malachi: A Literary and Theological Commentary* (Macon: Smith & Helwys, 2016), 133–135.

30 (Roberts)	60 (Gärtner)
33 (Bosshard)	62 (Berges, Dietrich, Low)
34–35 (Bosshard, Roberts)	64 (Ryoo)
37 (Berges, Low)	65 (Dietrich, Steck, Tuell)
40–55 (Albertz, Gärtner, Sweeney)	66 (Dietrich, Gärtner, Ryoo, Steck, Tuell)

Defining that relationship is, however, a very different venture. The relationship between Zeph 3 and Isaiah is often assumed as self-evident, or mentioned with only a passing reference to the parallel text(s) in Isaiah. As such, it can be difficult to assess the strength of these claims. Further, not all relationships are the same. Some scholars refer to shared phrases, others to shared concepts. Some presume the relationship shows an awareness of a literary form of the text. Others presume the relationship refers merely to a common tradition, or to a common sociological milieu. Given the different contexts in which the above references appear, it seems quite plausible to suggest that Zeph 3 and Isaiah overlap with one another. Using the scholarly principle of *ubi fumo ignis* ("where there is smoke, there is fire"), and a long history of working on the scrolls of Isaiah and the Twelve, I admit to a certain predisposition toward this question. In all probability, both the possible preexilic forms of Isaiah and Zephaniah that may have existed before 587 B.C.E. and the process that led to the final forms of both books were shaped in an intellectual milieu that shared many common assumptions and traditions. This conviction does not, however, prove that such overlap can be interpreted as the *intentional* borrowing of one text from another. Such claims can only be explored on a case by case basis.

The "case" I would like to explore in this essay arises from the second preliminary issue. What is the "concluding section" of Zephaniah? Scholars have made cases that one should treat the primary unit as the entire chapter (3:1–20), the salvific themes grouped together in 3:9–20, the eschatologically oriented message of 3:14–20, or some combination of 3:11–20 as the book's concluding unit.[2] In my estimation, this question is complex and could be the subject of an essay on its own

---

2 Sweeney treats the primary unit as 2:1–3:20, but sees 3:1–20 as a major segment (Marvin A. Sweeney, *The Twelve Prophets: Volume Two: Micah, Nahum, Habakkuk, Zephaniah, Haggai, Zechariah, Malachi*, Berit Olam: Studies in Hebrew Narrative & Poetry (Collegeville: Liturgical Press, 2000), 494; 518). Zimmerli deems 3:9–14 as the early salvific ending to the book that was later expanded with 3:15–20: Walter Zimmerli, "Vom Prophetenwort zum Prophetenbuch," *Theologische Literaturzeitung* 104 (1979): 481–496. Rudolph argues that early sayings go back to a prophet prior to the time of Josiah while the majority of 3:1–15* were joined editorially during the exile and 3:15–20 represent a postexilic expansion: Wilhelm Rudolph, *Micha – Nahum – Habakuk – Zephanja*, Kommentar zum Alten Testament 13/3 (Gütersloh: Gerd Mohn, 1976), 255–256.

merit.[3] That being said, I will focus upon 3:11–20 as the passage for two reasons. First, I think the rhetorical purposes of these verses cohere relatively consistently, despite some tensions within the unit (especially in 3:20). Second, these verses demonstrate awareness of traditions concerning Lady Zion, traditions that play with certain motifs to convey messages about the fate of Jerusalem to the readers of the respective books.[4]

I will first describe the rhetorical logic of Zeph 3:11–20 in terms of how it draws upon traditional concepts of Lady Zion (i. e., what it does and does not draw from this tradition). Next, I will survey the texts in Isa 40–55 that address Lady Zion directly followed by those in 56–66. Finally, I will conclude with some observations regarding the similarities *and* differences one finds in the treatment of Lady Zion in Zeph 3:11–20 and Isaiah. My hope is that this intertextual comparison

---

3 Compare, for example, these complexities in three recent commentaries. All three see a break between 3:1–13 and 3:14–20: Roberts, *Nahum, Habakkuk, Zephaniah*, 204; 222; Berlin, *Zephaniah*, 17–20; and Sweeney, *The Twelve Prophets*, 518–524. Roberts describes 3:1–20 as a "compositional unity" that may include older oracles but one cannot sort them out because the unity has been so thoroughly imposed upon the chapter. Nevertheless, he distinguishes Zeph 3:1–13 and 3:14–20 from one another based upon the thematic shift from judgment and purification (3:1–13) to rejoicing (3:14–20), so that he also sees the chapter as "two units." Roberts admits, however, that the second unit is aware of the first. Berlin notes that the division of Zephaniah as a whole and the third chapter in particular has always been problematic since both the ancient codexes (Aleppo, Leningrad, Cairo, and Petersburg) and modern translations see the divisions quite differently. She opts to follow the Leningrad Codex and divide the units into 3:1–13 and 3:14–20, but sees them as part of a rhetorical and structural unity, not a collection of individual oracles. Sweeney understands 3:1–20 as the description of a three-fold process that moves from Jerusalem's desolation (3:1–4) to the "punishment of Israel's oppressors and gathering of Israel's exiles" (3:5–13), and then concludes by announcing the imminent restoration of Jerusalem and Israel. Nevertheless, Sweeney divides his presentation of this unit into two main sections (3:1–13 on pp. 519–523 and 3:14–20 on pp. 523–524). Hence, even though these three commentators recognize that the chapter shifts in 3:14–20, they differ markedly in how they see the structure and rhetoric.
4 I presuppose discussions of בת ציון (Lady Zion) in the works of Fitzgerald, Schmidt, Biddle, and Maier which draw attention to the ways that בת ציון appears as a Judean adaptation of a west Semitic tradition wherein cities are personified as a woman who is a consort deity to the male deity. Aloysius Fitzgerald, "Mythological Background for the Presentation of Jerusalem as a Queen and False Worship as Adultery in the OT," *CBQ* 34 (1972): 403–416; John J. Schmitt, "The Motherhood of God and Zion as Mother," *RB* 92 (1985): 557–569; Mayer I. Gruber, "The Motherhood of God in Second Isaiah," *RB* 90 (1983): 351–359; Mark E. Biddle, "The Figure of Lady Jerusalem: Identification, Deification and Personification of Cities in the Ancient Near East," in *Biblical Canon in Comparative Perspectives*, eds. B. Batto and W. Hallo (Lewiston, NY: Edwin Mellen, 1991): 173–194; Odil Hannes Steck, "Zion als Gelände und Gestalt: Überlegungen zur Wahrnehmung Jerusalems als Stadt und Frau im Alten Testament," *ZTK* 86 (1989): 261–281; and Christl Maier, *Daughter Zion, Mother Zion: Gender, Space, and the Sacred in Ancient Israel* (Minneapolis: Fortress, 2008).

opens up the creative use of the tradition in the two scrolls. They share much, especially in the ways that the texts utilize the tradition to offer hope, but the differences are equally instructive as they are more tied to the aims of the individual scroll than to an intentional borrowing from one another.

1 Zephaniah 3:11–20

Zephaniah 3:11–20 represents a composite unit designed for at least two purposes: initially the end of the Book of the Four and as the final "preexilic" book in the Book of the Twelve. Zephaniah 3:11–20 does not represent a completely homogenous text, but these verses offer a hopeful, salvific message addressed to Zion personified. These verses divide into three rhetorical subsections: 3:11–13, 14–17, and 18–20.

These three subsections are set off from the preceding verses. Zephaniah 3:1–8 offers words of judgment against Jerusalem by summarizing the accusations against the city and its leaders from chapter 1 and by anticipating the coming judgment against the nations that has been the focus of 2:4–15. Verses 9–10 change the focus from judgment to hope, setting the stage for the message of 3:11–20, but they do not utilize the second feminine singular address forms that dominate beginning with 3:11.

All three of these subsections are generally dated to a time after the destruction of Jerusalem, largely based upon the topic of the remnant that features prominently, though a significant number of commentators see some parts of these verses as later than others.[5] Nevertheless, these verses appear in the book of a seventh-century prophet, so that one should not ignore this setting when describing the literary function of these verses. In this sense, Zeph 3 shares this charac-

---

5 For example, consider the presentations of Roberts, *Nahum, Habakkuk, and Zephaniah*, 204–223, and Dietrich, *Nahum Habakkuk Zephaniah*, 191–192; 246–249. Roberts avoids any serious attempt to date Zeph 3. He claims there is no way to reconstruct the original logia because "a compositional unity has been imposed" (p. 204) on the original units to such a degree that no criteria can convincingly portray the original contours of the settings. He divides 3:1–13 from 3:14–20 merely on the grounds that v. 13 seems like an ending while the change to an imperative style in 3:14 starts something new. Dietrich, by contrast, considers 3:9–20 as a "joyful conclusion" comprised of sayings added sometime in the middle or late Persian period (i.e. fifth or fourth century B.C.E.). He separates 3:9–10 and 3:20 and refers to them as a (composite) introduction and a (composite) solemn conclusion respectively while he describes 3:11–19 as a collection of individual logia linked by the fact that they either address or speak about Lady Zion.

teristic with Isa 40–55 and 56–66. They deal with hope for the Persian period as a message from a prophetic character who lived prior to Jerusalem's destruction.

Verses 11–13 address Lady Zion concerning the remnant and describe the current situation in relatively mild terms. These verses depict the time of restoration as a future event ("on that day") when the boastful and haughty people in Zion have been removed (3:11), leaving a remnant people who are "humble and lowly" and who "seek refuge in the name of YHWH" (3:12). The lives of this population left behind are characterized by their ethical propriety and the peaceful normalcy that results from their behavior (3:13).

In 3:14–17, five observations expose the difficulties of reading prophetic texts, especially those in the Book of the Twelve. First, in these verses, the syntactical marker of the second feminine singular address to Lady Zion continues, but the formal speaker changes. In 3:11–13 (and 3:18–20), YHWH speaks directly to Lady Zion, while in 3:14–17 YHWH appears only in third-person references, meaning that, conceptually, the prophet speaks in these verses. Second, the content shifts from the remnant in Jerusalem in 3:11–13 to the relationship between Lady Zion and YHWH in 3:14–17. To be sure, these latter verses continue the general theme of Jerusalem's restoration, but they use different motifs and foci to describe the restoration. These verses focus upon YHWH's decision to return as king and to defeat her enemies because the time of punishment has ceased (3:15). This subsection admonishes Lady Zion to rejoice (3:14) and not to fear (3:16) because the warrior king resides in her midst, rejoices over her, renews his love, and breaks into song (3:17). Third, verses 14–17 manifest a very tight, thematic structure, providing these verses with their own organic unity.[6] Fourth, despite their thematic continuity and their structural cohesion, any relationship to the preceding verses has to be inferred from the context. No particles, conjunctions, or causal statements provide the reader/hearer with a clue to explain how these verses relate to 3:11–13. While the direct address of Lady Zion continues from 3:11–13, verses 14–17 only refer indirectly to the deliverance of the inhabitants of Jerusalem as a remnant *if* one assumes a relationship to the preceding verses.[7] Finally, the vocab-

---

[6] See James D. Nogalski, *The Book of the Twelve: Micah – Malachi*, SHBC 18b (Macon: Smyth & Helwys, 2011), 747–748.

[7] Herein lies another methodological decision. Every reader of prophetic literature must determine how to understand verses in relationship to their surrounding context, given the change of focus, the tight structure, and the lack of any statement of purpose by an author or editor. Such similarities amid changes are ubiquitous. See James D. Nogalski, "Where Are the Prophets in the Book of the Twelve?," in *The Book of the Twelve and New Form Criticism*, eds. Mark J. Boda, Michael H. Floyd, and Colin M. Toffelmire, Ancient Near East Monographs (Atlanta: SBL, 2015): 163–182.

ulary of this subsection overlaps with portions of Isaiah more than other sections of Zeph 3.[8]

Verses 18–20 comprise the third subsection of 3:11–20. The first verse has some syntactical difficulties that one must resolve. The speaker changes back to the first-person divine speech as in 3:11–13, even as the second feminine singular address to Lady Zion continues in 3:18–19a. Moreover, the content concerns those who have survived (i.e., the humbled remnant), also in much the same fashion as 3:11–13. Finally, whereas 3:19b speaks to Lady Zion but refers to this restored population using a third-person masculine plural pronoun, 3:20 addresses this remnant directly using second-person masculine plural pronouns while essentially repeating the content of 3:19b.

Significantly, Zeph 3:19 draws upon Mic 4:6–7 to predict the restoration of the lame and the outcast, terms which refer respectively to those who suffer in the environs of Jerusalem and to those who have vacated the land under duress.[9] Two observations regarding Zephaniah's adaptation of the promise seem relevant. First, in Zeph 3:19, the perspective has been enlarged with respect to the outcast. In Mic 4 (cf. 4:6,10) the outcast is defined as those taken to Babylon (without specifying whether that means 597, 587, or following Gedaliah's assassination). By contrast, Zeph 3:19 anticipates the restoration from "all your oppressors," a change that may suggest awareness of the OAN in Zeph 2:5–15. Second, the chronological formulation that begins 3:19 articulates the promise with a syntactical construction that emphasizes the nearness of the action (הנני + participle: "Behold, I am about to ...").[10] By comparison, Mic 4:6 places the promise in the more distant future. These subtle changes align with the position of Zephaniah in the broader corpus, as the last book in the Twelve explicitly set in the time of a Judean monarch.

Stepping back and looking at the stylistic and material characteristics of these three subunits, several things stand out. First, all three subunits consistently refer to Lady Zion using direct address (2fs). Second, the content of the first and third subunits align more closely with one another. These subunits convey their message using divine first-person speech (as opposed to the third-person references about YHWH in 3:14–17). Third, the second subunit focuses upon the divine warrior's relationship to Lady Zion without explicitly mentioning Zion's children (i.e., the population of the city), though restoration of the relationship

---

8 See Erich Bosshard, "Beobachtungen zum Zwölfprophetenbuch": 34–35.

9 James D. Nogalski, *Literary Precursors to the Book of the Twelve*, BZAW 217 (Berlin: de Gruyter, 1993), 204–211.

10 GKC § 116p.

between Lady Zion and YHWH obviously would have implicit ramifications for the people. Fourth, despite the common theme of restoration and the direct address to Lady Zion, the stylistic and content variations of the three subunits raise the question of how they are intended to be read. The commonalities suggest that they belong together, but the change of speakers and the switching pronouns give the reader pause and suggest that these verses reflect more than one compositional hand. Fifth, and finally, 3:19 borrows the language of Mic 4:6–7, which raises the question whether this citation reflects awareness of Zephaniah's function as the conclusion to the Book of the Four and/or Zephaniah's function as the final "pre-exilic" book within the Book of the Twelve that is explicitly set in the time of a king of Judah prior to Jerusalem's destruction.

2 Lady Zion in Isa 49–55

Isaiah 49–55 contains three extended passages addressing Lady Zion directly. The husband/wife relationship and references to Zion's children appear prominently in all three. These passages include: 49:14–26; 51:17–52:8; and 54:1–17.

Isaiah 49:14–26. This passage represents a speech by YHWH to Lady Zion in which he responds to her accusations that he has abandoned her (42:14). YHWH proceeds to prove his love by depicting himself in motherly terms (Isa 49:15). He describes the blue prints of her walls that will be rebuilt (vv. 16–17). YHWH promises Lady Zion that her children will soon return (49:18). The building process will have trouble keeping up with all the inhabitants whose return will crowd the city (19–20). She will be astounded at the size of her population (49:21). Her children (i. e., the city's population) will be carried to her by kings and queens of the nations (49:22–23). Her oppressors will themselves be destroyed and all the nations will see YHWH's power in these events (49:24–26). The imagery assumes Lady Zion as wife, mother, and city. YHWH comforts her by refuting her charge that he abandoned her.

Isaiah 51:17–52:8. These fourteen verses speak directly to Lady Zion and blend images of her as mother and city in two major units: 51:17–23 and 52:1–8. The content of the first unit starts with an oracle announcing a change of status for her (51:17–23).

The unit begins with a call to Lady Zion to rouse herself from where she has fallen after drinking from YHWH's cup of wrath (51:17–20). The oracle first describes the current situation (51:17–20): she has no leader (v. 18); she suffers from destruction and famine (v. 19); and her children have fainted in every street (v. 20). These images depict Zion's situation after 587 B.C.E. The second portion of the oracle describes YHWH's decision to punish those who have tormented her (51:21–23). This pronouncement assumes YHWH's decision to change her fate relates to the cup of wrath that began the unit (51:21–23, cf. v. 17). YHWH will remove the cup from her and force her "tormentors" to drink from it instead. These tormentors refer to foreign powers. The cup of wrath tradition plays a major role in Jeremiah's OAN, where its logic assumes that Jerusalem's punishment is the first thing to happen before YHWH punishes the other countries.[11]

The Zion imagery alludes briefly to Zion's children (the punishment of the population of the city in v. 20), but the major focus is on her role as the capital city of Judah. She has no leader (v. 18), a reference to the ongoing loss of the king. She suffers from destruction and the lack of food (v. 19). The devastation is described as the wrath of YHWH (v. 20), meaning that she was deemed responsible by YHWH. Nevertheless, YHWH has now decided to reverse the punishment and punish those who have attacked her.

The Zion imagery in 52:1–8 advances the picture of Zion's restoration with a pronouncement of YHWH's return to her. The verses unfold in three subsections: commands to Zion to awaken and get dressed (52:1–2), YHWH's soliloquy regarding the restoration of the people (52:3–6), and the description of the sentinel's vision of YHWH's return (52:7–8).

The first subsection (52:1–2) calls for Zion to get ready. Whereas Zion is portrayed as a humiliated city lying in the dirt in 51:23, YHWH tells her to stand up and shake the dust off of herself (52:2) and to don her "beautiful garments" (52:1). The Zion imagery in 52:1–2 assumes Zion as the city, but also assumes she is the wife of YHWH. The speaker announces that the uncircumcised (i. e., foreigners) will no longer enter Zion because she is a holy city. At the same time, the imagery of arising and dressing in her finest clothes assumes that she is getting dressed to greet her husband.

YHWH speaks in 52:3–6 regarding the people whom he is restoring. These verses do not address Zion directly. Stylistically, they appear like a parenthetical aside, as YHWH announces his intention to redeem his people from "the Assyrian" just as he did when Israel went to Egypt to reside as aliens (52:4). The Assyrian here should be understood as an allusion to the Assyrian oppression in addition to the current Mesopotamian (i. e., Babylonian) setting presumed in these chapters.[12] The exodus allusion presumes a return to the land by the population

---

11 So, for example Blenkinsopp, *Isaiah 56–66*, 341.

12 Note, for example, discussions in H. G. M. Williamson, *The Book Called Isaiah: Deutero-Isaiah's Role in Composition and Redaction* (Oxford: Clarendon Press, 1994), 127–128; and Claus

that has been outside the land. The three events (oppression in Egypt, oppression by Assyria, and the current setting in Babylon) are thus interrelated.

The third subsection 52:7–8 returns to addressing Lady Zion directly, but these verses announce the arrival of the messenger who tells her, "your God reigns" while the sentinels see YHWH returning to Zion. In this sense, the verses continue the scene from 52:2 as YHWH returns to Zion, who is ready to receive him. The Zion imagery in these verses assumes that Zion is waiting for her husband's imminent return.

Isaiah 54:1–17. This chapter presents an extended address to Lady Zion that presumes several things: the arrival of a new population creates the need for Jerusalem to expand its living space (54:1–3); YHWH has restored Zion's role as wife and mother (54:4–8); a comparison of her restoration to the time after Noah (54:9–10); and pronouncements of great wealth and security for the city (54:11–17).

Verses 1–3 call for Lady Zion to sing because her children have returned to take up space within her, but the number of children is greater than she has space to support so she must expand her tent. Verses 4–8 tell her not to worry since the shame of her widowhood will be gone because YHWH has returned as her husband. She was cast off (i. e., divorced) by YHWH in his wrath (54:6), but he has shown compassion for her and returned as her husband (54:5). YHWH admits to abandoning her for a short time, but promises that his *ḥesed* will continue forever (54:7).

Verses 9–10 compare the "covenant of peace" with Zion to the time of Noah after the flood waters receded. YHWH's *ḥesed* will last forever (cf. 54:8).[13] The monumental significance of the restoration of the relationship between YHWH and Lady Zion is thus emphatically placed on par with YHWH's decision to establish a covenant with the earth that he would never again destroy the world by flood.

Verses 11–17 portray life after the return of YHWH and Zion's children by blending images of Zion as city, wife, and mother. YHWH will provide her with

---

Westermann, *Isaiah 40–66*, trans. David M. G. Stalker, Old Testament Library (Philadelphia: Westminster, 1969), 248. Westermann sees 52:4–6 as a "marginal gloss" that seeks to connect the dots between the experience of the exiles in Babylon with the prior examples of foreign oppression: slavery in Egypt and Assyrian domination of the eight and seventh centuries. Williamson, like others, draws a correlation to the unusual combination of Egypt and Assyria that also appears in Isa 11:15–16 and Isa 19:23–24. He considers the passage to have been added to Isa 11 when Deutero-Isaiah himself composed texts to help link early portions of Isa 1–39 with his own composition.
13 The allusion to Gen 9 mirrors the use of an allusion to the exodus in the comparison of the people's return in 51:3–4.

jewels for her gates and pinnacles, and YHWH will teach her children himself so that they live in prosperity (54:13). Zion herself will be established in righteousness (54:14) and no longer experience oppression (54:14–15). The passage concludes with YHWH's affirmation of protection by threatening anyone who stirs up trouble for her. This passage presupposes a restored relationship between Zion, her children, and YHWH, meaning she is again wife and mother. Still, her role as city plays a major role as well — especially in references to her gates and pinnacles covered with rubies and precious stones (54:11–12) and the expansion of her tent to house her children (54:2–3).

3 Lady Zion in Isa 56–66

In Isa 56–66, the following passages speak to Lady Zion directly: 57:6–13; 60:1–22; 62:1–12.

Isaiah 57:6–13. This passage takes up the motif of Lady Zion as wanton woman in order to condemn her idolatry. The charges of adultery articulate the accusations of idolatry. Such imagery is well attested in Hos 2, Jer 2–6*, and Ezek 16 and 23. Isaiah's depiction in 57:6–13 has some unique (and salacious) details that add to the severity of her guilt. The imagery and message of this text differ markedly from Isa 40–55. She opens her bed for her lovers to gaze upon their nakedness. She is accused of opening her bed of sacrifice upon high and lofty places (57:7–8) and of offering drink offerings and grain offerings (57:6) to Molech and other deities, including those of the underworld (57:9). Moreover, the passage ends with YHWH's rejection of Lady Zion because of her lack of remorse. YHWH tells her tale as the story of betrayal and sarcastically tells her to let her idols save her (57:13). The remainder of chapter 57, however, abandons the direct address to Zion for her past and points instead to the future when YHWH will revive the contrite and humble (57:15). YHWH will provide them comfort (57:18) and peace (57:19). In this sense, the rhetoric of the accusations against Lady Zion functions as an explanation for YHWH's past punishment, not future events. Further, this passage fits the general tenor and message of chapters 56–59* which seek to admonish Zion and the people for past misdeeds which have "created a barrier" between YHWH and YHWH's people (59:1–2). The more negative attitude toward Zion is consistent with the general tenor of Isa 57–59, a fact that fits well with recent models of Isaiah that distinguish the origins of these chapters from 60–62 (or 63–66).[14]

---

[14] See the summary of recent redaction historical studies in Berges, *The Book of Isaiah*, 29–34.

Isaiah 60:1–22. The two extended passages in Isa 60 and 62 that involve Lady Zion as the addressee both tend to highlight her function as the city, but also as mother. Isaiah 60 begins with the prophet addressing Lady Zion with the command to stand up and look around because the nations are returning her sons and daughters (i. e., the population of the city) back to her (60:1–5). YHWH is mentioned in the third person (61:1,2,6,9), but the style of address changes in verse 14. There, divine first-person speech becomes the norm for the remainder of the chapter. In 60:14–22, YHWH is mentioned on several occasions, but always as YHWH referring to himself in the third person (60:14, cf. vv. 13,19–20,21–22). The nations specifically mentioned include near and distant lands to the east and west of Judah. Midian and Ephah (60:6) presumably refer to the Sinai region. Shebah (60:6) refers to distant lands beyond Sinai.[15] Kedar and Nebaioth (60:7) represent the desert tribes descended from Ishmael, also east of Judah. By contrast, the coastlands and Tarshish (60:9) refer to the distant parts of the Mediterranean west of Judah. All of these nations are depicted as returning Zion's children and contributing to her restoration from their own wealth. The resources they provide will be used to rebuild Zion (60:10) and to outfit the temple (60:13) to fit her status as YHWH's city (60:14). YHWH will provide treasures for Zion (60:17) and peace and righteousness will characterize her fate and the behavior of her children (60:17–22). This passage, thus, addresses Lady Zion as both city and mother, though the function of Zion as city takes center stage. Her children (the population) will be returned from a wide array of foreign territories on either side. Moreover, foreign kings and queens will contribute from their own wealth to restore the splendor of Zion and they will bow down before her.

Isaiah 62. The style of chapter 62 is difficult to define. Isaiah 62:1–12 presents as a complex unit, alternating both speakers (the prophetic voice and YHWH) and terms for Zion/Jerusalem (62:1)/Lady Zion (62:11). A first-person speech begins with 62:1, but almost every verse thereafter refers to YHWH or God in the third person. Verses 1 and 10 do not specifically mention the deity, and v. 7 refers to YHWH with a 3ms suffix. YHWH speaks directly in verses 8 and 11, but both times the short speech is introduced by the narrator (i. e., the prophetic voice). The content of 62:1, however, sounds more like a divine speech even though it leads directly into 62:2 where YHWH appears in the third person.

The content of chapter 62 utilizes Lady Zion imagery to focus first upon the marital relationship before offering extensive treatment of Lady Zion as the city of Jerusalem. The marital imagery appears quite explicitly in verses 4–5 which twice

---

15 So, for example, Berges interprets these names as indicating the distant West and East: Berges, *The Book of Isaiah*, 412.

describe Zion's status as married (to YHWH). Additionally, the dual references to Zion as YHWH's delight certainly adds to the sense of the groom's pleasure with his bride, and verse 5 makes this comparison explicit by comparing God's joy to the joy of the bridegroom who looks upon his bride. Given this marital language, the language in verses 2–3 become clearer. These verses characterize Zion using royal terminology (righteousness, glory, crown, diadem), while addressing Lady Zion directly with second feminine singular pronouns and verbs. Hence, indirectly, these verses articulate the relationship between YHWH and Zion as that of the king and queen.

Despite the marital imagery, the dominant imagery in this chapter focuses heavily upon Zion as the city, the capital of the land, and the place where YHWH dwells. From 62:6 forward, the marital imagery subsides as the focus of Zion as city comes to the fore. Sentinels will be placed upon her walls (62:6); her grain and wine will not be given to other nations, but will be gathered at YHWH's house (62:8–9). People are commanded to enter her gates (62:10), for YHWH's return will mean the return of people to the city (62:11–12).[16] The picture that develops from 62:6–12 presupposes 62:1–5 in which the restoration of Lady Zion as YHWH's queen leads to the restoration of the city: the sentinels on the walls, the return of the grain and the wine to the temple (YHWH's palace), and the return of a holy people to populate the city so that she receives a new name: forsaken no more (62:12).

Excursus: Isa 35 and Zeph 3:14–17. According to Erich Bosshard, similarities between Isa 35 and Zeph 3:14–17 appear more prominently in Zeph 3:14–17 than in the surrounding verses. Bosshard argues that Zephaniah depicts a universal expansion of judgment against all people and nations similar to Isa 34. In addition, he argues that Zeph 3:14–18 parallels Isa 35 too closely to denote merely a common tradition.

Rather, according to Bosshard, one has to understand the relations as a literary relationship.[17] For Bosshard, the lexical clustering connecting Zeph 3:14–18

---

16 Additionally, the text-critical problem of 62:5 should not be overlooked. The MT makes little sense when it points בניך as the plural construct of "son," causing several versions to re-point the word as a plural participle from the verb "to build." The resulting translation "those building you will marry you" also makes little sense, but NRSV and NIV assume that the original reading would have been a singular pronoun. Both versions translate the verse, consequently, as "your builder will marry you."

17 See the essay by Erich Bosshard, "Beobachtungen zum Zwölfprophetenbuch": 30–62. Bosshard argues for a common structural arrangement in which the Twelve parallel the major lines of Isaiah. He argues that several texts in the Twelve contain literary parallels to texts in Isaiah and mirror the position of that text in Isaiah, including Zeph 3:14–18 drawing upon (pp. 34–35).

to Isa 35 involves the following: רני/רנן (Zeph 3:14/Isa 35:2); שמחת/שמחי (Zeph 3:14/
Isa 35:10); אל תיראי/אל תיראו (Zeph 3:16/Isa 35:4); ידיך ירפו/רפות ידים (Zeph 3:16/Isa
35:3), שוש גיל, רנה/רנן (Zeph 3:17/Isa 35:1f.); ברנה, שמחה, שוש/ששון (Zeph 3:17/Isa
35:10); יגה/יגון (Zeph 3:18/Isa 35:10). No other such grouping appears in the Old
Testament and when that is combined with the theme of the return of the diaspora
(Zeph 3:19/Isa 34–35), Bosshard argues one can hardly see this combination as
accidental. The question of intentionality, however, requires more evidence. What
purpose would such parallels play? One could suggest that Isa 35 functions as part
of the bridge to Isa 40–55, as a literary foreshadowing of the restoration of Zion.
Unlike Zeph 3:14–17, however, Isa 35 does not address Zion directly. It begins (vv.
1–2) by drawing attention to territory in the former northern kingdom (Lebanon,
Carmel, Sharon), but by the end of the chapter (vv. 8–10) depicts a highway prepared for the "ransomed of YHWH" who will return to Zion with joy and gladness.
This imagery certainly anticipates Isa 40 ff., but nothing in Zeph 3:14–17 speaks
of such a highway. By contrast, Zeph 3:19 takes up Mic 4:6–7, but does so with a
grammatical formulation that presumes a more imminent restoration of the blind
and the lame than one finds in Mic 4:6–7.[18] In the end, one can say that the two
passages demonstrate a thematic parallel (the restoration of Zion). Both passages,
however, link themselves to other passages within their respective scrolls. So, one
can say that while both Isa 35 and Zeph 3:14–17 demonstrate a strong interest in
the restoration of Zion, their literary horizons, in my opinion, are more strongly
rooted in the content of the scrolls in which they appear than Bosshard would
allow when he claims an intentional parallel between Isaiah and the Twelve.

Vocabulary overlap may represent allusions in some places, but not clearly
so. More likely, the overlap comes in the form of common traditions (e. g., word
pairs or specific constellations like Lady Zion). For example, the noun "king" and
the 2fs address to Lady Zion represent types of parallels between Zeph 3:14–17 and
Isaiah, especially passages in Isa 40–55 and 60–62, some of which have lexical
parallels as well.

The noun "king" refers to YHWH in Zeph 3:15 whose presence in Zion ("in
your midst") after turning away Lady Zion's enemies reestablishes a reason not
to fear. These phrases depend upon the concept of the divine warrior fighting on
Jerusalem's behalf. The presence of YHWH in the city means the enemies have
been defeated. By contrast, the term "king" does not appear in the Lady Zion
passages in Isa 40–55. The term appears only three times (41:21; 43:15; 44:6) in

---

18 Note that Mic 4:6 begins with "in that day," a formula that points back to t the time in Mic
4:1 (which is labeled as the "latter days"), whereas in Zeph 3:19 YHWH is "about to act" (הנני +
participle).

Isa 40–55. Two of these references to the king appear in conjunction with YHWH as creator combined with an anti-idolatry polemic (41:21–26; 43:14–17), while the third draws attention to the divine warrior at creation (43:15–17). Isaiah 52:7 comes the closest to Zeph 3:14–17 when it refers to YHWH's reign that will return to Zion. Certainly, the image of YHWH as king evokes a sense of power, but there is no implicit military threat as in Zeph 3:15.

The second feminine singular form רני calling upon Lady Zion to sing appears in Isa 12:6; 54:1; and Zeph 3:14. This unusual form appears only one other time in prophetic texts, notably in the restoration vision recounted in Zech 2:14.[19] Dietrich and others correctly call attention to this call to rejoice in Zeph 3:14 as a response to the removal of the preceding announcements of judgment against Jerusalem.[20] Rarely, however, do they pause to consider the character's gender and its effect upon the reader.[21] The recognition of gender accentuates Zion's role as mother and spouse (especially in Isaiah).

4 Comparisons and Implications

Several things become clear from this survey of Zion texts in Zephaniah and Isaiah. Certainly, the two texts share a number of characteristics. The personification of Jerusalem as Lady Zion appears in both texts. Both texts convey a salvific message from YHWH that calls upon Lady Zion to rejoice. Both texts draw upon traditions of the divine warrior battling the nations. A significant number of scholars date both texts to the Persian period. Given the small size of Jerusalem's population, there are strong reasons to suspect those compiling the Isaiah scroll and those constructing the Twelve had some kind of awareness of the developing scrolls.

---

19 It never appears in Jeremiah or Ezekiel, and appears only one other time in the Old Testament: Lam 2:19. In the Lamentations text, however, the call to cry out in context refers to cries of mourning, not rejoicing.
20 See Dietrich, *Nahum Habakkuk Zephaniah*, 244–245; and Sweeney, *The Twelve Prophets*, 523.
21 See O'Brien, *Nahum Habakkuk Zephaniah Haggai Zechariah Malachi*, 125. O'Brien astutely distinguishes between the masculine plural terms for Israel and the feminine singular terms to Lady Zion and Lady Jerusalem. She describes the effect of this gendered imagery as the attempt to juxtapose the (helpless) woman with the savior figure of YHWH as king: "With a mighty (male) protector, she need not fear evil anymore." Additionally, the references to Lady Zion and Lady Jerusalem have the potential to accentuate more intimately the city and her relationships to YHWH (her husband) and the population of the city (her children). These relationships are explored more fully in the Isaiah texts while they remain in the background in Zephaniah.

These similarities are important, but one must also be clear that differences between the two texts also need to be delineated. Lady Zion is not personified in the same way in Zephaniah and Isaiah. Isaiah utilizes the personified city to explore relationships in familial terms. In Isaiah, the relationship between YHWH and Zion unfolds as the restoration of the marital covenant. The restoration of Zion's children plays a more prominent role and intersects with the family imagery. Relatedly, Isaiah uses aspects of the personified city to focus upon Zion as spouse and mother. Also, the Lady Zion texts in Isaiah and Zephaniah assume different attitudes to the nations. In Isaiah, the nations recognize YHWH's power. They return Zion's children as an act of gracious subservience in the face of divine power rather than defeat/annihilation (the implication of YHWH as victorious warrior in Zephaniah). Thus, it is worth highlighting the salient characteristics of Lady Zion as wife and mother and as a cipher for the fate of the city.

Wife and Mother. Isaiah 49–55 contains a number of passages addressing Lady Zion directly, and most of these presuppose a husband/wife relationship. YHWH denies that he has divorced her or forgotten her children (Isa 50:1,2ff.). The Zion material in Isa 49–55 tends to refer to the population as her children (49:20,25; 51:18,20; 54:1,13), while Zeph 3:14–20 refers to the population in other, non-familial terms (e. g., a humble and lowly people in 3:11–12; the remnant in 3:13; and the lame and the outcast in 3:19).[22] Ultimately, in Isaiah, YHWH acknowledges that he abandoned her and hid his face from her for a time but will now have compassion upon her (54:6–7).

The role of Zion in 60–62 as wife and mother corresponds closely with the imagery in 40–55. In a certain sense, one could read Isa 60 and 62 as continuations of the interaction between YHWH and Zion.[23] By contrast, Isa 57 exhibits a much darker picture of the relationship as it focuses upon Zion's former behavior as wanton woman who would sleep with anyone. Rhetorically, this castigation strengthens accusations of idolatry, as is often the case in the Latter Prophets. This critique of Lady Zion is unusual, however, for 40–66, but does fit the darker tone of 57–59 that most redactional models of the last decades have noted.

In contrast to the Isaiah texts, Zeph 3 does not draw upon Lady Zion imagery in relational terms that highlight her role as wife or mother, except indirectly. Her personification as city remains the focal point throughout. Zephaniah 3:14–17, in

---

22 Even when Lady Babylon is addressed, her role as mother also figures prominently (cf. Isa 47:8–9).

23 For example, Zion is told to arise at the beginning of Isa 60:1. She had been told by the nations in 51:23 to lie down so they could walk on her.

particular, highlights YHWH's role as warrior king who has returned triumphant after defeating Zion's enemies.

Zion as City. In several texts in 40–55 and 56–66, the mother imagery recedes and the city imagery comes to the fore. These texts still use the second feminine singular address to speak directly to Lady Zion, and the direct address evokes sympathy and tenderness. The punishment of Zion is acknowledged as the cup of YHWH's wrath (51:17) which YHWH is now removing from her and passing to her tormentors who have tread over her outstretched body (51:22–23). YHWH calls to her to awaken, to adorn herself with her beautiful garments, and to stand up and shake the dust from herself (52:1–2) because YHWH reigns (52:7) and will return to her (52:8). Restoration implies expanding and rebuilding the city in grand style (see 54:2–3,12). The city walls and the temple become part of the focus in these texts.

The city plays the central role in Zeph 3:11–20, but the role of her population is more nuanced. The population includes the proud, exultant, and haughty who rebelled against YHWH and who will be removed from the city (3:11). It also anticipates a humble, lowly remnant that seeks refuge from YHWH (3:12). Zephaniah 3:19–20 also refer to the salvation of the lame and the gathering of the outcast (3:19) by YHWH. These final metaphors likely refer to those who remained in the land (the lame) and some of those driven from the land.

In Isa 40–66, YHWH's relationship with Lady Zion presents itself in more relational terms. YHWH does not stand "in the midst" of Zion. Rather, YHWH speaks to her as his wife and talks with her about her children. Nevertheless, Lady Zion serves as a cipher for the fate of the city. Her roles as wife and mother consistently appear more prominent than is the case in Zeph 3:11–20, where these motifs are more muted.

Zephaniah's personified Zion does not emphasize these relational qualities, but still presumes the concept of Lady Zion as the consort of YHWH. The image of YHWH differs in how Zeph 3:14–17 draws upon militaristic and royal traditions. *Isaiah's YHWH* seeks to return Zion's children and restore his relationship to her. *Zephaniah's YHWH* returns to Jerusalem as the triumphant king. Jerusalem's population does not participate in the personified husband/wife relationship. Zephaniah's restored population is portrayed as humbled and wounded inhabitants of the city.

Bibliography

Ahn, John J., "Zephaniah, a Disciple of Isaiah?," in *Thus Says the Lord: Essays on the Former and Latter Prophets in Honor of Robert R. Wilson*, eds. John J. Ahn and Stephen L. Cook, LHBOTS 502 (London: T&T Clark, 2010): 292–307.

Albertz, Rainer, "Exile as Purification: Reconstructing the Book of the Four (Hosea, Amos, Micah, Zephaniah)," *SBLSP* 41 (2002): 213–233.

Berges, Ulrich, *The Book of Isaiah: Its Composition and Final Form*, trans. Millard C. Lind, HBM 46 (Sheffield: Sheffield Phoenix, 2012).

Berlin, Adele, *Isaiah 56–66*, AB 19B (New Haven: Yale University Press, 2000).

Berlin, Adele, *Zephaniah*, AB 25A (New York: Doubleday, 1994).

Biddle, Mark E, "The Figure of Lady Jerusalem: Identification, Deification and Personification of Cities in the Ancient Near East," in *Biblical Canon in Comparative Perspectives*, eds. B. Batto and W. Hallo (Lewiston, NY: Edwin Mellen, 1991): 173–194.

Blenkinsopp, Joseph, *Isaiah 1–39*, AB 19 (New York: Doubleday, 2000).

Blenkinsopp, Joseph, *Isaiah 56–66*, AB 19B (New York: Doubleday, 2004).

Bosshard, Erich, "Beobachtungen zum Zwölfprophetenbuch," *BN* 40 (1987): 30–62.

Dietrich, Walter, *Nahum Habakkuk Zephaniah*, IECOT (Stuttgart: Kohlhammer, 2016).

Fitzgerald, Aloysius, "Mythological Background for the Presentation of Jerusalem as a Queen and False Worship as Adultery in the OT," *CBQ* 34 (1972): 403–416.

Gärtner, Judith, "Jerusalem — City of God for Israel and for the Nations in Zeph 3:8, 9–10, 11–13," in *Perspectives on the Formation of the Book of the Twelve: Methodological Foundations, Reactional Processes, Historical Insights*, eds. Rainer Albertz, James D. Nogalski, and Jakob Wöhrle, BZAW 433 (Berlin: de Gruyter, 2012): 269–283.

Ginsberg, H. L., "Some Emendations in Isaiah," *JBL* 69 (1950): 51–60.

Gruber, Mayer I., "The Motherhood of God in Second Isaiah," *RB* 90 (1983): 351–359.

Hadjiev, Tchavdar S., "Zephaniah and the 'Book of the Twelve' Hypothesis," in *Prophecy and Prophets in Ancient Israel: Proceedings of the Oxford Old Testament Seminar*, ed. John Day (London: T&T Clark, 2010): 325–328.

Holladay, William L., "Reading Zephaniah with a Concordance: Suggestions for a Redaction History," *JBL* 120 (2001): 671–684.

King, Greg A., "The Message of Zephaniah: An Urgent Echo," *Andrews University Seminary Studies* 32 (1996): 211–222.

Low, Maggie, *Mother Zion in Deutero-Isaiah: A Metaphor for Zion Theology* (New York: Peter Lang, 2013).

Maier, Christl, *Daughter Zion, Mother Zion: Gender, Space, and the Sacred in Ancient Israel* (Minneapolis: Fortress, 2008).

Nogalski, James D., *The Book of the Twelve: Micah – Malachi*, SHBC 18b (Macon: Smyth & Helwys, 2011).

Nogalski, James D., *Literary Precursors to the Book of the Twelve*, BZAW 217 (Berlin: de Gruyter, 1993).

Nogalski, James D., "Where Are the Prophets in the Book of the Twelve?," in *The Book of the Twelve and New Form Criticism*, eds. Mark J. Boda, Michael H. Floyd, and Colin M. Toffelmire, ANEM (Atlanta: SBL, 2015): 163–182.

O'Brien, Julia, *Nahum Habakkuk Zephaniah Haggai Zechariah Malachi*, AOTC (Nashville: Abingdon, 2004).

Roberts, J. J. M., *Nahum, Habakkuk, and Zephaniah*, OTL (Louisville: Westminster John Knox, 1990).

Rudolph, Wilhelm, *Micha – Nahum – Habakuk – Zephanja*, KAT 13/3 (Gütersloh: Gerd Mohn, 1976).

Ryoo, Daniel Hojoon, *Zephaniah's Oracles against the Nations: A Synchronic and Diachronic Study of Zephaniah 2:1–3:8*, BibInt 13 (Leiden: Brill, 1995).

Sadler, Rodney Steven, *Can a Cushite Change His Skin? An Examination of Race, Ethnicity, and Othering in the Hebrew Bible*, LHBOTS 425 (London: T&T Clark, 2005).

Schmitt, John J., "The Motherhood of God and Zion as Mother," *RB* 92 (1985): 557–569.

Steck, Odil Hannes, "Zion als Gelände und Gestalt: Überlegungen zur Wahrnehmung Jerusalems als Stadt und Frau im Alten Testament," *ZTK* 86 (1989): 261–281.

Steck, Odil Hannes, "Zu Zef 3:9–10," *BZ* 34 (1990): 90–95.

Sweeney, Marvin A., *The Twelve Prophets: Volume Two: Micah, Nahum, Habakkuk, Zephaniah, Haggai, Zechariah, Malachi*, Berit Olam: Studies in Hebrew Narrative & Poetry (Collegeville: Liturgical Press, 2000).

Sweeney, Marvin A., *Zephaniah: A Commentary*, Hermeneia (Minneapolis: Augsburg Fortress, 2003).

Tuell, Steven, *Reading Nahum—Malachi: A Literary and Theological Commentary* (Macon: Smith & Helwys, 2016).

Westermann, Claus, *Isaiah 40–66*, trans. David M. G. Stalker, OTL (Philadelphia: Westminster, 1969).

Williamson, H. G. M., *The Book Called Isaiah: Deutero-Isaiah's Role in Composition and Redaction* (Oxford: Clarendon Press, 1994).

Zimmerli, Walter, "Vom Prophetenwort zum Prophetenbuch," *TLZ* 104 (1979): 481–496.

II Analyses Concerning the Relationships between Later Layers of Isaiah and Later Layers of the Book of the Twelve

Burkard M. Zapff
Second Isaiah and the Twelve

1 The references to the Book of Isaiah in the Book of the Twelve

In his little known paper published in *Biblische Notizen* (1987), Erich Bosshard makes some observations on the parallels between the Book of the Twelve and the Book of Isaiah[1]. In his dissertation, published ten years later, these observations lead him to the thesis that at certain times there have been common redactional processes in both text corpora, more precisely in Isa 1–39 and the Book of the Twelve.[2] According to Bosshard–Nepustil, these serve the purpose of aligning the Book of the Twelve with this part of the Book of Isaiah at a certain time of the formation of the latter. It is now undeniable that there are a number of striking correspondences between the two text corpora, which far surpass those commonalities which exist between the Book of Isaiah and the Book of Jeremiah, irrespective of form.

These points of contact, which sometimes obviously are direct literary dependencies,[3] cannot be overlooked even by those who do not want to read and understand the Book of the Twelve as single book but merely as a compilation of

---

[1] Erich Bosshard, „Beobachtungen zum Zwölfprophetenbuch", *Biblische Notizen* 40 (1987), 30–62.

[2] Erich Bosshard–Nepustil, *Rezeptionen von Jesaja 1–39 im Zwölfprophetenbuch. Untersuchungen zur literarischen Verbindung von Prophetenbüchern in babylonischer und persischer Zeit*, Orbis biblicus et Orientalis 154, (Freiburg/Schweiz: Universitätsverlag; Göttingen: Vandenhoeck & Ruprecht, 1997). On page 465 Bosshard–Nepustil describes the essence of his thesis: „Das wohl wichtigste Ergebnis der Arbeit ist, daß sich im Corpus propheticum längst vor der Kanonisierung von Nebiim nicht nur an den Rändern, sondern in der Folge des jeweiligen Textbestands überhaupt bücherübergreifende literarisch–sachliche Zusammenhänge feststellen lassen, die zwar Veränderungen zulassen und v. a. für Erweiterungen offen sind, die aber bereits ein erstaunliches Maß an kohärentem Sachprofil und feste Bücherabfolge zu erkennen geben."

[3] E. g. Isa 2: 1–4 and Mi 4: 1–3; for the different judgements of the literary dependency see Burkard M. Zapff, *Redaktionsgeschichtliche Studien zum Michabuch im Kontext des Dodekapropheton*, BZAW 256 (Berlin – New York: Walter de Gruyter, 1997), 65–74; Ludger Schwienhorst-Schönberger, „Zion – Ort der Tora. Überlegungen zu Mi 4,1–3" in *Zion – Ort der Begegnung*, Festschrift für Laurentius Klein zur Vollendung des 65. Lebensjahres, ed. Ferdinand Hahn, Frank-Lothar Hossfeld, Hans Jorissen and Angelika Neuwirth, Bonner Biblische Beiträge 90 (Bodenheim: Athenäum Hein Handstein, 1993), 110 ff.; Rainer Kessler, *Micha*, Herder Theologischer Kommentar Altes Testament (Freiburg, Basel, Berlin: Herder, 1999), 179.

https://doi.org/10.1515/9783110705799-005

twelve writings which, in their opinion, are not directly related to each other, be it in terms of content or literary correspondences.[4] All in all, it is noteworthy that the coincidences between Isaiah and the Book of the Twelve are not only restricted to some of the most prominent writings in the Book of the Twelve – here the most noteworthy example would be the Book of Micah[5] – but are also found in most writings of the Dodekapropheton. A few examples for illustration: At the beginning of the Book of the Twelve, it is striking, that the superscription in Hos 1: 1 contains the same sequence of kings as the Book of Isaiah.[6] Both are dated at the time of the Judaen kings Uzziah, Jotam, Ahaz and Hezekiah, and both prophets are defined by the names of their fathers. In the Book of the Twelve, the latter can only be found in connection with the prophets Jonah, Zephaniah and Zechariah. However, there are differences as well. The superscription of the Book of Hosea, for example, mentions the northern king Jeroboam II in addition to the four kings; and in contrast to Hosea (Hos 1: 1) where the "word of YHWH" came to the prophet, the superscription of the Book of Isaiah characterizes the prophecy as a "vision" which the prophet "saw". On the other hand, in Mic 1: 1a the prophet Micah is not only portrayed chronologically as the younger contemporary of Isaiah, but also, as with Hosea, as one to whom the word of YHWH came. At the same time, Mic 1: 1b connects the prophet with regard to the reception of the word of YHWH with Isaiah insofar as, according to Isa 2: 1, the prophet Isaiah also "saw" the word.[7] In general, Micah, as already briefly indicated, has a whole series of relationships with Isaiah. These, as I have stated in several recent papers[8], are obviously not to

---

4 E. g. Marvin A. Sweeney, "Synchronic and Diachronic Concerns in Reading the Book of the Twelve Prophets" in *Perspectives on the Formation of the Book of the Twelve. Methodological Foundations – Redactional Processes – Historical Insights*, ed. Rainer Albertz, James D. Nogalski, Jakob Wöhrle, BZAW 433 (Berlin–Boston: Walter de Gruyter, 2012), 21–33.

5 Burkard M. Zapff, „Wie Micha zu Jesaja wurde" in *Historia magistra vitae, Festschrift für Johannes Hoffmann zum 65.Geburtstag*, cd. Anselm Blumberg, Oleksandre Petrynko (Regensburg: Verlag Friedrich Pustet, 2016), 539–555.

6 Bosshard, „Beobachtungen", 31.

7 Zapff, „Micha", 542.

8 *Ibid.*, „Micha"; Burkard M. Zapff, „Ist Micha der Amos des Südreiches?" in „*Darum, ihr Hirten, hört das Wort des Herrn" (Ez 34,7.9). Studien zu prophetischen und weisheitlichen Texten, Festschrift für Bernd Willmes zum 65. Geburtstag*, ed. Christoph Gregor Müller and Matthias Helmer, Fuldaer Studien 21 (Freiburg–Basel–Wien: Herder, 2017): 142–155; Burkard M. Zapff, „Why is Micah similar to Isaiah", *ZAW* 129/4 (Berlin–New York: Walter de Gruyter, 2017): 536–554; Burkard M. Zapff, „Rückschlüsse aus der Entstehung der Michaschrift auf das Werden des Zwölfprophetenbuches" in *The Books of the Twelve Prophets. Minor Prophets – Major Theologies*, Bibliotheca Ephemeridum Theologicarum Lovaniensium 295, ed. Heinz–Josef Fabry (Leuven–Paris–Bristol: Peeters, 2018), 79–101.

be explained biographically, as if Micah were a disciple of Isaiah.[9] Rather, these correspondences to Isaiah are most likely the result of a deliberate alignment of the prophecies of Micah with those of Isaiah. Not least, this assumption is supported by the fact that some of the references that the Book of Micah makes to prophecies in the Book of Isaiah are simultaneously combined with references to the prophecies of Hosea and Amos[10]. This in turn means that on the one hand Micah appears as a contemporary of Isaiah and thus a kind of representative of Isaiah's theology in the Book of the Twelve and on the other hand as the successor of Amos but with the southern kingdom as his addressee.[11] Apart from Micah, who obviously has a special function at a central place in the Book of the Twelve, the Joel–script has clear references to the Book of Isaiah.[12] This is especially true with regard to the striking reception of the motif of the Day of YHWH in Joel 2. This is accompanied by the quotation of Isa 13[13], but leaves behind the limitation on Babylon as an object of the judgement of YHWH. Finally, the oracles of the nations in the Book of Isaiah, especially in Isa 13–23, also find an echo in the Book of the Twelve, if one thinks of the cycle of the judgement on the foreign nations in Amos 1 and 2: 1–3 and Zeph 2: 4–15. In particular, the Book of Zephaniah has a similar structure to the Book of Isaiah: judgment on Jerusalem (Zeph 1: 2–2: 3) – judgment on the nations (Zeph 2: 4–15) and salvation for Israel (Zeph 3: 9–20). Compare the sequence of Isa 1–12; 13–23 and Isa 40–66! Beyond that, the almost literal correspondence between Hag 2: 7 and Isa 60: 5–7 is well known.[14] That the end of the Book of Isaiah contains a whole series of correspondences to the end of the Book of the Twelve was already established by Odil Hannes Steck in his study *„Der Abschluss der alttestamentlichen Prophetie"* published in 1991.[15] In particular, both text–corpora lead into chronologically phased eschatological schemes

---

9 In this way e. g. John T.Willis explains the similarities; e. g. id., „The Authenticity and Meaning of Micah 5,9–14", *ZAW* 81 (1969), 353–368.

10 E. g. Mi 2: 11; cf. Zapff, „Michaschrift", 95.

11 Zapff, „Amos", 147–152.

12 Bosshard, „Beobachtungen", 31 f.; the recent research usually assumes a literary dependence of Joel 1: 1–2: 11 on Isa 13 and other texts; e. g. Bosshard–Nepustil, Rezeptionen, 296; Burkard M. Zapff, *Schriftgelehrte Prophetie – Jes 13 und die Komposition des Jesajabuches. Ein Beitrag zur Erforschung der Redaktionsgeschichte des Jesajabuches* (Würzburg: Echter, 1995); Anna Karena Müller, *Gottes Zukunft, Die Möglichkeit der Rettung am Tag JHWHs nach dem Joelbuch* (Neukirchen–Vluyn: Neukirchener Verlag, 2008), 69–98.

13 E. g. Joel 2: 1/Isa 13: 6; Joel 2: 6/Isa 13: 8; Joel 2: 10/Isa 13: 10.

14 Bosshard, „Beobachtungen", 35.

15 Odil Hannes Steck, *Der Abschluß der Prophetie im Alten Testament. Ein Versuch zur Frage der Vorgeschichte des Kanons*, BThSt 17 (Neukirchen–Vluyn: Neukirchener Verlag, 1991).

in the end.[16] In addition to the divorce between the righteous and the wicked in Israel, such a divorce also takes place within the nations. For the Book of Isaiah, Steck postulates for the Book of Isaiah three and for the Book of the Twelve two so-called „redaktionelle Fortschreibungen", which can be traced back to similar theological circles of prophetical scribes.[17] With their „redaktionelle Fortschreibungen", they respond to certain contemporary developments and seek to cope with them. Steck dates these editorial adaptations to the Hellenistic period with the aim of stylizing both corpora as largely similar witnesses of the prophetic word that YHWH spoke at the time. According to Steck, the purpose of the alignment of these written prophetic corpora was to provide a standard and a perspective for Israel's self-understanding of its past, present and future in relation to the widespread prophetic and oracular system of the Hellenistic period.[18] Through the alignment of these two corpora at their very end, the corpora of the later prophets namely the Book of Isaiah, Jeremiah, Ezekiel, and the Book of the Twelve are framed by two corpora corresponding to one another. In his afore mentioned study „Rezeptionen von Jes 1–39 im Zwölfprophetenbuch", Erich Bosshard–Nepustil sought to prove that the Book of Isaiah and the Book of the Twelve were not only aligned at their ends, as Steck had suggested. Beyond that he argues the Book of the Twelve as a whole at least temporarily served as a kind of mirror of the historic editorial formation process of the Book of Isaiah.[19]

Bosshard–Nepustil refers in particular to Isa 1–39 and seeks to demonstrate that the editorial processes of formation of the Book of Isaiah can be found in the Book of the Twelve as well. According to his thesis, these literary connections between the two corpora should be dated to the Babylonian and Persian periods.[20] For both theses, namely the formation of the Book of Isaiah and the Book of the Twelve by editors who worked in both corpora, the mentioned similarity of the endings, the almost identical size, the correspondences in content as well as the similar chronology of both text corpora can be taken as arguments. In both cases, they contain prophetic words that cover the period from the middle of the eighth century (Hosea, Proto–Isaiah) to the end or the completion of the world (Zech 9–14/Mal and Isa 56–66). In fact, it is not only that a number of books in the Dodecapropheton and Isaiah have substantive correspondences that extend to the textual level, but also that the sequence of contents of both corpora share

---

16 Cf. Steck, Abschluß, 105–111.

17 Ibid., 25–60.

18 Ibid., 169.

19 Bosshard–Nepustil, Rezeptionen, 277–407.

20 Ibid., 408: „Assur/Babel-Red.[Jes] etwas nach 562 v. Chr. – Assur/Babel-Red.[XII] bald danach – Babel-Red.[Jes] kurz vor 539 v. Chr. – Babel-Red.[XII] um 520 v. Chr."

a similarity that is not confined to the abovementioned eschatological schemata found at the ends of the Book of Isaiah and the Book of the Twelve. Thus, in the Book of the Twelve the section from Hosea to Micah includes the judgment on Samaria and Jerusalem, comparable to Isa 1–11. In Isaiah, however, the main focus is placed particularly on the judgment on Jerusalem. However, the current sequence from Hosea to Micah, which culminates in Mi 3: 12, where the desolation of the mountain of the house of the Lord is announced, also points towards the judgment on Jerusalem. The turn of events in Isa 12/13, from the judgment on Jerusalem and Israel to the judgment on the nations, has an echo in the sequence of Micah–Nahum–Habakkuk. Here, too, it is noteworthy that in the center of the Book of the Twelve, the Book of Micah plays a decisive role, which, as already mentioned, is influenced by the theology of the Book of Isaiah. It marks a central change from the judgment to the salvation of Zion and – according to Mi 7 – to the downfall of its enemy. In this sequence, Mi 7: 8–20 could fulfill a function similar to that of Isa 12.[21]Like the text in Isaiah this chapter was always seen as a kind of psalm–like structure.[22] The following books, Nahum and Habakkuk, are devoted to the downfall of Assur and the Chaldeans, thus reflecting Isa 13 and 14, albeit in the reverse and therefore actual chronological order.

A problematic element is the following Book of Zephaniah. Looking at its headline, it covers a period that strikingly has no equivalent in the Book of Isaiah. It is well known that the Book of Isaiah has a chronological gap between the time of King Hezekiah in Isa 39 at the end of the eighth century B.C. and the end of the exile described in Isa 40.[23] However, Zeph 3: 10.19 f. seems to refer to the latter in a

---

21 Already Hans–Peter Mathys, *Dichter und Beter, Theologen aus spätalttestamentlicher Zeit*, Orbis Biblicus et Orientalis 132 (Freiburg Schweiz: Universitätsverlag/Vandenhoeck & Ruprecht, 1994): „Jes 12 (insbesondere V 1 f.) weist enge inhaltliche Berührungen mit diesen drei Psalmen auf (scil. Mi 7:8–20, remark from me)"; Burkard M. Zapff, „Jesaja 12 – Dank am Ende und am Anfang", in: Dankbarkeit. Ein interdisziplinäres Projekt in Literaturwissenschaft, Theologie und Religionspädagogik, ed. Ingrid Wiedebroth-Gabler, Gottfried Orth, Jürgen Wehnert (Berlin 2020: EB-Verlag), 45–71, esp. 67–69.

22 Bernhard Stade, „Streiflichter auf die Entstehung der jetzigen Gestalt der alttestamentlichen Prophetenschriften", *ZAW* 23 (1903), 153–171; Hermann Gunkel, „Der Micha–Schluß. Zur Einführung in die literaturgeschichtliche Arbeit am AT", *ZS* 2 (1924): 145–178; also Bo Reicke, „Liturgical Tradition in Mic 7", *HThR* (1967), 349–367.

23 Cf. Ulrich Berges, *Jesaja. Der Prophet und das Buch.* Biblische Gestalten, (Leipzig: Evangelische Verlagsanstalt, 2010), 91: „Eine der größten Besonderheiten des Jesajabuches besteht darin, dass die Exilsereignisse nicht geschildert werden, obwohl die Ankündigung der Deportation des königlichen Hauses (39,6 f.) das hätte erwarten lassen können." A connection between the time of King Hezekiah and the announcement of the end of the exile in Isa 40:1 is made by Isa 39: 6 f. which announce the Babylonian exile, cf. Ulrich Berges, *Das Buch Jesaja. Komposition und Endgestalt*, Herder Biblische Studien 16 (Freiburg–Basel–Wien: Herder, 1998): 316: „Der Verweis auf

characteristic way. The rebuilding of the temple and the pilgrimage of the nations to Mount Zion in Hag 2 again, have, as already mentioned, a correspondence in Isa 60–62. The eschatological judgment of YHWH and the resulting divorce within Israel and the nations in Zech 9–14/Mal and Isa 65/66, the striking similarity of which Steck had pointed out, have already been mentioned. However, it should be noted here that Judith Gärtner in her dissertation[24] was also able to point out significant differences between the ends of the two corpora. When comparing the sequence of the Book of the Twelve with that of the Book of Isaiah in its present form, one will note, as was done in a cursory manner, striking correspondences and similarities that reach down to the level of content and text. At the same time, one will also notice that one part of the Book of Isaiah plays little or no role in this sequence, namely the second major section of the Book of Isaiah, which is referred to as „Deutero–Isaiah" in the Old Testament research. According to a broad consensus, this section not only refers to the time of the Babylonian exile but also originated in this period to a considerable extent.[25] However one defines the extent of the Deutero–Isaiah corpus, be it Isa 40–48, if we follow numerous recent exegetical publications, or beyond this up to Isa 52: 7–10,[26] this section, which distinctly shows an exilic background due to its various historical allusions, has no direct correspondence as such in the Book of the Twelve. While the Book of Isaiah has a chronological gap between the period of King Hezekiah and the end of the exile, the Book of the Twelve has a gap between the days of Joshiah in Zeph. 1: 1 and the "second year of King Darius" in Hag 1: 1. Also, a look at the biblical registers of recent exegetical publications on the Book of the Twelve[27] shows that texts from Deutero–Isaiah play only a very limited role in

---

das Exil in 39:6–8 bestätigt zum einen die prophetischen Qualitäten Jesajas und ist zum anderen die einzige Stelle im Buch, an der explizit von den Ereignissen von 587 gesprochen wird. Das Exil, in 39 angekündigt, ist in 40,1 bereits Vergangenheit."

24 Judith Gärtner, *Jesaja 66 und Sacharja 14 als Summe der Prophetie. Eine traditions- und redaktionsgeschichtliche Untersuchung zum Abschluss des Jesaja- und des Zwölfprophetenbuches*, WMANT 114 (Neukirchen–Vluyn: Neukirchener Verlag, 2006), 93–101.

25 Cf. one of the latest publications on the topic: Alexander Weidner, *Das Ende Deuterojesajas*, Forschung zum Alten Testament 2.Reihe 94 (Tübingen: Mohr Siebeck, 2017), esp. 235–237.

26 See the discussion of this question in Weidner, „Deuterojesajas", 233.

27 E. g. Jakob Wöhrle, *Die frühen Sammlungen des Zwölfprophetenbuches, Entstehung und Komposition*, BZAW 360 (Berlin–New York: Walter de Gruyter, 2006; Id., *Der Abschluss des Zwölfprophetenbuches. Buchübergreifende Redaktionsprozesse in den späten Sammlungen*, BZAW 389 (Berlin–New York: Walter de Gruyter, 2008); Aaron Schart, „Die Entstehung des Zwölfprophetenbuchs. Neubearbeitungen von Amos im Rahmen schriftenübergreifender Redaktionsprozesse", BZAW 260 (Berlin–New York: Walter de Gruyter, 1998).

the Book of the Twelve, although the latter, as shown, is otherwise marked by Isaianic theology and references to the Book of Isaiah to a considerable extent. At the most, the exile is mentioned in Mic 4: 10 which says that "you", meaning the inhabitants of Zion, will come to Babylon and will be saved there.[28] In general, it is striking that "Babylon" is only mentioned twice in the Book of the Twelve (Mic 4: 10 and Zach 2: 11), and the "Chaldeans" only once (Hab 1: 6). As I have said, besides the quoted text Mic 4: 10, there is only one very general allusion to the theme of exile in Zeph 3: 19, which speaks of a collection of the scattered וְהַנִּדָּחָה אֲקַבֵּץ in accordance with Mic 4: 6. However, according to the concordance, the term הַנִּדָּחָה can not only refer to those exiled to Babylon, but also those who were scattered among the nations and fled towards Egypt (cf. Jer 43: 5). Yet according to James Nogalski's observations, the perspective here is "broader, and reflects a time when the deportees had returned"[29]. Thus, the scattered ones "is very close to a *terminus technicus* for dispersed Jews."[30] In this way Zeph 3: 18–20 serves as the prelude to Haggai and beyond.[31] It can therefore be said that the Book of the Twelve, whose sequence shows a great similarity with that of the Book of Isaiah, shows a clear gap during the period of exile and the return from exile, which at most is bridged by the end of the Book of Zephaniah. Although at first sight this text seems to be reminiscent of Deutero–Isaiah on a linguistic level in quite a number of instances, it rather alludes to the atmosphere of the so–called Trito–Isaiah content-wise.[32] Why, however, does Deutero–Isaiah only play an obviously minor role in the sequence of the Book of the Twelve, whereas the Book of Isaiah as a whole is a particularly important source of reference for the Book of the Twelve? Is Deutero–Isaiah important for the Book of the Twelve at all, and if so, how? In the following, I want to pursue these questions and in particular determine the texts of the Book of the Twelve in which Deutero–Isaiah plays a role, as well as the motifs in Deutero–Isaiah that are adopted by the

---

28 According to Jörg Jeremias, *Die Propheten Joel, Obadja, Jona, Micha*, Altes Testament Deutsch 24,3 (Göttingen: Vandenhoeck & Ruprecht, 2007), 179, reflects Mi 4: 9f. and 4: 14 the distress of the final weeks before the destruction of Jerusalem.

29 James Nogalski, *Literary Precursors to the Book of the Twelve*, BZAW 217 (Walter de Gruyter: Berlin–New York 1993), 209. Similarly Walter Dietrich, *Nahum, Habakuk, Zefanja*, Internationaler Exegetischer Kommentar zum Alten Testament (Stuttgart: Kohlhammer, 2014), 253: „V. 19 erwartet die Rückkehr von Golajuden, …"

30 Nogalski, *Precursors*, 209.

31 *Ibid.*, 215: „The answer implied by the Zephaniah text is that only with the unification of all the people of YHWH, the remnant and the dispersed, will YHWH truly glorify Zion. In this manner, Zeph 3:18ff. introduces Haggai, but looks beyond Haggai as well. The story is not finished with the reconstruction of the temple."

32 Cf. Isa 60:4.9.

Book of the Twelve or not. Thus, I want to work out a profile of the Book of the Twelve in relation to Isaiah. Before proceeding further, however, there is another thesis of Bosshard–Nepustil's pertaining to our enquiry which deserves some attention.

2 An explanation of the missed reference to Deutero–Isaiah in the sequence of the Book of the Twelve – The thesis of Bosshard–Nepustil

As the title of Bosshard–Nepustil's dissertation makes clear, he limits himself in his research to the literary connections between Isa 1–39 and the Book of the Twelve. According to him, the Book of the Twelve is a reliable reflection of the „*Redaktionsgeschichte*" of Isa 1–39 at a certain time. The fact that there are no influences of Deutero–Isaiah here results from Bosshard–Nepustil's assumption that "Deutero–Isaiah" was not originally a part of the Book of Isaiah, but only later connected with it.[33] He refers to a thesis by Odil Hannes Steck published in the 1985 volume „*Bereitete Heimkehr*".[34] In this work, Steck seeks to give reasons for the thesis that Isa 35 is a bridge chapter which had been added in Proto–Isaiah to connect a Proto– with a Deutero–Isaiah corpus and in this way creates a so–called „*Groß–Jesajabuch*". Bosshard–Nepustil develops this thesis insofar as, according to him, the original arrangement of the prophetic books in the *corpus propheticum* was different from the one present today. Accordingly, in former times, the Book of Jeremiah and then Deutero–Isaiah followed after Proto–Isaiah[35], whatever its original extent was. This thesis seems to be attractive, not least because it would explain the strange temporal gap between Isa 39 and Isa 40.[36] In contrast, the book of Jeremiah would fill this gap by introducing the reader to the pre–exilic period and the circumstances that led to exile, the

---

33 Bosshard Nepustil, *Rezeptionen*, 450 464.

34 Odil Hannes Steck, *Bereitete Heimkehr. Jesaja 35 als redaktionelle Brücke zwischen dem Ersten und Zweiten Jesaja*, Stuttgarter Bibelstudien 121 (Stuttgart: Verlag Katholisches Bibelwerk GmbH, 1985).

35 Bosshard–Nepustil, *Rezeptionen*, 450–452.

36 *Ibid.*, 460, writes: „Jes *36–39 zielte in IJes ursprünglich auf Jer, und Jes 40,1ff. schloß literarisch einmal an Jer 50f./52 an". First this thesis was formulated by Reinhard Gregor Kratz, „Der Anfang des Zweiten Jesaja in Jes 40,1f. und das Jeremiabuch", *ZAW* 106 (1994), 243–261.

end of which is then announced by Deutero–Isaiah. With regard to Proto– and Deutero–Isaiah, the book of Jeremiah would approximately fill the chronological gap which occupies the time of the prophecy of Zephaniah in the Book of the Twelve. Moreover, this thesis would explain why there is barely any mentioning of the exile and Deutero–Isaiah in the Book of the Twelve. This would mean that, as Bosshard–Nepustil points out, the Book of the Twelve was aligned with the Book of Isaiah at a time when the Deutero–Isaiah Corpus was not yet part of the Book of Isaiah, and therefore could not be relevant for the content and formation of the Book of the Twelve, which was based on Isaiah, namely Isa 1–39. When, in the Hellenistic period, the ends of both corpora were formatted by theologically related editors according to Steck's thesis, they were no longer interested in the problems and theological questions that still moved Deutero–Isaiah during the exilic time. Rather, they sought to answer the theological and challenging problems of their own time in the manner described by Steck. Adding the theological answers of Deutero–Isaiah in this period would have been anachronistic.

Although this thesis seems quite plausible at first, I cannot agree with it. The following points in the thesis of Bosshard–Nepustil appear problematic to me, or at least, in need of modification. The first concerns the relationship of Deutero–Isaiah to Proto–Isaiah. The thesis that the core of Deutero–Isaiah was originally a kind of a "consolation booklet" of a former temple–singer group, was supported by good arguments brought forward by Ulrich Berges in his Deutero–Isaiah commentary in HBS.[37] Despite the fact that it has some theological characteristics of an already existing Proto–Isaiah corpus, this booklet may initially have circulated independently. It also may have been a kind of answer to the Book of Lamentations, with which there are many interconnections.[38] The connection to Proto–Isaiah, however, was made by the supplementing text Isaiah 40: 1–8,[39] as various recent studies on Deutero–Isaiah suggest[40]. As we know, Isa 40 is related to Isa 6

---

37 Ulrich Berges, *Jesaja 40–48, Herder Theologischer Kommentar zum Alten Testament* (Freiburg–Basel–Wien: Herder, 2008), 42.

38 *Ibid.*, 41.

39 Jan van Oorschot, *Von Babel zum Zion*, BZAW 206 (Berlin–New York. Walter de Gruyter, 1993), 105; Ulrich Berges, *Das Buch Jesaja. Komposition und Endgestalt*, Herder Biblische Studien 16 (Freiburg u. a.: Herder 1998), 368.

40 In this way e. g. Burkard M. Zapff, „Jes 40 und die Frage nach dem Beginn des deuterojesajanischen Corpus" in *Gottes Wege suchend. Beiträge zum Verständnis der Bibel und ihrer Botschaft, Festschrift für Rudolph Mosis zum 70.Geburtstag*, ed. Franz Sedlmeier (Würzburg: Echter, 2003), 355–373; Berges, *Jesaja 40–48*, 83: „Wie kaum eine zweite Passage sind diese elf Verse (scil. Isa 40:1–11, remark from me) mit den vorangehenden und nachfolgenden Texten des Jesajabuches intratextuell verwoben, was ihre zentrale Stellung unterstreicht."

in a number of ways.[41] In other words, I assume a unity of Proto– and Deutero–Isaiah already in the time of the early Persian period, and not, as Steck believes, only from Hellenistic times.

The second point concerns the editing of the Book of the Twelve referring to Isaiah. In my opinion, the Book of Micah plays a crucial role here. In contrast to Bosshard–Nepustil, who considers the reference of the Book of Micah to Isaiah as a revision of an already existing collection of prophetic texts,[42] I think that the Book of Micah as such was from the outset written from a perspective oriented to Isaiah on the one hand and Amos and Hosea on the other hand. A few existing prophecies of a historical prophet Micah may have already existed as a foundation.[43] This formation of the Book of Micah, which can be seen not only in the headline of the Book of Micah and the related pilgrimage of the nations to Mount Zion in Mi 4: 1–3 but also in the common references to Isaiah, Amos and Hosea[44] has not a pre-exilic or Babylonian background but refers to the Persian period. Here, again, the political and therefore theological situation was different from that in the last third of the 6th century, so that the theology of Deutero–Isaiah was no longer considered the answer to the pressing questions of the time. Therefore, Deutero–Isaiah was only eclectically quoted depending on the theological necessity. Below, I shall illustrate how this is implemented and that this assumption is very probable. First of all, I will show – *ex negativo* so to speak – which motives and theological questions of Deutero–Isaiah do not play a part in the Book of the Twelve.

3 Which motifs and theological questions of Deutero–Isaiah do not play a role in the Book of the Twelve?

As already stated, the so–called *„Grundschrift"* of the Deutero–Isaiah corpus can be dated relatively well due to various historical references. One of these points of

---

41 E. g. Rolf Rendtorff, „Jesaja 6 im Rahmen der Komposition des Jesajabuches", in *The Book of Isaiah, Bibliotheka Ephemeridum Theologicarum Lovaniensium 81*, ed. Jacques Vermeylen (Leuven: Peeters, 1989), 73–82, esp. 79–81; Christopher Seitz, "The Divine Council: Temporal Transition and New Prophecy in the Book of Isaiah", *JBL 109* (1990): 229–246; Zapff, „Jes 40", 359–365.
42 Bosshard-Nepustil, *Rezeptionen*, 434, reckons „mit einer weitgehend getrennten Entwicklung der je auf eine Prophetengestalt zurückgehenden Schriften IJes, Hos, Am und Mi".
43 Zapff, „Rückschlüsse", esp. 98 f.
44 Cf. *Ibid.*: 85–91; e. g. Mi 1: 6; Mi 2: 6.11.

reference is the mention of "Cyrus". This refers to the Persian king Cyrus II, who is known to us[45]. Although Cyrus is mentioned only twice in Deutero–Isaiah (Isa 44: 28; 45: 1), he is not mentioned in the Book of the Twelve at all. This coincides with the observation that exile, i. e. the Babylonian exile and the release from this exile, does not play any role in the Book of the Twelve apart from the already mentioned text in the Book of Micah. A central theological statement relating to the mention of Cyrus is that of YHWH's power to act in historical and political affairs (cf. Isa 41: 1–4). This competes with the power of foreign gods, notably the Babylonian deities and cult of the stars, to predict future political events (cf. Isa 41: 21–29). Foreign gods, as potentially important figures, do not appear in the Book of the Twelve. YHWH does not have to prove, so to speak, that he is the one and only acting God, as is done in the judgment speeches of Deutero–Isaiah. Although in the Book of the Twelve there are phrases that emphasize the uniqueness of YHWH which have strong reminiscences of deutero–isaianic statements, such as Hos 13: 2,4 (cf. Isa 43: 11 and 45: 21) or Joel 2: 27 (cf. Isa 42: 8), these do not serve, as in Deutero–Isaiah, to emphasize the uniqueness of YHWH against other possible gods. We will see which role they play in the Book of the Twelve. One theme in the Book of the Twelve is Israel's apostasy to foreign gods or the problem of images of the gods, but not the question of whether YHWH is in fact the only God who is acting in historical or political affairs. This in turn points to the religious–political background of Deutero–Isaiah, in which YHWH had to prove himself master of the world in the face of the competitive pressure of Babylonian theology. This is also true with regard to the theology of creation. In combination with the theology of YHWH's acting in history, this plays a prominent role for the strategy of argumentation in the deutero–isaianic „*Grundschrift*" (cf. Isa 40: 22–26).[46] Although there are statements of theology of creation in the Book of the Twelve – I only recall the hymnic fragments in Am 4: 13; 5: 8 and 9: 5 –, these do not stand, as in

---

45 Cf. Berges, *Jesaja 40–48*, 43–45.
46 Cf. Matthias Albani, *Der eine Gott und die himmlischen Heerscharen. Zur Begründung des Monotheismus bei Deuterojesaja im Horizont der Astralisierung des Gottesverständnisses im Alten Orient.* Arbeiten zur Bibel und ihrer Geschichte 1 (Leipzig: Evangelische Verlagsanstalt, 2000), esp. 123–255, 253: „Insgesamt ist festzuhalten, daß die politische und religiöse Krise am Ende des babylonischen Reiches unter Nabonid sich in der Begründung des Monotheismus bei DtJes widerspiegelt: Zum einen hat der Aufstieg des Kyros, der zum Fall Babylons führte, im Weissagungsbeweis seinen Niederschlag gefunden [...], während sich die religiöse Auseinandersetzung zwischen Marduk–Kult und Sîn–Kult um den Anspruch auf die höchste göttliche Position besonders in DtJes' schöpfungstheologischer Unvergleichlichkeitsargumentation widerspiegelt [...]. Die Formulierung des monotheistischen Bekenntnisses bei DtJes ist auf diesem historischen und religiösen Hintergrund am wahrscheinlichsten."

Deutero–Isaiah, in competition with the Babylonian theology of creation,[47] but testify without any polemics to the sublimity of YHWH, who is unrivaled here from the outset. Again, there is no sign of the conflict with Babylonian theology. Thus, the Book of the Twelve obviously assumes a more or less self–evident monotheism, even if Hosea, for one, is concerned with the implementation of the exclusive worship of YHWH in Israel (the so called monolatry). Finally, in Deutero–Isaiah, the former exodus from Egypt is used as a paradigm of the return from Babylon. Of course, the Book of the Twelve is also familiar with the exodus tradition (e. g. Amos 2: 10; 3: 1), but it is not related to the return from the Babylonian exile (cf. Isa 43: 14–21).[48] Rather, it is understood as either the once ideal time of the intimate relationship between YHWH and his people (cf. Hos 12: 10) or as a paradigm of the return of the entire Diaspora (cf. Zeph 3: 18–20). Although the term "servant" is occasionally also found in the Book of the Twelve, it does not play a prominent role there: neither as a symbolic figure for Israel as a whole, nor as a possible title of the King Cyrus, nor as a figure causing salvation for Israel and possibly also the nations.[49]

This short overview confirms what has been said so far. The basic lines of the theology of Deutero–Isaiah only find a very weak echo in the Book of the Twelve. In particular, all aspects which can be understood against the background of Babylonian exile and testify to a dispute between exiled Jewish theologians and Babylonian theology are missing. Here too, it is true that the Babylonian exile and the theological issues that it raises play no part in the Book of the Twelve. After this initially sobering finding, the counter–question is posed: Where do Deutero–Isaiah and aspects of his theology play a role in the Book of the Twelve? Is the silence absolute or are there some hints of the reception of deutero–isaianic ideas in the Book of the Twelve, such that also this part of the Book of Isaiah has had some influence on the Book of the Twelve?

4 Which aspects from Deutero–Isaiah are adopted in the Book of the Twelve?

As already briefly indicated, there are two formulations in the Book of the Twelve which emphasize the uniqueness of YHWH and cite deutero–isaianic ideas. The

---

47 Cf. Albani, *Der eine Gott*, 241.
48 Berges, *Jes 40–48*, 296 f.
49 Cf. Burkard M. Zapff, *Jesaja 40–55*, Neue Echterbibel (Würzburg: Echter, 2001), 225.

first one is found in Hos 13: 2.4. So it says in v. 2a.b: וְעַתָּה יוֹסִפוּ לַחֲטֹא וַיַּעְשׂוּ לָהֶם מַסֵּכָה מִכַּסְפָּם כִּתְבוּנָם עֲצַבִּים מַעֲשֵׂה חָרָשִׁים כֻּלֹּה "And now they sin more and more and make for themselves molten images. Idols skillfully made from their silver. All of them the work of craftsmen."[50] In v. 4, on the other hand, YHWH presents himself to be the true god when he says: וְאָנֹכִי יְהוָה אֱלֹהֶיךָ מֵאֶרֶץ מִצְרָיִם וֵאלֹהִים זוּלָתִי לֹא תֵדָע וּמוֹשִׁיעַ אַיִן בִּלְתִּי "Yet I *have been* YHWH your God since the land of Egypt; And you were not to know any god except Me, For there is no savior besides Me." By the keywords "craftsman" חרש and the material used כסף "silver", the technique of casting נסך and the derived noun "picture" מסכה Hos 13: 2.4 clearly refers to the theme of the production of idols[51], which is unfolded in Isa 40:19 as such: הַפֶּסֶל נָסַךְ חָרָשׁ וְצֹרֵף בַּזָּהָב יְרַקְּעֶנּוּ וּרְתֻקוֹת כֶּסֶף צוֹרֵף "As for the idol, a craftsman casts it, a goldsmith plates it with gold, and a silversmith fashions chains of silver."

Likewise, the phrases וֵאלֹהִים זוּלָתִי לֹא תֵדָע and וְאָנֹכִי יְהוָה אֱלֹהֶיךָ מֵאֶרֶץ מִצְרָיִם as well as וּמוֹשִׁיעַ אַיִן בִּלְתִּי in Hos 13: 4 evidently are a mixed quote from the shortened self–introduction of YHWH in Exod 20: 2 and Deut 5: 6 with an allusion to Isa 45: 5; 43: 11b and 45: 21.[52] So in Exod 20: 2 and Deut 5: 6, one finds the phrase אָנֹכִי יְהוָה אֱלֹהֶיךָ אֲשֶׁר הוֹצֵאתִיךָ מֵאֶרֶץ מִצְרָיִם "I am YHWH your God, who brought you out of the land of Egypt", in Isa 45: 5a זוּלָתִי אֵין אֱלֹהִים "Besides me there is no God", in Isa 43: 11b וְאֵין מִבַּלְעָדַי מוֹשִׁיעַ "And there is not beside me a savior" and in Isa 45: 21 וּמוֹשִׁיעַ אַיִן זוּלָתִי "And a savior is not beside me".

The deutero–isaianic texts are concerned with YHWH's competition with other gods, particularly his ability to announce future events and the past (see Isa 43: 9), or his being the only God who shapes history (cf. Isa 45: 5.21). On the other hand, in the text of Hosea – at least in today's context – the worship of idols competes with YHWH. Worship of the images of other gods is thus seen as apostasy from YHWH, who alone can claim to be God. While the identity of the real God in Israel – and possibly also beyond – still has to be demonstrated in Deutero–Isaiah, this is already clear in Hos 13.

Another emphasis on YHWH's uniqueness with a possible reference to Deutero–Isaiah is found in Joel 2: 27.[53] It says in v. 27b וַאֲנִי יְהוָה אֱלֹהֵיכֶם וְאֵין עוֹד: "and I am YHWH your God and none else". Here, reference is also made to Isa 45:

---

50 Translation according the New American Standard Bible (1995).
51 Wöhrle, *Sammlungen*, 234, points to the terminological parallels with the dtn./dtr. literature, esp. 2 Kgs 17: 16 and draws the conclusion that Hos 13: 3 is dependent on this text.
52 That this is a mixed quote, is usually ignored. For example, Jeremias says that this is the „älteste datierbare Zeugnis im Alten Testament für die Verbindung von Selbstvorstellung Jahwes [...] und erstem Gebot", Jörg Jeremias, *Der Prophet Hosea*, Altes Testament Deutsch 24/1 (Göttingen: Vandenhoeck & Ruprecht, 1983), 163.
53 Cf. Jeremias, *Propheten*, 39.

5a,6c,18c with each אֲנִי יְהֹוָה וְאֵין עוֹד. While the topic of Isa 45 is the actual historical action of YHWH by Cyrus,[54] the topic here is YHWH's power over the enemy from the North mentioned in v. 20 and his concern for the future fertility of the land, which leads to the salvation of Israel.[55] The statement of YHWH's uniqueness in a specific historical situation in Deutero–Isaiah now becomes a fundamental statement in the face of the final salvation of his people.

A reference to the theme of idols, as it is treated in detail in Deutero–Isaiah, can also be found in Hab 2: 18 f. There it says: מָה־הוֹעִיל פֶּסֶל כִּי פְסָלוֹ יֹצְרוֹ מַסֵּכָה וּמוֹרֶה שָׁקֶר כִּי בָטַח יֹצֵר יִצְרוֹ עָלָיו לַעֲשׂוֹת אֱלִילִים אִלְּמִים: הוֹי אֹמֵר לָעֵץ הָקִיצָה עוּרִי לְאֶבֶן דּוּמָם הוּא יוֹרֶה הִנֵּה־הוּא תָּפוּשׂ זָהָב וָכֶסֶף וְכָל־רוּחַ אֵין בְּקִרְבּוֹ׃ "What profit is the idol when its maker has carved it, Or an image, a teacher of falsehood? For its maker trusts in his own handiwork when he fashions speechless idol. Woe to him who says to wood, 'Awake!' To a dumb stone, 'Arise!' that is a teacher? Behold, it is overlaid with gold and silver, And there is no breath at all inside it." Here, Isa 44: 9–20 could serve as the reference text in the background. There is talk as well of those who form a carving–image – יֹצְרֵי־פֶסֶל (v. 9) and that this is of no use: לְבִלְתִּי הוֹעִיל (v. 10). Lothar Perlitt also refers to Isa 42: 17.[56] Not only is the מַסֵּכָה cast–picture mentioned there, but it is also discussed about those who trust in the idol בַּפֶּסֶל הַבֹּטְחִים. Finally, as the third reference text, Jer 2: 27 comes into view,[57] at least in terms of content, because there, too, the materials of wood and stone are connected with the criticism of idols: אֹמְרִים לָעֵץ אָבִי אַתָּה וְלָאֶבֶן אַתְּ יְלִדְתִּנִי "Who say to a tree, 'You are my father', And to a stone, 'You gave me birth'." According to the context of the criticism of idolatry in Isa 44: 9–20, the topic is about the false confidence in the idols in the face of YHWH, who in Isa 44: 8 is called "the only rock". Similarly, in Isa 42: 17 the theme again is the false trust in idols in the face of YHWH's action in history and creation (see Isa 42: 10–16). On the other hand, in the text of Habakkuk, the topic is the grandeur of YHWH, before whom all the world must be silent while

---

54 Berges, *Jes 40–48*, 401, points to the concentration of the formula, "I am YHWH – no god is beside me" in the Cyrus–chapter of Isa 45. This is motivated not only by the polemic against the cults of foreign gods, „sondern weist zudem die propersische Euphorie in die Schranken [...]. Kyrus bringt zwar das Ende der babylonischen Gefangenschaft, aber von der Erkenntnis des wahren Gottes ist und bleibt er weit entfernt."
55 Jeremias, *Propheten*, 39: „In der Nähe dieses Gottes ist Israel vor aller Feindgefahr geschützt, und zwar für alle Zeiten".
56 Lothar Perlitt, *Die Propheten Nahum, Habakuk, Zephanja*, Altes Testament Deutsch 25,1 (Göttingen: Vandenhoeck & Ruprecht, 2004), 79.
57 *Ibid.*, 79.

the false idols are mute.[58] This makes the criticism of idols a theme that now also refers to the nations, while in Deutero–Isaiah the criticism is addressed to Israel.[59]

In two cases, direct quotes from Deutero–Isaiah are included in the Book of the Twelve, but inserted into a new context. The first is Nah 2: 1 although the literary dependence is controversial in the literature. For example, Heinz–Josef Fabry advocates the priority of the Nahum version, which deals with the consequences of the fall of Assyria in the 7th century B.C.[60] It should be considered, however, that Nah 1: 14, which precedes Nah 2: 1, again shows idol–polemics, which also refers to the terminology of Deutero–Isaiah (cf. פֶּסֶל וּמַסֵּכָה). In any case, Nah 2: 1 and Isa 52: 7 are almost identical. In Isa 52: 7 the verse is: מַה־נָּאווּ עַל־הֶהָרִים רַגְלֵי מְבַשֵּׂר מַשְׁמִיעַ שָׁלוֹם "How lovely on the mountains Are the feet of him who brings good news, Who announces peace". Nah 2: 1 renders the verse with "Behold, on the mountains the feet of him who brings good news, Who announces peace!" If one assumes a priority of the deutero–isaianic text, then the topic in Nahum no longer is the announcement of YHWH's return to Zion, but the consequence of the downfall of Nineveh. The quote from Isaiah is then generally understood as an indication of a new time of salvation. Nineveh is no longer the former capital of the Assyrian Empire but serves as the epitome of the oppression of Judah by a hostile power. The previous destruction of the idols could then refer to idols of other nations, so that here a kind of universalization is emerging, which also affects the idol worship of other nations.[61] This seems to be similarly the case in Zeph 2: 15, where a quotation (v. 8aβ.b) from the mocking song about Babylon in Isa 47: 8–10 is adopted, but now is connected with Nineveh – again understood

---

58 Oskar Dangl, *Das Buch Habakuk*, Neuer Stuttgarter Kommentar Altes Testament 25/1 (Stuttgart: Verlag Katholisches Bibelwerk, 2014), 108, interprets the verse as an expression of the universal sovereignty of YHWH; possibly there is also reference to a liturgical context (e. g. Zeph 1: 7), cf. Perlitt, Propheten, 81.

59 Wöhrle, *Abschluss*, 309, supposes that a basic script of Habakkuk, which also included vv. 19–20, was originally directed against grievances in the society of Israel and was later addressed to an external enemy by supplements.

60 Heinz–Josef Fabry, *Nahum*, Herder Theologischer Kommentar zum Alten Testament (Freiburg–Basel–Wien: Herder, 2006), 151 f.; he follows Wilhelm Rudolph, *Micha – Nahum – Habakuk – Zephanja*, Kommentar zum Alten Testament XIII,3 (Gütersloh: Gütersloher Verlagshaus, 1975), 163; for the opposite position cf. Wöhrle, *Abschluss*: 37. In remark 47 he insinuates to those who argue for a priority of the Nahum version that this „auf den Willen zurückgehen (dürfte), Nah 2,1 noch vor DtJes zu datieren, um diesen Vers so dem meist in vorexilischer Zeit angesetzten Grundbestand des Nahumbuches zuweisen zu können."

61 Cf. Hab 2: 18 f.; Wöhrle, *Abschluss*, 28, however supposes that the cleansing from idols refers to the temple of Jerusalem.

as the epitome of enemy power par excellence.[62] There, Nineveh is referred to as a once happy and safe city that speaks in its heart: "I am, and there is no one besides me." הַיּוֹשֶׁבֶת לָבֶטַח הָאֹמְרָה בִּלְבָבָהּ אֲנִי וְאַפְסִי עוֹד. Again, a word originally related to a particular historical situation, namely the distress by Babylon, now becomes a general characterization of an anti–Israel city.

5 Conclusions

The examination of the texts with regard to the question to what extent Deutero–Isaiah and his theology shape the Book of the Twelve has led to the following results.

1. The main topics of Deutero–Isaiah, such as the Babylonian exile and the return of the exiled, play only a very minor role in the Book of the Twelve.

2. The confrontation with other gods and the question of who determines the course of history and the world is also barely present in the Book of the Twelve.

3. Theological statements concerning creation, which emphasize YHWH being the creator of the cosmos, and thus also master over the stars – highly esteemed as gods in Babylonian theology – are likewise not found in the Book of the Twelve. An exception are the hymns in the Book of Amos, which, however contain no polemics but serve to highlight the power of YHWH.

4. If there are literal correspondences between deutero–isaianic texts and texts in the Book of the Twelve, then they are, in the majority of cases in the Book of the Twelve mixed quotes from different texts. Thus, however, the direction of literary dependency is virtually evident. The Book of the Twelve is derivative, while Deutero–Isaiah is the origin.

5. The following correspondences are adopted: a) statements regarding the uniqueness of YHWH; b) polemics against idolatry; c) announcements of salvation; d) formulation documenting the arrogance of Babylon; e) statements on the gathering and return of the Babylonian Golah.

6. It is striking that the statements are no longer used according to their original context. This is especially true for the quarrel with Babylon and the return of the Golah. Rather, the quotations from Deutero–Isaiah are being re–contextualized and related to a changed theological and political situation.

---

62 According *Ibid.*, 227, Zeph 2: 12–25 belongs to the so called „Fremdvölkerschicht I", which became a part of Zephaniah in the postexilic time („fortgeschrittene persische Zeit").

7. In my opinion, these observations result in the following conclusion concerning the „*Redaktionsgeschichte*". When speaking of an alignment of the Book of the Twelve with the Book of Isaiah and assuming at the same time that Deutero–Isaiah was an integral part of the Book of Isaiah relatively early, it must be assumed, that this alignment took place under changed theological conditions no earlier than in the time after the exile. Deutero–Isaiah, with its very situational theology, played a minor role here. On the other hand, there is a considerably stronger relationship to ideas of the so–called Trito–Isaiah (see for example, Mic 7: 1–7 and Isa 59: 2–8).[63]

8. This coincides with my previously stated assumption that the Book of Micah never existed independently in its present form but was probably created in the Persian period in relation to Hosea and Amos on the one hand and Isaiah on the other hand. In this way, it was the center and the starting–point of an "Isaianisation" of the Book of the Twelve.

Bibliography

Albani, Matthias, *Der eine Gott und die himmlischen Heerscharen. Zur Begründung des Monotheismus bei Deuterojesaja im Horizont der Astralisierung des Gottesverständnisses im Alten Orient*. Arbeiten zur Bibel und ihrer Geschichte 1 (Leipzig: Evangelische Verlagsanstalt, 2000).

Berges, Ulrich, *Das Buch Jesaja. Komposition und Endgestalt*, Herder Biblische Studien 16 (Freiburg–Basel–Wien: Herder, 1998).

Berges, Ulrich, *Jesaja. Der Prophet und das Buch*. Biblische Gestalten, Evangelische Verlagsanstalt (Leipzig: Evangelische Verlagsanstalt, 2010).

Berges, Ulrich, *Jesaja 40–48*, Herder Theologischer Kommentar zum Alten Testament (Freiburg–Basel–Wien: Herder, 2008).

Bosshard, Erich, „Beobachtungen zum Zwölfprophetenbuch", *Biblische Notizen* 40 (1987), 30–62.

Bosshard–Nepustil, Erich, *Rezeptionen von Jesaja 1–39 im Zwölfprophetenbuch. Untersuchungen zur literarischen Verbindung von Prophetenbüchern in babylonischer und persischer Zeit*, Orbis biblicus et Orientalis 154, (Freiburg/Schweiz: Universitätsverlag; Göttingen: Vandenhoeck & Ruprecht, 1997).

Dangl, Oskar, *Das Buch Habakuk*, Neuer Stuttgarter Kommentar Altes Testament 25/1 (Stuttgart: Verlag Katholisches Bibelwerk, 2014).

Decorzant, Alain, *Vom Gericht zum Erbarmen*, Forschungen zur Bibel 123 (Würzburg: Echter, 2010).

---

63 Cf. Alain Decorzant, *Vom Gericht zum Erbarmen*, Forschungen zur Bibel 123 (Würzburg: Echter, 2010), „Mi 6 f weist aber auch eine Verwandtschaft mit zahlreichen Jesaja–Stellen auf, besonders aus dem letzten Teil des Buches (c 56–66)".

Dietrich, Walter, *Nahum, Habakuk, Zefanja*, Internationaler Exegetischer Kommentar zum Alten Testament (Stuttgart: Kohlhammer, 2014).

Fabry, Heinz–Josef, *Nahum*, Herder Theologischer Kommentar zum Alten Testament (Freiburg–Basel–Wien: Herder, 2006).

Gärtner, Judith, *Jesaja 66 und Sacharja 14 als Summe der Prophetie. Eine traditions– und redaktionsgeschichtliche Untersuchung zum Abschluss des Jesaja– und des Zwölf-prophetenbuches*, Wissenschaftliche Monographien zum Alten und Neuen Testament 114 (Neukirchen–Vluyn: Neukirchener Verlag, 2006).

Gunkel, Hermann, „Der Micha–Schluß. Zur Einführung in die literaturgeschichtliche Arbeit am AT", ZS 2 (1924), 145–178.

Jeremias, Jörg, *Der Prophet Hosea*, Altes Testament Deutsch 24/1 (Göttingen: Vandenhoeck & Ruprecht, 1983).

Jeremias, Jörg, *Die Propheten Joel, Obadja, Jona, Micha*, Altes Testament Deutsch 24,3 (Göttingen: Vandenhoeck & Ruprecht, 2007).

Kessler, Rainer, *Micha*, Herder Theologischer Kommentar Altes Testament (Freiburg, Basel, Berlin: Herder, 1999).

Kratz, Reinhard Gregor, „Der Anfang des Zweiten Jesaja in Jes 40,1f. und das Jeremiabuch", *ZAW* 106 (1994), 243–261.

Mathys, Hans–Peter, *Dichter und Beter, Theologen aus spätalttestamentlicher Zeit*, Orbis Biblicus et Orientalis 132 (Freiburg Schweiz: Universitätsverlag/Vandenhoeck & Ruprecht, 1994).

Müller, Anna Karena, *Gottes Zukunft, Die Möglichkeit der Rettung am Tag JHWHs nach dem Joelbuch* (Neukirchen–Vluyn: Neukirchener Verlag, 2008).

Nogalski, James, *Literary Precursors to the Book of the Twelve*, BZAW 217 (Berlin–New York: Walter de Gruyter, 1993).

Perlitt, Lothar, *Die Propheten Nahum, Habakuk, Zephanja*, Altes Testament Deutsch 25,1 (Göttingen: Vandenhoeck & Ruprecht, 2004).

Reicke, Bo, „Liturgical Tradition in Mic 7", HThR (1967), 349–367.

Rendtorff, Rolf, „Jesaja 6 im Rahmen der Komposition des Jesajabuches", in *The Book of Isaiah, Bibliotheka Ephemeridum Theologicarum Lovaniensium 81*, ed. Jacques Vermeylen (Leuven: Peeters, 1989), 73–82.

Rudolph, Wilhelm, *Micha – Nahum – Habakuk – Zephanja*, Kommentar zum Alten Testament XIII,3 (Gütersloh: Gütersloher Verlagshaus, 1975).

Schart, Aaron, D*ie Entstehung des Zwölfprophetenbuchs. Neubearbeitungen von Amos im Rahmen schriftenübergreifender Redaktionsprozesse*, BZAW 260 (Berlin–New York: Walter de Gruyter, 1998).

Schwienhorst-Schönberger, Ludger, „Zion – Ort der Tora. Überlegungen zu Mi 4,1–3" in *Zion – Ort der Begegnung*, Festschrift für Laurentius Klein zur Vollendung des 65. Lebensjahres, ed. Ferdinand Hahn, Frank–Lothar Hossfeld, Hans Jorissen and Angelika Neuwirth, Bonner Biblische Beiträge 90 (Bodenheim: Athenäum Hein Hanstein, 1993), 107–125.

Seitz, Christopher, "The Divine Council: Temporal Transition and New Prophecy in the Book of Isaiah", *JBL 109* (1990), 229–246.

Stade, Bernhard, „Streiflichter auf die Entstehung der jetzigen Gestalt der alttestamentlichen Prophetenschriften", *ZAW* 23 (1903), 153–171.

Steck, Odil Hannes, *Bereitete Heimkehr. Jesaja 35 als redaktionelle Brücke zwischen dem Ersten und Zweiten Jesaja*, Stuttgarter Bibelstudien 121 (Stuttgart: Verlag Katholisches Bibelwerk GmbH, 1985).

Steck, Odil Hannes, *Der Abschluß der Prophetie im Alten Testament. Ein Versuch zur Frage der Vorgeschichte des Kanons*, BThSt 17 (Neukirchen–Vluyn: Neukirchener Verlag, 1991).

Sweeney, Marvin A., "Synchronic and Diachronic Concerns in Reading the Book of the Twelve Prophets" in *Perspectives on the Formation of the Book of the Twelve. Methodological Foundations – Redactional Processes – Historical Insights*, ed. Rainer Albertz, James D. Nogalski, Jakob Wöhrle, BZAW 433 (Berlin–Boston: Walter de Gruyter, 2012), 21–33.

van Oorschot, Jan, *Von Babel zum Zion*, BZAW 206 (Berlin–New York: Walter de Gruyter, 1993).

Weidner, Alexander, *Das Ende Deuterojesajas*, Forschung zum Alten Testament 2.Reihe 94 (Mohr Siebeck: Tübingen, 2017).

Willis, John T., "The Authenticity and Meaning of Micah 5,9–14", *ZAW* 81 (1969), 353–368.

Wöhrle, Jakob, *Der Abschluss des Zwölfprophetenbuches. Buchübergreifende Redaktionsprozesse in den späten Sammlungen*, BZAW 389 (Berlin–New York: Walter de Gruyter, 2008).

Wöhrle, Jakob, *Die frühen Sammlungen des Zwölfprophetenbuches, Entstehung und Komposition*, BZAW 360 (Berlin–New York: Walter de Gruyter, 2006).

Zapff, Burkard M., "Jesaja 12 – Dank am Ende und am Anfang", in: Dankbarkeit. Ein interdisziplinäres Projekt in Literaturwissenschaft, Theologie und Religionspädagogik, ed. Ingrid Wiedenbroth-Gabler, Gottfried Orth, Jürgen Wehnert (Berlin: EB-Verlag, 2020), 45–71.

Zapff, Burkard M., *Jesaja 40–55*, Neue Echterbibel (Würzburg: Echter, 2001).

Zapff, Burkard M., "Jes 40 und die Frage nach dem Beginn des deuterojesajanischen Corpus" in *Gottes Wege suchend. Beiträge zum Verständnis der Bibel und ihrer Botschaft, Festschrift für Rudolph Mosis zum 70.Geburtstag*, ed. Franz Sedlmeier (Würzburg: Echter, 2003), 355–373.

Zapff, Burkard M., *Redaktionsgeschichtliche Studien zum Michabuch im Kontext des Dodekapropheton*, BZAW 256 (Berlin–New York: Walter de Gruyter, 1997).

Zapff, Burkard M., *Schriftgelehrte Prophetie – Jes 13 und die Komposition des Jesajabuches. Ein Beitrag zur Erforschung der Redaktionsgeschichte des Jesajabuches* (Würzburg: Echter, 1995).

Zapff, Burkard M., "Wie Micha zu Jesaja wurde" in *Historia magistra vitae, Festschrift für Johannes Hoffmann zum 65.Geburtstag*, cd. Anselm Blumberg, Oleksandre Petrynko (Regensburg: Verlag Friedrich Pustet, 2016), 539–555.

Richard J. Bautch
Isaiah 10 as an Intertext that Informs a Unified Reading of Zechariah 11 (Zech 11:1–3 and 11:4–17)

1 Introduction

I am grateful to Burkard Zapff and Joachim Eck for inviting me to present this study of Zechariah at "Isaiah and the Twelve," the international conference that they hosted at the Katholische Universität Eichstätt-Ingolstadt. With collegiality and rigor, the scholars who gathered in Eichstätt began painting a picture of Isaiah as a vital influence on the Book of the Twelve. The picture exists now in outline, although the details that have been put in place are significant and shed valuable light on individual prophetic books in the collection of the Twelve. In the coming years, the picture will become clearer and more complete as we refine our understanding of Isaiah's relationship to the Twelve. Crucial to this understanding is the book of Zechariah, whose oracles reflect key developments among the Judeans in the province of Yehud during the Persian period. Zechariah owes a certain debt to the book of Isaiah, especially in one of Zechariah's later chapters where the prophet critiques the community and its leadership from two distinct vantage points.

Zechariah 11 comprises an oracle followed by an extended allegory. The oracle, in 11:1–3, envisions a Lebanon where the great cedars go up in flames and fall far to the ground. In response, other trees howl, and presently shepherds and lions bewail a similar loss of their glorious habitat. Such is the scene in Zech 11:1–3. The account of natural destruction serves as a polemic against a certain group or class of people. The individuals implicated by the oracle give rise to a question: Are they related to the failed leaders in the allegory of vv. 4–17, which also refers unflatteringly to shepherds? At the climax of the allegory, the prophet breaks a covenant that he has made with all the people (11:10). He breaks it only after he snaps in two a rod with which he had cared for the people, also known as the flock, and he snaps the rod only after he has lost patience with the flock's previous shepherds, and they with him. The allegory holds more questions than answers. All we know for certain is that initially YHWH tells the prophet to go and "shepherd the flock (marked for) slaughter," (11:4) and YHWH adds that divine mercy has been withheld from this flock (11:6). Of Zech 11:4–17, Samuel Rolles Driver famously remarked that it is the most enigmatic passage

https://doi.org/10.1515/9783110705799-006

in the entire Old Testament, and a century later scholars are still citing Driver's words.[1]

To be certain, recent studies have clarified aspects of Zech 11. Raymond Person has studied an intertextual connection between Zech 11 and the book of Jeremiah. Reading for Deuteronomistic language and themes, Person finds a surfeit of Jeremian influence in the oracle about the fiery destruction of Lebanon cedars that begins Zech 11:2.[2] The devastated cedars are a metaphor for the society's once noble leaders now in ignominy. Person finds another concentration of Jeremian influence in Zech 11:9–10, that portion of the allegory where the shepherd snaps the first of his two rods and breaks his covenant with all the people.[3] Although the two passages, Zech 11:1–3 and 11:9–10, draw from different chapters in Jeremiah, the fact that Jeremiah's Deuteronomistic theology influences both passages but informs little else in Zech 11 suggests a connection between the Lebanon cedars ablaze early in the chapter and later the broken rod expressing failed leadership on the part of the Jerusalem based shepherd/prophet.[4]

Given the placement of the Jeremian material in Zechariah 11, this study explores the full range of resonance between the arboreal oracle that begins the chapter and the broken staffs signaling a voided covenant in later verses. I argue that it is an extensive and polyphonous resonance due to the fact that beyond Jeremiah there are additional intertexts, Isaiah 10 and Nehemiah 10, that lend cohesion to the two parts of Zech 11. The intertexts from Isaiah and other biblical books indicate that there is indeed a resonant bridge between the oracular critique that begins chapter 11 and the biting allegory that concludes it. To show the bridge in greater detail, this study returns to Jeremiah and the prophet's articulation of covenant. The covenant in Jeremiah 11 takes as its image a tree set ablaze

---

1 Samuel Rolles Driver, *The Minor Prophets: Nahum, Habakkuk, Zephaniah, Haggai, Zechariah, Malachi*. Century Bible (Edinburgh: T. C. & E. C. Jack, 1906), 23.
2 Raymond F. Person, *Second Zechariah and the Deuteronomic School*, JSOTSup 167 (Sheffield: Sheffield Academic Press, 1993), 124. In addition to Person, many other studies demonstrate how Zech 11 is dependent on Jeremiah; see Rex Mason, *The Books of Haggai Zechariah and Malachi* (Cambridge: Cambridge University Press, 1977), 103; 105; David L. Petersen, *Zechariah 9–14 and Malachi* OTL (Louisville: Westminster John Knox, 1995), 84.
3 *Ibid.*, 126–128.
4 Resolving the larger question of the oracle's relationship to the narrative further involves the text's significant images and vocabulary. In Zech 11, תאכל serves as a key note and signals all-consuming devastation. Zech 11:1 reports that fire consumes (וְתֹאכַל) Lebanon's cedars. תאכל is as well a catchword that recurs in the subsequent allegory of the shepherd (Zech 11:4–17); Zech 11:9 describes a state of anarchy in which a neighbor eats her neighbor's flesh (תֹּאכַלְנָה). The catchword suggests a lexical connection between the oracle and the allegory similar to that indicated previously by the catchword "shepherd" and by the Jeremian linkage.

by God's anger, which becomes a symbol of covenant lost. In the final section of this study, the intertext Isaiah 10 again comes into play to help explain the wage that the leaders pay the shepherd as a show of their worldly power. Unexpectedly, the wage of coins is destroyed by fire in the smelter of the Jerusalem Temple. Here and throughout Zechariah 11, the imagery of fiery destruction recalls Isaiah and other intertexts as it secures the oracle (11:1–3) to the allegory (11:4–17) in order to underscore burning issues in the community.

2 Preliminary Issues

2.1 Dating and Historical Context

In terms of dating, it suffices to say that the texts dealt with here are all late, likely from the second half of the Persian period. In the case of Isaiah, the passages 10:16–19 and 10:33–34 are especially relevant. While certain commentators date the passages to the monarchic era, there is ample support for locating these two, interrelated segments in the Persian period. In the case of 10:16–19 it appears to be a Persian period text inasmuch as the reference to Assyria is so oblique that it is likely metaphorical and not literal.[5] Casting Assyria as a cipher is a common practice in the Persian period.[6] In the case of 10:33–34, Hugh Williamson argues convincingly that this anti-Assyrian oracle originated in monarchic times but was placed in its present location during the final stages of the compilation of the book of Isaiah.[7] It is functionally a Persian period text. Given that the two Isaiah texts

---

[5] A similar conclusion is reached in a host of commentaries; see for example Hans Wildberger, *Jesaja: Kapitel 1–12*, BKAT 10.1 (Neukirchen-Vluyn: Neukirchener, 1972), 408; George B. Gray, *The Book of Isaiah*, ICC (Edinburgh: T&T Clark, 1949), 199. Using an essentially ahistorical approach, Csaba Balogh holds that Isa 10:16–19 is secondary in the sense that it "was relocated from a different context." See his "Inverted Fates and Inverted Texts: Rationales of Reinterpretation in the Compositional History of the Isaianic Prophecies, with Special Emphasis on Isaiah 10, 16–19 and Its Context," *ZAW* 128/1 (2016): 80.

[6] For example, Nah 2:1 treats the fall of Assyria and its capital Nineveh, which occurred in the seventh century. A critical reading of the verse, however, indicates that for the postexilic author of Nah 2:1, "Nineveh is no longer the former capital of the Assyrian empire, but serves as the epitome of the oppression of Judah by a foreign power." Burkard M. Zapff, "Second Isaiah and the Twelve," p. 91 in this volume.

[7] H. G. M. Williamson, *A Critical and Exegetical Commentary on Isaiah 1–27*, vol. 2, *Isaiah 6–12*, ICC (London: T&T Clark, 2018), 635. Williamson's view is like that of Balogh (see n. 5 on Isa 10:16–19): the short Isaian pericope was secondarily added.

and the material in Zech 11 were all in use at roughly the same time and share a common provenance, postexilic Judah, one rightly envisions the sharing of terms and terminology as well as images and concepts that belonged to the contemporary prophetic idiom.

What was the social milieu from which Zech 11 emerged? Because the account of natural destruction in Zech 11:1–3 polemicizes against a certain group or class of people, some commentators refer to the oracle as a "taunt song."[8] In biblical literature, the Lebanon cedar can symbolize a nation such as Assyria (Ezek 31:3, 16–17) or Judah's king (Ezek 17:3). In Zech 11:1 the Lebanon cedars suggest Jerusalemite leaders during the Second Temple period. These individuals are likely indicated as well in 11:3, by the reference to "shepherds" bereft of their glory. The term "shepherds" need not speak of royalty or kings *per se*. Paul Redditt has suggested that the "shepherds" approximate influential people from the leading families, while stressing the Priestly character of the historical figures represented here.[9] Redditt infers that they were priests, in fact that they were Temple functionaries "in collusion with the actual overlords, the Persians."[10] The point is well taken, especially in light of the widespread Priestly influence in late Persian period textuality. Priestly influence, writes David Carr,

> appears not only in texts such as Chronicles or the Ezra traditions, but also in ways that link with late Isaiah traditions, both in Sabbath emphasis and in subtle signs of potential Levitical authorship. [...] This rise in Priestly elements in the late Persian period reflects the increasingly exclusive domination of literary textuality in the Persian period by groups related to the Jerusalem temple and its priesthood.[11]

It is plausible that priests are responsible for Zech 11, and that these authors are targeting rival priests. While Redditt suggests that the target is Temple priests in collusion with the Persians, evidence of such collusion around the Temple mount is lacking. Another scenario to consider would be the authors of Zech 11 fulminating against local Priestly elites, or "shepherds," in political alliances with agents of the crown at a site such as Ramat Raḥel. Ramat Raḥel is located southwest of

---

8 Paul L. Redditt, *Zechariah 9–14*, IECOT, (Stuttgart: Kohlhammer, 2012), 17.
9 Paul L. Redditt, "Zechariah 9–14: The Capstone of the Book of the Twelve," in *Bringing out the Treasure: Inner Biblical Allusion in Zechariah 9–14*, eds. Mark J. Boda and Michael H. Floyd, JSOTSup 370 (London/New: Sheffield Academic Press, 2003): 305–323, here 321.
10 Redditt, *Zechariah 9–14*, 84.
11 David M. Carr, "Criteria and Periodization in Dating Biblical Texts to Parts of the Persian Period," in *On Dating Biblical Texts to the Persian Period: Discerning Criteria and Establishing Epochs*, eds. Richard J. Bautch and Mark Lackowski, FAT II 101 (Tübingen: Mohr Siebeck, 2019): 11–18, here 14.

the City of David, and excavations indicate that it was an administrative center for late Iron Age Judah and Persian period Yehud. Importantly, it reached its apex of activity during the fifth – fourth centuries, when its outstanding feature was its garden. Oded Lipschits describes the garden of Ramat Raḥel in detail:

> The hallmark of royal architecture and grandeur was the unique garden. This well-watered imperial garden and its original flora originated in the Persian homeland and surrounding areas, and its magnificence [sic] location in this relatively arid environment must have left a lasting indelible impression on visitors to the royal site. Its imported trees from far-off lands, aromatic plants and impressive fruit trees, together with its aesthetic architectural features, symbolized the power and affluence of the local rulers who represented the Persian Empire.[12]

Ramat Raḥel may well stand in the background as Zech 11 passes judgment on both shepherds and plant life. The destruction of trees from distant lands (11:1–3) would serve as a polemic against the Persian Empire and those Judeans who would do its bidding from Ramat Raḥel. The author's ire, trained on local Priestly leaders in league with the Persian authorities, would find expression in a fiery allegory with great trees going up in flames, other trees howling, and shepherds along with lions bewailing the loss of their glorious garden. The likelihood of this literary scenario is even greater in light of studies that align other oracles in Zechariah with the Achaemenid garden at Ramat Raḥel.[13] It has been suggested that certain of the prophet's visions in Zech 1–8 are set in the *paradeisos* at Ramat Raḥel, in particular the first vision (Zech 1:1–8), with its reference to myrtles located near a pool.[14] The imagery replicates one of the pools at Ramat Raḥel, where myrtles grew nearby. While the evidence is not yet conclusive, one can imagine that the shepherds criticized in Zechariah 11 were complicit with the Persian authorities at Ramat Raḥel.

---

12 Oded Lipschits, Yuval Gadot, and Dafna Langgut, "The Riddle of Ramat Raḥel: The Archaeology of a Royal Persian Period Edifice," *Trans* 41 (2012): 57–79, here 77. See also Yuval Gadot, Oded Lipschits, and Manfred Oeming, "Tieferes Verstehen: Erwägungen zur Epistemologie der Archäologie am Beispiel der Ausgrabung von Ramat Rahel (Jerusalem)," *Trumah* 18 (2008): 33–55; Oded Lipschits, Yuval Gadot, Benjamin Arubas, and Manfred Oeming, "Palace and Village, Paradise and Oblivion: Unraveling the Riddles of Ramat Raḥel," NEA 74, (2011): 2–49.
13 Christine Mitchell, "A Paradeisos at Ramat Rahel and the Setting of Zechariah," *Trans* 48 (2016): 77–91.
14 *Ibid.*, 87–88.

2.2 Methodology

Methodologically, this study is aligned with those scholars of Zechariah who focus on inner biblical allusion in order to attend to both the diachronic and synchronic aspects of the text. Rex Mason, Michael Floyd, and Mark Boda, among others, have established and refined this interpretive framework, keyed to allusions and intertexts.[15] The present study aims to describe the incorporation of an intertext into the host text. The host text is Zech 11, and the intertexts include two passages from Isaiah 10, as well as material from Neh 10. With this mode of study, a key datum is language that is repeated across texts.[16] On that basis, the fact that Isa 10:33–34, for example, has many lexical points of contact with Zech 11 is significant for intertextuality. As is shown in the next section, roughly 25 percent of the language in Isa 10:33–34 recurs in Zech 11.

The crucial issue, methodologically, is burden of proof.[17] Whereas literary dependence may be proven by instances of verbatim phrasing, there is a different burden of proof to establish an intertextual relationship between, in this case, Isaiah and Zechariah. To prove that there is intertextuality or an allusion or an echo, one looks to the key datum of language repeated across texts, but repeated in a way that is more piecemeal and subtle. The connection between the two texts consists of resembling expressions, as opposed to quotations. The verbal similarities involve individual words or at most partial phrases, while there are often synonymic and thematic links that enhance the prophet's message of judgment. In sum, the lexical connections between the texts are in no way accidental and would not have been lost on informed readers in antiquity.

---

15 Rex A. Mason, "The Use of Earlier Biblical Materials in Zechariah IX-XIV: A Study in Inner Biblical Exegesis" (Ph.D. diss., University of London, 1973); Michael H. Floyd, "Deutero-Zechariah and Types of Intertextuality," in *Bringing out the Treasure*, eds. Boda and Floyd: 225–244; Mark J. Boda, *Exploring Zechariah*, vol. 1, *The Development of Zechariah and its Role within the Twelve*, ANEM 16, (Atlanta: SBL Press, 2017), 17–18; 26.

16 Richard L. Schultz, *The Search for Quotation: Verbal Parallels in the Prophets*, JSOTSup 180, (Sheffield: Sheffield Academic Press, 1999), 232–233.

17 The following discussion draws from Richard J. Bautch, "Intertextuality in the Persian Period," in *Approaching Yehud: New Approaches to the Study of the Persian Period*, ed. Jon L. Berquist, SemeiaSt 50 (Atlanta: Society of Biblical Literature, 2007): 25–35.

3 Isaiah 10:33–34

3.1 Introduction

Isaiah 10:33–34 contains a vivid oracle that begins with יְהֹוָה צְבָאוֹת הָאָדוֹן, the Lord God of hosts, lopping off large branches with terrifying force (בְּמַעֲרָצֶה). God can-opies the trees, and each bough that is cut away, each פֻּארָה, recalls the Akkadian word *per'u*, a term for Assyrian royalty. The oracle next describes persons of stature being chopped down as if they were trees. They are cut, גְּדוּעִים, the passive participle of גדע, and the *qal* binyan is here noteworthy. Based on the previous action, lopping off branches, one might expect גדע in the *pual*, as in Isa 9:9, where sycamore trees are hewn apart. The *qal*, in contrast, denotes an article of wood that is broken in two. This fine distinction between hewing apart or breaking in two notwithstanding, the action is then restated in patently Isaian terms: Isa 10:33b concludes by announcing that the lofty ones will be brought low, as in humbled. The oracle continues in 10:34, stating that he will cut down the thickets of the forest with an axe, literally with iron. Then, to conclude the oracle, there is a terse pronouncement that Lebanon in majesty will fall. Majesty, expressed בְּאַדִּיר, presents a challenge for translation and is rendered variously, including the NRSV's "Lebanon with its majestic trees," a reference to the great forests of Lebanon as a metonymy. I translate it literally, "Lebanon in majesty," without supplying a substantive or, as is sometimes done, a pronominal suffix.

3.2 Isaiah 10:33–34 as Intertext

3.2.1 Lexical Evidence

Between Isa 10:33–34 and Zech 11, there is significant overlap of terms and ter-minology. The short passage Isa 10:33–34 contains five terms the roots of which are attested in Zech 11:1–3 or in 11:4–17: (גדע) גְּדוּעִים; (יער) הַיַּעַר; (ולבנון) וְהַלְּבָנוֹן; (אדר) בְּאַדִּיר; (נפל) יִפּוֹל;. Roughly 25 percent of the vocabulary in Isa 10:33–34 appears in Zech 11. The fact of shared, specialized vocabulary is noteworthy, and equally significant is the fact that the words shared by Isa 10:33–34 and Zech 11 are attested in both the oracle and the allegory of the eleventh chapter in Zechariah. It is not the case that only the oracle contains evidence of a connection to Isa 10, or that only the allegory has links to Isa 10. They both do so, and in fairly specific ways. First, the expression גְּדוּעִים, the *qal* passive participle of גדע, in Isa 10:33b, reads: "The tallest trees are cut down." It was noted that this verb is used in *qal* when a wooden structure is broken in two; such action is never associated with the *niphal* or *piel/pual* forms. In the allegory of Zechariah 11, the shepherd breaks in two both of his staffs (Zech 11:10, 14), actions that are described in the *qal* imperfect converted of the verb גדע (וָאֶגְדַּע). "And I took my staff, Noam, and I snapped it in two."

A related question is: what is broken in two? Williamson tracks the verbal root גָּדַע to three other verses in Isa: 9:9; 14:12; and 22:25.[18] Isa 9:9, he argues, relates to the destruction of timber in a building as opposed to the felling of trees. He discerns a similar usage in 22:25; and he notes that 14:12 is not related to wood at all, but rather to the son of dawn who is cut down to the ground. The point is that in Isaiah גדע is not used univocally, and the referent, that thing which is broken in two, can take different forms. In fact, what is broken in two need not even be made of wood, although it typically is, with Isaiah's tall trees a textbook example. In Zech 11, the shepherd breaks in two both of his מַקְלוֹת staffs (Zech 11:10, 14). He does not split the wood or shear it apart: he breaks it in two. To the objection that these are staffs, not trees, a difference that could mitigate the correspondence between Zechariah and Isaiah, recall that in Isaiah this verb is multivocal and applies to a range of breakable objects. Why not staffs, at least in theory? And, to restate an earlier finding, the shepherd himself narrates the action, and the first-person form of the verb is in the *qal* binyan, which connotes a breaking into two pieces, in Isaiah and elsewhere. In Zech 11, the מַקְלוֹת are snapped clean, broken in two. The usage of גדע in Zechariah is eminently consistent with its usage in Isaiah.

While גדע secures a connection between Isa 10:33–34 and the allegory in Zech 11, the expression בְּאַדִּיר links Isa 10:33–34 and the oracle that begins Zech 11. It was observed that בְּאַדִּיר in Isa 10:34b is an adjective that is subject to different translations and that a literal translation conveys a certain elegance: "Lebanon in majesty." Zechariah employs an adjectival form of this root as well in Zech 11:2. The only difference is that the adjective in Zechariah is plural, אַדִּרִים. In Zech 11:2 אַדִּרִים is typically translated as either "the mighty" or "the glorious trees." In short, these are the best subjects of the realm, Lebanon's finest, personified as great trees. In the next verse, Zech 11:3, the root אדר recurs with the same verb, but here as a feminine noun (אַדַּרְתָּם) whose referent is the wailing shepherds. The shepherds' majesty has been ravaged, with אַדַּרְתָּם perhaps indicating a mantle or cloak similar to that worn by the false prophets in Zech 13:4. In both Isaiah and Zechariah, that which is majestic relates to Lebanon.

In short, of the many echoes between Isa 10:33–34 and Zech 11:1–17, two in particular are in the same pitch, with the same key signature. Isaiah's גְּדוּעִים and בְּאַדִּיר each find an uncanny likeness in Zech 11. As an intertext, Isa 10:33–34 con-

---

18 Williamson, *Isaiah 1–27*, 639.

firms and clarifies aspects of both the oracle in Zech 11:1–3 and the allegory in Zech 11:4–17. In this role as intertext, Isa 10:33–34 further reifies the bridge in Zech 11 between the oracle that begins the chapter and the allegory that concludes it.

3.2.2 Further Parallels between Zech 11:1–3 and Isa 10:33–34

There are further parallels between Zech 11:1–3 and Isa 10:33–34, although they are not as compelling as the lexical parallels in the previous section. When joined with the lexical parallels, however, these further, *prima facie* parallels advance the argument. (1) Both texts are judgment oracles that clearly begin a new literary unit, and they ostensibly connect to the section that follows them. They begin a new unit, but what they begin does not end with them. In the case of Isaiah, Isa 10:33–34, the cutting down of Assyria/Lebanon, is joined to Isa 11:1–9, which paints a positive future for Israel. In 11:1–9, a wholly new Davidic scion brings forth a harmony within nature whereby predators and prey dwell together in peace and security. Similarly, the oracle in Zech 11:1–3 leads directly to the allegory of 11:4–17, which approximates the Isaiah text except that here the tribulations of Israel are extended rather than reversed. In Zechariah, the animals, sheep in a herd, are mistreated, abused, and denied any pity. The figure of the shepherd struggles to provide leadership, and his tale ends badly when he is called to be a shepherd of foolishness (11:17). It is a case of *coincidentia oppositorum*. (2) These are two Persian period texts, Zech 11:1–3 self-evidently and Isa 10:33–34 by virtue of its placement through a redactional process, as noted earlier. It is not merely that the Isaian oracle's placement is a Persian period effect, but that it has been placed in a sequence with the postexilic Isa 11:1–9, which presupposes the fall of the Davidic dynasty, after which a new scion appears. In this vein, the divine spirit functioning in Isa 11:2 to inspire the Davidic figure is a theological development that speaks of a later time after the exile. (3) The Isaian oracle in 10:33–34, about lopping off boughs and cutting down trees, should be read in light of Isa 10:16–19, where the sovereign, the Lord of Hosts, turns the light of Israel into a fire that burns thorns and briars before burning down the majority of the trees in God's glorious forest. Not only is the arboreal content of 10:16–19 parallel to that of 10:33–34, but the sequencing of these two oracles in terms of what precedes and what follows is strikingly similar, as Kirsten Nielsen has noted.[19] If the compiler of Isa 10 has made a match between these two oracles about demolishing

---

19 Kirsten Nielsen, *There is Hope for a Tree: The Tree as Metaphor in Isaiah*, JSOTSup 65, (Sheffield: JSOT Press, 1989), 123–144.

trees, it solidifies the connection between Isaian imagery *as an assemblage* and the incendiary oracle that begins Zech 11. (4) As reading Isa 10:33–34 in light of Isa 10:16–19 illumines the analysis of Zech 11, there are additional parts within the book of Isaiah that frame the intertextual connection between Isa 10 and Zech 11. For example, Isa 2:13 describes the day of the Lord as ruination coming upon all the cedars of Lebanon, high and lifted up, and upon all the oaks of Bashan. The terms "Lebanon cedar" and "oaks of Bashan" recur in Zech 11:1–2, which also contains the motif of God humbling that which is high and haughty. In the analysis of Risto Nurmela, Isa 2:13 constitutes a "possible allusion" to Isaiah in Zechariah; in fact, the author of Zech 11:1–3 alludes to Isa 10, with Isa 2:13 framing the allusion.[20]

4 Nehemiah 10

4.1 Nehemiah 10 as Intertext

The Hebrew expression אַדִּיר in Zech 11:2, 3 expresses the mighty trees or the glorious trees as personifications of Lebanon's finest individuals. In Neh 10, another postexilic text, the Hebrew root denoting majesty or glory (אדר) again indicates a class of leaders or distinguished people in postexilic Judea. In Neh 10:30 the אחיהם אדיריהם are "noble kinsmen" who swear an oath to follow Torah, thereby sealing an אמנה, a (non-*bĕrît*) covenant kept within the postexilic community. The covenant is a bi-lateral agreement that mandates the performance of certain commands or מצות (Neh 10:30,33) which pertain to intermarriage or to the Sabbath.[21] These tasks also include more mundane tasks such as bringing wood to the temple on certain days. Thus, the groups involved in this covenant are focused on specific behaviors in a local context, while at the same time understanding themselves very globally. How? As Neh 10:30 makes clear, the members of these groups bind themselves together in a covenant in order to follow *all the laws of Moses*. The covenant of Neh 10, then, is an iteration of the Mosaic covenant in its totality with an innovation: The covenant interrelates global/universal and local/particular senses of the law. The universal sense or Mosaic sense is articulated in Neh 10:30, 33, and the particular sense is the application of specific

---

20 Risto Nurmela, *Prophets in Dialogue: Inner-Biblical Allusions in Zechariah 1–8 and 9–14* (Åbo: Åbo Akademi University Press, 1996), 132–133.

21 See Joseph Blenkinsopp, *Essays on Judaism in the Pre-Hellenistic Period,* BZAW 495 (Berlin: de Gruyter, 2017), 218.

mandates, like bringing wood to the temple, to certain groups on certain days. Thus, the covenant is a mixture of different types of elements.[22] The question then becomes: is there comparability between the mixed covenant of Neh 10 and the covenant established by the leaders or אדיריהם of Zech 11? Because there is a third and crucial attestation of אדר in Zech 11:13, which falls within the framework of the allegory, the question will be pursued in a later section (5.2). Here it is important to note that Neh 10 expands the intertextual network previously established between Isa 10: 33–34 and Zech 11, and it serves as another instance in which intertextual language bridges the oracle of Zech 11:1–3, where אדר is attested twice, and the allegory of Zech 11:4–17, where a noble sum, אֶדֶר הַיְקָר, is exchanged after the covenant is broken.

4.2 Preliminary Conclusions

To sum up the discussion thus far, there is copious evidence of a connection between the oracle of the felled cedars in Zech 11:1–3 and the breaking of the shepherd's rod and his covenant (with all the peoples) in Zech 11:10. The connection is manifest via intertexts such as Neh 10:30–33 and especially Isa 10:33–34. Isaiah reports the destruction of Lebanon's majestic cedars, described as the snapping of a vertical shaft. Earlier in Isa 10, a forest of trees is devoured in flames (10:16–18). By alluding to Isaiah's oracles, the writer of Zech 11 foregrounds two of his most salient images, Lebanon's burned, broken cedars (11:1–2) and the snapped rod and broken covenant (11:10). The allusion to Isaiah in turn unifies the bipartite ch. 11 of Zechariah. This is significant literarily, and beyond the literary effect, there is the historical detailing of failed leadership that leaves the community in an abyss. The short oracle (11:1–3) encapsulates the travail of the shepherd and those associated with him before the same plot is elaborated in the allegory of Zech 11:4–17. The compiler responsible for this text provides insight into the Second Temple period at a point when polity fell short of its aims and a covenant was broken.

---

22 In the mixed covenants of the Persian Period, the dual senses of covenant (particular and universal) relate to issues of identity. The particular and universal are conjoined so that covenant may express both group identity within Judean society as well as a "national" identity for Judeans who are subjects of the Persian empire. See Richard J. Bautch, *Glory and Power, Ritual and Relationship: The Mosaic Covenant in the Postexilic Period*, LHBOTS 471, (London: T&T Clark, 2009), 109–114; Maria Häusl, "Searching for Forces of Group Cohesion in the Books of Nehemiah and Isaiah," in *Ṣedaqa and Torah in Postexilic Discourse*, eds. Susanne Gillmayr-Bucher and Maria Häusl, LHBOTS 640 (London: T&T Clark, 2017): 55–70, here 63.

5 Jeremiah 11:1–17

5.1 The Mosaic/Sinaitic Covenant in Jer 11:1–7

In the oracle that begins Zech 11, the destruction of the cedars anticipates the shepherd's career. Specifically in 11:10, the shepherd snaps the rod called pleasantness, an echo of the Lebanon cedars snapping in two, and he breaks "my covenant which I made with all the people."

The language of covenant in 11:10b is distinctive but not unique:

לְהָפֵיר אֶת־בְּרִיתִי אֲשֶׁר כָּרַתִּי אֶת־כָּל־הָעַמִּים׃

"To break the covenant that I made with ..." is an expression found three times in the Hebrew Bible. In addition to Zech 11:10, there are two Deuteronomic references in Deut 31:16,20 and another reference in Jer 11:10. Deut 31:16 falls within the unit Deut 31:16–22, where God addresses Moses shortly before the prophet's death. God tells him that after he dies, the people will serve foreign gods "and forsake me and break the covenant that I made with them." In the context of Zechariah, the prophet could be identifying with Moses, whose best attempt to lead the people did not keep them from falling into lawlessness.[23] In this sense, the writer is aligning the covenant of Zech 11:10 with the Mosaic or Sinaitic covenant. The covenant broken in Zech 11:10 is typologically the same as that broken in Deut 31:16, 20.

The phrase "to break the covenant that I made with ..." also occurs in Jer 11:10, the center of a distinct literary unit, the covenant sermon in Jer 11:1–17. In this Deuteronomic oracle from the seventh century, Jeremiah is portrayed as preaching the covenant. But the peoples of Israel and Judah become rebellious and idolatrous. In Jer 11:10, they "break the covenant that I made with their forefathers," and YHWH pronounces judgment against them.[24] Jeremiah is then told not to pray for the rebellious people of Israel and Judah (11:14), thereby severing his relationship with them, just as the shepherd in Zechariah 11 becomes alienated from all of the people.

---

23 Within Deuteronomy, this treatment of Moses likely dates to the time of Zech 11's composition. Deuteronomy 31:16–22, 24–29 "show features typical of a redactional addition, which can be ascribed to a late postexilic *Fortschreibung* to the Pentateuchal redaction." Benedetta Rossi, "Conflicting Patterns of Redaction: Jer 31, 33–34 and its Challenge to the Post-Mosaic Revelation Program," *Bib* 98 (2017): 202–225, here 221.
24 To compare this breaking of the covenant with that in Deut 31:16, 20, see Rossi, "Conflicting Patterns": 220, n. 81.

The reason why Jeremiah's intercession would be fruitless is given in Jer 11:16–17. In these crucial verses, Israel and Judah are likened to a beautiful olive tree that YHWH planted to bear fruit. But because Israel and Judah made offerings to Baal, they provoked the anger of YHWH (להבעסני) who in response set fire to the olive tree. The fire blazed until with a shattering sound the tree's branches were all broken and the tree was destroyed. In this Deuteronomic oracle, there is a fundamental connection between "breaking the covenant that I made with" the forefathers of Israel and Judah and the fiery destruction of an otherwise healthy tree. The writer of Zechariah depicts the same sort of dissolution: Israel and Judah, who are mentioned explicitly in Zech 11:14, are typified by their worthless leaders who were once tall and promising like Lebanon's cedars or the olive tree of Jeremiah, but are now the objects of destruction. The lexical correlation between Zechariah's oracle (11:1–3) and the allegory (11:4–17) on the crucial issues of leadership and covenant is again amplified, in this instance by intertextual allusions to Jeremiah.

5.2 The Community's Covenant in Zech 11:4–17

While the covenant in Zech 11:10 is based upon the Mosaic/Sinaitic covenant, it is no less a sign of the relationship between this particular shepherd and his flock, a certain group of Judeans.[25] In the words of Redditt, "within the passage itself, the most obvious covenant is the one implied in v. 7 when the narrator agreed to shepherd the flock."[26] In fact, the pact may have contained some particular understandings between the shepherd and the group or groups he sought to lead as well as between him and other leaders in the community. In such cases, the community-specific מצות subsist within the Mosaic covenant. In Zech 11, some unstated issue may be regulated covenantally to enhance the quality of life for those under the shepherd's authority. Of course, one would like to know more, such as what exactly the shepherd's covenant stipulated.[27] The fact that he refers

---

25 See n. 22.

26 Redditt, *Zechariah 9–14*, 85.

27 The shepherd may have hoped to provide a pleasant life to those within his covenant. In this scenario, the shepherd is drawing on proverbial material in which נעם is pleasantness, one of the many benefits of wisdom. In Proverbs, for example, the person who lives in accord with wisdom receives all the goods that a wisely constructed world can offer. This would be a true alternative to the anarchic world of Zech 11. Moreover, Prov 3:17, which describes wisdom as peaceful and pleasant (נעם), is followed by a remarkable comparison between wisdom and the tree of life (Prov 3:18, see Gen 2:9). The world of Proverbs and its life-giving flora contrasts sharply with the

to it as "my covenant" (בריתי) that "I created" (כרתי) indicates that the agreement bears his imprint, making the covenant particular to this shepherd and linked in all likelihood to the issues that he helped the community to confront.

The fact that the shepherd's allegory of Zech 11:4–17 includes a particular understanding within the agreement suggests that the pact is in fact a mixed covenant, the design of which was discussed earlier in this study. The mixed covenant has two dimensions, with the first expressing the Israelite covenant par excellence, the Mosaic/Sinaitic covenant. The Sinaitic legal tradition retained its value despite the exile and is one dimension of the mixed covenant. The other dimension is the particular, the specific מצות that galvanize a given community. Although this dimension is unspecified in Zech 11:10, it is no leap to say that there is particular content in the shepherd's mixed covenant because there are examples from other Persian period texts. The examples, from Nehemiah and Haggai, are explored next in 5.2.1 and 5.2.2.

5.2.1 Mixed Covenants in Neh 10 and Neh 5

Recall the mixed covenant of Neh 10 as it contained the mundane matter of a common schedule for bringing wood to the temple. Wood for sacrifice represents the type of particular issue that could be taken up in a postexilic covenant that is Mosaic/Sinaitic in its larger design. In Neh 5, a debate about debt slavery is fueled by sharp differences of opinion among Judeans as to how they should treat their non-Judean "brothers" from the land. Some commentators have described these "brothers from the land" as Israelites. Through a covenant, the figure of Nehemiah establishes a common practice for dealing with "brothers" who fall into financial arrears (Neh 5: 11–13). It is an ad-hoc covenant with a sure bottom line: prohibiting debt slavery. Eibert Tigchelaar likens the situation depicted in Neh 5 to that found in the shepherd's allegory of Zech 11:4–17.[28] Tigchelaar even suggests that the flock entrusted to Zechariah's shepherd are the "Israelites" or mixed-bloods looked down upon in Neh 5 and vulnerable to debt slavery except for the protections of a covenant forged by Nehemiah. This suggestion may overreach the evidence available in Zech 11:4–17 and is in any case difficult to corrob-

---

landscape of Zech 11, where great forests are denuded and the shepherd's staffs are broken. It contrasts as well with Ramat Raḥel if the lush garden there were a symbol of corruption to the author of Zech 11.

28 E. J. C. Tigchelaar, *Prophets of Old and the Day of the End: Zechariah, the Book of the Watchers and Apocalyptic*, OtSt 35 (Leiden: Brill, 1996), 113.

orate. Nevertheless, Tigchelaar's view of the matter is intriguing in that it points to particular social issues that may have subsisted in the covenant of Zech 11:10. The sheep of the flock in Zechariah were not necessarily subject to debt slavery, but whatever made their lives wretched was likely addressed in the covenant by which they lived for a time, until conditions worsened and the shepherd took it upon himself to annul the pact.

5.2.2 A Mixed Covenant in Haggai

Alongside the agreements in Neh 5 and 10, another example of the mixed covenant occurs in Haggai. As John Kessler has shown, on the one hand, "Haggai views the Sinai covenant as a foundational constitutive element of the community's relationship with Yahweh" (1:2–11).[29] On the other hand, the prophet preaches first and foremost rebuilding the temple, a directive that is "markedly absent from other covenant stipulations preserved in the Hebrew Bible."[30] In Kessler's words, "Haggai blurs the broader details of the tradition complex and picks up a single element within the [covenant] tradition and elevates it to central importance."[31] Might not the prophet/shepherd of Zech 11 be doing something similar? In his analysis of Haggai and the covenant, Kessler distinguishes between plot content and ideological purpose. Haggai's plot content is reconstruction of the temple, whereas the prophet's ideological purpose is "a rich theology of divine-human interaction."[32] In a word, the covenant is Haggai's ideological purpose, with rebuilding the temple his specific directive. Haggai's approach to the covenant exhibits the type of mixed covenant seen in Nehemiah and Zechariah.

In Zech 11, there is a mutual understanding that the shepherd has established between himself and the flock. This understanding may include unspecified content that facilitates the shepherd's leadership and constitutes the particular

---

29 John Kessler, "Tradition, Continuity and Covenant in the Book of Haggai," in *Tradition in Transition: Haggai and Zechariah 1–8 in the Trajectory of Hebrew Theology*, ed. Mark J. Boda and Michael H. Floyd, LHBOTS 475, (New York: T&T Clark, 2008): 1–39, here 26.

30 *Ibid.*, 17.

31 *Ibid.*, 27. Kessler elsewhere revisits the imperative to rebuild the temple in Haggai. His analysis of this single element within the tradition of the Mosaic covenant is consistent with his earlier work, although his later work describes the delay in rebuilding the temple as a violation *in* covenant, as opposed to a violation *of* covenant. See his "Curse, Covenant and Temple in the Book of Haggai," in *Covenant in the Persian Period: From Genesis to Chronicles*, eds. Richard J. Bautch and Gary N. Knoppers (Winona Lake, IN: Eisenbrauns, 2015): 229–254, here 240.

32 *Ibid.*, 35.

dimension of the covenant, which is Mosaic in its broader outlines. The text does not disclose what the shepherd's covenant stipulated, whereas in Haggai and Nehemiah the covenant's specific contents are enumerated.

6 Denouement

It remains only to interpret the puzzling verse Zech 11:13a:

וַיֹּאמֶר יְהוָֹה אֵלַי הַשְׁלִיכֵהוּ אֶל־הַיּוֹצֵר אֶדֶר הַיְקָר אֲשֶׁר יָקַרְתִּי מֵעֲלֵיהֶם

Then YHWH said to me, send to the smelter this princely sum at which they valued me.

The verse continues in 11:13b, "And I took (the) thirty shekels and I sent the sum to the smelter (in) the temple." A key term is אל-היוצר, which Rex Mason understands to be a smelter, a person forging metals by fire in a workshop within the Temple.[33] This reading finds support in 1 Kgs 7:15 and Isa 44:9–10. With Mason, I read the MT over and against a Syriac version that translated the *yod* as an *ʾalep* to render the word "treasury." The prophet/shepherd brings his princely wages to the Temple smith so that they might be liquidated. But why should money, in this case the shepherd's wages, be liquidated? Typically, commentators read this verse as ironic. YHWH required of the people not payment to a third party, the shepherd, but obedience to the laws and the covenant. The people were not covenant-compliant, however, and as a result their paying the shepherd is ironic and futile, ultimately of no account. But within the allegory, is this interpretation plausible? The parties at fault are the leaders, not the people as a whole. The allegory polemicizes against the upper echelon, against the owners, merchants, and shepherds, including the prophet/shepherd who speaks in the first person. One might imagine merchants, their business thriving as a result of their political connections at the lavish Ramat Raḥel, located not far from the city of David or from the Temple.[34] To the point in Zech 11:13, the discourse about wages subtly indicts the leaders, yet again, by way of the Hebrew word אדר. Readers first encountered

---

33 Rex Mason, "Zechariah 11:4–17," in *Bringing out the Treasure,* Boda and Floyd, 93–116, here 113.

34 Apropos of the discussion in section 2.1, if the shepherd were in conflict with priests at the Jerusalem Temple, an order to take his wages to the Temple for liquidation by the smith would not make sense. If, however, he were paid his wages at Ramat Raḥel, he would indeed need to take them from there to the Temple mount for their disposal.

אדר in the intertext Isa 10:34b, "Lebanon in majesty." The Hebrew root אדר was also prominent in the oracle Zech 1:1–3, where "majestic ones" (אדרים) in 11:2 is echoed by the word "glory" (אדרתם) in 11:3. Verse 3 refers to the lost glory of the shepherds; the devastation of the great trees will cause shepherds and the lions in the jungle of the Jordan to howl. Here in 11:13 something very similar takes place. The princely wage paid out by the leaders as a show of their worldly glory is literally destroyed by fire, now at the hand of the smelter in the Jerusalem Temple. Glory gone up in flames is the last word on the leaders of this day, just as it was the last word in Zech 11:2. They are all failed shepherds, the prophet first and foremost. In the allegory's final verses, 11:15–17, the prophet is called anew, but this time to be a shepherd of foolishness (11:15, רעה אולי). So ends the allegory of the prophet/shepherd in Zech 11.

A subsequent passage, Zech 13:7–9, may have once followed the allegory directly, with 12:1–14 and 13:1–6 being later interpolations.[35] In this case, there would be a continuation of Zech 11:13, with its Temple imagery of a smelter, in Zech 13:9, a reference to the people being refined as silver and tried as gold. Zech 13:9 reads:

> And I will bring the third part through the fire, and will refine them as silver is refined, and will try them as gold is tried; they shall call on my name, and I will answer them; I will say: "It is my people," and they shall say: "YHWH is my God."

The images of the smelter in Zech 11:13 and of the refined silver and gold in 13:9 are congruous. The possibility that 13:9 served as an *inclusio* to Zech 11:4–17 increases in light of the final words of 13:9: "I will say, 'It is my people,' and they shall say: 'YHWH is my God.'" The covenantal language serves as a response to the broken covenant of Zech 11:11. God will institute and ensure the right relationship with the people that the prophet and his community could not sustain. Although their covenant was broken and anarchy ensued, God restores the covenant with God's people.[36]

---

35 Bernhard Stade, "Deuterozacharja: Eine kritische Studie," *ZAW* 1 (1881): 1–96, here 29.

36 Postexilic biblical literature offers the theologically complex perspective of a covenant's re-adoption alongside the implicit termination of an earlier covenant. See, for example, two of the sources that influenced Zechariah, Jeremiah (30:22; 31:31, 33; 32:38) and Ezekiel (36:28). Saul Olyan has characterized this perspective as an "anti-rejectionist" position, and he lays emphasis on God's readopting the people, over and against the termination of an earlier covenant (Saul Olyan, "The Status of Covenant During the Exile," in *Berührungspunkte: Studien zur Sozial- und Religionsgeschichte Israels und seiner Umwelt: Festschrift für Rainer Albertz zu seinem 65. Geburtstag*, eds. Ingo Kottsieper, Rudiger Schmitt, and Jakob Wöhrle, AOAT 350 (Münster: Ugarit Verlag, 2008): 333–344, here 342–343. "Anti-rejectionist" aptly describes the redactor of Zech 9–14. This

7 Summary and Conclusion

This study of Zech 11 has employed intertexts from Nehemiah, Jeremiah and Isaiah to adduce connections between the oracle of the felled cedars in Zech 11:1–3 and the allegory of the shepherd that follows (11:4–17). Intertextually, the social critique of leadership in the oracle extends to the allegory. While commentators have posited various lines of relationship between the two parts of Zech 11, a unified reading of the chapter gains clarity and cogency in light of the intertexts.

The text in question, Zech 11, has intertextual relations with other biblical texts not included here. I have refrained from analyzing every intertext in order to make a focused argument about the role of Isa 10:33–34 as an intertext. The most important intertextual connection yet to be discussed is that which exists between Zech 11 and the oracles of Ezekiel. Zech 11:4–16 rearticulates material from Ezekiel (34:1–31 and 37:15–28) by taking the two sticks of Ezek 37 as the basis for the two staffs wielded by the shepherd of Zech 11. Whereas Ezekiel joins his two sticks to symbolize new unity between Judah and Joseph/Ephraim, Zechariah snaps the second staff just as he did the first, thereby breaking the fraternity (האחוה) between Judah and Israel (11:14). Following Ezekiel's fusing of the two sticks, the narrative continues to elaborate how God saved the people and set the shepherd David over them as king. In sharp contrast, Zechariah depicts the shepherd/leader as an abject failure. The passage in Ezek 37 concludes with a renewal of the divine-human relationship as God makes a "covenant of peace" with the people (37:23): they will be God's people and God will be their God. The covenantal language of Ezek 37:23 is echoed in Zech 13:9, the prophet's reference to his covenant which he made with all the people.

It is remarkable that Zech 11 enjoys intertextual connections with Isaiah, Jeremiah and Ezekiel. These major prophets are each associated with a prophetic corpus. As such, the three major prophets each have literary relations extending throughout the Book of the Twelve, the twelve so-called minor prophets. But it is uncommon, to say the least, that one of the Twelve, in this case Zechariah, would have substantial intertextual contact with all three, Isaiah, Jeremiah and Ezekiel, and in the same chapter at that. On these grounds Zech 11 qualifies not as the most enigmatic text, but as an exemplar of intertextuality.

---

biblical writer highlights the rejection of covenant as dramatized by the broken ברית in Zech 11:10 while casting the restoration of the covenant as a possibility in the future. Zech 13:9 points toward that future: "I will say: 'It is my people', and they shall say: 'YHWH is my God.'"

Bibliography

Bautch, Richard J., *Glory and Power, Ritual and Relationship: The Mosaic Covenant in the Postexilic Period* (LHBOTS 471; London/New York: T & T Clark, 2009).

Bautch, Richard J., "Intertextuality in the Persian Period," in *Approaching Yehud: New Approaches to the Study of the Persian Period,* ed. Jon L. Berquist (SemeiaSt 50; Atlanta: Society of Biblical Literature, 2007), 25–35.

Blenkinsopp, Joseph, *Essays on Judaism in the Pre-Hellenistic Period* (BZAW 495; Berlin: de Gruyter, 2017).

Boda, Mark J., *Exploring Zechariah,* vol. 1, *The Development of Zechariah and its Role within the Twelve* (ANEM 16; Atlanta: SBL Press, 2017).

Balogh, Csaba, "Inverted Fates and Inverted Texts. Rationales of Reinterpretation in the Compositional History of the Isaianic Prophecies, with Special Emphasis on Isaiah 10, 16–19 and Its Context," *ZAW* 128/1 (2016).

Carr, David M., "Criteria and Periodization in Dating Biblical Texts to Parts of the Persian Period," in *On Dating Biblical Texts to the Persian Period: Discerning Criteria and Establishing Epochs,* ed. Richard J. Bautch and Mark Lackowski (FAT II 101; Tübingen: Mohr Siebeck, 2019), 11–18.

Driver, Samuel Rolles, *The Minor Prophets* (Century Bible; Edinburgh: T. C. and E. J. Jack, 1906).

Floyd, Michael H., "Deutero-Zechariah and Types of Intertextuality," in *Bringing out the Treasure: Inner Biblical Allusion in Zechariah 9–14,* ed. Mark J. Boda and Michael H. Floyd (JSOTSup 370; London/New York: Sheffield, 2003), 225–244.

Gadot, Yuval/Lipschits, Oded/Oeming, Manfred, "Tieferes Verstehen. Erwägungen zur Epistemologie der Archäologie am Beispiel der Ausgrabung von Ramat Rahel (Jerusalem)," *Trumah* 18 (2008), 33–55.

Gray, George B., *The Book of Isaiah* (ICC; Edinburgh: T & T Clark, 1949).

Häusl, Maria, "Searching for Forces of Group Cohesion in the Books of Nehemiah and Isaiah," in *Ṣedaqa and Torah in Postexilic Discourse,* ed. Susanne Gillmayr-Bucher and Maria Häusl (LHBOTS 640; London/New York: Bloomsbury T & T Clark, 2017), 55–70.

Kessler, John, "Curse, Covenant and Temple in the Book of Haggai," in *Covenant in the Persian Period: From Genesis to Chronicles,* ed. Richard J. Bautch and Gary N. Knoppers (Winona Lake, IN: Eisenbrauns, 2015), 229–254.

Kessler, John, "Tradition, Continuity and Covenant in the Book of Haggai," in *Tradition in Transition: Haggai and Zechariah 1–8 in the Trajectory of Hebrew Theology,* ed. Mark J. Boda and Michael H. Floyd (LHBOTS 475; New York/London: T & T Clark, 2008), 1–39.

Lipschits, Oded/Gadot, Yuval/Arubas, Benjamin/Oeming, Manfred, "Palace and Village, Paradise and Oblivion: Unraveling the Riddles of Ramat Rahel," *NEA* 74/1 (2011), 2–49.

Lipschits, Oded/Gadot, Yuval/Arubas, Benjamin/Oeming, Manfred/Langgut, Dafna "The Riddle of Ramat Rahel: The Archaeology of a Royal Persian Period Edifice," *Trans* 41 (2012), 57–79.

Mason, Rex, *The Books of Haggai Zechariah and Malachi* (Cambridge: Cambridge University Press, 1977).

Mason, Rex, "The Use of Earlier Biblical Materials in Zechariah IX-XIV: A Study in Inner Biblical Exegesis" (Ph D diss., University of London, 1973).

Mason, Rex, "Zechariah 11:4–17," in *Bringing out the Treasure: Inner Biblical Allusion in Zechariah 9–14,* ed. Mark J. Boda and Michael H. Floyd (JSOTSup 370; London/New York: Sheffield, 2003), 93–116.

Mitchell, Christine, "A Paradeisos at Ramat Rahel and the Setting of Zechariah," *Trans* 48 (2016), 77–91.

Nielsen, Kirsten, *There is Hope for a Tree: The Tree as Metaphor in Isaiah* (JSOTSup 65; Sheffield: JSOT Press, 1989).

Nurmela, Risto, *Prophets in Dialogue: Inner-Biblical Allusions in Zechariah 1–8 and 9–14* (Åbo: Åbo Akademi University Press, 1996).

Olyan, Saul, "The Status of Covenant During the Exile," in *Berührungspunkte: Studien zur Sozial- und Religionsgeschichte Israels und seiner Umwelt: Festschrift für Rainer Albertz zu seinem 65. Geburtstag*, ed. Ingo Kottsieper, Rudiger Schmitt, and Jakob Wöhrle (AOAT 350; Munster: Ugarit Verlag, 2008), 333–344.

Person, Raymond F., *Second Zechariah and the Deuteronomic School* (JSOTSup 167; Sheffield: Sheffield Academic Press, 1993).

Petersen, David L., *Zechariah 9–14 and Malachi* (OTL; Louisville: Westminster John Knox, 1995).

Redditt, Paul L., *Zechariah 9–14* (IECOT; Stuttgart: Kohlhammer, 2012).

Redditt, Paul L., "Zechariah 9–14: The Capstone of the Book of the Twelve," in *Bringing out the Treasure: Inner Biblical Allusion in Zechariah 9–14*, ed. Mark J. Boda and Michael H. Floyd (JSOTSup 370; London/New York: Sheffield, 2003): 305–323.

Rossi, Benedetta, "Conflicting Patterns of Redaction: Jer 31, 33–34 and its Challenge to the Post-Mosaic Revelation Program," *Bib* 98/1 (2017), 202–225.

Schultz, Richard L., *The Search for Quotation: Verbal Parallels in the Prophets* (JSOTSup 180; Sheffield: Sheffield Academic Press, 1999).

Stade, Bernhard, "Deuterozacharja: Eine kritische Studie," *ZAW* 1 (1881), 1–96.

Tigchelaar, E. J. C., *Prophets of Old and the Day of the End: Zechariah, the Book of the Watchers and Apocalyptic* (OtSt 35; Leiden/New York/Cologne: Brill, 1996).

Wildberger, Hans, *Jesaja: Kapitel 1–12* (BKAT 10.1; Neukirchen-Vluyn: Neukirchener, 1972).

Williamson, H. G. M., *A Critical and Exegetical Commentary on Isaiah 1–27*, vol. 2, *Isaiah 6–12* (ICC; London/New York: Bloomsbury T & T Clark, 2018).

Zapff, Burkard M., "Second Isaiah and the Twelve," 77–95 (in this volume).

J. Todd Hibbard
Zechariah 14 and the final section of Isaiah

1 Introduction

Scholars have long noted that Zech 9–14, so-called Deutero-Zechariah, uses earlier texts and traditions at various points. In the last century, this feature of these chapters was noted and studied extensively by Sæbø,[1] Willi-Plein,[2] and Mason,[3] among others. Numerous scholars since then have taken up their work as starting points for examining this element of Zech 9–14.[4] Of particular interest in this study is Zech 14, the final chapter both in this section of Zechariah and of the book as a whole. Zech 14's use of other texts has been studied in detail by Schaefer, who identifies extensive allusions to other texts throughout the Hebrew Bible.[5] Of special importance are redactional allusions connected to earlier texts in Zechariah, but he and others argue that the chapter cites or alludes to other texts throughout the Hebrew Bible with regularity.[6] Such connections clearly position Zech 14 as an inner-Zecharian development. Additionally, Wöhrle has, importantly, shed light on the redactional connections between Zech 14 and other texts within the Book of the Twelve, though his redactional conclusions about the Book of the Twelve and Zechariah have not garnered universal assent.[7]

---

1 Magne Sæbø, *Sacharja 9–14: Untersuchungen von Text und Form*, WMANT 34 (Neukirchen–Vluyn: Neukirchener Verlag, 1969), 108–127; 282–309.
2 Ina Willi-Plein, *Prophetie am Ende: Untersuchungen zu Sacharja 9–14*, BBB 42 (Cologne: Peter Hanstein, 1974).
3 Rex Mason, "The Use of Earlier Biblical Material in Zechariah 9–14: A Study in Inner Biblical Exegesis" (Ph.D. diss., University of London, 1973); repr. in Mark J. Boda and Michael H. Floyd, eds., *Bringing out the Treasure: Inner Biblical Allusion in Zechariah 9–14*, JSOTSup 370 (Sheffield: Sheffield Academic Press, 2003): 3–208.
4 See the numerous essays in Boda and Floyd, *Bringing out the Treasure*.
5 Konrad R. Schaefer, O.S.B., "Zechariah 14: A Study in Allusion," *CBQ* 57 (1995): 66–91; see also, Konrad R. Schaefer, "The Ending of the Book of Zechariah: A Commentary," *RB* 100 (1993): 165–238 and "Zechariah 14 and the Composition of the Book of Zechariah," *RB* 100 (1993): 368–398.
6 In addition to Schaefer's studies, see Paul L. Redditt, *Zechariah 9–14*, IECOT (Stuttgart: W. Kohlhammer, 2012), 144–145; James D. Nogalski, "Zechariah" in *The Book of the Twelve: Micah–Malachi*, SHBC (Macon: Mercer University Press, 2011), 969–988.
7 Jakob Wöhrle, *Der Abschluss des Zwölfprophetenbuches*, BZAW 389 (Berlin: de Gruyter, 2008), esp. 112–138.

https://doi.org/10.1515/9783110705799-007

One trend in scholarship has been the focus on the relationship between Zech 14 and the later portion of Isaiah, especially Isa 66. Given that these are the two concluding chapters in their respective books, we might reasonably suspect that such a connection, if existent, bears more significance than others since conclusions often exhibit important signs of intentional theological and literary shaping.[8] Additionally, since Zech 14 occupies a place near the end of the Twelve, its addition along with any existing intertextual associations might also be significant to the collection as well.

In this paper, I intend to examine the evidence for Zech 14's invocation of Isa 66 as well as Isa 56:1–8 and 65:1–25, that is, the latest layer of Trito-Isaiah. Key questions will include how and why Zech 14 is associated with this material. Other issues will be dealt with along the way.

2 The latter portion of Isaiah (56:1–8; 65:1–66:24) in the book of Isaiah

Before we consider how that late sections of Trito-Isaiah and Zech 14 exhibit associations with each other, it is first necessary to understand the origin and function of each layer or chapter in its respective literary placement.[9] That is, I agree with Gärtner that we must first come to some understanding of how Isa 66 originated and functions in Isaiah and how Zech 14 originated and functions in Zechariah. Only then is it possible to address how they are related to each other. In the limited space of this modest study our reflections on this issue will necessarily be brief. With that in view, let us turn first to a consideration of the relevant portions in Isaiah.

Most scholars of Isa 56–66 argue that this final section of the book represents a composite development.[10] There is broad agreement that the earliest material

---

8 Additionally, several scholars think that Isa 2:2–4 has played a role in the composition of Zech 14:20–21 since both texts present the pilgrimage of the nations to Zion. See, among others, Nogalski, *Redactional Processes in the Book of the Twelve*, BZAW 218 (Berlin: de Gruyter, 1993), 241–242.
9 In this respect I agree with Gärtner, who makes a similar argument; Judith Gärtner, *Jesaja 66 und Sacharja 14 als Summe der Prophetie*, WMANT 114 (Neukirchen-Vluyn: Neukirchener Verlag, 2006), 5–7.
10 Though taking very different views of the section, both Goldingay and Blenkinsopp affirm this. See John Goldingay, *Isaiah 56–66*, ICC (London: Bloomsbury, 2014), 6–7; Joseph Blenkinsopp, *Isaiah 56–66*, AYB19B (New Haven: Yale University Press, 2003), 54–66. One should also consult the numerous works of Odil Hannes Steck on this question and his argument in favor

is to be found in chs. 60–62, with the latest material occurring in the outer texts: 56:1–8 and 65:1–66:24.[11] Additionally, 56:1–8 forms an inclusio with 66:15–24, strongly suggesting coordinated redaction.[12] Evidence has also been put forward that the first and last chapters of the book, especially its last section (66:18–24), have been shaped in light of each other.[13] Recently, Sweeney has documented the literary connections between Isa 1 and 65–66 that demonstrate their coordination.[14] Additionally, it is clear that Isa 1 and 66 have been shaped to serve as both introduction and conclusion to the book, whatever ch. 1's earlier shape and role might have been.[15] Beyond this, however, scholars disagree over the authorship of Isa 65–66, with some arguing in favor of single authorship while others see two or more layers.[16] I agree with the analysis of Stromberg, who concludes that chs. 65–66 represent a single composition. The two chapters present a twofold divine address, with 65:1–66:2 addressed to the wicked and 66:3–24 addressed to the righteous.[17] While Stromberg and others correctly note the role of the two chapters as a divine response to the lament in 63:7–64:11[12], the chapters also constitute the last words of the book, giving them additional importance.

Assigning dates to the material in Trito–Isaiah is a fool's errand in many respects. The text lacks historical allusions that permit one to anchor the text securely to any particular historical context. Nevertheless, broad agreement exists among scholars that the earliest core likely dates to early in the restoration period; beyond this one finds broad disagreement.[18] The greatest variation in propos-

---

of viewing the growth of the chapters as a process of *Fortschreibung*; see O. H. Steck, *Studien zu Tritojesaja*, BZAW 203 (Berlin: de Gruyter, 2001).

11 Most scholars think the material in 56:9–59:21 and 63:1–64:11 [12] represents redactional development in between the composition of the central and outer panels. For an overview of the section's redaction, see Jacob L. Stromberg, *Isaiah After Exile: The Author of Third Isaiah as Reader and Redactor of the Book* (Oxford: Oxford University Press, 2011), 40–67.

12 Blenkinsopp, *Isaiah 56–66*, 132.

13 See David M. Carr, "Reading Isaiah from Beginning (Isaiah 1) to End (Isaiah 65–66): Multiple Modern Possibilities," in *New Visions of Isaiah*, eds. Roy F. Melugin and Marvin A. Sweeney (Sheffield: Sheffield Academic Press, 1996): 188–218.

14 Marvin Sweeney, *Isaiah 40–66*, FOTL 19 (Grand Rapids: Eerdmans, 2016), 380–381. See also Shalom M. Paul, *Isaiah 40–66*, Eerdmans Critical Commentary (Grand Rapids: Eerdmans, 2012), 610. Sweeney also documents extensive intertextual connections between Isa 65–66 and the rest of the Isaianic corpus, especially chs. 1–39 (*Isaiah 40–66*, 381–4).

15 For Isa 1 as a redactional collection that re-configures earlier Isaianic oracles, see H. G. M. Williamson, *Isaiah 1–5*, ICC (London: Bloomsbury, 2006), 7–11.

16 For a consideration of the issue, see Stromberg, *Isaiah After Exile*, 42–67.

17 Stromberg documents the numerous uses of first person forms in the two chapters which underscores the fact that this is unmistakably a divine address; see *Isaiah After Exile*, 46.

18 On the problems of dating material in Isa 56–66, see Blenkinsopp, *Isaiah 56–66*, 42–54.

als revolves around the date assigned to the latest stages of the composition. For reasons that will not be explored here (principally because I do not wish to test the reader's patience), I will simply affirm what I find to be most likely: that Isa 56:1–8 and 65:1–66:24 probably originate around the time of the missions of Ezra and Nehemiah, (that is, ca. mid- to late-5th century).

3 Zechariah 14 in the book of Zechariah

Just as it is necessary to understand Isa 66's place within the book of Isaiah, it is equally necessary to understand Zech 14 within its literary home.[19] Given the composite nature of the book of Zechariah, we must address this question at multiple levels. First, as is well known, scholars recognize Zech 1–8 and 9–14 as fundamentally different compositions originating in different contexts. Zech 9–14 comprise two separate units, chs. 9–11 and chs. 12–14, each called a משא.[20] Zech 14 comprises the final section of the second משא. Hence, the relationship with chs. 12 and 13, as well as with chs. 9–11, must be addressed when considering the origin and function of the chapter. Second, the chapter comprises the final chapter in the book of Zechariah, which means its function as the book's finale must also be discussed. Finally, Zech 14's place in the Book of the Twelve should also be addressed, given its origin as one of the latest additions to the collection. Space does not permit a full consideration of each of these, so brief comments must suffice.

The addition of Zech 9–14 to Zech 1–8 (we might include Malachi in this addition as well) should be viewed analogous to the addition of Isa 56–66 to the existing book of Isaiah. Each addition constituted an effort to bring the prophetic message into a new period. The process was reflective of ongoing concerns to understand matters religious, historical, and social from within the literary and thought worlds created by those books. This is the reason it is necessary to under-

---

19 I agree with the argument put forward by, among others, Jakob Wöhrle that we must first understand the redaction development of each book within the Twelve before we can understand its development and place in the Twelve as a whole; Jakob Wöhrle, "So Many Cross-References! Methodological Reflections on the Problem of Intertextual Relationships and their Significance for Redaction Critical Analysis," in *Perspectives on the Formation of the Book of the Twelve: Methodological Foundations–Redactional Processes–Historical Insights*, eds. Rainer Albertz, James D. Nogalski, and Jakob Wöhrle (Berlin: de Gruyter, 2012): 3–20.
20 The beginning of Malachi is also labeled משא, suggesting a three-part sequence.

stand the composition of Zech 14 as an inner-Zecharian effort first (as articulated by Gärtner).

When we turn to Zech 12–14, we note that most scholarship on these chapters argues that the final משׂא of Zechariah developed in two stages. Chs. 12–13 envision Jerusalem's purge and YHWH's vindication of the city. The references to the house of David are conspicuous (12:7–13:1), suggesting that the chapters were composed at a time when people still expected the Davidic dynasty to be re-constituted. To this is added a strong denunciation of prophets, likely because of their complicity in the downfall of Jerusalem (13:2–6). The last section, 13:7–9, represents a transitional section that bridges chs. 12–13 and ch. 14. Hanson's view that Zech 14 represents "full-blown apocalyptic" refracted liturgically through the ancient pattern of the conflict myth has generally been abandoned.[21] Peterson describes it as a montage organized around the repeated "on that day" refrain, a more cautious but literarily likely perspective.[22]

The dates assigned to Zech 14 in scholarship range from the sixth century B.C.E. to third century B.C.E., and many points in between. Nogalski helpfully identifies three primary options for all of Zech 9–14: the late sixth century, the mid-fifth century, and the third century.[23] Again, for the sake of space I will not respond to the arguments favoring various dates. I note simply that I find a date in the mid- to late-5th century (that is, roughly contemporaneous with but slightly later than that for the end of Trito-Isaiah) or slightly later likely, for reasons that will be explored below.

4 Is Zechariah 14 dependent on Isaiah 66?

Steck, Bosshard, Bosshard and Kratz, Nogalski, and others have argued that Zech 14 reveals important connections with Isa 66.[24] This is especially the case with respect to Zech 14:16–21 and Isa 66:18–24, as noted by both Bosshard and Nogal-

---

21 Paul Hanson, *The Dawn of Apocalyptic* (Philadelphia: Fortress, 1975), 369–401.

22 David L. Petersen, *Zechariah 9–14 and Malachi*, OTL (Philadelphia: Westminster John Knox, 1993), 139.

23 Nogalski, *The Book of the Twelve: Micah–Malachi*, SHBC (Macon, GA: Smyth & Helwys, 2011), 808.

24 Erich Bosshard and Reinhard G. Kratz, "Maleachi im Zwölfprophetenbuch," *BN* 52 (1990): 27–46.

ski among others.[25] Their argument is based primarily on thematic and narrative similarities. For example, Bosshard noted that both texts present peoples/nations coming to Jerusalem to worship (Zech 14:16–17; Isa 66:23) and that both texts evidence a concern for sacred objects (Zech 14:20–21; Isa 66:20–21). Additionally, Nogalski has noted connections between Zech 14 and Isa 2:2–4 on the theme of the nations' coming to Jerusalem to worship, suggesting that the scribe of Zech 14 read both the beginning and end of Isaiah, an issue to which we will return below.[26] These connections all point to the same motif: "a purified, elevated Zion [that] will serve as salvation for all the world."[27] It is interesting, however, that most scholars see very little in the way of specific association based on shared vocabulary. This is the case with *most* of the connections that many scholars see between Zech 14 and Isa 66. So, along these lines, Steck has argued more broadly that in concluding the prophetic corpus, scribes intentionally included similar *ideas* at the conclusions of Isaiah and Zechariah as part of the process of creating an emerging canon.[28] For both Bosshard and Steck, Isaiah influenced the content of Zechariah such that the book adopted some of its themes and traditions, especially its particular eschatological view of the pilgrimage of the peoples to Jerusalem, but not necessarily its specific vocabulary.

More recently, Gärtner has noted not only similarities between the two but also important differences that affect both the conception of the two designs (i. e., Zech 14 and Isa 56:1–7,8/Isa 65–66) and their redactional processes.[29] She argues that the themes in the relevant Isaiah chapters are worked out primarily *within* the book of Isaiah. Among these are what she designates as the כבוד concept and the theme of the peoples.[30] While she sees these themes present in Zech 14, she notes that their appearance there differs from the latter passages in Trito-Isaiah. Despite the differences, however, she insists that each one attempts to describe the overall will of YHWH ("Gesamtwillen Jhwhs") as the summation of prophecy

---

25 Erich Bosshard, "Beobachtungen zum Zwölfprophetenbuch," *BN* 40 (1987): 30–62, here 31; James L. Nogalski, *Redactional Processes in the Book of the Twelve*, BZAW 218 (Berlin: de Gruyter, 1993), 242–247.
26 This Isaian passage appears in nearly duplicate form in Mic 4:1–3. Nogalski argues that the connection is likely with the Isaian version for two reasons: first, Zech 14 draws on other sections of Isaiah, but not Micah; second, the role of the horses in Zech 14:20–21 "make[s] sense when read against the threat in Isa 2:7" (*Ibid.*, 243).
27 *Ibid.*, 243. See also Bosshard and Kratz, "Maleachi" 44–45.
28 Odil Hannes Steck, *Der Abschluss der Prophetie im Alten Testament: Ein Versuch zur Frage der Vorgeschichte des Kanons*, BThSt 17 (Neukirchener–Vluyn: Neukirchener, 1991), 108.
29 Gärtner, *Jesaja 66 und Sacharja 14*, 329–331.
30 *Ibid.*, 329.

from within their respective traditions.[31] This comports with Steck's view that in terms of function, the end of the prophetic corpus reveals an essential unity of hermeneutical perspective — namely, to articulate an eschatological view in which YHWH reveals the salvation of the people of God.[32] Hence, it is quite likely that we are dealing with a similar redactional process affecting both Isaiah and the Book of the Twelve.[33] But the degree to which the former has influenced the latter remains far from certain in my view. As an alternative, it is possible that the texts bear witness to a complementary process whereby each sought to articulate similar ideas from within its own literary and theological traditions. This explains more adequately Zech 14's primary connection to the Book of Zechariah. That there may have been broad coordination on the part of the author of Zech 14 with concluding developments in the Isaiah tradition is possible, though if so, apparently this did not create specific *intertextual* connections. In my view, this is evidence against over-interpreting a putative connection between Zech 14 and the end of Isaiah.

Indeed, Zech 14's *literary* connections with Isaiah point more clearly to chapters 1–39. For example, Zech 14 contains seven occurrences of ביום ההוא, "on that day," (14:4,6,8,9,13,20,21).[34] This number hardly seems coincidental, especially since the phrase constitutes the last words of the chapter/book. As is generally well known, this phrase occurs over forty times in Isa 1–39. Second, Zech 14 uses the title יהוה צבאות in 14:16,17,21. To be sure, the title is found throughout Zechariah[35] but its importance in Isaiah, especially Isa 1–39, is unmistakable. Of equal importance is the fact that the title *never* occurs in Trito-Isaiah. Third, as noted above Zech 9–14 constitute two משא oracles (9:1; 12:1). This recalls the nine משאות of Isa 13–23 introducing the oracles against the nations.[36] Fourth, while the reference to plunder, שלל, in 14:1 links with Zech 2:8,9, it is also suggestive of the use

31 *Ibid.*, 331: "Sie wollen am Buchschluss den ›Gesamtwillen Jhwhs‹ festhalten und ziehen deswegen aus der ihnen jeweils vorliegenden Tradition die Summe."
32 Steck, *Der Abschluss der Prophetie*, 118–119.
33 Bosshard and Kratz ("Maleachi") have addressed how and where Malachi fits into this canonical development.
34 The phrase occurs elsewhere in Zechariah as well. See 3:10; 6:10; 9:16; 11:11; 12:3,4,6,8,9,11; 13:1,2,4. While the phrase does occur throughout the prophetic corpus, Isaiah and Zechariah contain the two largest concentrations of the phrase by a wide margin.
35 1:3,4,6,12,14,16,17; 2:12,13,15; 3:7,9,10; 4:6,9; 5:4; 6:12,15; 7:3,4,9,12,13; 8:1,2,3,4,6,7,9,11,14,18,19, 20,21,22,23; 9:15; 10:3; 12:5; 13:2,7. Meyers and Meyers call it a "hallmark of the Haggai-Zechariah-Malachi corpus"; see Carol L. Meyers and Eric M. Meyers, *Zechariah 9–14*, AYB25C (New Haven: Yale University Press, 1993), 466.
36 Of course, the title also stands at the beginning of Habakkuk (1:1) and Nahum (1:1); see also Isa 30:6 and Ezek 12:10.

of the same term as part of the symbolic child's name in Isa 8 (cf. Isa 9:3). Fifth, Zech 14:2 is nearly a quotation of Isa 13:16.[37] Sixth, Zech 14's emphasis on YHWH's kingship finds an analogue in Isa 1–39 (as well as 40–55), but not 56–66.[38] I do not mean to suggest that all of these literary features of Zech 14 come from Isa 1–39 nor that Zech 14 does not display associations with the end of Isaiah; rather, I only wish to draw attention to the fact that the chapter's literary evidence recalls the first part of the book more than the latter portion.[39] In light of the conclusions by Mason and Schaefer noted above, this should not be surprising.

5 Zechariah 14 and the end of Isaiah: scenes from late post-exilic prophecy

Given that the chapter fails to make many explicit literary references to Isa 66, how should we think about its connection to the chapter? Here I want to suggest that both Zech 14 and the beginning and end, that is, the last section of Isaiah's development, share similar thematic concerns. In this sense, I want to affirm the work of Steck, Bosshard, Gärtner, and Nogalski, among others, while also cautioning against over-reading the evidence. In the remainder of this paper, I wish to build on their conclusions to offer some observations about how and why these prophetic books end as they do by drawing attention to three shared themes: inclusion of the peoples in worship; glorification of Jerusalem; and YHWH's retribution on his enemies. We will conclude by examining a theme that is present in both texts, but of unequal importance to the two texts.

The first theme that I wish to draw attention to is the inclusion of the peoples in worship. As is generally well-known, a dispute about the place of foreigners in the worshiping community emerged in the Persian period. Two opposing views are recognizable in the extant literature.[40] The exclusivist position, which debarred foreigners from the YHWH cult in Jerusalem, can be found most readily in Ezra 9–10

---

37 See Mark J. Boda, *The Book of Zechariah*, NICOT (Grand Rapids: Eerdmans, 2016), 750–751.
38 Isa 6:5; 24:23; 33:22; see also 41:21; 43:15; 44:6; 45:1.
39 It is of some surprise to me that no connections are noted in the thorough study of the reception of Isa 1–39 in the Book of the Twelve by Bosshard-Nepustil (Erich Bosshard-Nepustil, *Rezeptionen von Jesaia 1–39 im Zwölfprpohetenbuch: Untersuchngen zur literarischen Verbindung von Prophetenbüchern in babylonischer und persischer Zeit*, OBO 154 [Göttingen: Vandenhoeck & Ruprecht, 1997]).
40 On this broader issue, see Dalit Rom-Shiloni, *Exclusive Inclusivity: Identity Conflicts between the Exiles and the People who Remained (6th-5th Centuries BCE)*, LHBOTS 543 (London: Bloomsbury, 2013).

and Neh 13:23–31.[41] This attitude apparently drew its inspiration from Deut 7:1–5, which prohibited intermarriage with the notorious seven nations, and Deut 23:3–6, which debarred Ammonites and Moabites from the community in perpetuity and Edomites and Egyptians to the third generation. Ezra and Nehemiah extended this to include all foreigners, a move that forms the intellectual backdrop for the mandatory divorce policy implemented by Ezra as well as Nehemiah's expulsion policy.

Against this, both Isaiah and Zechariah envision ways in which the nations may comprise part of the people of YHWH. Isa 56:3–8 announces that both eunuchs and foreigners "who attach themselves to YHWH" (הנלוה אל יהוה) have a place in the community. Later, Isa 66:18–23 speaks of foreigners transporting exiled Judeans back to the land (v. 20), but goes beyond this to note that all flesh (כל בשר) will worship (להשתחות) YHWH as part of Jerusalem's regular cultic activities (v. 23). Of an even more remarkable nature, v. 21 envisions foreigners serving as Levites.[42] These emphases in Trito-Isaiah are echoed near the beginning of the book as well, in Isa 2:2–4, where we read that the nations will come to Zion to learn torah and peace. When we turn to Zech 14 we see a similar emphasis at the end of the chapter on the nations coming to Jerusalem yearly (מדי שנה בשנה) to celebrate the festival of booths (vv. 16, 18, 19). Zech 14:16 specifies that the nations come to Jerusalem to worship YHWH (להשתחות) using the same terminology as we find in Isa 66:23, one of the few instances of shared terminology between the two texts. As noted earlier, Zech 14 constitutes the third portrayal of a pilgrimage of the nations in Zechariah; the first is found in 2:15 [2:11] where many nations "join themselves to YHWH" (נלוו) and the second occurs at the end of the book's first half (8:20–23), where the peoples come to seek YHWH. Hence, we see that both Isaiah and Zechariah develop this theme as part of discourses in their own respective books at both the beginning and the end. Thus, Nogalski's point that Isa 2 and 66 provide evidence of Isaiah's influence on Zechariah is possible,[43] but it is equally likely that Zechariah ends as it does as a development of the way the *first* part of the book began and ended (which might also be an imitation of Isaiah).

It is also likely, in my view, that Zechariah's emphasis on the nations celebrating *sukkot* develops in light of the celebration of this festival as portrayed in Nehemiah (cf. Ezra 3:4). Neh 8:14–17 depicts the *golah* community discovering the instructions about the festival of *sukkot* in the law of Moses, after which

---

41 See Joseph Blenkinsopp, *Ezra-Nehemiah*, OTL (Louisville: Westminster John Knox, 1988), 173–201, 361–366. For a broader and more comprehensive discussion of these issues see Dalit Rom-Shiloni, Exclusive Inclusivity: Identity Conflicts between the Exiles and the People Who Remained (6th–5th Centuries BCE), LHBOTS 543 (London: Bloomsbury, 2015).
42 The meaning of this verse is highly debated. See Stromberg, *Isaiah After Exile*, 135–141.
43 Nogalski, *Redactional Processes*, 242.

they build the necessary huts to celebrate the festival. Neh 8:17 notes that those who celebrated were כל הקהל השבים מן השבי, "all the assembly of those who had returned from captivity." This implies that foreigners were not among the celebrants. It seems quite reasonable to see Zech 14's inclusion of the nations as a reaction against this restrictive view in Nehemiah. Additionally, the connection between *sukkot* and Yhwh's kingship provides a setting for the nations' acclamation of Yhwh's sovereignty.[44]

At this point we must note a significant difference between the last section of Isaiah and Zech 14 with respect to the nations. As just noted in Zech 14, they are included (coerced?) as part of the worshiping community, but not before Yhwh has gathered them to fight against Jerusalem (14:2,11). Zech 14 outlines a narrative scenario in which the nations attack Jerusalem,[45] only to have Yhwh arise to inflict a great defeat on these nations (14:3,12–15). Scholars disagree over whether the attack portrayed in v. 2 should be viewed as an event in the past or the future.[46] This need not detain us at the present; I draw this to our attention for two reasons. First, those from among the nations who come to Jerusalem to worship Yhwh are said to be the survivors of Yhwh's attack (14:16). Hence, their worship is not entirely voluntary. Additionally, given the threat that Yhwh will withhold rainfall (גשם) from those who fail to worship him — or in the case of Egypt, to inflict plague (מגפה) — it is not entirely incorrect to see this is a type of coerced obeisance.

This note of coercion appears to be lacking in the depiction of the nations' worshiping Yhwh in Isa 66 (and 2:2–4). This is related to the second shared theme: the identity of those who are the objects of Yhwh's ire in the two texts. Isa 65–66 describe Yhwh dealing retribution on his enemies, a theme shared with Zech 14, but the identity of these enemies differs in important ways. In Isa 65 and 66:6,14–16,24, the recipients of Yhwh's retribution are members of the Judean community. For example, in Isa 66:6, Yhwh's voice is heard dealing retribution on his enemies, but those enemies must be identified with those who hate those who tremble at the word of Yhwh (66:5).[47] This comports with the emphasis on the division within the community that characterizes Isa 65–66 between the righteous and the wicked.[48] These categories are generally mapped onto the internal

---

44 The question of whether Zech 14's emphasis on *sukkot* should be linked with its assertion of Yhwh's kingship (14:8; see below) as part of Mowinckel's highly questionable reconstruction of the New Year's celebration remains doubtful. See Boda, *Zechariah*, 777–778.

45 Verse 11 describes Jerusalem as subject to חרם, the ban (see Isa 43:28; Mal 3:24[4:6]).

46 Petersen, *Zechariah 9–14 and Malachi*, 139 argues that it refers to a future attack while Meyers and Meyers, *Zechariah 9–14*, 411 see it as both, with the emphasis on the past.

47 See Blenkinsopp, *Isaiah 56–66*, 296–297.

48 See Brooks Schramm, *The Opponents of Third Isaiah: Reconstructing the Cultic History of the Restoration*, LHBOTS 193 (London: Bloomsbury, 1995).

life of the Judean community. The situation is quite different in Zech 14, where the Jewish community is depicted as a unity. Its enemies are from without, not within. While the two texts are broadly similar, the relationship between YHWH and the nations registers differently in Zech 14. For example, as I noted earlier, in vv. 12–15, YHWH sends a plague (מגפה) upon the nations that attack Jerusalem, causing the rot of flesh, eyes and tongues. A few verses later, we read that YHWH will withhold rainfall from the nations failing to worship him (v. 17). Egypt is singled out for special threats (vv. 17–19). While Isa 66:16 does envision YHWH's sword executing judgment on "all flesh," this universal threat seems almost like a stereotypical afterthought in the larger context where "all flesh" come to worship YHWH (66:23).

A third shared theme appears in both texts' concern for the glorification of Jerusalem. Given that the book of Isaiah's most consistent theme is the status and welfare of Jerusalem, this comes as little surprise for Isaiah. Rather, it is the way in which the latter portion of Isaiah states this theme that is of interest here. Isa 65:18–20 describes Jerusalem's restoration using new creation language and 66:7–13 features maternal birthing imagery. Both texts reflect expectations about Jerusalem's future, suggesting the city's restoration has been incomplete at the point of writing. Zech 14's presentation of Jerusalem's glorification sounds some of the same notes, though important differences also exist. For example, as mentioned earlier, the beginning of the chapter envisions the nations gathering for attack against the city. Acting as divine warrior, YHWH delivers the city in dramatic fashion (see also 66:15–16). Accompanying this deliverance are cosmic and terrestrial acts meant to highlight Jerusalem's prestige: the Mount of Olives splits in two and waters from east and west flow out of Jerusalem and the city is elevated above the rest of landscape (14:8,10). Verse 11 looks forward to the city's habitation and security, suggesting that at the moment of writing both of those elements are lacking. Hence, Isaiah and Zechariah look forward to Jerusalem's ultimate restoration, though each depicts that restoration in its own idiom.[49]

Finally, I note one additional shared theme, YHWH's kingship. To be sure, YHWH's role as king receives more emphasis in Zech 14; but it is also noted, if somewhat in passing, in Isa 66 as well. In Zech 14, the first assertion of this claim occurs in the central panel of the chapter: "And YHWH will be king over the whole land; on that day YHWH will be one and his name one" (14:9). The second half

---

49 Both are usually referred to as eschatological portrayals, however, in my view, this term does not represent the proper category. Biblical scholars have, generally, regarded future expectations in late prophecy as eschatological, but the rationale for this seems to be lacking. Eschatology designates a specific notion about "the end" that these texts do not possess. Rather, these are future expectations.

of the verse alludes to the *Shema* (Deut 6:4–9) and the result is a connection between Yhwh's unity and kingship never made in Deuteronomy.[50] Later, vv. 16–17 emphasize Yhwh's kingship over the survivors from the nations defeated by Yhwh earlier.[51] These texts establish that Yhwh's divine kingship serves as an important theme in this final chapter of Zechariah, undoubtedly as a way of asserting divine sovereignty over the nations in a context also devoid of an actual Judean monarch. By contrast, Isa 66:1 gestures toward Yhwh's divine rule, but that is not the primary emphasis of the passage: "Thus says Yhwh: Heaven is my throne and the earth is my footstool; where[52] is the house you would build for me and where is my resting place?" The language in the first part of the verse obviously draws on monarchic imagery (throne, footstool) but as the second half of the verse and the next several make clear, the context is primarily concerned with questions about worship in the Jerusalem temple. Beyond its appearance in 66:1, the theme does not explicitly occur in the latter portions of Isaiah. Hence, we may note that while Yhwh's kingship does appear here, it is secondary to issues stemming from the proper definition and conduct of the worshiping community. Zech 14, on the other hand, imagines a different set of issues in which Yhwh as conquering king is front and center. Yhwh subdues and defeats the nations, which easily leads to the assertion of his royal control over them. Hence, Zech 14 foregrounds Yhwh's royal portrayal, an image present but not emphasized in the latter portions of Isaiah.[53]

6 Conclusion

We return, then, to where we began, with the question of the association of the final part of Isaiah, here defined as Isa 56:1–8 and 65:1–66:24, with Zech 14. Our analysis has shown that similar concerns guided the development of these

---

50 See Nathan MacDonald, "The Beginnings of Oneness Theology in Late Israelite Prophetic Literature," in *Monotheism in Late Prophetic and Early Apocalyptic Literature*, eds. Nathan MacDonald and Kevin Brown, FAT II/72 (Tübingen: Mohr Siebeck, 2014): 103–123, esp. 119–122.
51 The phrase מלך יהוה צבאות, "King, Yhwh of hosts," is unique to this passage.
52 On translating אי זה in 66:1, see Stromberg, *Isaiah After Exile*, 18–19.
53 Yhwh's kingship is prominent in Isa 24–27 (e. g., Isa 24:23), a section of Isaiah the dates of which are highly contested. If one assigns a late date to this material, it would provide an analogue to Zech 14 on this matter that would have arisen in a context that is closer chronologically. For two contrasting views on the issue in Isa 24–27, see William D. Barker, *Isaiah's Kingship Polemic*, FAT II/70 (Tübingen: Mohr Siebeck, 2014), esp. 208–218; and J. Todd Hibbard, *Intertextuality in Isaiah 24–27*, FAT II/16 (Tübingen: Mohr Siebeck, 2006), 70–91.

respective materials. In particular, we have drawn attention to each text's interest in developing notions of the nations' participation in the worship of YHWH, of YHWH's retribution on his enemies, of Jerusalem's glorification, and, of a more minor nature, YHWH's kingship. In this sense, the finales of Isaiah and Zechariah share similar interests.[54] However, as we also demonstrated, the particular manner in which each text develops those themes differs in important ways. The question, then, is: does Zech 14's development of these themes suggest the influence of late Isaiah? My answer here is: Yes and no. It is entirely possible that Zech 14 identified these themes as coming from Isaiah (among others) but in my view, the particular way in which Zech 14 develops them suggests little influence from Isaiah

Bibliography

Barker, William D., *Isaiah's Kingship Polemic*, FAT II/70 (Tübingen: Mohr Siebeck, 2014).

Blenkinsopp, Joseph, *Ezra-Nehemiah*, OTL (Louisville: Westminster John Knox, 1987).

Blenkinsopp, Joseph, *Isaiah 56–66*, AYBC19B (New Haven, CT: Yale University Press, 2003).

Boda, Mark J., *The Book of Zechariah*, NICOT (Grand Rapids: Eerdmans, 2016).

Boda, Mark J./Floyd, Michael H., eds., *Bringing Out the Treasure: Inner-Biblical Allusion in Zechariah 9–14*, JSOTSup 370 (Sheffield: Sheffield Academic Press, 2003).

Bosshard, Erich, "Beobachtungen zum Zwölfprophetenbuch," *BN* 40 (1987): 30–62.

Bosshard–Nepustil, Erich, *Rezeptionen von Jesaja 1–39 im Zwölfprophetenbuch: Untersuchungen zur literarischen Verbindung von Prophetenbüchern in babylonischer und persischer Zeit*, OBO 154 (Freiburg: Universitätsverlag, 1997).

Floyd, Michael, "Deutero-Zechariah and Types of Intertextuality," in *Bringing Out the Treasure: Inner Biblical Allusion in Zechariah 9–14*, eds. Mark J. Boda and Michael H. Floyd, JSOTSup 370 (Sheffield: Sheffield Academic Press, 2003): 225–244.

Floyd, Michael, *Minor Prophets, Part 2*, FOTL XXII (Grand Rapids: Eerdmans, 2000).

Goldingay, John, *Isaiah 56–66*, ICC (London: Bloomsbury, 2014).

Hanson, Paul, *The Dawn of Apocalyptic* (Philadelphia: Fortress, 1975).

---

54 An apparent shared concern with matters of cultic purity and disposition also appears in both Isa 65–66 and Zech 14. Isa 65:3–7,11; 66:3,17 rail against cultic improprieties of various sorts while Isa 66:20 associates the nations who transport exiles back to Jerusalem with ritual purity. Scholars have drawn attention to the latter as an especially important for understanding Zech 14:20–21, which speaks horses with bells (?) inscribed "holy to YHWH" and clean cooking pots (סירות). While the general language about ritual purity occurs in both, the specific language differs. More importantly, the point of each set of texts seems hardly the same. This makes it hard to imagine that Zech 14's portrayal derives from Isa 66.

Harrelson, Walter, "The Celebration of the Feast of Booths according to Zech xiv 16–21," in *Religions in Antiquity: Essays in Memory of E. R. Goodenough*, ed. J. Neusner, SHR (Leiden: Brill, 1968): 88–96.

Hibbard, J. Todd, *Intertextuality in Isaiah 24–27*, FAT II/16 (Tübingen: Mohr Siebeck, 2006).

Jeremias, Jörg, *Theophanie*, WMANT 10 (Neukirchen-Vlyn: Neukirchner, 1965).

Mason, Rex, "The Use of Earlier Biblical Material in Zechariah 9–14: A Study in Inner Biblical Exegesis" (Ph.D. diss., University of London, 1973).

Meyers, Carol L. and Eric M. Meyers, *Zechariah 9–14*, AYBC25C (New York: Doubleday, 1993).

Nogalski, James D., *The Book of the Twelve: Micah–Malachi*, SHBC (Macon, GA: Mercer University Press, 2011).

Nogalski, James D., *Redactional Processes in the Book of the Twelve*, BZAW 217 (Berlin: de Gruyter, 1993).

Petersen, David L., *Zechariah 9–14 and Malachi*, OTL (Louisville: Westminster John Knox, 1993).

Nurmela, Risto, "The Growth of the Book of Isaiah Illustrated by Allusions in Zechariah," in *Bringing Out the Treasure: Inner Biblical Allusion in Zechariah 9–14*, eds. Mark J. Boda and Michael H. Floyd, JSOTSup 370 (Sheffield: Sheffield Academic Press, 2003): 245–259 [sees one connection b/w Zech 14 and Isaiah: Zech 14:12,16 and Isa 66:23,24; sees Isaiah as dependent on Zechariah.]

Reddit, Paul L, *Zechariah 9–14*, IECOT (Stuttgart: W. Kohlhammer, 2014).

Rudolph, Wilhelm, *Haggai, Sacharja 1–8, Sacharja 9–14, Maleachi*, KAT XIII/4 (Gütersloh: Gütersloher Verlagshaus Mohn, 1976).

Schaefer, Konrad R., O.S.B., "The Ending of the Book of Zechariah: A Commentary," *RB* 100 (1993): 165–238.

Schaefer, Konrad R., "Zechariah 14: A Study in Allusion," *CBQ* 57 (1995): 66–91.

Schaefer, Konrad R., "Zechariah 14 and the Composition of the Book of Zechariah," *RB* 100 (1993): 368–398.

Steck, Odil Hannes, *Studien zu Trito-Jesaja* (Berlin: de Gruyter, 1991).

Steck, Odil Hannes, *Der Abschluss der Prophetie im Alten Testament: Ein Versuch zur Frage der Vorgeschichte des Kanons*, BThSt 17 (Neukirchener–Vluyn: Neukirchener, 1991)

Stromberg, Jacob, *Isaiah After Exile: The Author of Third Isaiah as Reader and Redactor of the Book*, Oxford Theological Monographs (Oxford: Oxford University Press, 2011).

Tiemeyer, Lena-Sophia, *Priestly Rites and Prophetic Rage: Post-Exilic Prophetic Critique of the Priesthood*, FAT II/19 (Tübingen: Mohr Siebeck, 2006).

Williamson, H. G. M, *Isaiah 1–5*, ICC (London: Bloomsbury, 2006).

Wöhle, Jakob, *Der Abschluss des Zwölfprophetenbuches: Entstehung und Komposition*, BZAW 360 (Berlin: de Gruyter, 2006).

Wolters, Al, *Zechariah*, Historical Commentary on the Old Testament (Leuven: Peeters, 2014).

Christopher B. Hays

Isa 24–27 and Zephaniah Amid the Terrors and Hopes of the Seventh Century: An Intertextual Analysis

The late seventh century B.C.E. was a political and theological maelstrom for Judah. The enormous Assyrian empire, which had flooded over the land on its way to conquering Egypt and the "four corners of the earth," began to crumble from within, and the world was changing rapidly. As at other moments of social and political turmoil, Hebrew prophets played a role in these events. This is widely recognized in the cases of Jeremiah and Zephaniah. But within the book of Isaiah, the formation of which spans from the eighth century to at least the fifth, there is another Josianic prophetic text: Isa 24–27. Its historical setting can be recognized, among other ways, by its striking resemblances to Zephaniah.

My new book, *The Origins of Isaiah 24–27: Josiah's Festival Scroll for the Fall of Assyria*, unpacks and retells the story of Isa 24–27 in its seventh-century context.[1] In the present essay, a brief summary of the book's arguments sets the stage for the exposition of the extensive intertextual connections between the two books. This analysis confirms and fleshes out the occasional passing observations of the similarity between the two books, leading to a consideration of the scribal realities and ideologies underlying the texts' production.

1 Isa 24–27 as a Josianic text

When Josiah was handed the kingship in an uprising in 640, Judah was firmly in the hands of Assyria. Within living memory, Assyria had devastated Judah, inflicting extensive destruction at many sites, and imposing an imperial administration that benefited a few while frustrating many. Taxation was heavy, which may have caused the unrest that elevated Josiah. A couple of decades later, things looked very different. Threats from Babylonia and Media cost Assyria its ability to administer its outlying territories. Judah felt itself restored from a state of death. Josiah propagated an exclusivist and somewhat radical law collection that called

---

1 Christopher B. Hays, *The Origins of Isaiah 24–27: Josiah's Festival Scroll for the Fall of Assyria*. (Cambridge: Cambridge University Press, 2019). Excerpts that have been incorporated into the present essay are reprinted with permission.

https://doi.org/10.1515/9783110705799-008

for faithfulness to Yahweh alone, with all the people's heart, soul and might (Deut 6:4–5) — which would have had the effect of centralizing more power and authority in Jerusalem. It was a moment of ascendant Judahite nationalism and heated rhetoric.

Isaiah 24–27 begins with a scene of widespread destruction of the land:

> The land mourns and withers,
>   the earth suffers and withers;
>   the heights suffer with the land.
> The land is polluted under its inhabitants,
>   for they have transgressed teachings (תורת),
> swept aside statute (חק),
>   broken the ancient covenant (ברית).

This claim is entirely consistent with what is known about Josiah's ideology. Josiah is said to have torn his garments "because our ancestors did not obey the words" of the "scroll of the *torah*" (2Kgs 22:11–13). Each of the three Hebrew terms above is pervasive in Deuteronomy. *Torah* and *berit* are specifically mentioned in connection with Josiah's religious reforms in 2Kgs 23.

In earlier scholarship, Isa 24–27 was often described as an apocalypse. However, it has scarcely any of the characteristic features of that Hellenistic genre, and this has been generally recognized in recent years.[2] Instead, it shares many elements of ancient Near Eastern royal propaganda: The failure (esp. in Isa 24) of the natural order in earthquakes, darkening of the heavenly lights, and failure of water sources and agricultural fertility were all used by ancient kings to characterize the awful state of the land before their reigns. Such propagandistic claims are consistently attested from Mesopotamia, Egypt, and even the Levant from early periods. When stripped of their historical context through redaction, however, such texts could easily be dehistoricized and appear "apocalyptic." This process has been empirically demonstrated with the Potter's Oracle.[3]

---

2 Christopher B. Hays, "From Propaganda to Apocalypse: An Empirical Model for the Formation of Isaiah 24–27," *Hebrew Bible and Ancient Israel* 6 (2017): 120–144.
3 Hays, "From Propaganda to Apocalypse," 141–144; J. Z. Smith, "Wisdom and Apocalyptic," in *Map Is Not Territory* (repr. ed.; Chicago: University of Chicago Press, 1993): 80; J. J. Collins, "The Sibyl and the Potter: Political Propaganda in Ptolemaic Egypt," in *Religious Propaganda and Missionary Competition in the New Testament World: Essays Honoring Dieter Georgi*, ed. L. Bormann, K. D. Tredici, and A. Standhartinger (Leiden: Brill, 1994): 63.

The subsequent scene of feasting on Zion in Isa 25:6–8 reflects a characteristic act of a victorious (or simply successful) ruler.[4] Like a human ruler who won a war, YHWH is given credit for the downfall of the Assyrians and the deliverance of the land and people. The feast thus expresses a will to power on the part of its authors, whether or not they really wielded it. It was an ambitious attempt to shape reality.

The references to the defeat of death and the dead rising in 25:8 and 26:19 are not, as has often been said, late texts reflecting Hellenistic beliefs about resurrection. Rather, they take part in ancient Near Eastern literary/theological traditions that extend back into the Bronze Age, in which political deliverance is described as salvation from a state of death. Both gods and human kings were regularly said to have raised the dead. This motif appears repeatedly in Hittite and Egyptian texts from the Late Bronze Age, among others, and extends into numerous letters to Neo-Assyrian kings, and into preexilic biblical texts (e. g., Hos 6:1–3). In Isa 24–27, the theme of revivification reflects a belief that YHWH had saved his people from imperial oppression.

One of the most important images in Isa 24–27 is that of the once-lofty city that had fallen (24:10–12; 25:2; 26:5; 27:10). The ongoing challenge of identifying the city has largely thwarted historical interpretation of the pericope. On the basis of recent archaeological publications, my book argues that the city in question was the Assyrian citadel at Ramat Rahel, built on a lofty hill near Jerusalem, and a site of imperial splendor and power that would naturally have been resented by the Judahites. The author pointed to the desertion of that city by the retreating Assyrians as a symbol of the possibility of a new political order.

In Isa 27, YHWH invites Jacob/Israel to "make peace with me," and it has previously been recognized that this is a Josianic overture to the territory of the former northern kingdom to reunite itself with Judah.[5] There is no evidence that Josiah ever achieved anything of the sort (and indeed his failure to do so offers one pos-

---

4 Hays, *The Origins of Isaiah 24–27*, chapter 2; Jacob L. Wright, "Commensal Politics in Ancient Western Asia: The Background to Nehemiah's Feasting," *ZAW* 122 (2010): 212–233, 333–352; Peter Altmann, *Festive Meals in Ancient Israel: Deuteronomy's Identity Politics in Their Ancient Near Eastern Context*, BZAW 424 (Berlin: de Gruyter, 2011); Andrew T. Abernethy, *Eating in Isaiah: Approaching the Role of Food and Drink in Isaiah's Structure and Message*, BibInt Series 131 (Leiden: Brill, 2014).
5 Marvin A, Sweeney, *King Josiah of Judah: The Lost Messiah of Israel* (Oxford: Oxford University Press, 2001), 247–48, 327–29; and see the review of scholarship in the introduction to Christopher B. Hays, *The Origins of Isaiah 24–27: Josiah's Festival Scroll for the Fall of Assyria* (Cambridge: Cambridge University Press, 2019 (pp.) 1–9.).

sible reason that he no longer appears in the text[6]), but there are numerous indications that he was interested in doing so—in 2 Kings, Zephaniah, and Jeremiah. It has even been argued that much of Isa 24–27 was written in a northern dialect of Hebrew that was intended both to reach out to northerners and to model what their response to YHWH's invitation might sound like.[7]

Isaiah 24–27 also does not show any meaningful frequency of Late Biblical Hebrew features. Its Hebrew is no less classical than other prophetic texts that are generally thought to be preexilic, such as Isa 3–6 and Amos. By contrast, prophetic texts that are generally agreed to be postexilic on other grounds, such as Isa 40–66, Malachi, and Haggai, all show rates of LBH features that are multiple times as high. The use of Hebrew diachrony to date texts remains experimental, but it has value when correlated with other data.[8]

All of these observations provide impetus to reconsider the date of Isa 24–27.

2 Isaiah 24–27 and Zephaniah in intertextual perspective

Increasingly in recent years, intertextual analyses of Isa 24–27 have been the only substantive rationales given for dating the book to a late period. In short, it is generally argued that the book had numerous intertextual connections with a wide variety of biblical texts, and that this must be because the author was working near the end of the biblical period and had access to a wide range of texts. Some of these studies have advanced new theories about the book's overall formation,[9] while others have built on preceding views or simply not pursued diachronic redactional questions.[10]

---

6 It is not the only possible reason. Notably, there is no mention of Josiah in Deuteronomy, either, and he appears in Zephaniah only in the editorial superscription.

7 Scott B. Noegel, "Dialect and Politics in Isaiah 24–27," *AuOr* 12 (1994): 177–192.

8 While the analysis of Hebrew diachrony within the Bible remains a controversial topic, the LBH features in the prophetic texts have most often been identified initially in postexilic prose texts, so that the process is not circular.

9 Marvin A. Sweeney, "Textual Citations in Isaiah 24–27: Toward an Understanding of the Redactional Function of Chapters 24–27 in the Book of Isaiah," *JBL* 107 (1988): 39–52; H. G. M. Williamson, *The Book Called Isaiah: Deutero-Isaiah's Role in Composition and Redaction* (Oxford: Oxford University Press, 1994), 156–183; Reinhard Scholl, *Die Elenden in Gottes Thronrat. Stilistisch-kompositorische Untersuchungen zu Jesaja 24–27*, BZAW 274 (Berlin: de Gruyter, 2000).

10 Donald C. Polaski, *Authorizing an End: The Isaiah Apocalypse and Intertextuality*, BibInt 50 (Leiden: Brill, 2001); J. Todd Hibbard, *Intertextuality in Isaiah 24–27: The Reuse and Evocation of*

The intertextual "landscape" of Isa 24–27, however, does not support a late date in any clear way. In the first place, Josiah's reign is widely agreed to be one of the greatest periods of literary ferment in the formation of the Hebrew Bible. No less important is the fact that the intertextual allusions themselves are consonant with the period and interests described above: Some of the most significant allusions are to oracles that are taken from prophetic books such as Hosea and Amos that originated in the eighth century and against the Northern Kingdom or Assyria.[11] Proto-Isaianic traditions from the same period are also significant in Isa 24–27. Where it has intertextual connections with Jeremiah, the latter may be contemporaneous or dependent upon Isaiah, since the book of Jeremiah was demonstrably much more textually fluid in a later period than Isaiah.

In the case of Zephaniah, the intertextual connections are overwhelming. Indeed, the relationship between Zephaniah and proto-Isaiah has not gone unremarked. Robert Wilson pointed out that "scholars have long noted Zephaniah's affinities with Jerusalemite prophetic and cultic traditions."

He went on: "At points the theology of Zephaniah resembles that of Isaiah, and in particular Zephaniah's ideas about the Day of Yahweh (Zeph 1:7–2:3) develop those found in Amos, Isaiah, and Micah. The vocabulary of Zephaniah has roots within the Jerusalemite tradition, and in his words there are echoes of Judean prophets such as Isaiah and Amos."[12]

Kent Richards observed that Zephaniah seems to have been aware of the prophetic traditions condemning injustice in Judah, and added, "some have suggested that Zephaniah may have been a disciple of Isaiah."[13]

Later, in Wilson's *Festschrift*, John Ahn reported a conversation with Wilson about echoes of Isaiah in Zephaniah; the senior scholar had said that he expected there were "more similarities between the two than what's currently available."[14] Noting that the topic had never been fully investigated, Ahn took up Wilson's

---

Earlier Texts and Traditions, FAT II/16 (Tübingen: Mohr Siebeck, 2006). See also Hibbard, "Isaiah 24–27 and Trito-Isaiah: Exploring Some Connections," in *Formation and Intertextuality in Isaiah 24–27*, ed. J. T. Hibbard and H. C. P. Kim (Atlanta: Society of Biblical Literature, 2013): 183–199.

11 See esp. John Day, "The Dependence of Isaiah 26:13–27:11 on Hosea 13:4–14:10 and Its Relevance to Some Theories of the Redaction of the 'Isaiah Apocalypse'," in *Writing and Reading the Scroll of Isaiah*, ed. Craig C. Broyles and Craig A. Evans (Leiden: Brill, 1997): 357–368.

12 Robert Wilson, *Prophecy and Society in Ancient Israel* (Philadelphia: Fortress, 1984), 280.

13 Kent Harold Richards, "Zephaniah," in *The HarperCollins Study Bible: Fully Revised and Updated*, ed. Harold W. Attridge (New York: HarperCollins, 1993): 1402.

14 John Ahn, "Zephaniah, a Disciple of Isaiah?" in *Thus Says the Lord: Essays on the Former and Latter Prophets in Honor of Robert R. Wilson* (New York/London: T & T Clark, 2009): 293.

comment about the "day of Yahweh,"[15] and added material on the "outstretched arm" motif, which is prominent in both First Isaiah and Zephaniah.[16]

Ahn begins by stating that "Zephaniah may have been the redactor (for at least some portions of Isa 5–11) or ... the editor(s) who worked on Isa 5–11 (12) was/were also responsible for editing or linking this seminal section [Zeph 2:13] to the core of Zephaniah that condemns Assyria."[17] He quickly escalates to simply calling Zephaniah "the editor of First Isaiah,"[18] and he closes with a flourish: "So, is Zephaniah a disciple of Isaiah (cf. Isa 8.16)? I would be surprised if he wasn't."[19]

Rather than calling Zephaniah a "disciple," it might be better to return to a formulation closer to Wilson's, namely that Zephaniah may have been an Isaianic *tradent*—one who considered himself to be carrying on the Isaianic tradition.[20] Nevertheless, the aforementioned observations capture the sense that there is some relationship between the two.

In light of the pervasive similarities and intertextual connection between the book of Zephaniah and Isa 24–27, the lack of coordination between the study of the two is quite remarkable. The intertextual connections are scarcely noted in major studies of either.[21] Even Adele Berlin, who promises an intertextual approach to

---

15 The phrase "on that day" occurs in Zeph 1:9–10; 3:11,16; and 34 times in Isa 2–31, not counting the occurrence in 22:8, which is to a past day rather than a future one. The specific phrase "day of the Lord" occurs in Isa 13:6,9 and Zeph 1:7,14.

16 Isa 5:25; 9:12,17,21; 10:4; 14:26–27; 23:11; 31:3; Zeph 1:4; 2:13.

17 Ahn, "Zephaniah," 297.

18 *Ibid.*, 298.

19 *Ibid.*, 307.

20 "Disciple" can mean various things, but Ahn's reference to Isa 8:16 is at risk of being understood to mean that the two were contemporaries. I do not think Ahn himself meant this, and it is scarcely possible. There are no prophecies of Isaiah ben Amoz that can be firmly dated to the seventh century, while the superscription of Zephaniah suggests that he was four generations removed from the time of Hezekiah, and did not appear until the reign of Josiah, which began in 640. So the careers of the two prophets were separated by more than half a century, and perhaps as much as 70 years, and it is almost certainly not possible to consider Zephaniah a disciple of Isaiah in any direct sense.

21 Zephaniah is relegated almost entirely to passing footnotes by Hibbard. Polaski considers certain shared themes such as YHWH's discipline (מוסר; *Authorizing an End*, 272–275) and the reproach (חרפה; *Authorizing an End*, 188–192) of the peoples but does not report on the more numerous connections. Some of these same themes are noted briefly by the authors in *Formation and Intertextuality*. E. g., Carol Dempsey, "Words of Woe, Visions of Grandeur: A Literary and Hermeneutical Study of Isaiah 24–27," in *Formation and Intertextuality in Isaiah 24–27*, ed. J. T. Hibbard and H. C. P. Kim (Atlanta, GA: Society of Biblical Literature, 2013): 218–219 discusses the "day of YHWH" theme in the two books.

Zephaniah in her commentary, mentions a verse from Isa 24–27 only once.[22] Only a few scattered essays and articles touch on (narrow) comparisons.[23]

There is some risk that in the listing that follows, of the numerous specific words and phrases shared between the two books, one will miss the forest for the trees. There is a nearly comprehensive overlap between the themes of Isa 24–27 and Zephaniah: Yнwн's widespread judgment of the earth; the need for repentance on the part of the people; the removal of the shame brought on by the other nations; and their reduction to wilderness; divine feasting; the problem of the city; and the regathering and restoration of Israel. There is little that either text says that is not said in some similar way by the other.[24]

Theme	Isa 24–27	Zephaniah
widespread judgment	24:1–23; 26:20–27:1	1:2–18
repentance	26:7–19	2:1–3
removal of shame	25:1–8	2:8–10
reduction to wilderness	27:10–11	2:4–7,11–14
divine feast	25:6–8	1:7; 3:18
problem of the city	26:5–6; 27:10–11	2:15–3:7
regathering/restoration	27:1–9,12–13	3:10–20

These thematic similarities are not skin-deep, but are borne out by extensive intertextual similarities at the level of lexicon and phraseology.

3 Isaiah 24–27, Zephaniah, and the Origins of Apocalyptic

One significant cluster of intertextual connections relates to the supposedly apocalyptic material in Isa 24–27. As noted above, this theme has roots in ANE royal propaganda and is understandable as Josianic rhetoric after Assyrian power

---

22 Adele Berlin, *Zephaniah*, AB 25A (New York: Doubleday, 1994), 117.

23 E. g., Ihromi, "Die Häufung der Verben des Jubelns in Zephanja 3:14 f, 16–18: *rnn*, *rw'*, *śmḥ*, *'lz*, *śwś* und *gîl*," *VT* 33 (1983): 106–110.

24 The structures of Zephaniah and Isaiah as a whole have been studied by, e. g., Brevard S. Childs, *Introduction to the Old Testament as Scripture* (Philadelphia: Fortress, 1979), 458; Otto Kaiser, *Introduction to the Old Testament: A Presentation of Its Results and Problems* (Minneapolis: Augsburg, 1977), 230; Ehud ben Zvi, "Understanding the Message of the Tripartite Prophetic Books," *Restoration Quarterly* 35 (1993): 93–100; but see also the critique by Marvin Sweeney, "Dating Prophetic Texts," *Hebrew Studies* 48 (2007): 70–73.

receded. The book of Zephaniah opens in 1:2–2:3 with an apocalyptic-sounding scene of judgment that is exceedingly similar: the divine devastation of the land and the humbling and abasement of its inhabitants.

The most numerous intertextual connections involve the language of judgement. As noted above, the two scenes participate in the ancient and widespread motif of the day of Yahweh (יום יהוה). Warnings (and occasionally promises) about the day of YHWH pervade both: Zeph 1:7,8,9,10,14 (x2),15 (x6),16,18; 2:2 (x2),3; 3:8,11,16 and Isa 24:21; 25:9; 26:1; 27:1,2,8,12,13. The day of YHWH was of course a prophetic motif of significant antiquity, used frequently in Amos (1:14; 2:16; 3:14; 4:2; 5:18, 20; 6:3; 8:3; 8:9–13) and Hosea (1:5; 5:9; 9:7),[25] and it is used in Zephaniah in a classical way.

Although the hand (יד) of Yahweh is not specifically outstretched (with the verb נטה) in Isa 24–27, as in Zeph 1:4; 2:13, the divine hand is powerful in judgment (26:11) and protection (Isa 25:10); and in both texts, it wields a sword (חֶרֶב; Zeph 2:12; Isa 27:1).

Many other images of divine judgment are shared between Isa 24–27 and Zephaniah. The devouring fire of YHWH's zeal is mentioned in both texts in similar phrases (Zeph 1:18; 3:8 and Isa 26:11; cf. 24:6; 27:11).[26] In both Zephaniah 1:2–3 and Isaiah 24:1, the "face of the earth/ground" (פני האדמה) is threatened. YHWH punishes (פקד) various entities in both texts (Zeph 1:8,9,12; 2:7; 3:7 and Isa 24:21,22; 26:14,16,21; 27:1,3). The "inhabitants" (ישבי [הארץ]) of the land are threatened (Zeph 1:4,18 and Isa 24:1,5,6,17; 26:9,18,21), as are their "houses" (בתים in Zeph 1:13 and Isa 24:10). Related terms for distress, צר(ה)/צרר, appear in Zeph 1:15,17 and Isa 25:4; 26:16. Those to be punished will be "gathered" (אסף) in each case (Zeph 1:2 and Isa 24:22) and "shattered" (רעע in Zeph 1:12 and Isa 24:19). "Cities" (עיר/ערים) are also singled out for judgment in both texts (Zeph 1:16; 2:15; 3:1,6 and Isa 24:12; 25:2; 26:1; 27:10), including "fortified cities" (בצורה in Zeph 1:16 [plural] and Isa 25:2; 27:10).

In some cases, the same vocabulary appears but with a different significance, such as "drinking wine" (שתה יין) in Zeph 1:13 and Isa 24:9, or the themes of "fin-

---

25 Some comment on these lists of texts may be necessary, since there is apparently disagreement about what constitutes a reference to the "day of Ywh." It will not due to limit the consideration only to those texts that actually contain the phrase יום יהוה; rather, this was a long-running and malleable concept used in various phrasings to express expected divine judgment. I presume that the positive uses of the day of Yhwh (e. g., Hos 2:18; Amos 9:11) are derived from an originally negative/military use and were meant to be a refreshing rhetorical surprise; whether this was within the vision of early prophets is beyond the scope of this essay.

26 Zeph 1:18: באש קנאתי תאכל כל־הארץ; 3:8 באש קנאתו תאכל כל־הארץ; Isa 26:11: קנאת־עם אף־אש צריך תאכלם; 24:6: אלה אכלה ארץ.

ishing off" (כלה) in Zeph 1:18 and Isa 24:13. In other cases, slightly different terms are used to similar effect—for example, אדם in Zeph 1:3,17 vs. אנוש in Isa 24:6; and Zeph 1:11 and Isa 24:2 both include lists of social roles or trades as bound for suffering.

In both texts, Yhwh is wrathful (זעם; Zeph 3:8; Isa 26:20), and his punishment is forever (עולם; Zeph 2:9; Isa 25:2).[27] Both contain numerous references to the peoples and nations (גויים/עמים), including Moab (מואב; Zeph 2:8–9; Isa 25:10), the coastlands (איים; Zeph 2:11; Isa 24:15), and the western regions of the sea (ים; Zeph 2:5–6; Isa 24:14–15; 27:1[?]). These are a source of shame (חרפה; Zeph 2:8; 3:18; Isa 25:8). The punished nations will be abandoned (עזב; Zeph 2:4; Isa 27:10), destroyed (אבד; Zeph 2:5,13; Isa 26:14; 27:13), and plundered (בזז; Zeph 2:9; Isa 24:3); they will shrivel (רזה; Zeph 2:11; Isa 24:16) and experience Yhwh's correction (מוסר; Zeph 3:2,7; Isa 26:16). They will become wilderness (מדבר; Zeph 2:13; Isa 27:10) and pastureland (רעה; Zeph 2:6–7; Isa 27:10) where animals will lie down (רבץ; Zeph 2:14–15; Isa 27:10). They will be without inhabitant (יושב; Zeph 2:5; Isa 24:6), their streets desolate (חוצות; Zeph 3:6; Isa 24:11). This is because of the adversaries' transgression (פשע; Zeph 3:11; Isa 24:20), treachery (בגד; Zeph 3:4; Isa 24:16), unrighteousness (עול; Zeph 3:5; Isa 26:10); and self-exaltation (גאוה; Zeph 3:11; Isa 25:11 and גאון; Zeph 2:10).[28] In the end, the "exultant ones" will be punished (עליזים; Zeph 2:15; 3:11; Isa 24:8),[29] and the nations will bow down (*hishtaphel* of חוה; Zeph 2:11; Isa 27:13) to Yhwh.

In light of all this, the bodies of scholarship on Isaiah and Zephaniah provide an interesting case study. Whereas the supposedly apocalyptic elements of Isa 24–27 have brought it under scrutiny as a late text, this argument has been made mostly around the fringes of Zephaniah scholarship. It was argued in a brief article in 1950 that Zephaniah should be considered contemporaneous with Daniel,[30] but Duane Christensen remarked decades afterward that "[n]o scholar of competence on the contemporary scene accepts" that conclusion.[31] Today, despite the inevitable debates, Zeph 1—with its destruction of "everything from the face of the earth"—is the section of the book most widely dated to the seventh century.

---

27 עולם is also used, but differently, in Isa 24:5 and 26:4.

28 גאון is also used with a positive connotation in Isa 24:14. From a conceptual standpoint, terms such as מרום and נשגב in Isa 24–27 and גבה in Zeph 1:16; 3:11 are also relevant here.

29 Although עלי is positive in Zeph 3:14.

30 L. P. Smith and E. R. Lacheman, "The Authorship of the Book of Zephaniah," *JNES* 9 (1950): 137–142. They argued mostly on the basis of its apocalyptic themes and intertextual connections to the three major prophets—without, it should be noted, arguing for the priority of the other prophetic texts in question (on which, see chapter 6).

31 D. L. Christensen, "Zephaniah 2:4–15: A Theological Basis for Josiah's Program of Political Expansion," *CBQ* 46 (1984): 669.

Even redactional analyses tend to include all or most of it as part of the so-called authentic core.[32] As Marvin Sweeney has demonstrated, "the book does not presuppose the world-wide perspective that is attributed to postexilic eschatology. Zeph 1:2–3 does employ cosmic reversal of creation language, but such language appears frequently in the prophets in contexts that cannot be understood in an eschatological sense. They merely refer to the inseparable relationship between human behavior and the welfare of the natural world."[33] Sweeney thus emphasized Zephaniah's this-worldly character, and the same is true of Isa 24–27.[34]

4 Other intertextual connections

There are numerous other lexical and phraseological connections between Isa 24–27 and Zephaniah. Some of these are fairly common points of Yahwistic theology that might ordinarily not occasion speculation about literary relationships, but in the wider context of the similarities they take on additional interest.

In both texts, Yhwh dwells on his holy mountain (הר קדשי; Zeph 3:11; הר הקדש; Isa 27:13; and הר; Isa 24:23; 25:6–7,10).[35] In both, Yhwh hosts a sacrificial feast, although the one in Zeph 1:7–8 has a decidedly darker cast than that in Isa 25:6–8, and זבח is not used in the latter (see also Zeph 3:18–19). Both texts are concerned with Zion (ציון; Zeph 3:14,16; Isa 24:23) and Jerusalem (ירושלם; Zeph 1:4,12; 3:14,16; Isa 24:23; 27:13). And in both texts, Yhwh and other gods have their "places" (מקום; Zeph 1:4; 2:11; Isa 26:21) from which they may come forth.

---

32 John S. Kselman, "Zephaniah, Book of," *ABD* 6:1078 notes that the most extreme reduction of the book's original core "saw only chap. 1 and 2:12–15 as authentic material by the prophet of the Josianic era." Some reduce the book even more, although with the preponderance of original material still in chapter 1, e. g., Wilhelm Rudolph, *Micha–Nahum–Habakuk–Zephanja*, KAT 13.3 (Gütersloh: Gerd, 1975); William L. Holladay, "Reading Zephaniah with a Concordance: Suggestions for a Redaction History," *JBL* 120 (2001): 671–84; Lothar Perlitt, *Die Propheten Nahum, Habakuk, Zephanja*, ATD 25/1 (Göttingen: Vandenhoeck & Ruprecht, 2004), 96; and Tchavdar S. Hadjiev, "The Theological Transformations of Zephaniah's Proclamation of Doom," *ZAW* 126 (2014): 506–520.
33 Marvin A. Sweeney, "A Form-Critical Reassessment of the Book of Zephaniah," *CBQ* 53 (1991): 404.
34 Marvin A. Sweeney, "Zephaniah: Prophet of His Time—Not the End Time!" *BRev* 20:6 (December 2004): 34–40.
35 This motif seems to have both early and late manifestations. Early?: cf. Ps 2:6, 3:5; 15:1; 43:3; 48:2; etc. Late?: Isa 11:9; 56:7; 57:13; 65:11,25; 66:20; Dan 9:16,20. Outside this phrase, Zephaniah evinces more concern for holiness, e. g., "he has consecrated those he called" (Zeph 1:7) and "priests have profaned what is holy" (Zeph 3:4).

YHWH is described as a savior in both texts (ישע; Zeph 3:17,19; Isa 25:9) who works (עשׂה; Zeph 1:18; 3:5,19; Isa 25:1,6; 27:11 and פעל;[36] Isa 26:12). The people are expected to trust in YHWH (בטח; Zeph 2:15; 3:2; Isa 26:4), although they do not always. YHWH removes sin and judgment (*hiphil* of סור; Zeph 3:11,15; Isa 25:8; 27:9). The people respond with shouts, joy and gladness (רנן; Zeph 3:14; Isa 24:14; 26:19; שׂמח; Zeph 3:14; Isa 25:9; and גיל; Zeph 3:17; Isa 25:9), and God answers back with gladness (שׂמחה) and a shout of joy (רנה) in Zeph 3:17. YHWH is concerned for his people (עם; Isa 25:8; 26:11[?]; 26:20; Zeph 2:8, 9, 10). In both texts, those who are saved are the poor and oppressed (עני/דל; Zeph 3:12; Isa 25:4; 26:6), as well as the scattered (נדח[ים]; Zeph 3:19; Isa 27:13).

YHWH's name (שֵׁם) is prominent in both texts (Zeph 3:9,12,19,20; Isa 24:15; 25:1; 26:8,13), as is his word (דבר; Zeph 1:1; 2:5; Isa 24:3; 25:8). Both texts refer to YHWH's just judgments (משפט[ים]; Zeph 2:3; 3:5,8,15; Isa 26:8–9) and, strikingly, both describe the violation or transgression of the "teaching" (חמס תורה; Zeph 3:4 and עברו תורת; Isa 24:5). Many of the same titles for God are used in both Isa 24–27 and Zephaniah, such as "YHWH the Righteous One" (צדיק; Zeph 3:5; Isa 24:16; 26:7).[37]

Zephaniah and Isa 24–27 even share certain literary features such as the device of using first-person forms of אמר to introduce direct quotation of the speaker's thoughts (Zeph 3:7 [cf. 1:12; 2:15]; Isa 24:16) and the theophanic use of הנה pointing to God (Zeph 3:19; Isa 24:1; 25:9; 26:21).

Numerous other shared lexical items can be catalogued, although their different usage in the two texts precludes hypothesizing about their intertextual significance.[38]

There are more than 80 shared lexical items listed here, and many have multiple occurrences. That seems an exceedingly high density of shared terminology for two texts that comprise only forty-three verses (Zephaniah) and sixty-nine verses (Isa 24–27), respectively.[39]

---

36 פעל occurs with a human subject in Zeph 2:3.

37 More common titles also appear: "My Lord Yhwh" (אדני יהוה; Zeph 1:7; Isa 25:8), "Yhwh God" (יהוה אלהים: Zeph 2:7; 3:17; Isa 24:15; 25:1), "Yhwh of Hosts" (יהוה צבאות; Zeph 2:9–10; Isa 24:23; 25:6), "God of Israel" (אלהי ישראל: Zeph 2:9; Isa 24:15), etc.

38 Particularly interesting are the common usage of שופר (Zeph 1:16; Isa 27:13) and כרם (Zeph 1:13; Isa 27:2). Also כהנ(ים) (Zeph 1:4; 3:4; Isa 24:2), דם (Zeph 1:17; Isa 26:21), עפר (Zeph 1:16; Isa 25:12; 26:5; 26:19), נוע (Zeph 2:15; Isa 24:20), בוש (Isa 24:23; 26:11; Zeph 3:11), יסף (Zeph 3:11; Isa 24:20; 26:15), and שׂים (Zeph 2:13; 3:19; Isa 25:2; 27:9).

39 It would be desirable to have a computerized analysis of these various corpora to confirm this sense, as was recently done for Jeremiah vs. Ezekiel and for P vs. non-P strata in the Pentateuch, as in Idan Dershowitz et al., "Computerized Source Criticism of Biblical Texts," *JBL* 134 (2015): 253–271.

5 Zephaniah Among the (Isaianic) Prophets

The similarities between Isaiah 24–27 and Zephaniah are such that one is driven back to the questions raised by Wilson, Richards, and Ahn: What sort of relationship is this? There are a number of potential answers that could be given, each of which deserves to be weighed:

(1) There was no direct connection between the two; instead, both participated in a common Jerusalemite prophetic tradition that happened to employ a common stock of rhetoric and terminology at different times. Against this theory, the cumulative effect of all the shared themes and intertextual connections catalogued above is overwhelming. There is too much in common to resort to merely a common subculture.

(2) Zephaniah consciously adopted existing Isaianic language in the late seventh century; Isa 24–27 provides another set of examples, like the outstretched hand and the day of the Lord, in which the later prophet adopted the earlier. Against this theory, it has proven almost impossible to maintain with critical integrity that Isa 24–27 dates to the eighth century. I have noted elsewhere that there may be fragments that predated their incorporation into the rhetoric of the whole passage (notably the prophecy of future destruction in Isa 25 and the Moab fragment in 25:10b–12), but for most of it I have never read a convincing argument for its "authenticity."

(3) Either Isa 24–27 or Zephaniah or both were postexilic—part of a great scribal invention of pre-exilic Israel and Judah. Thus one was created by copying the other, or both were created in a complex process of copying among various biblical texts. Since this theory holds a kernel of truth, the arguments against it are more complicated.

In the case of Isa 24–27, I have shown elsewhere that its Hebrew is not characteristic of the postexilic period, to the best of our current ability to discern; it has roughly the same low number of late Hebrew features as prophets generally agreed to be preexilic, and many fewer than postexilic prophets, including Isa 40–55.[40] And I have argued at length that it fits best in the context of Josiah's reign, and that the lofty city that had fallen in time, to which it repeatedly refers, was the Assyrian imperial citadel at Ramat Rahel. (I have also found myself unable to explain satisfactorily why such a lengthy interlude as Isa 24–27 would have been inserted in the middle of the book when there were simultaneously large additions being made to the end of the book. Why not simply locate it with the added material in Isa 40–66? But this is a topic that still requires additional work.)

---

40 Hays, *The Origins of Isaiah 24–27*, 176–212.

In the case of Zephaniah, the theory that it is mostly or entirely postexilic sets aside concrete data in favor of speculation. The book of Zephaniah is dated by its superscription to the reign of Josiah (1:1). Superscriptions to prophetic books are sometimes of doubtful historical value, but in the case of Zephaniah it has seemed logical that the prophet's words were delivered and compiled in a period of Deuteronomistic ideology, given their references to Deuteronomistic themes such as the condemnations of Baal, idolatrous priests, and the host of heaven (Zeph 1:4), as well as worship on rooftops (1:5). Furthermore, the curse in Zeph 1:13 may be compared with Deut 28:30.[41] There is some doubt about the identity of the prophet,[42] but there is fairly broad agreement that the core of the book reflects the concerns and interests of the late seventh century, perhaps even before the time of Josiah's attempted reform.[43]

Two passages in Zephaniah have particularly been associated with Josiah. The first is the set of oracles against the nations in 2:4–15, which threatens a divine campaign of retribution against Philistia, Moab, Ammon, and Assyria.[44] This is not a characteristically postexilic list; it comprises nations that surrounded and conflicted with Judah during the Neo-Assyrian period. Duane Christensen argued in an influential article that the passage "presents a theological basis for Josiah's program of political expansion at the expense of Assyria."[45] Christensen

---

41 John S. Kselman, "Zephaniah, Book of," *ABD* 6:1077 and Johannes Vlaardingerbroek, *Zephaniah*, HCOT (Leuven: Peeters, 1999), 17–24. Beginning with a far different understanding of Josiah's reform — as a political rebellion against Assyria — Anselm Hagedorn, "When Did Zephaniah Become a Supporter of Josiah's Reform?" *JTS NS* 62 (2011): 453–475, still finds Josianic material in the book, albeit different material.

42 The name "Zephaniah" was common in the monarchic period, attested on numerous seals and ostraca. In the late monarchic and exilic periods, there are as many as three different Zephaniahs: the prophet, a "second priest" (2Kgs 25:18; Jer 21:1; etc.), and the father of Josiah, who received gold and silver from Zechariah in the Persian period (Zech 6:10,14). Donald L. Williams, "The Date of Zephaniah," *JBL* 82 (1963): 77–88 argued that all three of these were the same person, but that has not been widely accepted.

43 In addition to the literature cited elsewhere in this chapter, see the overview by Barry A. Jones, "The Seventh-Century Prophets in Twenty-First Century Research," *CurBR* 14 (2016): 136, who notes that "the historical context of Zephaniah appears more straightforward" than those of Nahum and Habakkuk.

44 Hagedorn, "When Did Zephaniah Become a Supporter," 453–475; On the problem of Cush in a text slightly later than one would expect, see Robert D. Haak, "'Cush' in Zephaniah," in *The Pitcher is Broken: Memorial Essays for Gösta W. Ahlström* (Sheffield: Sheffield Academic, 1995): 238–251, although the conclusion of Marvin A. Sweeney, *Zephaniah: A Commentary*, Hermeneia (Minneapolis: Fortress, 2003), 145–148 is to be preferred.

45 Duane L. Christensen, "Zephaniah 2:4–15: A Theological Basis for Josiah's Program of Political Expansion," *CBQ* 46 (1984): 678; Marvin A. Sweeney, "A Form-Critical Reassessment of the

goes too far in assuming that Josiah actually carried out the program, but it is plausible that this passage expressed his ambitions.[46] The second passage is the call for the "remnant of Israel" (שארית ישראל) to "seek refuge in the name of YHWH" (Zeph 3:12–13), which Sweeney argues should be understood as a Josianic overture to the northern kingdom to "reunite ... under the rule of the Davidic monarchy."[47] Other occurrences of the "remnant of Israel" support this theory because they do plausibly refer to survivors of the Northern Kingdom (esp. Mic 2:12; Jer 6:9). Furthermore, 2Chr 34:9, although late, connects this group to the remnants of the Northern Kingdom precisely in Josiah's time: it describes the temple offering Josiah "collected from Manasseh and Ephraim and from all the remnant of Israel," as distinct from "all Judah and Benjamin and from the inhabitants of Jerusalem."[48]

Book of Zephaniah," *CBQ* 53 (1991): 405–406; and Adele Berlin, "Zephaniah's Oracle against the Nations and an Israelite Cultural Myth," in *Fortunate the Eyes That See: Essays in Honor of David Noel Freedman in Celebration of his Seventieth Birthday*, ed. A. B. Beck et al. (Grand Rapids, MI: Eerdmans, 1995): 175–184. More recently, Eric L. Welch, "The Roots of Anger: An Economic Perspective on Zephaniah's Oracle against the Philistines," *VT* 63 (2013): 471–485 has called attention to the specifically seventh-century character of parts of the passage.

46 J. J. M. Roberts, *Nahum, Habakkuk, and Zephaniah*, OTL (Louisville, KY: Westminster John Knox, 1991), 195; Sweeney, *Zephaniah*, 14; Vlaardingerbroek, *Zephaniah*, 17–22, 130. I was recently reminded of Josiah's ideology by Jenni Russell, "No Dunkirk Spirit Can Save Britain from Brexit Defeat," *New York Times* online, July 28, 2017, https://www.nytimes.com/2017/07/28/opinion/dunkirk-christopher-nolan-brexit.html?_r=0: who warned Great Britain against its ambitions to leave the European Union (i. e., Brexit): "We hear much about American exceptionalism, but Britain feels it, too. We are the nation of empire, whose ancestors once controlled a quarter of the globe; we are the mother of parliaments; we stood alone against Hitler; we have not been conquered for a thousand years. We feel remarkable. The Brexit vote was driven by the belief that Britain was hobbled by being shackled to a moribund, bureaucratic group of nations. The Brexiteers convinced enough of the electorate that we needed only to be set free from Europe, with its tiresome regulations, restrictions and pesky immigrants, to become a proud, swashbuckling, dominant and richer country again. This promise is a stunning misunderstanding of who we are, what we are capable of and where we stand in the world." Josiah's Judah, too, surely felt exceptional.

47 Sweeney, *Zephaniah*, 191–192.

48 The other passages in which שארית ישראל appears are Jer 31:7; Ezek 9:8; 11:13; 1Chr 12:39. This interpretation of Zeph 3:12–13 flies in the face of much recent scholarship, which understands the passage to be at least postmonarchic if not extremely late and eschatological. For example, in Ezekiel, the term "Israel" is usually used in the sense of "God's chosen people." Even Roberts, *Nahum, Habakkuk, and Zephaniah*, 222, who is sanguine about a seventh-century date for much of Zephaniah, takes the view that this passage is later. Dietrich, *Nahum, Habakkuk, Zephaniah*, 244 does not even deem the point necessary to support. If, however, one is asking about the passage's original composition rather than its editorial history, Sweeney's view deserves con-

Zephaniah scholarship in the twentieth century followed the lines of scholarship on more prominent books.[49] Broadly speaking, this has meant a bifurcation into a continental European tradition that identifies smaller literary layers and more late redactional activity[50] and an Anglophone tradition that, while allowing for redactional activity, emphasizes the historical identity and rhetorical goals of the prophet and the relationship of the book to the prophet's own period.[51] As B. A. Jones has pointed out in his recent overview, "[t]he complex and disparate results of redactional analyses suggest a need for a more constrained and limited analysis."[52] In recent years, Ehud Ben Zvi has sought to support a wholly postmonarchic date for Zephaniah,[53] but it has not exercised great influence over

---

sideration. It is widely agreed that Zephaniah, like other prophetic texts, was reinterpreted over the centuries so that many of its early sections came to mean something quite different from what they initially did. But new meanings are often found in existing texts. Times change, and referents shift in new historical contexts. "Israel" came to mean something different, and it is not difficult to imagine that Zephaniah preserves a preexilic call for restoration that simply took on new meaning after the exile. See Tchavdar S. Hadjiev, "The Theological Transformations of Zephaniah's Proclamation of Doom," *ZAW* 126 (2014): 517–518. Hadjiev is speaking of Zeph 1:2–2:3, but the same may be true for 3:12–13.

49 See the overview in Marvin A. Sweeney, "Zephaniah: A Paradigm for the Study of the Prophetic Books," *CurBS* 7 (1999): 119–145.

50 Note especially Wilhelm Rudolph, *Micha-Nahum-Habakuk-Zephanja*, KAT 13/3 (Gütersloh: Gerd, 1975); Walter Dietrich and Milton Schwantes, eds., *Der Tag wird kommen: Ein Interkontextuelles Gespräch über das Buch des Propheten Zefanja*, SBS 170 (Stuttgart: Katholisches Bibelwerk, 1996); Heinz-Dieter Neef, "Vom Gottesgericht zum universalen Heil: Komposition und Redaktion des Zephanjabuches," *ZAW* 111 (1999): 530–546; Hubert Irsigler, *Zefanja*, HThKAT (Freiburg: Herder: 2002); Lothar Perlitt, *Die Propheten Nahum, Habakuk, Zephanja*, ATD 25/1 (Göttingen: Vandenhoeck & Ruprecht, 2004); Anselm C. Hagedorn, *Die Anderen im Spiegel: Israels Auseinandersetzung mit den Völkern in den Büchern Nahum, Zefanja, Obadja und Joel*, BZAW 414 (Berlin: de Gruyter, 2011), 111–168; and Walter Dietrich, *Nahum, Habakkuk, Zephanja*, IECOT (Stuttgart: W. Kohlhammer, 2016), 188–192. This is not a unified tradition; note, e. g., Vlaardingerbroek, *Zephaniah*, which is very focused on the book's Josianic origins, and the careful attention to the relationship of Zephaniah to Josiah's reign and to Deuteronomism paid by Klaus Seybold, *Satirische Prophetie: Studien zum Buch Zefanja*, SBS 120 (Stuttgart: Katholisches Bibelwerk, 1985), 75–93.

51 Arvid S. Kapelrud, *The Message of the Prophet Zephaniah: Morphology and Ideas* (Oslo: Universitetsforlaget, 1975), 41–45; R. L. Smith, *Micah-Malachi*, WBC 32 (Waco, TX: Word, 1984); Elizabeth Achtemeier, *Nahum–Malachi*, Int (Atlanta, GA: John Knox, 1986); David W. Baker, *Nahum, Habakkuk, Zephaniah*, TOTC (Leicester: Inter-Varsity, 1988); and Roberts, *Nahum, Habakkuk, and Zephaniah*. Again, there are exceptions that take a more continental approach, e. g., Rex Mason, *Zephaniah, Habakkuk, Joel* (Sheffield: Sheffield Academic, 1994).

52 Jones, "Seventh-Century Prophets," 147.

53 Ehud Ben Zvi, *A Historical-Critical Study of the Book of Zephaniah*, BZAW 198 (Berlin: de Gruyter, 1991).

the authors of the most significant recent commentaries, who generally continue to place most of the book in the seventh century.[54] Even in theories that include various late redactions, Zeph 1:1–2:3, with its apocalyptic-seeming imagery, is generally taken to be the early core of the book.

If the traditional dating of much of Zephaniah to the seventh century is correct, then it provides an important point of comparison for Isa 24–27. I do not think that Zephaniah himself edited Isaiah, since that was not yet a period in which prophets wrote for themselves (see Jeremiah and Baruch). However, it is entirely plausible to me that whatever scribes were responsible for the original composition of the book of Zephaniah were also responsible for Isa 24–27.

There are excellent examples of scribal literary activity around prophetic texts in cognate literature such as the Deir 'Alla plaster texts and the compilations of Neo-Assyrian prophecy. These make it clear that ancient Near Eastern scribes were working with prophetic texts in literary form even before the seventh century. The major studies of ancient Near Eastern scribalism by Karel van der Toorn and David Carr have pointed precisely to the late seventh century as a point of origin for scribal work on prophetic texts.[55]

The intertextual implications of scribal activity seem broadly accepted among biblical scholars when it comes to later periods. It is taken for granted that postexilic prophets or Qumran compositions were written by scribes with their eyes and/or ears open to traditions. Less often is it asked: *How far back does 'scribal prophecy' reach?*

In the case of Isaiah, the original prophet's oracles were already being "preserved, collected, and redacted" in the time of Hezekiah (Isa 8:16; 30:8; and cf. the role in compilation attributed to the "men of Hezekiah" in Prov 25:1).[56] The empirical evidence of this very process with Neo-Assyrian oracles is well documented and now widely discussed, especially in connection with the book of

---

54 Marvin A. Sweeney, *Zephaniah: A Commentary*, Hermeneia (Minneapolis: Fortress, 2003) and Carol J. Dempsey, *Amos, Hosea, Micah, Nahum, Zephaniah, Habakkuk*, New Collegeville Bible Commentary 15 (Collegeville, MN: Liturgical Press, 2013). Adele Berlin, *Zephaniah*, AB 25A (New York: Doubleday, 1994), 43–47 was more noncommittal, taking the Josianic context seriously while remaining receptive to the possibilities introduced by Ben Zvi's challenge introduced.
55 Karel van der Toorn, *Scribal Culture and the Making of the Hebrew Bible* (Cambridge, MA: Harvard University Press, 2007), 173–204 and David M. Carr, *Writing on the Tablet of the Heart: Origins of Scripture and Literature* (Oxford: Oxford University Press, 2005), 141–151.
56 See also William M. Schniedewind, *How the Bible Became a Book: The Textualization of Ancient Israel* (Cambridge: Cambridge University Press, 2004), 89.

Isaiah.[57] The most interesting example is in Simo Parpola's collection *Assyrian Prophecies*. One compilation appears to have been created to support Esarhaddon during his difficult consolidation of power in 679; it was recompiled a little more than six years later when he named Assurbanipal as his successor in 672. In short, it appears that these supportive oracles concerning royal succession were reappropriated "to remind any potential critics of the decision—in the first place, Assurbanipal's elder brother, Šamaš-šum-ukin, and his supporters—of the fate of those who would try to usurp power against the will of the gods."[58] Although the six-year gap between composition and application to a new situation is small compared to those for the book of Isaiah, the principle involved is strikingly similar: An analogy is perceived between a past situation and the present situation, and the will of the gods is seen to be similarly relevant to both instances. Another collection (SAA 9.3) is attributed to a single prophet, Lā-dāgil-ili, whom Parpola described as "comparable to the great biblical prophets,"[59] and whose oracles were compiled and copied in 681–680.[60]

The existence of innerbiblical interpretation by Josiah's time is an inevitable conclusion from the common analyses of Deuteronomy's interaction with earlier biblical law, a process that stretched back into the cuneiform traditions of the Bronze Age.[61] The written word, in whatever form, had come to have the weight (and authority) of received tradition. In the case of law, that meant older traditions had to be reckoned with in various ways. Sometimes prophets, too, had to struggle with received ideas (e. g., Jer 31:29–20; Ezek 18:2; 20:25), but for them older traditions already had the potential to be harnessed and reinterpreted as sources of added authority. Dalit Rom-Shiloni has pointed out that the prophets' correlation of the present with the past, or invocation of "the enduring qualities of God," are "[t]he starting point of the exegetical process."[62]

---

57 Matthijs J. de Jong, *Isaiah among the Ancient near Eastern Prophets: A Comparative Study of the Earliest Stages of the Isaiah Tradition and the Neo-Assyrian Prophecies*, VTSup 117 (Leiden: Brill, 2007) and Christopher B. Hays, *Hidden Riches: A Sourcebook for the Comparative Study of the Old Testament and the Ancient Near East* (Louisville, KY: Westminster John Knox, 2014), 265–76.
58 Simo Parpola, *Assyrian Prophecies*, SAA 9 (Helsinki: Helsinki University Press, 1997), lxix–lxx.
59 Parpola, *Assyrian Prophecies*, li.
60 *Ibid.*, lxx.
61 Michael Fishbane, *Biblical Interpretation in Ancient Israel* (Oxford: Oxford University Press, 1985), 91–277; Bernard M. Levinson, *Deuteronomy and the Hermeneutics of Legal Innovation* (New York: Oxford University Press, 1998); and Jeffrey Stackert, *Rewriting the Torah: Literary Revision in Deuteronomy and the Holiness Legislation*, FAT 52 (Tübingen: Mohr Siebeck, 2007).
62 Dalit Rom-Shiloni, "Facing Destruction and Exile: Inner-Biblical Exegesis in Jeremiah and Ezekiel," *ZAW* 117 (2005): 204.

In more recent years, the textualization of revelation has been emphasized by a number of scholars. Carr and van der Toorn have been mentioned above. William Schniedewind notes that the Josianic reform begins with the announcement of the discovery of a written scroll (2Kgs 23) and points to the numerous references to the written form of the Deuteronomic law, which that scroll seems to have contained in some form (Deut 4:13; 5:22; 9:10; 10:2,4; 28:58,61; 29:19–20,26; 30:10; 31:9,24).[63] The people are even told to "write them on the doorposts of your house and on your gates" (6:9; 11:20), to have a copy made for the king (17:18), and to inscribe them on public monuments (27:3) and on the sacrificial altar itself (27:8)! Increasing importance of the written word in the late seventh century would accord well with Jeremiah's emphasis on having his own scribe, and particularly with the status of the scroll in Jer 36. There Jeremiah tells Baruch the scribe: "I am prevented from entering the house of YHWH; so you go yourself, and on a fast day in the hearing of the people in YHWH's house you shall read the words of YHWH from the scroll that you have written at my dictation" (Jer 36:5–6). Jehoiakim, failing to be chastened by Jeremiah's words, burns the scroll (Jer 36:23–24), an act that only confirms the perceived power of the written word. If the scroll didn't have power, it wouldn't need to be destroyed.

Even as the authority of writing grew, it came into tension with prophetic authority, as suggested by Jeremiah's own condemnation of the "lying pen of the scribes" (Jer 8:8) that falsifies the teachings and wisdom of YHWH.[64] The increasing use of writing in Judah in the seventh century B.C.E. would have made it a natural time for such conflicts to emerge.[65] Do such narratives reflect the reality of the late seventh century? A balanced view of Jeremiah's composition by van der Toorn concludes that "on occasion he did use writing as a means of communication," which may even have "created the reality of the writer-prophet."[66]

Here it is useful to refer to Berlin's comments about Zephaniah, a book much more commonly assigned to Josiah's period than Isa 24–27:

---

63 Schniedewind, *How the Bible Became a Book*, 109.

64 *Ibid.*, 116 and Rom-Shiloni, "Facing Destruction," 189–205.

65 Christopher A. Rollston, *Writing and Literacy in the World of Ancient Israel: Epigraphic Evidence from the Iron Age*, ABS 11 (Atlanta, GA: Society of Biblical Literature, 2010), 133. As Rollston notes, the rising use of writing is not to be confused with popular literacy.

66 Karel van der Toorn, "From the Mouth of the Prophet: The Literary Fixation of the Jeremiah's Prophecies in the Context of the Ancient Near East," in *Inspired Speech: Prophecy in the Ancient Near East*, ed. J. Kaltner, and L. Stulman, JSOTSupp 378 (London: T & T Clark, 2004): 201.

> The Book of Zephaniah is a study in intertextuality. A highly literate work, it shares ideas and phraseology with other parts of the Hebrew Bible to such an extent that at times it may appear as nothing more than a pastiche of borrowed verses and allusions ... The general effect is the creation of a strong link between this otherwise obscure prophet and the rest of the canon—not only the prophets, but also the Torah and the Psalms. Zephaniah participates in the textual world of the Bible. This suggests that the textual world, in one form or another, was known and accepted by the book's first audience (whether that audience was in the time of Josiah or later).[67]

Berlin thinks that a Josianic context for Zephaniah is quite possible, and this textual world is not hard to imagine in Josiah's time. The same period plausibly supplied the environment for Isa 24–27's "textual participation." Wilson recently made a similar point, that not only Second and Third Isaiah were "scribal creations," but First Isaiah was as well.[68]

In sum, then, the boundaries between spoken and scribal prophecy were already quite permeable in the seventh century—and not merely, as has long been widely accepted, in the postexilic period.[69] "[T]he phenomenon of prophecy as an oratory and performing art ... had to share the stage with prophecy ... as a literary genre."[70] In the late seventh century, scribes were compiling and editing prophetic texts, as well as adding to them (Jer 36:32). In adding to them, they naturally drew on traditions from their own times and earlier. Like any other author, they did not speak *ex nihilo*; but unlike many ancient authors, their sources and inspirations have survived, thanks to the very success of their work through Josiah's authorization of it.[71]

---

67 Berlin, *Zephaniah*, 13.

68 Robert R. Wilson. "Scribal Culture and the Composition of the Book of Isaiah," in *The Bible as a Human Witness to Divine Revelation: Hearing the Word of God through Historically Dissimilar Traditions*, ed. Randall Heskett and Brian Irwin, LHBOTS 469 (New York: T & T Clark International, 2010): 105.

69 On the permeable boundaries between oral and written literature, see Carr, *Writing*, 144–149 and, in the time of Josiah specifically, Lauren A. S. Monroe, *Josiah's Reform and the Dynamics of Defilement: Israelite Rites of Violence and the Making of a Biblical Text* (Oxford: Oxford University Press, 2011), 130–133.

70 Toorn, "From the Mouth," 201.

71 The possibility of a Josianic edition of the prophets was noted above. Cook, "Deliverance," 165 has taken as a given that "[a] corpus of authoritative, sacred writings was in place by postexilic times, to which Israel's early apocalyptic visionaries, such as the authors of the so-called Isaiah Apocalypse (Isa 24–27), made ready reference." The question is: Why only in postexilic times? Why not immediately before the exile as well?

6 Conclusion: Different perspectives on restoration

Isaiah 24–27 and Zephaniah have in common an exceptional amount of lexicon and their major themes, which are consonant with the sociopolitical context of the late seventh century. The examples of Iron Age IIB literary activity—both in extrabiblical prophetic texts and (as is generally acknowledged) in Josiah's court—indicate that "scribal prophecy" (the creation of prophetic oracles from existing literary traditions) had already begun by this time. While certainty is hard to come by, the similarities just noted are most economically attributed to a common period and even scribal source for the bulk of both pericopae. Both are early examples of scribal prophecy.

It is both curious and salient, given the enormous volume of shared vocabulary, that Zephaniah and Isa 24–27 do not share more phraseology. It seems to me that this argues against intertextual allusion as an explanation: A later prophet intending to mark his relationship to an earlier one might have been expected to do so more overtly. By contrast, a scribe composing two texts might be expected to draw, almost unconsciously, from a common stock of terminology that was characteristic of his ideology and theology.

If it is possible that a single scribe might have created both the core of Isa 24–27 and the core of Zephaniah, it is also clear that both Isaiah 24–27 and Zephaniah underwent additional editing in later periods. I have hypothesized elsewhere, on the basis of empirical data, that Isa 24–27 was reinterpreted after the perceived failure of Josiah's reign in 609; this might have effaced references to Josiah, if they were ever there.[72] But the great majority of what remains in Isa 24–27 can be explained as no later than the seventh century.

By contrast, shifts in terminology and ideology in the final verses of Zephaniah suggest to me a different editorial history, beginning with the opening formula כי־אז in 3:9 (and recurring in 3:11), which is very rare in the prophets.[73] There are linguistic signs of lateness in Zeph 3:9–20. The next construction in Zeph 3:9, סימע־לא דפהא, "I will change to (for?) the peoples (an expurgated speech)," is awkward; this is the only place such a construction is attested in BH.[74] This shifting use of prepositions is characteristic of LBH. And although the motif of unifying the nations' speech reverberates back into Iron Age Mesopotamian

---

72 Hays, "From Propaganda to Apocalypse," 120–144.
73 Elsewhere it occurs only in Jer 22:22
74 The usage of הפך אל in Josh 8:20 pertains to motion: "to turn back towards."

imperial ideology,[75] linguistic purity also was a concern of the Persian period (Neh 13:24). Furthermore, the specific term used to describe the speech (רוב) is highly characteristic of postexilic texts (Qoh 3:18, Isa 52:11; Dan 11:35; Dan 12:10; Neh 5:18; 1Chr 7:40; 9:22; 16:41).

Another telling indication of late redaction in the end of Zephaniah is its parallel use of Zion/Israel/Jerusalem in 3:14,16. By contrast, in Isa 27:6, Jacob and Israel are paired. Jacob/Israel commonly referred to the north in the preexilic period—thus the contrast between Israel and the house of David when the two divide in 2Kgs 12:16; thus the equations of Jacob/Israel/Bethel in Amos 3:13–14 and Jacob/Ephraim/Samaria in Isa 9:8–9. Like many terms of identity that are contested (e. g., what makes someone a "real American"?), "Jacob" and "Israel" had a complex history. They came to be adopted as terms of identity by postexilic groups. But they originally referred to the northern kingdom.

I suggest, then, that all or parts of Zeph 3:9–20 are additions by a tradent who perceived the intertextual connections between proto-Zephaniah and Isa 24–27, and applied Isa 27's promises to postexilic Jerusalem and Judah rather than to the preexilic northern kingdom (whether or not he understood their original context). As noted above, in various instances this redactor drew on additional elements of Isaianic terminology in light of the rich associations that already existed.[76]

From the standpoint of biblical theology, this comparison of Isaiah 24–27 and Zephaniah shows that seemingly apocalyptic language may mark periods of crisis, but not necessarily in the sense of persecution or suffering. Rather, both these texts have their roots in a period of epochal change when the Neo-Assyrian empire was crumbling, and new empires were rising. They announce in very similar ways that Yнwн has overseen the devastation of the land and the overthrow of the powers; and with the old order shattered, the people's allegiance to the One enthroned in Jerusalem must take its place.

Zephaniah's later shaping brought it into closer alignment with the positive message of Isa 27, demonstrating again the widely-recognized tendency that began within the Old Testament itself to dehistoricize texts by re-interpreting them.[77] Isaiah 24–27 and Zephaniah were thus reflective of two episodes in a stream that

---

75 Christoph Uehlinger, Weltreich Und "Eine Rede": Eine Neue Deutung Der Sogenannten Turmbauerzählung (Gen 11, 1–9); OBO 101 (Freiburg, Schweiz: Universitätsverlag, 1990).
76 This may be analogous in certain ways with the formation of the book of Isaiah as a whole, which includes similar themes. In my view, we might look similar settings for the final edition of Zephaniah as those of Isa 40–66.
77 Brevard S. Childs, *Introduction to the Old Testament as Scripture* (Philadelphia: Fortress, 1979), 325–326; John Goldingay, *A Critical and Exegetical Commentary on Isaiah 56–66*, ICC (London: Bloomsbury, 2014), 7; Marvin A. Sweeney, "Jesse's New Shoot in Isaiah 11: A Josianic Reading of

recurs throughout the Bible: The God of Israel does not only save once, but again and again; does not bring life out of death only once, but again and again; does not gather the outcasts only once, but again and again.

Bibliography

Abernethy, Andrew T., *Eating in Isaiah: Approaching the Role of Food and Drink in Isaiah's Structure and Message*, BibInt Series 131 (Leiden: Brill, 2014).

Achtemeier, Elizabeth, *Nahum–Malachi*, Int (Atlanta, GA: John Knox, 1986).

Ahn, John, "Zephaniah, a Disciple of Isaiah?" in *Thus Says the Lord: Essays on the Former and Latter Prophets in Honor of Robert R. Wilson* (New York/London: T & T Clark, 2009).

Altmann, Peter, *Festive Meals in Ancient Israel: Deuteronomy's Identity Politics in Their Ancient Near Eastern Context*, BZAW 424 (Berlin: de Gruyter, 2011).

Backer, David W., *Nahum, Habakkuk, Zephaniah*, TOTC (Leicester: Inter-Varsity, 1988).

Ben Zvi, Ehud, *A Historical-Critical Study of the Book of Zephaniah*, BZAW 198 (Berlin: de Gruyter, 1991).

Ben Zvi, Ehud, "Understanding the Message of the Tripartite Prophetic Books," *Restoration Quarterly* 35 (1993).

Berlin, Adele, *Zephaniah*, AB 25A (New York: Doubleday, 1994).

Berlin, Adele, "Zephaniah's Oracle against the Nations and an Israelite Cultural Myth," in *Fortunate the Eyes That See: Essays in Honor of David Noel Freedman in Celebration of his Seventieth Birthday*, ed. A. B. Beck et al. (Grand Rapids, MI: Eerdmans, 1995), 175–184.

Carr, David M., *Writing on the Tablet of the Heart: Origins of Scripture and Literature* (Oxford: Oxford University Press, 2005).

Childs, Brevard S., *Introduction to the Old Testament as Scripture* (Philadelphia: Fortress, 1979).

Christensen, Duane. L., "Zephaniah 2:4–15: A Theological Basis for Josiah's Program of Political Expansion," *CBQ* 46 (1984).

Collins, J. J., "The Sibyl and the Potter: Political Propaganda in Ptolemaic Egypt," in *Religious Propaganda and Missionary Competition in the New Testament World: Essays Honoring Dieter Georgi*, ed. L. Bormann, K. D. Tredici, and A. Standhartinger (Leiden: Brill, 1994).

Day, John, "The Dependence of Isaiah 26:13–27:11 on Hosea 13:4–14:10 and Its Relevance to Some Theories of the Redaction of the 'Isaiah Apocalypse'," in *Writing and Reading the Scroll of Isaiah*, ed. Craig C. Broyles and Craig A. Evans (Leiden: Brill, 1997), 357–368.

De Jong, Matthijs J., *Isaiah among the Ancient near Eastern Prophets: A Comparative Study of the Earliest Stages of the Isaiah Tradition and the Neo-Assyrian Prophecies*, VTSup 117 (Leiden: Brill, 2007).

Dempsey, Carol J., *Amos, Hosea, Micah, Nahum, Zephaniah, Habakkuk*, New Collegeville Bible Commentary 15 (Collegeville, MN: Liturgical Press, 2013).

the Prophet Isaiah," in *A Gift of G-d in Due Season: Essays in Scripture and Community in Honor of James A. Sanders*, ed. R. D. Weis and D. M. Carr; JSOTSup 225 (Sheffield: Sheffield Academic, 1996): 116–117.

Dempsey, Carol J., "Words of Woe, Visions of Grandeur: A Literary and Hermeneutical Study of Isaiah 24–27," in *Formation and Intertextuality in Isaiah 24–27*, ed. J. T. Hibbard and H. C. P. Kim (Atlanta, GA: Society of Biblical Literature, 2013).

Dershowitz, Idan et al., "Computerized Source Criticism of Biblical Texts," *JBL* 134 (2015), 253–271.

Dietrich, Walter, *Nahum, Habakkuk, Zephaniah*, IECOT (Stuttgart: W. Kohlhammer, 2016).

Dietrich, Walter/Schwantes, Milton, eds., *Der Tag wird kommen: Ein Interkontextuelles Gespräch über das Buch des Propheten Zefanja*, SBS 170 (Stuttgart: Katholisches Bibelwerk, 1996).

Fishbane, Michael, *Biblical Interpretation in Ancient Israel* (Oxford: Oxford University Press, 1985).

Goldingay, John, *A Critical and Exegetical Commentary on Isaiah 56–66*, ICC (London: Bloomsbury, 2014).

Haak, Robert D., "'Cush' in Zephaniah," in *The Pitcher is Broken: Memorial Essays for Gösta W. Ahlström* (Sheffield: Sheffield Academic, 1995), 238–251.

Hadjiev, Tchavdar S., "The Theological Transformations of Zephaniah's Proclamation of Doom," *ZAW* 126 (2014), 506–520.

Hagedorn, Anselm, "When Did Zephaniah Become a Supporter of Josiah's Reform?" *JTS NS* 62 (2011), 453–475.

Hagedorn, Anselm, *Die Anderen im Spiegel: Israels Auseinandersetzung mit den Volkern in den Buchern Nahum, Zefanja, Obadja und Joel*, BZAW 414 (Berlin: de Gruyter, 2011).

Hays, Christopher B., "From Propaganda to Apocalypse: An Empirical Model for the Formation of Isaiah 24–27," *Hebrew Bible and Ancient Israel* 6 (2017), 120–144.

Hays, Christopher B., *Hidden Riches: A Sourcebook for the Comparative Study of the Old Testament and the Ancient Near East* (Louisville, KY: Westminster John Knox, 2014).

Hays, Christopher B., *The Origins of Isaiah 24–27: Josiah's Festival Scroll for the Fall of Assyria.* (Cambridge: Cambridge University Press, 2019).

Hibbard, J. Todd, *Intertextuality in Isaiah 24–27: The Reuse and Evocation of Earlier Texts and Traditions*, FAT II/16 (Tübingen: Mohr Siebeck, 2006).

Hibbard, J. Todd, "Isaiah 24–27 and Trito-Isaiah: Exploring Some Connections," in *Formation and Intertextuality in Isaiah 24–27*, ed. J. T. Hibbard and H. C. P. Kim (Atlanta: Society of Biblical Literature, 2013), 183–199.

Holladay, William L., "Reading Zephaniah with a Concordance: Suggestions for a Redaction History," *JBL* 120 (2001), 671–684.

Ihromi, "Die Häufung der Verben des Jubelns in Zephanja 3:14 f, 16–18: *rnn, rw', śmḥ, 'lz, śwś* und *gîl*," *VT* 33 (1983): 106–110.

Irsigler, Hubert, *Zefanja*, HThKAT (Freiburg: Herder: 2002).

Jones, Barry A., "The Seventh-Century Prophets in Twenty-First Century Research," *CurBR* 14 (2016).

Kaiser, Otto, *Introduction to the Old Testament: A Presentation of Its Results and Problems* (Minneapolis: Augsburg, 1977).

Kapelrud, Arvid S., *The Message of the Prophet Zephaniah: Morphology and Ideas* (Oslo: Universitetsforlaget, 1975).

Kselman, John S., "Zephaniah, Book of," *ABD* 6.

Levinson, Bernard M., *Deuteronomy and the Hermeneutics of Legal Innovation* (New York: Oxford University Press, 1998).

Mason, Rex, *Zephaniah, Habakkuk, Joel* (Sheffield: Sheffield Academic, 1994).

Monroe, Lauren A. S. Monroe, *Josiah's Reform and the Dynamics of Defilement: Israelite Rites of Violence and the Making of a Biblical Text* (Oxford: Oxford University Press, 2011).

Neef, Heinz-Dieter, "Vom Gottesgericht zum universalen Heil: Komposition und Redaktion des Zephanjabuches," *ZAW* 111 (1999), 530–546.

Noegel, Scott B., "Dialect and Politics in Isaiah 24–27," *AuOr* 12 (1994), 177–192.

Parpola, Simo, *Assyrian Prophecies*, SAA 9 (Helsinki: Helsinki University Press, 1997).

Perlitt, Lothar, *Die Propheten Nahum, Habakuk, Zephanja*, ATD 25/1 (Göttingen: Vandenhoeck & Ruprecht, 2004).

Polaski, Donald C., *Authorizing an End: The Isaiah Apocalypse and Intertextuality*, BibInt 50 (Leiden: Brill, 2001).

Richards, Kent Harold, "Zephaniah," in *The HarperCollins Study Bible: Fully Revised and Updated*, ed. Harold W. Attridge (New York: HarperCollins, 1993).

Roberts, J. J. M., *Nahum, Habakkuk, and Zephaniah*, OTL (Louisville, KY: Westminster John Knox, 1991).

Rollston, Christopher A., *Writing and Literacy in the World of Ancient Israel: Epigraphic Evidence from the Iron Age*, ABS 11 (Atlanta, GA: Society of Biblical Literature, 2010).

Rom-Shiloni, Dalit, "Facing Destruction and Exile: Inner-Biblical Exegesis in Jeremiah and Ezekiel," *ZAW* 117 (2005).

Rudolph, Wilhelm, *Micha—Nahum—Habakuk—Zephanja*, KAT 13.3 (Gütersloh: Gerd, 1975).

Russell, Jenni, "No Dunkirk Spirit Can Save Britain from Brexit Defeat," *New York Times* online, July 28, 2017, https://www.nytimes.com/2017/07/28/opinion/dunkirk-christopher-nolan-brexit.html?_r=0.

Schniedewind, William M., *How the Bible Became a Book: The Textualization of Ancient Israel* (Cambridge: Cambridge University Press, 2004).

Scholl, Reinhard, *Die Elenden in Gottes Thronrat. Stilistisch-kompositorische Untersuchungen zu Jesaja 24–27*, BZAW 274 (Berlin: de Gruyter, 2000).

Seybold, Klaus, *Satirische Prophetie: Studien zum Buch Zefanja*, SBS 120 (Stuttgart: Katholisches Bibelwerk, 1985).

Smith, J. Z., "Wisdom and Apocalyptic," in *Map Is Not Territory* (repr. ed.; Chicago: University of Chicago Press, 1993).

Smith, L. P./Lacheman, E. R., "The Authorship of the Book of Zephaniah," *JNES* 9 (1950).

Smith, R. L., *Micah-Malachi*, WBC 32 (Waco, TX: Word, 1984).

Stackert, Jeffrey, *Rewriting the Torah: Literary Revision in Deuteronomy and the Holiness Legislation*, FAT 52 (Tübingen: Mohr Siebeck, 2007).

Sweeney, Marvin A., "A Form-Critical Reassessment of the Book of Zephaniah," *CBQ* 53 (1991).

Sweeney, Marvin A., "Dating Prophetic Texts," *Hebrew Studies* 48 (2007).

Sweeney, Marvin A., "Jesse's New Shoot in Isaiah 11: A Josianic Reading of the Prophet Isaiah," in *A Gift of G-d in Due Season: Essays in Scripture and Community in Honor of James A. Sanders*, ed. R. D. Weis and D. M. Carr; JSOTSup 225 (Sheffield: Sheffield Academic, 1996).

Sweeney, Marvin A., *King Josiah of Judah: The Lost Messiah of Israel* (Oxford: Oxford University Press, 2001).

Sweeney, Marvin A., "Textual Citations in Isaiah 24–27: Toward an Understanding of the Redactional Function of Chapters 24–27 in the Book of Isaiah," *JBL* 107 (1988), 39–52.

Sweeney, Marvin A., *Zephaniah: A Commentary*, Hermeneia (Minneapolis: Fortress, 2003).

Sweeney, Marvin A., "Zephaniah: A Paradigm for the Study of the Prophetic Books," *CurBS* 7 (1999), 119–145.

Sweeney, Marvin A., "Zephaniah: Prophet of His Time—Not the End Time!" *BRev* 20:6 (December 2004), 34–40.

Van der Toorn, Karel, "From the Mouth of the Prophet: The Literary Fixation of the Jeremiah's Prophecies in the Context of the Ancient Near East," in *Inspired Speech: Prophecy in the Ancient Near East*, ed. J. Kaltner, and L. Stulman, JSOTSupp 378 (London: T & T Clark, 2004).

Van der Toorn, Karel, *Scribal Culture and the Making of the Hebrew Bible* (Cambridge, MA: Harvard University Press, 2007).

Vlaardingerbroek, Johannes, *Zephaniah*, HCOT (Leuven: Peeters, 1999).

Welch, Eric L., "The Roots of Anger: An Economic Perspective on Zephaniah's Oracle against the Philistines," *VT* 63 (2013), 471–485.

Williams, Donald L., "The Date of Zephaniah," *JBL* 82 (1963), 77–88.

Williamson, H. G. M., *The Book Called Isaiah: Deutero-Isaiah's Role in Composition and Redaction* (Oxford: Oxford University Press, 1994).

Wilson, Robert, *Prophecy and Society in Ancient Israel* (Philadelphia: Fortress, 1984).

Wilson, Robert, "Scribal Culture and the Composition of the Book of Isaiah," in *The Bible as a Human Witness to Divine Revelation: Hearing the Word of God through Historically Dissimilar Traditions*, ed. Randall Heskett and Brian Irwin, LHBOTS 469 (New York: T & T Clark International, 2010).

Wright, Jacob L., "Commensal Politics in Ancient Western Asia: The Background to Nehemiah's Feasting," *ZAW* 122 (2010), 212–233, 333–352.

Joachim Eck

The Song of the Unfruitful Vineyard (Isa 5:1–7): Its Position in the Book of Isaiah and Its Reception in Late Layers of Isaiah and the Twelve

אָשִׁירָה נָּא לִידִידִי שִׁירַת דּוֹדִי לְכַרְמוֹ "Let me sing for my good friend a song about him, my dear one, regarding his vineyard …" (Isa 5:1a). Who would anticipate, when listening for the first time to these poetic lines, that they are the beginning of one of the harshest prophecies of doom in the Old Testament? The power, depth and rhetorical art of Isaiah's Song of the Unfruitful Vineyard (Isa 5:1–7) has fascinated listeners and readers from the very first moment. Therefore, it is no wonder that this poem already found its first echoes both in the book of Isaiah itself and the book of the Twelve, namely in Micah. At the same time, Isaiah's song is one of the most puzzling prophecies. For instance, the question of its genre is extremely hard to answer. Is it a love song, a lawsuit, a satirical polemic or simply a prophecy of doom, just to name four of the many proposals that have been considered? Since this matter is not primarily relevant when dealing with the reception of Isa 5:1–7 in late layers of Isaiah and Micah, the voluminous scholarly debate on this issue need not be recapitulated here.[1] We may therefore proceed with the structure, which stands out because it is both simple and complex.

---

1 For discussion of the topic see Rüdiger Bartelmus, "Beobachtungen zur literarischen Struktur des sog. Weinbergslieds (Jes 5,1–7). Möglichkeiten und Grenzen der formgeschichtlichen Methode bei der Interpretation von Texten aus dem corpus propheticum," in *Auf der Suche nach dem archimedischen Punkt der Textinterpretation: Studien zu einer philologisch-linguistisch fundierten Exegese alttestamentlicher Texte*, ed. Rüdiger Bartelmus (Zürich: Pano, 2002): 319–336 (here 319–325); Rebecca W. Poe Hays, "Sing Me a Parable of Zion: Isaiah's Vineyard (5:1–7) and Its Relation

---

Article note: I would like to express my gratitude to the École biblique et archéologique française de Jérusalem, which granted me a postdoctoral fellowship and thus supported the finalization of this article.
For discussion of the topic see Rüdiger Bartelmus, "Beobachtungen zur literarischen Struktur des sog. Weinbergslieds (Jes 5,1–7). Möglichkeiten und Grenzen der formgeschichtlichen Methode bei der Interpretation von Texten aus dem corpus propheticum," in *Auf der Suche nach dem archimedischen Punkt der Textinterpretation: Studien zu einer philologisch-linguistisch fundierten Exegese alttestamentlicher Texte*, ed. Rüdiger Bartelmus (Zürich: Pano, 2002): 319–336 (here 319–325); Rebecca W. Poe Hays, "Sing Me a Parable of Zion: Isaiah's Vineyard (5:1–7) and Its Relation to the 'Daughter Zion' Tradition," *JBL* 135 (2016): 743–761 (here 746–747); Hugh G. M. Williamson, *Isaiah 1–5*, ICC (London: T&T Clark, 2006): 327–328; John T. Willis, "The Genre of Isaiah 5:1–7," *JBL* 96 (1977): 337–362.

https://doi.org/10.1515/9783110705799-009

1 The Structure of Isa 5:1–7

The structure of the Song of the Unfruitful Vineyard[2] is marked by several changes of the identity of the speaker. In v. 1a, the prophet announces a song about[3] an intimate friend who owned a vineyard.[4] This introduction is followed by the first part of the song in vv. 1b–2, where the prophet recites in third person perspective the story of his dear friend who cultivated a vineyard with great diligence. But it yielded foul fruit instead of good grapes.[5]

In the subsequent verse 3, the particle וְעַתָּה marks the beginning of a new section.[6] The song proper already seems to be over[7] because the text now directly turns to the audience, who are addressed as the people of Jerusalem and Judah. They are asked to render judgment between "me and my vineyard". Quite unexpectedly, the prophet turns out to represent the voice of a different person here, namely that of his dear friend who owns the vineyard. He seems to represent him authentically and with full authority as he speaks on his behalf in first person singular. Here, the question arises by what authority he does this.[8] This refers to the next chapter, Isa 6, where the question is answered by Isaiah's prophetic voca-

---

to the 'Daughter Zion' Tradition," *JBL* 135 (2016): 743–761 (here 746–747); Hugh G. M. Williamson, *Isaiah 1–5*, ICC (London: T&T Clark, 2006): 327–328; John T. Willis, "The Genre of Isaiah 5:1–7," *JBL* 96 (1977): 337–362.

2 For a concise summary of the structure see Willem A. M. Beuken, *Jesaja 1–12*, HThKAT (Freiburg: Herder, 2003), 134. For fuller dicussion see Williamson, *Isaiah 1–5*, 325–327; Joachim Eck, "Isaiah's Song of the Unfruitful Vineyard (Isa 5.1–7) and the Biblical Concept of Justice and Righteousness," in *Faith and Reason. An Interdisciplinary Construction of Human Rights*, West-östliche Denkwege 25, eds. Marko Trajkovic and Joost van Loon (Sankt Augustin: Academia, 2016): 15–32 (here 17–23); Peter Höffken, "Probleme in Jesaja 5,1–7," *ZTK* 79 (1982): 392–410 (here 397–400); Hubert Irsigler, "Speech acts and intention in the 'Song of the Vineyard' Isaiah 5:1–7," *OTE* 10 (1997): 39–68 (here 45–47).
A concentric structure, which in its largest parts is not based on concentric repetitions of lexemes but on associations derived from content, is proposed by Beuken, *Jesaja 1–12*, 135, and Konrad Schmid, *Jesaja 1–23*, ZBK.AT 19.1 (Zürich: TVZ, 2011): 80.

3 The construct chain שִׁירַת דּוֹדִי is a *genitivus obiectivus*, see Irsigler, "Speech acts": 45–46.

4 Cf. Hugh G. M. Williamson, *Isaiah 1–5*, 326, who observes that the metre of the first line consists of 3 + 3, which is slightly longer than the following lines. It is thus characterized as an introductory rubric.

5 Cf. Rüdiger Bartelmus, "Beobachtungen": 328–329.

6 Cf. Williamson, *Isaiah 1–5*, 338, who notes that וְעַתָּה marks the shift from setting out the circumstances of the situation to the essence of the case. Here, it indicates the shift from tale to request for some sort of judgement.

7 Irsigler, "Speech acts": 46.

8 Cf. *Ibid.*, 46, who underlines that the abrupt change of roles "indicates a specific competence of the poet, to follow his friend's role directly" and argues that the interpretation of the metaphorical speech in v. 7 reveals the speaker's prophetic competence.

tion. Like Isa 5:1–2, the vocation account is also told from a first person singular perspective. Isaiah 5:4 then presents two questions to the audience for judgement. These, however, are rhetorical in nature[9] so that verse 4 prompts the direction of the judgement which the audience is asked to make by verse 3.[10] Since the prophet already gave testimony of the perfect diligence which the owner applied to his vineyard (v. 2), the answer to the question of verse 4a what else he could have done is obviously "nothing". Verse 4b is also rhetorical in meaning since the vineyard owner is clearly not interested in learning a variety of possible natural influences which cannot be controlled by an ordinary human wine-grower but may indeed cause a perfectly cultivated vineyard to yield bad fruit or even no fruit at all. Instead, the tone of the vineyard owner's question in v. 4b indicates the apodictic character of his expectation. He seems to have controlled and averted all possible influences that might have caused the vineyard to yield foul fruit. Thus, the rhetorical question in v. 4b gives a slight hint of the vineyard owner's universal divine power. The rhetorical questions in v. 4 do not ask what they ask but they raise questions about the vineyard owner who asks them.

The next section, vv. 5–6, is again introduced by the particle וְעַתָּה "now", which here marks the progress from the verdict, which is implied in v. 4, to the sentence.[11] Since the questions in v. 4 are rhetorical, the vineyard owner does not wait for the judgement he asked for but interrupts the judicial considerations of his audience and announces his own judgement against the vineyard. He intends to destroy its protection from wild animals, to stop all pruning and hoeing, and even to command the clouds not to rain upon it. The last-mentioned command already indicates that the vineyard owner must either be at least a prophet like Elijah, who successfully performed a ritual for rain after his triumph over the 400 prophets of Baal (1 Kings 18:41–46), or, more probable, God himself, whose commands the clouds obey.[12]

Nonetheless, the vineyard owner's identity remains obscure until it is clarified in v. 7, the last section of the song. Introduced by the emphatic particle כִּי, this final passage now speaks of כֶּרֶם יְהוָה צְבָאוֹת "the vineyard of YHWH Sabaoth", thus revealing the identity of the prophet's friend. Since verse 7 refers to the vineyard owner, who turns out to be YHWH Sabaoth, in third person singular, and since the same verse identifies his vineyard with the house of Israel and the people of Judah, it is also obvious that the speaker's identity has changed again. The prophet here speaks with his own voice as he did in the introduction and the first

---

9 Peter Höffken, *Das Buch Jesaja. Kapitel 1–39*, NSK-AT 18/1 (Stuttgart: Kath. Bibelwerk, 1993), 63.
10 Williamson, *Isaiah 1–5*, 339.
11 *Ibid.*, 339.
12 Höffken, *Jesaja 1–39*, 63–64.

section of the song (vv.1a and 1b–2).[13] The metaphorical meaning of the unfruit-fulness of the vineyard is then explained in v. 7b. While justice and righteousness (מִשְׁפָּט and צְדָקָה) should have grown in the society of Judah like good grapes in a well-cultivated vineyard, the foul fruit in fact produced stands for bloodshed and cries of distress (מִשְׂפָּח and צְעָקָה).

In sum, Isa 5:1–7 consists of five sections. After the introduction by the prophet (v. 1a), the following four main sections are characterized by a chiastic pattern which results from changes in the speaker's voice as illustrated in the chart below. Although the prophet's song proper already ends in v. 2,[14] the subsequent prophetic interaction cannot be separated from it as it is necessary to understand its meaning and vice versa. Therefore, the Isaiah 5:1–7 forms a literary unit.[15]

INTRODUCTION Verse 1a:	Prophet's voice	Announcement of a song about his dear friend, who had a vineyard
Verses 1b–2:	**Prophet's voice**	The story of the friend's efforts devoted to his vineyard and the disappointing results
Verses 3–4:	*Friend's voice*	Speaking with his friend's voice, the prophet requires his audience to render a judgment concerning his own and the vineyard's behaviour
Verses 5–6:	*Friend's voice*	Announcement of the prophet's friend that he will destroy and abandon the vineyard
Verse 7:	**Prophet's voice**	Identification of the friend with YHWH and of the vineyard with the people of Jerusalem and Judah, who yielded bloodshed and distress instead of law and justice

(SONG AND PROPHETIC INTERACTION — bracketing Verses 1b–2 through Verse 7)

---

13 Cf. Irsigler, "Speech acts": 46. Theoretically, verse 7 could also be spoken by a new anonymous voice. But considering that the first person singular voice of the prophet, who spoke in vv. 1–2, was implicitly replaced by the voice of the vineyard owner in v. 3, it is most natural to assume that the next implicit change of the speaker's voice between vv. 6 and 7 involves the same two persons as before. The fact that these changes in the speaker's identity happen without an introduction underlines the deep unity between the prophet and his intimate friend, who turns out to be YHWH himself in v. 7. Both speak with one voice although they represent different perspectives.
14 Williamson, *Isaiah 1–5*, 325–326;
15 Irsigler, "Speech acts": 43–44. Williamson, *Isaiah 1–5*, 329, rightly notes that the change of person at v. 3 is a simple ruse which heightens the tension and is certainly no reason for literary-critical surgery. The literary-critical distinctions proposed by Oswald Loretz, "Weinberglied und prophetische Deutung im Protest-Song Jes 5,1–7," *UF* 7 (1975): 573–576; Höffken, "Probleme in Jesaja 5,1–7": 404–410; Herbert Niehr, "Zur Gattung von Jes 5,1–7," *BZ NF* 30 (1986): 99–104; Uwe Becker, *Jesaja – von der Botschaft zum Buch*, FRLANT 178 (Göttingen: Vandenhoeck, 1997), 128–134, do not seem necessary considering the rhetoric and theological (see note 12) value of the oscillating identity of the speaker.

2 The Position of the Vineyard Song Isa 5:1–7 within Isa 1–12

Regarding the position of the Vineyard Song in the Book of Isaiah, it is important to note that this text is the first and only one in Isa 1–12 to explicitly announce to an assembly of the people of Judah that their kingdom will be completely destroyed. Therefore, it has a unique function in Isa – 12 and the whole book. The vineyard owner's verdict of annihilation, of course, raises the question of its reasons. In a general and theologically deep way, the Song of the Unfruitful Vineyard points out that the people of Judah and Jerusalem failed to yield justice and righteousness and, instead, brought forth bloodshed, violence and terror, as expressed by the Hebrew nouns מִשְׂפָּח "bloodshed" and צְעָקָה "cry of distress" (v. 7). This critique takes up and summarizes the preceding social-critical texts of Isa 1 (esp. vv. 2–4, 15b–17, 21–23, 27) and Isa 3:1–4:1 (esp. 3:9–16), and guides the understanding of the subsequent critique expressed in the woe-oracles in 5:8–23 and 10:1–4 as well as in 9:13–18.[16] There is one fundamental difference between the critique of Isa 1 and the other passages mentioned. Chapter 1 grants in vv. 16–17 and 18–20 the possibility to repent and return to a sound relationship to the Lord, and it urges not to miss this last chance. All other social-critical passages in Isa 1–12, however, announce the unconditional arrival of doom. It can no longer be averted by repentance.[17] The reason for this difference, which corresponds to the function of the superscription 2:1 as a dividing line, seems to be that the Day of YHWH, which is announced in Isa 2:10–22 as a present fact, has changed the situation. Since the Day of YHWH is described as a present phenomenon in Isa 2:10–22, i. e. it has already begun, repentance and conversion are no longer able to avert the doom but can only save individual persons who then become the group of Israel's remnant. On his Day, the Lord reveals himself as the only one who is exalted (v. 11b: וְנִשְׂגַּב יְהוָה לְבַדּוֹ בַּיּוֹם הַהוּא) and all other persons or things which are or deem themselves high and lofty are brought low. Yet, since the solemn proclamation of the Day of YHWY in Isa 2:10–22 does not tell why and how the announced exaltation and humiliations are going to happen and what the whole description of this day specifically means, it makes sense to read the subsequent chapters 3–10 as specifications of these open questions. This is confirmed by numerous references

---

16 Cf. Becker, *Jesaja*, 127–128.
17 See already Joachim Eck, "Divine Strategies against Abuse of Power in the Opening of the Book of Isaiah and the Exodus Story. Some Aspects where Micah is not Similar to Isaiah," *ZAW* 130 (2018): 4–25 (here 13–14).

to Isa 2:10–22, for example in 3:16; 5:15–16; 6:1 כסא רם ונשא as well as 9:8–10; 10:12 and 10:33–34.

Along these lines of thought, chapters 3, 5 and 10:1–4 as well as parts of chpt. 9 give evidence of the guilt of God's people by accusing them of sin and iniquity in the areas of society and, occasionally, cult. The Vineyard Song summarizes the core point of the accusation and proclaims the judgement. Justice and righteousness were perverted into violence and injustice. Since YHWH is exalted in justice and shows himself holy in righteousness (5:16), Israel's guilt results in a massive rejection of his divine kingship, which is revealed to Isaiah in chpt. 6. The execution of the destruction of Judah which Isaiah 5:5–6 metaphorically announces by depicting the imminent end of the Lord's vineyard is described in the subsequent chapters from two complementary perspectives. Isaiah 6 and Isaiah 7:1–17 focus on the description of its interiour aspects. By calling a prophet to harden the heart of God's people so that it can neither see nor hear nor understand (Isa 6:9–10), all exteriour perceptions and interiour functions of the heart are blocked so that a return to the Lord as the only true protector, healer and saviour is impossible, and the people continue their way towards death and destruction until the end. Isaiah 7:1–17 serves as a supreme example of the effects of the prophet's commission of hardening.[18] The exteriour aspect of the Day of YHWH and the resulting judgment against Israel is mainly described in the texts found between 7:18 and 10:34. Complementary to the prophet's commission of hardening, the Lord sends the Assyrian and some other nations, cf. chpt. 9, against his people and uses him as the rod in his outstretched hand to physically destroy the kingdoms of Israel. The described aspects of the Day of YHWH are shaped to form a basic theological unity by multiple cross-references, notwithstanding certain less consistent details.

The development from the judgment against Israel beginning with the Day of YHWH in Isa 2, towards the judgment against the nations in Isa 13–23, which is characterized by a resumption of the Day of YHWH in Isa 13, is marked by the arrogance of the Assyrian figure, who refuses to be an instrument in the hand of the Lord and considers himself to be superiour (10:5–19). Isa 11 and 12 as well as the preceding messianic texts open a positive perspective of salvation in spite of doom, which begins with the purification of the prophet from sin and iniquity and his ordination as a servant of the divine throne in Isa 6 and develops along the lines of a holy remnant and a righteous messianic leadership.

---

18 Cf. Becker, *Jesaja*, 57–58; Odil Hannes Steck, "Rettung und Verstockung. Exegetische Bemerkungen zu Jes 7,3–9," in *Wahrnehmungen Gottes im Alten Testament. Gesammelte Studien*, ed. Odil Hannes Steck, TB 70 (München: Kaiser, 1982): 171–186 (here 177).

3 The Reception of the Vineyard Song in Isa 7:23–25

Two chapters after Isa 5:1–7, some of its aspects are taken up in 7:23–25, which scholars agree is a late redactional addition.[19] The connection with the vineyard song is made explicit by several keywords.[20] Verse 23b speaks of places with 1000 valuable vines, cf. שֹׂרֵק in Isa 5:2 ("choice vines"),[21] which will become a property of briers and thorns (לְשָׁמִיר וְלַשַּׁיִת יִהְיֶה). Isaiah 7:24 describes that briers and thorns, which in the Vineyard Song (5:6) are the future vegetation growing on the devastated former vineyard, will cover the whole land so that men will carry weapons when they enter it. "Briers and thorns" are used as an image of a danger here which can be fought by weapons.[22] Similarly, verse 25 uses "briers and thorns" for a third time and describes them as something to be afraid of. Due to this wild vegetation, mountains which used to be hoed (יֵעָדֵרוּן, Ni. impf. of עדר) shall become impassable. This includes another reference to Isa 5:6, where the vineyard owner decides that the vineyard shall not be hoed any more (לֹא יֵעָדֵר, again Ni. impf. of עדר). Also the expectation of Isa 5:5bβ that it will be "for trampling down" (לְמִרְמָס) is taken up in the concluding remark of 7:25, according to which the place will be "for trampling down" (לְמִרְמָס).[23]

One question raised by a simple reading of the text is why briers and thorns, as plants which can hurt when one approaches them but are not aggressive by

---

[19] E.g. Hugh G. M. Williamson, *Isaiah 6–12*, ICC (London: T&T Clark, 2018), 181–182; Beuken, *Jesaja 1–12*, 188–191; Becker, *Jesaja*, 34–35, 214; Höffken, *Jesaja 1–39*, 94–95; Hans Wildberger, *Jesaja 1–12*, BK.AT X/1 (Neukirchen-Vluyn: Neukirchener, 1978), 302–303, 307; William McKane, "The Interpretation of Isaiah VII 14–25," *VT* 17 (1967): 208–219 (here 218).

[20] Cf. Beuken, *Jesaja 1–12*, 188, 209; Becker, *Jesaja*, 35; Höffken, *Jesaja 1–39*, 94; Williamson, *Isaiah 6–12*, 180, 190–192.

[21] Considering the fact that one shekel is a very high price even for an expensive vine, Wildberger, *Jesaja 1–12*, 308, understands the 1000 vines as a *pars pro toto* for a fine piece of land where this amount of vines can be planted.

[22] Wildberger, *Jesaja 1–12*, 308, thinks verse 24 does not mean that only armed warriors enter the land in order to chase away some last hidden enemies. According to him, those who enter it with bow and arrows must be hunters because the devastated land is left over to wild animals. However, the text says nothing about hunting or wild animals. The fact that bow and arrows *can* be used for hunting constitutes no evidence as they are also used in war. As verse 25 explicitly speaks of fear caused by briers and thorns, it is more probable that verse 24 means some danger to be fought by bow and arrows. Beuken, *Jesaja 1–12*, 209, speculates such a danger could be caused by wild animals.

[23] See already Hugh G. M. Williamson, "Poetic Vision in Isaiah 7:18–25," in *The Desert Will Bloom. Poetic Visions in Isaiah*, ed. A. Joseph Everson and Hyun Chul Paul Kim, Ancient Israel and Its Literature 4 (Atlanta: SBL, 2009): 77–89, here 81.

themselves, are used in vv. 24 and 25 as an image for someone or something which is actively aggressive so that defense by weapons is necessary. Moreover, while a cutting tool like a large knife can be helpful for the removal of thorny plants, bow and arrows is a kind of weapon most useless for such a purpose. The idea of shooting every single stalk with an arrow in a land covered with briers and thorns is quite funny. Obviously, this is to indicate that briers and thorns are an image for aggressive human enemies here. A solution to the question can be derived from the use of the same Hebrew lexemes "briers and thorns" in Isa 10:17. Since these plants pose no logical problems there, I consider it as the passage which motivated 7:24. Isaiah 10:27 says that the Light of Israel, i. e. YHWH, shall be for a fire and will burn "his thorns and his briers". Here, שִׁיתוֹ וּשְׁמִירוֹ means the allies or high officers of the arrogant King of Assyria, against whom doom is announced because he considers himself more powerful than Israel's God, the master who sent him (10:5–6). These allies or high officers are referred to in 10:16 as "his fat ones" מִשְׁמַנָּיו, and they are fought by the Lord by means of "leanness" (רָזוֹן) and fire (וְיֵקַד יְקֹד כִּיקוֹד אֵשׁ). Isaiah 10:17 adds to this that "his", i. e. the Assyrian king's, "briers and thorns" will be devoured by the fire of the Lord: וְהָיָה אוֹר־יִשְׂרָאֵל לְאֵשׁ וּקְדוֹשׁוֹ לְלֶהָבָה וּבָעֲרָה וְאָכְלָה שִׁיתוֹ וּשְׁמִירוֹ בְּיוֹם אֶחָד Thus, the metaphor of "briers and thorns" here represents the Assyrian invader's helpers who come over the country like a plague. This is taken up in 7:24, where the land is grown over by such hostile plants, and people only dare to enter it carrying bow and arrows. The double occurrence of "briers and thorns" שמיר ושית creates an *inclusio* between 7:24 and 10:17 which emphasizes, for one thing, the idea that the country is invaded by a foreign power, which in the light of 10:17 must be the Assyrians. In a very general sense which included not only Assyria but also Egypt as possible aggressors, this perspective was already expressed in 7:18–19 in the image of an insect plague called by YHWH to occupy the country. Whereas Isaiah 7:18–19 illustrates the moment of the conquest of the land, the image of briers and thorns in v. 24 describes the result of this occupation. A second aspect of the *inclusio* formed by "briers and thorns" שמיר ושית between 7:24 and 10:17 is that it encompasses all those texts which, in line with the view stated in 7:18, describe the Assyrian aggression as a judgement sent by YHWH against his people. Thus, it confirms the interpretation (explained above) that the texts between Isa 7:18 and 10:34 are mainly dedicated to the exterior aspect of the execution of the Day of YHWH.

A more general question is what the references to the Vineyard Song in chpt. 7 intend to express. Among the different parts of the Vineyard Song, the author(s) of 7:23–25 chose to take up the image of a vineyard planted with choice vines from 5:2, where the vineyard owner's particular care was described, and the image of an abandoned wasteland trampled down by animals and overgrown with thorns and briers from 5:5–6. So, the emphasis is on the idea that YHWH's care for the planting of his delight, i. e. his chosen people settled down in the promised land, leads to no better end than its complete destruction. Why put an emphasis on this at the end of Isa 7? At the same time, it strikes that the core message of the song, according to which God's people produced injustice instead of the good fruit of justice, seems to have no relevance for the story told in Isa 7:1–17. During the encounter of Ahaz and Isaiah, prophetic social critique simply does not occur. The only obvious point of contact between the Vineyard Song and Isa 7:1–17 is that both the conduct of God's people, as generally described in 5:1–7, on the one hand, and Ahaz's behaviour as described in 7:1–17, on the other hand, are judged as utterly negative and therefore lead to announcements of doom. Since the end of the Immanuel story in Isa 7:17 is somewhat obscure,[24] one of the intentions of the redactions found in vv.18–25 will have been to clarify that doom is announced. But why do so by reference to the Vineyard Song? What is the meaning of the resulting inclusion between Isa 5:1–7 and 7:23–25?

One parallel aspect in Isa 5:1–7 and chpt. 7 lies in the situation of the persons exposed to aggression by superior political enemies. The Vineyard Song concludes in 5:7b that instead of righteousness (צְדָקָה) there was only a cry of distress (צְעָקָה). The word צְעָקָה "outcry" plays a prominent role in the vocation account of Moses in Ex 2:23–4:17. It is twice used for the cry of the oppressed Israelites (Ex 3:7,9), a cry which is heard by YHWH and urges him to call Moses to lead Israel out of Egypt. As pointed out in my article on Isaiah and the Exodus,[25] the vocation account of Isaiah (Isa 6) stands in a similar context because it relates YHWH's call of a prophet in response to the outcry of the oppressed mentioned at the end of the Vineyard Song. The downfall of the people of God as a whole and their upper class in particular, which is prophecied in 5:13–17 with reference to the Day of YHWH (see 5:15–16 and 2:10–22), puts an end to the injustice and violence prevailing in the society of Judah and opens the possibility for a new start for a remnant which comprises the prophet himself, his sons Shear-jashub (7:3) and Maher-shalal-hash-baz (8:1–4), and the disciples mentioned in 8:16–18.[26] The birth of a new royal child in 9:1–6 (MT) opens to the remnant a perspective of a future which is free from the former burden and yoke (9:4) and blessed with a peaceful government in accordance with divine justice and righteousness.

---

24 Höffken, *Jesaja 1–39*, 92, who states that verse 17 announces a disaster in relatively obscure words ("in relativ dunklen Worten"); Wildberger, *Jesaja 1–12*, 297.

25 Eck, "Divine Strategies against Abuse of Power."

26 Cf. the discussion of the meaning of the name שְׁאָר יָשׁוּב (Isa 7:2) and the idea of a remnant by Wildberger, *Jesaja 1–12*, 277–279.

When we now compare the situation of the distressed whose cry is heard by YHWH when he in vain looks for the fruit of righteousness in his vineyard (Isa 5:7) with the situation of Ahaz in Isa 7, it can be noted that the Judean king is in distress, too. He is confronted with a military attack by two of his neighbour kings who were together more powerful than him.[27] And more, they plan to snatch his lawful kingship away from him and give it to the son of Tabe-el, who was obviously willing to co-operate with Pekah and Remaljah in the matter of their anti-Assyrian plans.[28] They were even prepared to dethrone the dynasty of David. In reaction to this danger, the hearts of the Davidic king and his people shake as trees shake before the wind (7:2). So, the situation of Ahaz in this matter of foreign policy may be compared with the distress of the poor and weak within the society of Judah as described in chpt. 5. Ahaz, too, is exposed to despotic and unlawful decisions of more powerful political stakeholders. YHWH, as a God who sees the affliction of those in distress, comes to his aid by sending the prophet Isaiah to him with a prophecy of salvation (7:3–9) which in its concluding part reminds him of the existential importance of firmly trusting his God. When the required confidence is put to the test in another word of God inviting him to ask for a sign according to his wish (7:10–11), Ahas fails this test as he refuses to accept the divine word (v. 12).[29] It has long been noted that Isa 7 can be read as an example of the effect of Isaiah's commission of hardening in Isa 6.[30] Ahas rejects the offer of a sign although the divine word is advantageous to him. The reason seems to be that his heart is hardened by Isaiah's prophetic message (cf. Isa 6:9–10). His faith in God ends as soon as this would influence his political decisions. He refuses to accept a sign (7:12), which, if granted, would oblige him to seriously rely on YHWH's sovereignty and trust him alone.

---

27 In particular, the king of Aram had a predominant position, see Beuken, *Jesaja 1–12*, 192–193; Höffken, *Jesaja 1–39*, 83.

28 *Ibid.*, 87–88. Concerning the possible historic identity of Tabeel, see Beuken, *Jesaja 1–12*, 197–198. Otto Kaiser, *Das Buch des Propheten Jesaja. Kapitel 1–12*, ATD 17 (Göttingen: Vandenhoeck, 1981⁵), 144–145, however questions whether the figure of Tabeel might not rather have emerged from contemporary disputes instead of historical memories.

29 Cf. Beuken, *Jesaja 1–12*, 201, who admits that the new scene beginning in verse 10 can be set off from the preceding one as a different literary unit on the basis of literary-critical considerations but, at the same time, is clearly a continuation of the preceding scene (see also Höffken, *Jesaja 1–39*, 82, 87–88). For literary-critical arguments qualifying Isa 7:10–17 as a secondary addition resulting from a process of literary growth, see Kaiser, *Jesaja 1–12*, 151–152.

30 E.g. Rudolf Kilian, *Jesaja 1–12*, NEB (Würzburg: Echter, 1999²), 56; Hubert Irsigler, "Gott als König in Berufung und Verkündigung Jesajas," in *Ein Gott, eine Offenbarung: Beiträge zur biblischen Exegese, Theologie und Spiritualität. Festschrift für Notker Füglister OSB zum 60. Geburtstag*, ed. Friedrich V. Reiterer (Würzburg: Echter, 1991): 127–154 (here 151); Williamson, *Isaiah 6–12*, 106.

The presence of Isaiah's son Shear-jashub in the scene (7:3) is an already visible sign which invites Ahaz to become part of the small community of those who return to YHWH and are therefore his remnant.[31] But he does not even notice this exhortation which is implicit in the son's presence. In the context of foreign policy, which is the theme of Isa 7, conversion to YHWH would mean that Ahas would have to give up strategies for increasing his military strength by making alliances with more powerful foreign nations. Instead, he would have to fully trust God's advice given through Isaiah in 7:4. He would have to take heed and be quiet and fearless because the Lord himself promises that the enemies' plans will not succeed (7:4–9b). In sum, Ahas' rejection of the divine offer of a sign is a refusal to acknowledge YHWH's divine kingship as relevant for the political agenda.

Although the foreign affairs Ahaz has to deal with are a matter substantially different from the corrupt condition of the Judean society criticized in Isa 5, the wrongful attitudes of the Judean upper class and King Ahaz who is their head, are quite near to each other. The perversion of justice and righteousness into exploitation and oppression of the poor is an attack against YHWH's divine throne and his rule.[32] In a similar way, the rejection of his help against exterior enemies implies a denial of the divine kingship since the protection from exterior enemies is an indispensable royal task of any king.[33] But as YHWH's kingship is real and cannot

---

31 Concerning the much-disputed meaning of שְׁאָר יָשׁוּב, I follow Wildberger, *Jesaja 1–12*, 278–279, who understands the name in the context of the situation of Isa 7:1–9. Since Isaiah's son is already several years old here, he might have received his name during Isaiah's early ministry in order to underline his message. The name warns the Judeans that only a remnant will return to YHWH. Some who follow this invitation will be saved, most will fail to do so. A different proposal is made by Hugh G. M. Williamson, *Isaiah 6–12*, 121–123. While acknowledging the ambiguity of the name, he argues that its purpose must be some kind of encouragement as Isaiah's son appears in the context of the proclamation of an oracle of salvation. Therefore, he proposes that the presence of Shear-jashub means only a remnant of the enemies will return home after battle. In this case, the name שְׁאָר יָשׁוּב represents a hope given to those who are willing to fully trust YHWH by expecting salvation only from him (cf. v. 9b). Isaiah and his son represent a small group of Judeans who indeed have this faith. Still being a child, the son lacks strength to defend himself, and thus he ideally represents a person whose only hope of salvation is YHWH. Ahas is invited to join Isaiah and his son by trusting YHWH in the same way. The name שְׁאָר יָשׁוּב promises that such faith will not be in vain. For full discussion and further literature, see the two quoted authors.

32 The relevance of justice and righteousness for the divine kingship is more fully outlined by Eck, "Song of the Unfruitful Vineyard": 28, and Joachim Eck, "Divine Strategies": 10–13. Biblical texts such as Isa 9:6; 11:3–5; Ps 72:1–4 testify that these values are crucial to kingship in general.

33 See e. g. Pss 2; 110 concerning messianic kingship, and Pss 47; 48 concerning divine kingship. See also Michael Pietsch, "König/Königtum AT," *WiBiLex* (online https://www.bibelwissenschaft. de/stichwort/23844/, 2014, cited 3 October 2019): esp. paragraphs 1.2 and 3.2.

be rejected, God grants a sign of his own choice to confirm the prophecied defeat of Judah's enemies (7:13–16).

This interpretation is confirmed by the fact that the theophany in Isa 6 presents YHWH as divine king of the cosmos, and thus forms a bridge from chpt. 5 to chpt. 7. This line of thought is further emphasized by the resumption of the divine judgment against the unfruitful vineyard (5:5–6) in the concluding passage of Isa 7:23–25. Since King Ahas as the highest representative of the Judean society yielded the foul fruit of scepticism against YHWH's promise of salvation, and failed to yield the good fruit of belief (7:9b), the Davidic kingdom is bound to fall and the land will turn into wilderness. Yet, a remnant protected by the Lord will be able to survive there. The central intention of the late redactional addition 7:23–25, as it appears to me, is to underline that the rejection of the Lord's help by Ahaz for lack of belief marks the first and most crucial step in the historical development of the kingdom of Judah towards its complete destruction as announced in Isa 5:1–7. After Isaiah's vocation and his commission of hardening in Isa 6, the arrogance of the oppressors of the poor and weak, which is explicitly condemned in Isa 5:14–15, a passage referring back to Isa 2:10–22, becomes an irreversible attitude. The vocation of Isaiah begins to show its first effects. In line with Isa 6.9b–10, the Judean King, who is the head of the upper class accused in Isa 5, rejects the offer of divine salvation out of an educated (cf. 7:12) but arrogant blindness.

4 The New Vineyard Song of Isa 27:2–6

The probably most famous reception of Isa 5:1–7 in late layers of the Book of Isaiah is found in Isa 27:2–6, the New Vineyard Song in a composition also called the Apocalypse of Isaiah.[34] For reasons of space, I will limit myself to a few remarks. The introductory verse speaks of a pleasant vineyard and invites in 2nd person plural speech to sing of it. This is in contrast to the 1st person singular self-exhortation to sing in Isa 5:1. While the prophet was an isolated individual confronted

---

34 Most commentators agree that Isa 24–27 is of postexilic origin, see e.g. the discussions by Joseph Blenkinsopp, Isaiah 1–39, AB 19 (New York: Doubleday, 2000), 347–348; Otto Kaiser, *Das Buch des Propheten Jesaja. Kapitel 13–39*, ATD 18 (Göttingen: Vandenhoeck, 1973), 141–145, and Willem A. M. Beuken, *Jesaja 13–27*, HThK.AT (Freiburg: Herder, 2007), 313–314. In the present volume, Christopher B. Hays, "Isa 24–27 and Zephaniah Amid the Terrors and Hopes of the Seventh Century: An Intertextual Analysis," presents arguments for a late pre-exilic date of this composition. For Isa 27 alone, see also Beuken, *Isaiah 13–27*, 397, who thinks a late pre-exilic date of this chapter cannot be excluded. The term "Apocalypse" is meanwhile rejected by many interpreters, see *ibid.*, 310.

with an audience to whom he had to announce doom, the speaker of the New
Vineyard Song of Isa 27:2–6 is the Lord himself, and those invited to sing are a
larger group. The vineyard is no longer unfruitful but pleasant. In vv. 3–6, all
aspects of judgement which had been announced in Isa 5:5–6 are reversed and
transformed into positive statements.[35] There is peace between the Lord and the
vineyard, which could be a new Israel grown out of the remnant. The final verse 6
proclaims that Jacob and Israel will take root, blossom and put forth shoots in
future. The vineyard will yield an immensely rich harvest, filling the face of the
whole world with fruit (27:6b: וּמָלְאוּ פְנֵי־תֵבֵל תְּנוּבָה). In the background of this image
is the fullness of the whole earth, which is YHWH's glory according to Isa 6:3
(מְלֹא כָל־הָאָרֶץ כְּבוֹדוֹ). One day, the fruitful vineyard of Israel will no longer be a
frustration to YHWH but a particularly valuable evidence of his glory.

The New Vineyard Song of Isa 27:2–6 does not mention justice and righteousness, which are key notions in Isa 5:1–7. Instead, it announces peace, which is
the consequence resulting from justice and righteousness (cf. Isa 32:16–17).[36]
Thus, the New Vineyard Song sums up the positive developments described in
the preceding song Isa 26:1–19, where the Lord's justice and righteousness are
praised as the way to peace by a repentant community who confess that the Lord
is now their only God.

There are further allusions to Isa 5:1–7 in the Book of Isaiah which would be
interesting to analyse and discuss in detail. For reasons of space, however, it is
necessary to leave this task to later studies, noting that Isa 32:11–20; Isa 61; 60:21
and probably also 65:8 are further prominent examples of a reception of Isaiah's
Song of the Unfruitful Vineyard in later layers of the book.

5 Elements of Isaiah's Vineyard Song in the Book of Micah

5.1 Micah 1:6

A reader who first comes across the Book of Micah will soon find a divine word
against Samaria which proclaims that it will be made "a heap in the open country,

---

35 For details, see Blenkinsopp, *Isaiah 1–39*, 374–375; Beuken, *Jesaja 13–27*, 398–401.
36 Therefore, I would not fully agree with Blenkinsopp's view, *Isaiah 1–39*, 374, that the metaphor of Isa 5:1–7 is left behind as YHWH waits for שָׁלוֹם "peace" instead of "justice and righteousness" מִשְׁפָּט וּצְדָקָה.

a place for planting a vineyard" (לְעִי הַשָּׂדֶה לְמַטָּעֵי כָרֶם). Since the opening chapter of the Book of Micah includes a superscription as well as several prophetic words that recall Isaiah,[37] a sensitive reader or listener might immediately associate the catchword "vineyard" with Isaiah's Song of the Unfruitful Vineyard in Isa 5:1–7. However, the expression "plantings of a vineyard" מַטָּעֵי כָרֶם in Mi 1:6 is not at all a metaphor of a kingdom like the vineyard recalling Judah in Isa 5:1–7, but it is a description of the complete destruction that awaits Samaria. The land where Samaria once stood can now be used for an agricultural plantation. Nonetheless, the association of Samaria's destruction with Isaiah's Vineyard Song is legitimate insofar as this song also prophecies destruction, namely that of Judah and Jerusalem. The text of Mi 1:6 itself also contains a hint that it implies some meaning which goes beyond a simple description of a complete disaster. If we were to consider the parallelism of עִי הַשָּׂדֶה "a heap of rubble in the field" and מַטָּעֵי כָרֶם "plantings of a vineyard" as strictly synonymous, the second colon would appear inadequate because it does not simply describe a deserted spot after destruction as does the first colon. Rather, an area fit for planting a vineyard requires excellent soil and climate, and wine, as the excellent and valuable product of such plantings, is not at all associated with a destroyed and abandoned place. YHWH's statement that he will turn Samaria into plantings for a vineyard therefore indicates that the present sinful civilization will be destroyed in order to replace it with a new and wholesome culture. The plural "plantings" combined with the singular "of a vineyard" might point to some kind of an envisaged reunification of Samaria and Jerusalem. Although this might seem speculative, it is clear from the preceding v. 5 that this text contemplates the parallel fates of both Samaria and Jerusalem. This is confirmed by the fact that 1:6, as has often been noted, is closely related to 3:12, which announces the complete destruction of Jerusalem with similar imagery.[38] Since Judah and Jerusalem on the one hand and Jacob and the house of Israel on the other hand are presented as equally sinful in 1:5, which is immediately before the keyword "vineyard" occurs in 1:6, the mere use of this word in this context should be able to create an association with Isaiah's Song of the Unfruitful Vineyard[39] because in this song, the accusation is also directed

---

37 For the superscriptions Isa 1:1 and Mi 1:1 see Eck, *Jesaja 1 – Eine Exegese der Eröffnung des Jesaja-Buches: Die Präsentation Jesajas und JHWHs, Israels und der Tochter Zion*, BZAW 473 (Berlin etc.: De Gruyter, 2015), 28–58; Burkard M. Zapff, "Why is Micah similar to Isaiah?," *ZAW* 129 (2017): 536–554, here 537–538; for other shared motifs in Isa 1 and Mi 1 see *ibid.*, 538–545.
38 See e. g. Jörg Jeremias, *Die Propheten Joel, Obadja, Jona, Micha*, ATD 24,3 (Göttingen: Vandenhoeck, 2007), 136, 166.
39 Always provided that Isaiah's well-known prophecy of doom, cf. its reception in Isaiah, is older than Mi 1:6, which most exegetes assume.

against the "inhabitants of Jerusalem and men of Judah" (Isa 5:3) or, respectively, the "house of Israel" and "people of Judah" (Isa 5:7). Thus, Mi 1:5 resumes all transgressors mentioned in Isaiah's song, i. e. "the house of Israel", "Judah" and "Jerusalem", and adds Jacob and Samaria. Now it is strange that the image of plantings for a vineyard refers to Samaria in Mi 1:6 and not to Judah and Jerusalem. And the vineyard is neither used as a metaphor of Samaria nor does it represent an originally valuable but unfruitful piece of property that must be destroyed in the end. Rather, the vineyard points to a positive perspective which may follow after the destruction of Samaria. This positive sense of the vineyard image also exists in the Book of Isaiah, e. g. in the Vineyard Song of 27:2–6.

In spite of the above evidence, a proposal to understand the "plantings of a vineyard" in Mi 1:6 as an expression pointing to a positive perspective following the destruction of Samaria would appear as an over-interpretation if there was no text in the book which describes such a perspective with more specific references to the vineyard metaphor. Indeed, the very last chapter of Micah does not only express such a positive perspective for God's people but also includes specific references to Isaiah's Vineyard Song and its imagery.

5.2 Micah 7

The structure of Mi 7 is complex as the speech perspective changes several times and the speakers' identities are not always clear.[40] Nonetheless, many agree that it consists of two parts, the first one comprising vv. 1–7 and the second one vv. 8–20.[41]

Mi 7:1–7 is spoken by a prophetic voice from the 1st person singular perspective, which explicitly occurs in vv. 1 and 7.[42] The prophet describes the ethical corruption of all the inhabitants of the earth and proclaims a day of punishment (vv. 2–4) which will lead to utter confusion and distrust even in the most intimate relationships.

---

40 For a full discussion of the structure of Mi 7, see Ehud Ben Zvi, *Micah*, FOTL 21b (Grand Rapids: Eerdmans, 2000), 165–170, 173–181; Hans Walter Wolff, *Dodekapropheton 4. Micha*, BK.AT 14/4 (Neukirchen: Neukirchener, 1982), 176–177, 189–192.

41 E. g. Jeremias, *Joel, Obadja, Jona, Micha*, 213, 219; Rainer Kessler, *Micha*, HThK.AT (Freiburg: Herder, 1999), 255; Wolff, *Micha*, 176–177. Ben Zvi, *Micah*, 165 and 173, however, as well as many of the older interpreters (see the literature quoted in Kessler, *Micha*, 286) draw the dividing line between v. 6 and 7. Francis I. Andersen and David N. Freedman, *Micah*, AB 24E (New York: Doubleday, 2000), 563, see the inclusion formed by the 1st person sing. speech in vv. 1 and 7, and note the repetition of צפה in vv. 4 and 7, but nonetheless treat vv. 1–6 as the first unit of Mi 7.

42 Cf. Kessler, *Micha*, 286; Andersen/Freedman, *Micha*, 563.

The second part of Mi 7, vv. 8–20, begins with a dialogue (vv. 8–13) between a female and a prophetic voice. The female voice warns her enemy not to rejoice over her present misfortune, confesses her sin and expresses hope of rising again, whereas her enemy will fall (vv. 8–10). The prophetic voice proclaims to her that her walls will be rebuilt and people from all over the earth will come to her. The earth, however, will be desolate (vv. 11–13). The second section, vv. 14–17, begins with a prayer which asks God to shepherd his people and let them graze in Bashan and Gilead as of old. It is answered by God (vv. 15–17) with a promise to show them marvelous things and to humiliate the formerly mighty nations. The chapter concludes with a praise of God (vv. 18–20) sung by the remnant of his people, who express their confidence that God will forgive them by his mercy because he delights in steadfast love since the days of his oath to Jacob and Abraham.[43]

Micah 7 is very rich in allusions to other biblical texts.[44] There are explicit links to the Exodus events (7:15) as well as to the patriarchs (7:20), and many similarities have been observed with Jeremiah and Isaiah 56–66[45] as well as the Psalms.[46] When I now focus on aspects of Isaiah's Vineyard Song in Mi 7, I do not exclude the possibility that even the same phrase may simultaneously have another parallel in a different text. Multiple allusions may either be intentional or due to complex traditio- or text-historical processes which can never be fully disentangled but only described in simplified models as far as sufficiently reliable data can be extracted from the texts.

5.2.1 Shared features in Mi 7 and Isa 5:1–7

In Mi 7:1, the prophet laments his own situation.[47] He is like someone who desires fruit but can find none. He desires grapes but there is no cluster to eat, like after gleaning. He wishes he could eat first-ripe figs but there are none, like after gath-

---

43 On the structure of Mi 7:8–20, cf. Kessler, *Micha*, 296; Jeremias, *Joel, Obadja, Jona, Micha*, 221; Wolff, *Micha*, 189–192; Burkard M. Zapff, *Redaktionsgeschichtliche Studien zum Michabuch im Kontext des Dodekapropheton*, BZAW 256 (Berlin: de Gruyter, 1997), 226–231. Andersen/Freedman, *Micah*, 574–576, 588–589, 595–596, consider 7:7–12, vv. 13–17 and vv. 18–20 as three separate sections.

44 See Zapff, *Redaktionsgeschichtliche Studien*, 165–205.

45 Kessler, *Micha*, 287; Wolff, *Micha*, 177–178; Jeremias, *Joel, Obadja, Jona, Micha*, 213–214.

46 Kessler, *Micha*, 292, 296–297; Wolff, *Micha*, 179, 183, 192; Jeremias, *Joel, Obadja, Jona, Micha*, 222–231.

47 For reasons why the speaker of 7:1 cannot be a collective, see Kessler, *Micha*, 287.

ering the summer-fruit. The language of this passage recalls Jer 6:9,[48] where God announces that further judgment will come up against Jerusalem: the remnant of Israel shall thoroughly be gleaned like a vine. The situation of Mi 7:1, however, corresponds to that of the vineyard owner in Isa 5:2–3, who hopes to find good grapes but only discovers foul fruit.[49] Quite similarly, the prophet in Mi 7:1 laments that there is no cluster or first-ripe fig to eat (אֵין־אֶשְׁכּוֹל לֶאֱכוֹל בִּכּוּרָה אִוְּתָה נַפְשִׁי). A semantic feature in Mi 7:1 which can remind the listener or reader of Isaiah's Vineyard Song is the use of the words בָּצִיר "vintage" and עֹלְלֹת "gleaning". Although the vocabulary itself is not used in Isa 5:1–7 but in Jer 6:9, the general semantic field of wine growing also allows for an association with the Vineyard Song. Both in Mi 7:1 and Isa 5:2–3 someone hoping to find fruit is disappointed. In both cases, the fruit is a metaphor which refers to similar things. As pointed out in Mi 7:2a, the fruit which the prophet desires are upright persons seeking God and abiding by his commandments (חָסִיד and יָשָׁר), but they all perished from the earth. In Isa 5:7, the prophet explains that the Lord had hoped the society of Jerusalem and Judah would yield the fruit of justice and righteousness. This would have required joint efforts of godly and upright persons in the sense of Mi 7:1, but the faithless people of God only brought forth violence and injustice. If the general semantic field of wine growing, and a report on the experience that no one lived in accordance with justice and righteousness, were the only features shared by Mi 7 and Isa 5:1–7, then the assumption of a conscious connection between the two texts would still lack a substantial basis. But the subsequent text of Mi 7 includes a number of other features known from Isa 5:1–7. Interestingly, their number increases in the middle of the chapter. I will now briefly mention these features and then try to interpret them step by step.

In v. 4, if the common interpretation of the consonantal text is correct,[50] "their righteous one is a thorn hedge" uses the rare expression מְסוּכָה "thorn hedge", which also occurs in Isa 5:5 with a slightly different spelling (שׂ instead of ס) but the same meaning. Also in v. 4, the particle עַתָּה "now" highlights the negative consequence of the ethical corruption described in vv. 2–4a. This particle occurs once more in v. 10, where it introduces a sudden turn in the situation of the female voice speaking from v. 8 on. Her repentance of sins and patient acceptance

---

48 Jeremias, *Joel, Obadja, Jona, Micha*, 214.
49 Cf. Andersen/Freedman, *Micah*, 568; Zapff, *Redaktionsgeschichtliche Studien*, 166–167.
50 MT יָשָׁר מִמְּסוּכָה is probably erroneous insofar as the first מ is more likely to be a 3rd person masculine plural Suffix of יָשָׁר than an enclitic form of the preposition מִן attached to מְסוּכָה. Therefore, the text should be read strictly parallel to v. 4aα (טוֹבָם כְּחֵדֶק), as follows: יָשְׁרָם מְסוּכָה. See Zapff, *Redaktionsgeschichtliche Studien*, 145; Wolff, *Micha*, 175. Jeremias, *Joel, Obadja, Jona, Micha*, 212, assumes a haplography.

of the Lord's indignation as well as her trust in his justice prepare the way for the demise of her presently triumphant enemy, see v. 10b: עַתָּה תִּהְיֶה לְמִרְמָס "now, she will be trampled down". A double use of עַתָּה is also found in Isa 5 vv. 3 and 5, where the particle marks two sudden changes of the situation. In addition, Micah 7:10 announces that the – equally feminine – enemy of the female voice "will be for trampling down" (תִּהְיֶה לְמִרְמָס). Again, this is an exact quotation from Isa 5:5, which concludes that the vineyard "will be for trampling down" (וְהָיָה לְמִרְמָס) after the vineyard owner alias YHWH has broken down its wall (פָּרֹץ גְּדֵרוֹ). Now, this last-mentioned catchword גָּדֵר "wall" also occurs in Mi 7:11, where a prophetic voice addresses the female voice of the preceding verse and cries to her that her walls shall be built.[51] This means the judgement against the vineyard will be reversed with respect to the female voice, who now turns out to be a city with walls that had shared the fate of the vineyard.

Another important link between the Vineyard Song and Mi 7 is the occurrence of the terms "justice" מִשְׁפָּט and "righteousness" צְדָקָה in v. 9, which are the theological key terms used in Isa 5:7.[52] But whereas, in Isa 5:1–7, the society of Judah fails to yield justice and righteousness and is therefore condemned to destruction, the female voice of Mi 7:8–10 has already experienced destruction (v. 11) but now confesses her sin and hopes with regard to her enemy that the Lord will execute justice (מִשְׁפָּט) for her so that she can look upon his righteousness (צְדָקָה), v. 9.

I consider the above evidence as sufficient to assume that Mi 7 intentionally refers to Isa 5:1–7. Yet, these references do not follow a simple pattern like confirmation or reversal of the judgement pronounced in Isa 5:7 but are much more complex.

5.2.2 Interpretation of the references in Mi 7:1–7 to Isaiah's Vineyard Song

The general picture is that the first part of Mi 7, i.e. vv. 1–7, seems to confirm the judgement pronounced in Isaiah's Vineyard Song. Like Isaiah's vineyard owner, the prophet finds no righteousness in his society. His perspective is that of an isolated individual in a corrupt society. The way this situation is depicted does not only recall Jeremiah, as often observed, but also and in particular Isaiah. Thus,

---

51 The shared vocabulary of Mi 7:10–11 and Isa 5:5 was already observed by Zapff, *Redaktionsgeschichtliche Studien*, 182–183.

52 The general importance of the notion מִשְׁפָּט for Isaiah and Micah was already noted by Gary Stansell, *Micah and Isaiah: A Form and Tradition Historical Comparison*, SBLDS 85 (Atlanta: Scholars Press, 1988), 102–117, 120–121.

the description of vv. 2b–3 reminds of the social-critical passages Isa 1:15b–17,21–23. In Isa 1, God rejects all ongoing cultic activities (Isa 1:11–15a) because the hands of the people of Jerusalem are full of blood (v. 15b: יְדֵיכֶם דָּמִים מָלֵאוּ). In Mi 7:2, Isaiah's critique seems to have been inefficient because all people on earth lie in wait for bloody deeds (v. 2b). In Isa 1:16, God commands the Jerusalemites to remove the evil of their works from the sight of his eyes (הָסִירוּ רֹעַ מַעַלְלֵיכֶם), to stop doing evil (חִדְלוּ הָרֵעַ) and instead, v. 17, to learn to do good (לִמְדוּ הֵיטֵב). When looking at Micah's description in 7:3aα of what people made of Isaiah's preaching, I find a good deal of bitter irony in it. They seem to have understood there is something they should do better, but since that what is truly good is completely beyond their horizon, knowledge and will, they "improve" their methods of doing evil (עַל־הָרַע כַּפַּיִם לְהֵיטִיב).[53] The next evil criticized by Micah in 7:3aβ, "the prince and the judge ask for a bribe" (הַשַּׂר שֹׁאֵל וְהַשֹּׁפֵט בַּשִּׁלּוּם), recurs in Mi 3:11 but also reads like a summary of Isa 1:23, where Isaiah speaks against "princes" (שָׂרַיִךְ), who are at the same time judges (v. 23bα: יִשְׁפֹּטוּ), because they love a bribe (שֹׁחַד) and hunt after rewards. For "reward", Isa 1:23 uses שַׁלְמֹנִים, which is very similar to the more common word שִׁלּוּם used by Micah.[54]

In Mi 7:4, the use of מְסוּכָה "thorn hedge" as an image of the most upright person in the corrupt society is a debatable case. Taken as such, "thorn hedge" expresses the uselessness of this person, just as "briers and thorns" in Isa 5:6 describes the uselessness of the vineyard after its destruction. But since the rare word מְסוּכָה "thorn hedge" itself is also used in Isa 5:5, where, before being removed, it had the specific function of protecting the valuable vineyard against wild animals and thieves, a subtler reading might be allowed. In a high-value setting like a vineyard with finest vines, a thorn hedge is useful because it protects the vines although it is the least valuable plant compared to the others. In a corrupt society like the one described by Micah, where all values have vanished and no valuable objects are left, a thorn hedge is of relatively high value because of its potential usefulness although the absence of anything valuable renders it as useless as anything else. Thus, an intertextual reading of Micah's statement that the most upright in his corrupt community is a thorn hedge adds an ironical tone.

The advice given in Mi 7:5–6 is closest to Jer 9:3–4 and 12:6, where Jeremiah also warns his addressees not to trust their most intimate relatives and friends. But in the context of v. 4b, which prophesies confusion (מְבוּכָה), this advice to

---

53 In Isa 1:15a, the flat parts of the hands (כַּפֵּיכֶם) are spread out for prayer although they are bloody (v. 15b), which is an insult for the eyes of YHWH (v. 15aβ: אַעְלִים עֵינַי מִכֶּם). In Mi 7:3a, the flat parts of the hands (כַּפַּיִם) are eager to do evil.
54 Cf. Wolff, *Micha*, 180.

distrust everyone, even the closest relatives, is also a description of important details of this confusion. Although there are no catchword connections, the idea that general ethic corruption leads to chaotic social confusion is expressed in a comparable way in Isa 3:1–4:1.

Mi 7:7 is a first person singular speech which has no terminological links to Isaiah. Nonetheless, the situation of the prophet reminds of Isaiah's isolated situation described in 8:17, as Jörg Jeremias[55] notes. There, Isaiah waits for the Lord, who hides his face from the house of Jacob, and hopes in him. The above-explained numerous associations with Isaiah might even allow to read the word ישעי in Mi 7:7 as an allusion to Isaiah's name, just as the beginning of v. 18, מִי־אֵל כָּמוֹךָ could allude to Micah's[56] name. In sum, the overall function of the above-explained allusions to Isaiah's Vineyard Song in Mi 7:1–7 is to warn the listeners or readers that the present corruption of the society will inevitably lead to a disastrous judgement of the same kind as was proclaimed in Isaiah's Vineyard Song. The difference between this song and Mi 7:1–7 is that Micah does not yet pronounce such an irrevocable prophecy of doom as Isaiah's. At the same time, the prophet's hopeful outlook towards God (v. 7) in spite of his isolated situation is an encouragement to those among the people of God who find themselves in a similar situation.

5.2.3 Interpretation of the references to Isaiah's Vineyard Song in Mi 7:8–20

Whereas the description of the corrupt society in Mi 7:1–7 reminds of the causes which led to a severe judgment against the people of God, the city speaking in Mi 7:8–10 represents a community which has already experienced the judgment. They are now repentant of their sins and filled with the hope that God will deliver them from their present enemy. As the female voice is repentant and patiently bears her punishment (v. 9a), God's justice and righteousness, which had brought about the judgment against her (cf. Isa 5:7), now becomes the origin of her hope that God will deliver her from her enemy (Mi 7:8,9b).

The above-explained allusions to Isaiah's Vineyard Song have a double function. In Mi 7:10, they illustrate that the same judgment now awaits the enemy of the fallen city because she has mocked the God of Israel. In v. 11, the allusion underlines the fact that the verdict of complete destruction pronounced in Isa 5:5–6 will be reversed. The new prophetic word announces the rebuilding of the walls (v. 11) and describes a contrast between the city of the people of God, which will attract people from all over the earth (v. 12), and the rest of the earth, which will be deserted because of the evil deeds of its inhabitants (v. 13). This implies that the verdict of Isaiah's Vineyard Song, which had cast down Jerusalem and Judah as the first one of all kingdoms, is now directed against the rest of the world. In response to this turn of fates, the community of the city of God express their confidence in the Lord (Mi 7:14–17). They ask him to be their shepherd (v. 14) and to reveal his sovereignty over the nations (vv. 16–17), which is underlined by allusions to the Day of YHWH, cf. Isa 2:10,19.[57]

A conspicuous characteristic of Mi 7 is that it never mentions the name of the fallen and restored city of the people of God. The prophecy of Micah 4:10, which anticipates important contents of Mi 7:8–20, had announced in plain words that the Daughter of Zion had to go to Babylon, where she would later be redeemed by the Lord.[58] In v. 14, however, the praying community asks the Lord, their shepherd, to lead his flock, who dwell alone in a forest in the midst of a garden land, and to let them graze in *Bashan* and *Gilead*. These places, which are the only ones mentioned by name in Mi 7:8–20, belonged for the most part to the Kingdom of North Israel.[59] The statement that YHWH's flock dwells alone in a forest in the midst of a garden land refers back to Mi 3:12bβ, which prophesies in the context of the future destruction of Jerusalem that the mountain of the house (of the Lord) will become a wooded height (לְבָמוֹת יָעַר). Seen against this background, Micah 7:14 seems to propose that the future place where the people of God live does not have to be the city of Jerusalem and not even a city at all, but it may well be an open green field, even in the former Northern Kingdom, where they can graze. This observation brings me back to Mi 1:6, where Samaria is prophesied to become

---

57 In particular, note the motifs of hiding in מְעָרוֹת צֻרִים "rock caves" and holes of "dust" עָפָר in Isa 2:10a,19a. With similar vocabulary and comparable contents, Micah 7:17 speaks of the nations' licking "dust" עָפָר while "they come out of their holes" יִרְגְּזוּ מִמִּסְגְּרֹתֵיהֶם. In addition, Isaiah 2:10,19 speaks of the overwhelming פַּחַד יְהוָה "terror of the Lord" while Micah 7:17 announces that the nations "will turn in dread" יִפְחָדוּ to the Lord, the God of Israel (אֶל־יְהוָה אֱלֹהֵינוּ).
58 Cf. Zapff, *Redaktionsgeschichtliche Studien*, 176, who speaks of a "Tendenz zur Verallgemeinerung oder Anonymisierung" with regard to the female enemy addressed in Mi 7:8. The same tendency can also be observed with regard to the speaker herself.
59 See Ralph L. Smith, *Micah – Malachi*, WBC 32 (Waco: Word Books, 1984), 58–59, who discusses the proposal by Otto Eissfeldt, "Ein Psalm aus Nord-Israel. Micha 7,7–20," *ZDMG* 112 (1962): 259–268, and other earlier scholars that the female voice speaking in 7:8–10 could be Samaria because the names and traditions mentioned in 7:8–20 point to the Northern Kingdom. Bernard Renaud, *Michée, Sophonie, Nahum*, SB (Paris: Gabalda, 1987), 146–146, rightly underlines both the anonymity of the female speaker and the associations with the Daughter of Zion which result from Mi 1:13 and 4:9–13.

a place for "plantings of a vineyard". The new vineyard of the Lord, as it seems, is no longer bound to be the city of Jerusalem but may even spread in the open field where once Samaria stood.

6 Conclusion

In the book of Isaiah, the Song of the Unfruitful Vineyard (Isa 5:1–7) is the first unconditional prophecy which announces the complete destruction of Judah/the "house of Israel" through YHWH. It is preceded by the poem of the Day of YHWH in Isa 2:10–22, which proclaims that he alone shall be exalted on his Day (cf. 2:11b) whereas all ungodly arrogance is to be cast down. In this context, Isaiah's Vineyard Song accuses the society of Jerusalem and Judah/Israel of perverting justice and righteousness into unjust oppression. Since this is an assault against the divine sovereignty of YHWH, whose reign establishes justice and righteousness, his people are bound to fall on his Day, which after Isa 2:10–22 is a present reality. The Vineyard Song confirms this by prophesying the complete destruction of Judah/Israel. After Isa 5, YHWH renders his announced Day effective by calling the prophet Isaiah in chpt. 6 to harden the heart of his people and make them unable to conceive (Isa 6:9–11), and by sending the Assyrian power against them, as described in several pericopes between Isa 7:18 and 10:34.

The first text in the book which resumes Isaiah's Vineyard Song is Isaiah 7:23–25. The imagery of this song is evoked when places with a thousand valuable vines are mentioned in 7:23. Yet, not only one vineyard planted by YHWH but every place where vines grow in abundance, even the land as a whole (v. 24: כָּל־הָאָרֶץ) and all fertile hills (v. 25) will be destroyed, overgrown by useless briars and thorns (v. 23) and trampled down by cattle and sheep (v. 25). By this amplified prose version of the judgement which YHWH pronounced against Jerusalem and Judah in Isa 5:5–6, the concluding section of the narration of Isa 7 marks the behaviour of the Davidic king Ahaz in a situation of political distress as no less disappointing than the obstruction of justice and righteousness by the society of Judah. Only YHWH can save Ahaz who has to face two powerful opponents while feeling the grip of the Assyrian superpower on his neck. But Ahaz, refusing to put all his trust in God, ignores YHWH's divine sovereignty in an equally grave manner as those who seek secular advantages by turning divine justice upside down. Therefore, Isaiah 7:23–25 reminds that Judah is doomed to be destroyed. Seen against the hermeneutical background of Isa 6:9–11, the blind behaviour of King Ahaz also appears as a first result of Isaiah's commission to make God's people unable to conceive and understand. Thus, the reception of Isa 5:5–6 at the end of Isa 7 underlines the emerging realization of the divine decision to make an end to the unfruitful vineyard.

The New Vineyard Song in Isa 27:2–6, by contrast, proclaims in a triumphant voice that Israel has become a vineyard pleasant to the Lord. Enjoying God's full care and protection, it yields fruit to the whole world. The former judgement against the unfruitful vineyard (Isa 5:5–6) is reversed, and peace, which is the fruit of justice and righteousness (cf. Isa 32:16–17), crowns the relationship between the Lord and his people.

To Mi 1:6, the background of Isaiah's Song of the Unfruitful Vineyard is able to add deeper meaning. Samaria, other than Jerusalem in Isa 5:1–7, is neither compared to a vineyard nor expected to bear good fruit. Due to the weight of her crimes (Mi 1:5), she will be destroyed. Nonetheless, YHWH turns her former place in a potentially fruitful area where future vines can grow. Hence, the perspective arises that the place of Samaria might become what the vineyard owner of Isa 5:1–7 had wished for in vain. Micah 7:1–7 describes an atmosphere of injustice and ethical degeneration which is similar to the social conditions criticized in Isa 1; 3 and 5. By catchwords recalling Isa 5:1–7, the text evokes the same type of situation which had caused God's decision to destroy his vineyard in Isa 5:5–6. Without detailing the course of doom which occurred in the meantime, Micah 7:8–20 describes the circumstances after the disaster which the sins enumerated in Mi 7:1–7 had triggered. While the nameless city of YHWH shows repentance and is willing to accept her punishment (Mi 7:8–10), the arrogance of her enemy who had destroyed her leads to a reversal of the judgement. While the repentance of the city of YHWH and his people is rewarded by the secure hope that the Lord will grant them a new life under his full care and protection, the doom will now strike the enemy.

In sum, the reception of Isaiah's Song of the Unfruitful Vineyard circles around the judgement of Isa 5:5–6. Some texts such as Isa 7:23–25; Mi 7:1–7, and in a modified way probably also Mi 1:6, refer to this prophecy in order to show how negative attitudes or behaviour against YHWH will inevitably lead to its (repeated) fulfilment, i. e. to the destruction of those whose behaviour is an attack against YHWH's sovereignty. Other texts such as Isa 27:2–6 and Mi 7:8–20 depict how human repentance and full acknowledgement of YHWH's sovereignty can open the way to a reversal of the harsh judgement pronounced in Isa 5:5–6. Such a reversal may include both the enjoyment of a life in fullness under God's blessings and/or the destruction of arrogant enemies.

Bibliography

Andersen, Francis I./David N. Freedman, *Micah*, AB 24E (New York: Doubleday, 2000).

Bartelmus, Rüdiger, "Beobachtungen zur literarischen Struktur des sog. Weinberglieds (Jes 5,1–7). Möglichkeiten und Grenzen der formgeschichtlichen Methode bei der Interpretation von Texten aus dem corpus propheticum," in *Auf der Suche nach dem archimedischen Punkt der Textinterpretation: Studien zu einer philologisch-linguistisch fundierten Exegese alttestamentlicher Texte*, ed. Rüdiger Bartelmus (Zürich: Pano, 2002): 319–336.

Becker, Uwe, *Jesaja – von der Botschaft zum Buch*, FRLANT 178 (Göttingen: Vandenhoeck, 1997).

Ben Zvi, Ehud, *Micah*, FOTL 21b (Grand Rapids: Eerdmans, 2000).

Beuken, Willem A. M., *Jesaja 1–12*, HThK.AT (Freiburg: Herder, 2003), 134.

Beuken, Willem A. M., *Jesaja 13–27*, HThK.AT (Freiburg: Herder, 2007).

Blenkinsopp, Joseph, Isaiah 1–39, AB 19 (New York: Doubleday, 2000).

Eck, Joachim, "Divine Strategies against Abuse of Power in the Opening of the Book of Isaiah and the Exodus Story. Some Aspects where Micah is not Similar to Isaiah," *ZAW* 130 (2018): 4–25.

Eck, Joachim, "Isaiah's Song of the Unfruitful Vineyard (Isa 5.1–7) and the Biblical Concept of Justice and Righteousness," in *Faith and Reason. An Interdisciplinary Construction of Human Rights*, West-östliche Denkwege 25, eds. Marko Trajkovic and Joost van Loon (Sankt Augustin: Academia, 2016): 15–32.

Eck, Joachim, *Jesaja 1 – Eine Exegese der Eröffnung des Jesaja-Buches: Die Präsentation Jesajas und JHWHs, Israels und der Tochter Zion*, BZAW 473 (Berlin etc.: De Gruyter, 2015).

Eissfeldt, Otto, "Ein Psalm aus Nord-Israel. Micha 7,7–20," *ZDMG* 112 (1962): 259–268.

Höffken, Peter, "Probleme in Jesaja 5,1–7," *ZTK* 79 (1982): 392–410.

Höffken, Peter, *Das Buch Jesaja. Kapitel 1–39*, NSK-AT 18/1 (Stuttgart: Kath. Bibelwerk, 1993).

Irsigler, Hubert, "Gott als König in Berufung und Verkündigung Jesajas," in *Ein Gott, eine Offenbarung: Beiträge zur biblischen Exegese, Theologie und Spiritualität. Festschrift für Notker Füglister OSB zum 60. Geburtstag*, ed. Friedrich V. Reiterer (Würzburg: Echter, 1991): 127–154.

Irsigler, Hubert, "Speech acts and intention in the 'Song of the Vineyard' Isaiah 5:1–7," *OTE* 10 (1997): 39–68.

Jeremias, Jörg, *Die Propheten Joel, Obadja, Jona, Micha*, ATD 24,3 (Göttingen: Vandenhoeck, 2007).

Kaiser, Otto, *Das Buch des Propheten Jesaja. Kapitel 1–12*, ATD 17 (Göttingen: Vandenhoeck, 1981[5]).

Kaiser, Otto, *Das Buch des Propheten Jesaja. Kapitel 13–39*, ATD 18 (Göttingen: Vandenhoeck, 1973).

Kessler, Rainer, *Micha*, HThK.AT (Freiburg: Herder, 1999)

Kilian, Rudolf, *Jesaja 1–12*, NEB (Würzburg: Echter, 1999[2]).

Loretz, Oswald, "Weinberglied und prophetische Deutung im Protest-Song Jes 5,1–7," *UF* 7 (1975): 573–576.

McKane, William, "The Interpretation of Isaiah VII 14–25," *VT* 17 (1967): 208–219.

Niehr, Herbert, "Zur Gattung von Jes 5,1–7," *BZ NF* 30 (1986): 99–104.

Pietsch, Michael, "König/Königtum AT," *WiBiLex* (online https://www.bibelwissenschaft.de/stichwort/23844/, 2014, cited 3 October 2019).

Poe Hays, Rebecca W., "Sing Me a Parable of Zion: Isaiah's Vineyard (5:1–7) and Its Relation to the 'Daughter Zion' Tradition," *JBL* 135 (2016): 743–761.

Renaud, Bernard, *Michée, Sophonie, Nahum*, SB (Paris: Gabalda, 1987), 146–146.

Schmid, Konrad, *Jesaja 1–23*, ZBK.AT 19.1 (Zürich: TVZ, 2011).

Smith, Ralph L., *Micah – Malachi*, WBC 32 (Waco: Word Books, 1984).

Stansell, Gary, *Micah and Isaiah: A Form and Tradition Historical Comparison*, SBLDS 85 (Atlanta: Scholars Press, 1988).

Steck, Odil Hannes, "Rettung und Verstockung. Exegetische Bemerkungen zu Jes 7,3–9," in *Wahrnehmungen Gottes im Alten Testament. Gesammelte Studien*, ed. Odil Hannes Steck, TB 70 (München: Kaiser, 1982): 171–186.

Wildberger, Hans, *Jesaja 1–12*, BK.AT X/1 (Neukirchen-Vluyn: Neukirchener, 1978).

Williamson, Hugh G. M., *Isaiah 6–12*, ICC (London: T&T Clark, 2018).

Williamson, Hugh G. M., *Isaiah 1–5*, ICC (London: T&T Clark, 2006).

Williamson, Hugh G. M., "Poetic Vision in Isaiah 7:18–25," in *The Desert Will Bloom. Poetic Visions in Isaiah*, ed. A. Joseph Everson and Hyun Chul Paul Kim, Ancient Israel and Its Literature 4 (Atlanta: SBL, 2009): 77–89.

Willis, John T., "The Genre of Isaiah 5:1–7," *JBL* 96 (1977): 337–362.

Wolff, Hans Walter, *Dodekapropheton 4. Micha*, BK.AT 14/4 (Neukirchen: Neukirchener, 1982).

Zapff, Burkard M., "Why is Micah similar to Isaiah?," *ZAW* 129 (2017): 536–554.

Zapff, Burkard M., *Redaktionsgeschichtliche Studien zum Michabuch im Kontext des Dodeka-propheton*, BZAW 256 (Berlin: de Gruyter, 1997).

Carol J. Dempsey, OP

Divine and Human Kingships in the Books of Isaiah and the Twelve: A Kaleidoscope of Conflicting Yet Unifying Images

The Bible is an ancient cultural document that has influenced and continues to influence, in both positive and negative ways, contemporary culture. Because of its cultural nature and sphere of influence, the Bible must interface and be in dialogue with the global world and its many concerns. Only when this interface and dialogue occurs can the text be interpreted and critiqued appropriately by readers who give meaning to the text. No longer can the Bible be viewed simply as a reconstructed historical document, a work of ancient literature, or a theological work that gives personal meaning and direction to one's life. This essay explores the topic of kingship in selected poems from the book of Isaiah and the book of the Twelve. The essay highlights the connections between these two bodies of material and also investigates how various biblical texts on kingship have become a looking glass that shows how culture may or may not have changed from ancient times with respect to leadership, power, and corruption. Thus, the essay tries to answer these two questions, "What do we discover in the Bible, and specifically in the texts on kingship, that is oppressive, and what is liberating for readers then and now?" and "How can the vision contained within this ancient biblical document—a vision that transcends its own time and cultures—help to inform and transform our own global world today?" The essay approaches the topic from a literary, theological, and feminist-liberationist perspective.

1 Setting Sail to the New World from the Old Country

The Bible is a cultural document and a political artifact that has been shaped by many peoples' political, social, economic, and theological perspectives and world views. Robert Schreiter, C.PP.S. states that "the Bible itself has had a profound influence on shaping the cultures of Jews and Christians through the centuries, both within their immediate communities and in their wider societies, especially when either of these groups represented the majority of the popula-

https://doi.org/10.1515/9783110705799-010

tion."[1] From a contemporary ethical liberationist hermeneutical perspective and as they are related to the theme of this study on divine and human kingship, the questions then become not only what are the biblical connections between Isaiah and the Twelve but also, "What do we discover in the Bible, and specifically the texts on kingship, that is oppressive, and what is liberating for readers then and now?" "How does the Bible and the texts on kingship become a looking glass that shows us how culture has really not changed much, how ancient attitudes and mindsets, social and political structures that bound people centuries and centuries ago continue to do so now?" More importantly, "How can the vision contained within this ancient document—a vision that transcends its own time and cultures—help to inform and transform our own global world today that, in my mind, is in crisis and chaos?"

Given these questions and considerations, then, we need to bring the Bible and these texts on kingship into the world today and not leave them in their ancient times because the topic is too important. The Bible and these texts on kingship have been and can continue to be influential documents particularly for generations of people today who either take the Bible literally and follow it religiously or have no religious tradition "and live disconnected from religious institutions."[2] Thus, we live in a world of growing secularism on the one hand, and a growing evangelical fundamentalism on the other hand. The way various faith traditions have sometimes interpreted biblical texts and who gets privileged in the various readings and interpretations has sometimes led to some of the forms of oppression we experience today. Interestingly so, though, within the human community exists a hunger. This hunger is as much a spiritual one as it is a physical one. The search for the Divine in the world and in the biblical text is related to the spiritual hunger and related to how we understand the Divine, especially in relation to the theme of this study on divine and human kingship in Isaiah and the Twelve.

All of these thoughts have moved me out of my own comfort zone of looking at these texts in their ancient contexts alone because I am a member of the Dominican Order. I am a biblical scholar, but I am also a preacher, formed by the word and charged to bring the word into the world that aches to hear good news and longs to be freed from systemic oppression. Our current world situation compels me, as one who works with prophetic texts and as one who walks in the tradition of the prophets, to begin with our global political world in which we find

---

1 Robert J. Schreiter, C.PP.S., "The Bible and Culture," in *The Collegeville Pastoral Dictionary of Biblical Theology* (Collegeville: Liturgical Press), xlvii.
2 Susanne Scholz, *Sacred Witness: Rape in the Hebrew Bible* (Minneapolis: Fortress, 2014, paperback), 21.

ourselves and which is significant to my theme. The biblical world in which the prophets lived was their starting point, and so my current world in which I live must be my starting point as well. Biblical scholar Susanne Scholz reminds me time and again that anything I write today that does not deal with our contemporary world and its hunger and cry for justice is "immoral."

One of the hungers and cries for justice today is the need for a new understanding of leadership with new kinds of leaders who can begin to help us, a global community, transform our present world order into the new heavens and earth heralded by the ancient poet(s) of Isaiah whose vision we have yet to grasp and understand let alone put into practice. The books of Isaiah and the Twelve do present us with an alternative vision of leadership that is different from the leadership of the empire. This alternative vision is, to my way of thinking, a source of profound hope for a world that has always been plagued with the abuse of power, greed, and aggression. These forces now grip our planet more than ever, causing the most vulnerable to be devastated to the point of no return for some.

Thus, I begin this study from the perspective of a native born, white, American feminist-liberationist, Christian, Dominican woman who has experienced the kaleidoscope of leadership images, styles, and attitudes presented in this paper. I explore selected texts within the books of Isaiah and the Twelve from a literary, theological, feminist-liberationist perspective. I also deal with the texts from a synchronic perspective, with an eye toward how the books of Isaiah and the Twelve present the theme of divine and human kingship. Do thematic connections exist among the books? Does a cohesive or disparate picture emerge with regard to leadership? Finally, I listen to these texts in relation to our post-modern global world to see if Isaiah's vision of a new way of life is possible or if it is nothing more than dust in the wind.

2 Mysterium Tremendum: Regal, Royal, and Robed

Ever since civilization began, women and men of every generation have pondered the question "Who or what is God?" Artists have sketched portraits and wall hangings; mystics have crafted poems and stories; contemplatives have rested and sighed; theologians have written books and treatises; children have wondered and imagined; and biblical scholars have mined ancient historical documents. Contemporary novelist, essayist, and storyteller, Tom Mahon offers this advice:

> Instead of picturing God as a medieval monarch on a marble throne, imagine God as the living awareness in the space between the atoms, 'empty' space that makes up about 99.99 percent of the universe. Thinking of God that way gets us past some of the great theological divides of the past. Is God immanent or transcendent, internal or external, composed or compassionate? Like the question of whether the atom is wave or particle, the answer is: yes.[3]

Mahon's suggestion is a wise and noble one especially since we now live in the twenty-first century with a new cosmology and a new universe story. Ironically, however, many people are still fascinated with the image of the Holy One—whom some call God—as a king. In the books of Isaiah and the Twelve, God as "king"—royal, regal, and dressed in flowing robes—is a favorite image of the poets who wrote these biblical texts. This image of God as king emerged from the world of the empire, when nations and leaders were jockeying for power and position on the world stage. Supposedly, kingship was established in Israel according to the patterns found among other nations (1 Sam 8:5–20). The king was the military chief and primary decision maker.

In a world where male corrupt leaders are usurping lands and political power, where greed and injustice run rampant, where innocent people are killed as others become destitute, is it no wonder that the poets of the books of Isaiah and the Twelve depicted the Holy One as the King of kings, the Lord of lords, the Sovereign One who had to be more powerful than the most powerful male leader/king on earth? Thus, the metaphorical image of the Divine is one that emerged from and was a reflection of the male, hierarchal, and patriarchal leadership culture of the day, but also one that would be strong enough to address and do something about the injustices of the day, thereby giving a sense of hope to the most vulnerable in Israel. Indeed, their God—the Holy One of Israel--was on their side. As complex as the ancient culture was, so is the complexity of the image of God in this ancient text. Let us look now at the theme of divine kingship in select passages from the books of Isaiah and the Twelve.[4]

---

3 Tom Mahon, "The Spirit in Technology" in *The Hand of God: Thoughts and Images Reflecting the Spirit of the Universe*; ed. Michael Regan (Philadelphia: Templeton Foundation Press, 1999), 139.
4 The selection and arrangement of biblical texts chosen for this study is based on developing the study's theme and in no way aims to make any theological statements with respect to a Christian reading of the prophetic literature, i. e., how some Christian interpreters point to the "hidden Christ" in passages like Mic 5:2–5 and Zech 9:9–10. See, e. g., the work of Nancy Guthrie, *The Word of the Lord: Seeing Jesus in the Prophets* (Crossway: Wheaton, IL, 2014), Michael Cameron, *Christ Meets Me Everywhere: Augustine's Early Figurative Exegesis* (New York: Oxford University Press, 2012), and James L. Ferrell, *The Hidden Christ: Beneath the Surface of the Old Testament* (Deseret Book: Salt Lake City, 2012), among others.

2.1 Isaiah 6

In Isaiah 6, a poem that features several characters, namely, Isaiah, seraphs, and God, Isaiah receives an audio-visual call to be a prophet. At the outset of his "call," he experiences a breathtaking vision of God in the Temple (vv 1–3) who appears as a royal figure enthroned on a high and lofty regal throne. The seraphs refer to this God as "holy," a term distinct and separate from all creation, whose glory fills the earth. This God is also YHWH Sabaoth, translated as "Lord of hosts" (v 3) in most English Bibles (ie, NRSV, NAB, NEB). From the standpoint of the English translation, the term "Lord," analogous to human rulers, connotes authority and superiority over earthly and cosmic forces. The entire epithet presents God as divine king and divine warrior, a male hierarchical being superior to all in the earthly and cosmic realms. With the pivots on the thresholds shaking and the house filling with smoke, one could safely say that Isaiah's initial encounter with this God was like Dorothy, the Tin Man, the Lion, and the Scarecrow's initial encounter with the great and awesome Wizard of Oz until Toto tugged at the curtain and drew it back to reveal the true picture of the being behind all the extravaganza. The encounter with the Divine fills Isaiah with consternation and amazement and causes him to name this God "King."

Isaiah next experiences a cleansing that purifies his mouth, blots out his sin, and frees him from guilt. After this life-changing experience, he then hears the voice of God who issues the call: "Whom shall I send, and who will go for us?" (v 8a). Isaiah responds willingly and quickly replies, "Here I am, send me" (v 8b). His profound experience of the deity has moved him to respond positively, but how else could he respond to a God whom he now understands to be his "king"? Isaiah's posture toward this God is now one of subservience.

Having been cleansed, Isaiah next has to preach a hard word to the people (vv 9–13). The message foreshadows impending doom for all which will be completely orchestrated by God (vv 9–10). Some community members' disrespectful attitudes and injustices lead to the divine punitive chastisement of all, a situation of unjust "corporate punishment." Yet, the people are not without hope: a stump—a remnant—will remain, and that stump will be the holy seed (v 13) to be planted anew. Thomas Leclerc makes the observation that "the holiness of God celebrated in this classic passage (6:1–4) is sharply contrasted to human sinfulness (6:5–7)."[5] Leclerc states further that Isaiah's understanding of the people's

---

5 Thomas L. Leclerc, *Yahweh is Exalted in Justice: Solidarity and Conflict in Israel* (Minneapolis: Augsburg Fortress, 2001), 63.

sin and rebellion is tied to his own sin and both their sin and his sin are purged.[6] Hence, in this poem justice and holiness intersect. Holiness and ethical praxis define God's relationship with humanity, and holiness is no longer just a ritual practice.

The image of God in Isaiah 6 is a militaristic, "kyriarchal" one, and yet, this king—this Holy One, this Lord of Hosts—surprisingly, invites a wayward human being from a wayward community into the regal presence and abode in order to invite further this human being to participate in the divine mission of justice, the likes of which are almost totally devastating and punitive for a community but which the deity deems as necessary in order to re-establish justice and bring about a new way of life, or so this deity thinks. Isaiah becomes God's "subject," commissioned to serve the King. God entrusts Isaiah with the divine mission of working for justice on behalf of the King. The divine King's intentions for establishing justice, however, contain a retributive dimension which, in the context of the present-day global community, is troubling. This image of the divine King sets the tone and example for leadership and sends a message about how justice is to be established. In sum, the image of divine kingship thus far is a complicated and imperfect one.

2.2 Isaiah 43:1—44:8

The theme of divine kingship also appears in Isa 43:1—44:8. In this poem, God, the Holy One of Israel, becomes a source of hope for an exiled people who have lost their kingdom, monarchy, temple, land, and sense of identity. God promises to be their "savior" (43:3) to love them (43:3–4), to be with them in the midst of their fear and anxiety (43:5), and to liberate them (43:5b–14). In 43:14–15, the images of God converge. God, Israel's Redeemer and Holy One, will exert power over the Babylonians to free the exiles and to prove to them that their God is the Lord, their Holy One, the Creator of Israel, their King (43:15). Although this monarchal figure now has a personal relationship with the people, the display of divine power is self-serving and becomes an assertion of sovereignty over a people who are already disenfranchised. This male deity defines the relationship; the people do not. The relationship is hierarchical even though "mutuality" represented by covenant relationship has been the assumption.

Words of assurance and comfort turn to words of contention in Isa 43:22–28. Having given the exiled people two promises, God now has a bone to pick with the

---

6 *Ibid.*

captive ones (43:22–24). Yet, God is quick to remind the people of the gift of divine compassion that is theirs (43:25).

The image of God as King of Israel returns in Isa 44:6, along with the image of God as Lord, redeemer, and Lord of Hosts. Here the exiles once again receive comforting words in the midst of God declaring God's own sovereignty and incomparability (44:6–8). The image of divine kingship in Isa 43:1—44:8 remains the same as in Isaiah 6, but now in Isa 43:1—44:8, God's attitude toward Jacob/Israel appears warmer and more personal. As divine King, God is now redeemer, savior, comforter, and protector of a people who had earlier experienced tremendous suffering at the hand of this militaristic, kyriarchal God.

The image of divine kingship associated with the idea of comforter in Isa 43:1—44:8, particularly in Isa 43:1 and 5 where twice the phrase "do not fear" appears, is problematic. In one sense these words, that come from a warrior, commander-in-chief, Lord of Hosts, sovereign, kyriarchal God and spoken to a down-trodden Judean people who have experienced pain and suffering from this God on account of their transgressions (Isa 40:1–2), may only exacerbate the people's pain who have witnessed the violence committed by the Babylonians, a powerful empire (Isa 43:1–2, 14, 17; 54:4). Gilbert Lozano notes that the capture of Jerusalem, the destruction of the Temple, and the exile of many leaders was "a severe blow to the Judeans, for they marked the end of their nation."[7] Furthermore, he observes that "the actual splitting of a population into two groups namely, those who were allowed to remain in the land of Judah and those who were deported to Babylon, must have been horrendous in its own way."[8]

With all that has transpired in their lives and with their own faith in God now called into question, and especially since the royal family was now in Babylon, a situation that seems to undermine God's promises to the Davidic family (2 Sam 7:8–16), how could these exiles trust this kyriarchal King God? How could we?

2.3 Micah 2:12–13 and Zephaniah 3:14–20

In the Book of the Twelve, two poems that refer to divine kingship are Mic 2:12–13 and Zeph 3:14–20. In Mic 2:12–13 God the King will lead the people out of exile. The imagery echoes that of Isa 43:1—44:8. In Zeph 3:14–20, daughter Zion, now

---

7 Gilbert Lozano, "Words of Hope for Contemporary Exiles in South and Central America," in *Global Perspectives on the Bible*; eds. Mark Roncace and Joseph Weaver (NY: Pearson, 2014), 108.
8 *Ibid.*

painfully chastened and purified by God, her "father," receives a word of hope, salvation, and restoration. Verses 15–16 are significant. In v 15 God removes all judgments from Zion and turns away her enemies. Zion, portrayed as female, is the one judged by a male deity. This male deity is none other than "the king of Israel ... the Lord" (v 16) who will not cease to employ retributive justice. The next round will be meted out to Zion's enemies (vv 18b–19). Thus, the portrait of divine kingship in the books of Isaiah and the Twelve, as exemplified by this small sampling of texts, remains constant: the deity is a sovereign monarch whose holiness is tied to questionable ethical praxis, who as commander-in-chief over all the armies of the cosmic and earthly realms, exercises retributive and punitive justice in response to injustice and human transgression, and whose exertion of aggressive power only brings increased violence to the global scene and not peace. Furthermore, the selected poems of Isaiah and the Twelve become profoundly prophetic: this kind of leadership, and most especially the model held up as "divine," is ineffective and more troubling than transformative.

This metaphorical image of God gives a positive nod to political, religious, and social leaders today who exercise this ancient model of leadership deemed "divine." If God the King acts this way, then it must be OK for others in the human community to act this way. For evangelical fundamentalist Christian Right believers, many of whom are literalists with respect to the Bible, these texts only make the yearning for world leaders like God the King ever more desirable, especially for a country like the United States who, after all, is "One Nation Under God."

Interestingly, in an article entitled "Why Don't Christian Conservatives Worry about Climate Change? God," Lisa Vox cites US Rep. Tim Walberg (R-Mich) who stated: "As a Christian, I believe that there is a creator in God who is much bigger than us. And I'm confident that, if there's a real problem, he can take care of it."[9] Vox also points out that "nearly all evangelicals—88 percent, according to the Pew Research Center on Religion & Public Life—believe in miracles, suggesting a faith in a proactive God. And only 28 percent of evangelicals believe human activity is causing climate change."[10] These statistics lead Vox to make a further point: "Confidence that God will intervene to prevent people from destroying the world is one of the strongest barriers to gaining conservative evangelical support for environmental pacts like the Paris agreement."[11] For Americans today hearing these biblical texts concerning divine kingship, these points become clear: "as long as we *are* 'One Nation Under God,' and as long as we have a God who reigns over heaven and

---

9 See Lisa Vox, "Why Don't Christian Conservatives Worry About Climate Change? God.," in *The Washington Post* (June 2, 2017).
10 *Ibid.*
11 *Ibid.*

earth, then we have nothing to fear, nothing to worry about. We will be redeemed from the ecological disaster that the entire planet is experiencing because we have a Redeemer who is 'our Lord and Savior.' With reasoning like that which has just been stated, piety now trumps ethics, and justice becomes divorced from holiness. Human leaders can do whatever they want to do because as someone could argue, "God is in his heavens, seated on his throne, and all is and will be right with the world." Such thinking leads to the next section, human kingship.

3 Leaders and Kings Acting Godly?

In the past few decades, many of the world's nations have made great advancements in medical scientific research. For example, throughout the last five years, the US, the UK, Canada, India, and Taiwan have been developing tricorders which are portable tools that can diagnose health conditions and take real-time vital signs like blood pressure. Scientists have made tremendous progress in the area of T-cell immunotherapies, ultrasound therapy for Alzheimer's disease, and synthetic blood. In the field of astronomy, Steven Hawking has proven the existence of black holes. In 2017 archaeologists discovered a new Dead Sea Scrolls cave, and last but not least, Tesla has created and tested a driverless car.

Despite the world's many wonderful advancements and breakthroughs, the global community of human beings has yet to make significant advancement in global peace and the election of visionary, charismatic, and just leaders. Past and present profiles of heads of state bear this point out. Arnoldo Aleman, President of Nicaragua (1997–2002) embezzled more than $100 million of government funds. Slobadan Milosevic, President of Serbia/Yugoslavia (1989–2000) presided over the mayhem and mass murders that took place in Kosovo, Croatia, and Bosnia in the 1990 s. Bashar al-Assad, current President of Syria, has used chemical weapons against his own country's civilians, many of whom were women and children who died. Rodrigo Duterte, current President of the Philippines, has allegedly ordered death squads against his own people. Donald J. Trump, current President of the United States of America, faces sexual-assault allegations, beauty pageant scandals, racial housing discrimination, among other improprieties. Corruption among recent and current political world leaders invites a backward glance at the ancient NE world where we see that the corruption among leaders today was something that occurred in biblical times as well. Very specifically, former Iraqi President Saddam Hussein rose from an impoverished background to become one of the world's most feared leaders, but in 2003 after his 25-year reign of terror, he fell from power.

The poem in Isa 14:1–23 tells the story of the King of Babylon, a corrupt leader, one like Saddam Hussein, both of whom fell from power (vv 3–22). The poem is a taunt song against this human king who "struck down the peoples in wrath/with unceasing blows" (v 6a), ruled the nations in anger/with unrelenting persecution (v 6b), and declared he would make himself like the Most High (v 14).

Stories within Isaiah 36–39,[12] a distinct unit within the book of Isaiah, describe the encounter that takes place between the two kings, Hezekiah of Judah and Sennacherib of Assyria (Isaiah 36). Through the Rabshakeh (a chief cup-bearer or adviser), Sennacherib tries to make a wager with Hezekiah (v 8), but he is unsuccessful in his attempt. This poem describes Assyria's volley for power. Assyria tries to win over Judah, and thus defeat both the Egyptians and the Judahites. Here one king tries to usurp the power of another through deception. The quest for power on King Sennacherib's part is palpable in this poem. In the exchange between Kings Hezekiah and Sennacherib and their representatives, we see that strength does not always occur in numbers.

King Hezekiah continues his encounter with King Sennacherib in Isaiah 37. The series of rhetorical questions rehearse Assyria's power and highlight the ineffectiveness of the nation's gods. One king brutally tries to bully another king, and in doing so, attempts to undermine the power, confidence, and faith of one leader and his people. Psychological warfare is just as deadly as physical warfare.

Hezekiah's response to Sennacherib's bullying is laudable. Hezekiah takes the situation to prayer, does not cower in the face of threat and adversity, lets go to God, trusts in God's counsel and power (vv 14–20), and God responds favorably to Hezekiah (vv 21–35). A divine angel defeats the Assyrians, Sennacherib goes home to Nineveh and dies by the sword of his two sons (vv 36–38). Although a bully and his army experience defeat, this defeat gained through the assertion of divine power underscores the acceptability of the use of force to settle conflicts. This display of divine force gives support to those leaders today who continue to use brute force not only against their own people but also against the leaders and people of other nations. Finally, prayer and faith now become linked to the image of a conquering deity.

Thus, within Isaiah 36–39, two images of human kingship emerge. One king, Sennacherib, is self-serving, aggressive, and uses his power to try and usurp the power of another king, Hezekiah. Unlike Sennacherib, Hezekiah is a devout king who uses his power assertively. Hezekiah is prayerful, trusting, faithful, righteous, and pious. He enjoys God's favor, but the divine response to Hezekiah's request is as violent as the power asserted by corrupt human kings. This divine

---

12 The content of Isaiah 36–39 is almost identical to 2 Kings 18–20.

response begs a theological question: "Is the assertion of punitive power truly an 'answer to prayer'"?

One last king featured specifically in the book of Isaiah is Cyrus, King of Persia. In Isa 45:1–7, Cyrus debuts as God's "anointed one" who will free the exiles. Unlike Hezekiah, Cyrus will not rule in peace. He has been set up by Israel's God to rule like Israel's monarchal, kyriarchal God rules. Cyrus is to subdue nations, strip kings of their robes. Shalom Paul underscores Cyrus' use of aggressive power that will hallmark his reign. Paul states: "Cyrus was chosen to be God's instrument to execute the Deity's masterplan similar to the selection of Assyria in First Isaiah: 'The rod of my wrath" (Isa 10:5), and Nebuchadnezzar in the prophecies of Jeremiah: 'my servant' (Jer 25:9; 27:6)."[13] Furthermore, in order to prove to Cyrus that indeed he was "called by name" by Israel's God for the task of liberating the Israelites from exile while decimating another peoples, Israel's God promises to assert aggressive divine power (vv 2–3). Aggressive power marks God's divine kingship and will also mark Cyrus' human kingship, and herein lies one example of the intersection between divine-human kingship/leadership as described in the books of Isaiah and the Twelve. To be anointed by this monarchal, kyriarchal God, then, is to become one like this aggressive monarchal, kyriarchal God who appears to be obsessed with sovereignty (see vv 5, 6).

Interestingly, even though King Cyrus is long dead, might his spirit and style of leadership as a king live on in the US President Donald Trump? Benjamin Netanyahu seems to think so. In a recent meeting with Trump, and after Trump made Jerusalem the capital of Israel, Netanyahu made the following statement: "I want to tell you that the Jewish people have a long memory, so we remember the proclamation of the great king, Cyrus the Great, the Persian king 2,500 years ago. He proclaimed that the Jewish exiles in Babylon could come back and rebuild our Temple in Jerusalem. ..."[14] This image of Trump is particularly popular among evangelical Christians. Hence, we now have a democratic president being compared to a monarchal imperial king, and indeed, in light of poems and stories about ancient Near Eastern kings, Trump's leadership style does seem to be more monarchal and imperial than democratic. On the opposite end of the spectrum, however, the image of Hezekiah conjures up the memory of President Nelson Mandela of South Africa, who ruled democratically, who gained international acclaim for his

---

13 Shalom M. Paul, *Isaiah 40–66*; (Grand Rapids: William B. Eerdmans, 2012), 251–52.
14 See Andrew Silow-Carroll, "Who is King Cyrus, and Why did Netanyahu Compare Him to Trump?" in *The Times of Israel"* (March 8, 2018); see also Katherine Stewart, "Why Trump Reigns as King Cyrus," *New York Times* (Dec. 31, 2018).

activism on behalf of justice. The images of Hezekiah and Mandela leads into the third part of this essay that explores the vision of a new kind of leader.

4 Discovering a New Vision for Leadership: A Prophetic Response to Power, Politics, and Kings

Hunger, poverty, mass shootings, chemical warfare, floods, droughts, loss of precious ecosystems, melting and calving glaciers, rising sea levels, rising ocean temperatures, earthquakes, hurricanes, volcanic eruptions, dried up rivers, diminished water supplies—it is all happening on planet Earth and human and non-human life is being irreversibly affected to the point of, for some, extinction. Do we have global leaders who can jointly help the world communities change their course in life by implementing policy changes that go right to the heart of systemic change, inclusive of changes in attitudes and mindsets? Researchers tell us we only have a small window of opportunity.

Kim Bobo prays to claim God's vision of a new earth:

> O God, creator of the universe and architect of all things possible. Let me claim your vision of a new heaven and a new earth.
> In your vision, those who build houses will dwell in them. Those who plant vineyards will eat their fruit. No longer will they build houses and others live in them, or plant and others eat, says the prophet Isaiah (Isa 65:21–22)
> But we live in a society in which those who care for children struggle to afford child care.
> Those who provide home health care for seniors have no health care for themselves.
> Those who clean rooms in resort hotels can't afford to stay in a hotel.
> Day laborers who help build homes cannot live in them.
> And the children of those who plant and harvest our food go hungry.
> Please forgive my collusion with a twisted world that devalues work and hurts your people. I participate and sometimes benefit from this devaluing of work. Forgive me. Forgive me when my search for cheap deals encourages companies to cheat workers. Forgive me when I forget to recognize my food comes from workers' hands. Forgive me when I follow the market's standards instead of your standards.
> Lead me to a new heaven and a new earth. Remove my desire for more worldly goods in the midst of such poverty. Inflame my passion for justice. Create in me a vision of society in which those who build live and those who plant eat.[15]

---

15 Kim Bobo, "To Claim God's Vision of a New Earth" in *Prayers for the New Social Awakening*. Eds. Christian Iosso and Elizabeth Hinson-Hasty (Louisville: John Knox Westminster, 2008), 145.

Do we have global leaders today who can lead us into a new way of life? It seems doubtful that those who embrace the monarchal, kyriarchal models of leadership as portrayed by the Prophets' divine and human kings, together with all people, are going to be able to accomplish the critical task of the global transformation that is desperately needed to usher in the new heavens and the new earth. And yet, the theme of hope runs through several Isaian texts out of which a new vision of leadership emerges.

4.1 Isaiah 9:1–7; Isaiah 11:1–9; Isaiah 32

Three poems, among others, in the book of Isaiah describe an alternative vision of leadership. In Isa 9:1–7, the poet envisions a new kind of leader, one who will liberate the people from oppression and put an end to warfare (vv 1–5). This new leader, empowered and gifted by God, will work to establish lasting peace which will be the fruit of justice and righteousness, two virtues by which the leader will lead. Isaiah's vision addresses the type of leader needed for today's globalized world.

In Isa 11:1–9, the child who led God's people into the way of peace in Isa 9:6 will now lead the rest of creation into peace (Isa 11:6). A marvelous picture of a new creation that comes to birth through the exercise of justice and righteousness comes into focus in Isa 11:1–9, and a new kind of leader, one personally espoused to justice and righteousness (v 5) comes to the fore. The good governance of the new leader will usher in a new way of life. The hallmark of this new leader's power will be assertiveness and not aggression. The longing for a new kind of leader is as palpable today as it was for people in biblical times. The Isaian poem becomes a clarion call to present day leaders to recognize that the fate of humanity and the natural world—hence, the entire planet—is inextricably linked and that good governance demands from others the justice and respect that all communities of life so that all creation can thrive and not just one nation's economy over another.

In Isaiah 32 the poet describes a vision of a new type of leadership and governance (vv 1–8) and summons the upper class women to mourn what presently exists because what now exists is about to crumble (vv 9–15) as the spirit from on high is poured out, the effects of which will usher in a new way of life (vv 16–20). The women whom the poet summons receive direct commands to "rise up" (v 9a), to "listen" to the poet's speech (v. 9b), to "tremble," to "shutter," to "strip" and make themselves bare, to "put on sackcloth" on their loins (v. 11), and to "beat" their breasts (v 12). These actions denote a tone of lament and mourning which is to occur on account of the loss of the autumn fruit harvest--grapes, olives, figs (vv. 12–13), the depopulation of towns, inclusive of the city of Jerusalem (v. 14), and ultimately because nothing will be the same in Judah ever again when the new governance comes into effect.

Joseph Blenkinsopp notes that "lamenting for the lost harvest provides an entry point for the theme of reversion to the natural state that keeps on recurring throughout chs. 1–39."[16] Thus, these verses help to develop a particular theme within this first section of the book of Isaiah. The poem links the transformation of the human condition to the natural world. Only through God's spirit is life changed. Thus, social and ecological transformation goes hand in hand, a point supported by Blenkinsopp who also draws attention to the spirit of God as an agent of either "destructive" or "renovative" transformation (cf. 44:3–4).[17]

Furthermore, the poet refers to the women addressed in vv 9–15 as "complacent daughters," and even more directly, "you complacent ones," two phrases indicative of disdain. Of note, the poet neither addresses nor comments on any of the males who hold and wield power unjustly in the community. Only one class of women is singled out, upbraided, and asked to make an embarrassing and public display of mourning.

Although the poet delivers a somber message in vv 9–15, his final word ends on a note of hope. Or does it end on a word of hope? Just as Lebanon becomes a fruitful field, and the fruitful field a forest that would eventually be leveled (see Isa 29:17), so also the wilderness of Judah will become a fruitful field, and the fruitful field will be deemed a forest (v. 15). This mixed message leads into v. 16 which picks up the image of the fruitful field in relation to a new time that will dawn for Judah.[18]

The simplicity of expression and rich imagery present an idyllic picture of the land and the people abiding in peace, quietness, and trust forever, all of which will be the fruit of justice and righteousness in vv 16–20. This section of the poem complements verses 1–8 and continues the poet's vision that he shares with his people. When peace is established in the land, the forest will disappear completely, and the city will be utterly laid low (v. 19). The reference to the forest harkens back to verse 15 and to a similar image in Isaiah 29:17 (cf v. 13). Does the city represent Jerusalem? Does the forest signify what is to become of Judah? Perhaps everything must go to rack and ruin before a new way of life and governance can come into existence. With the forest and the city gone, the people will

---

16 Joseph Blenkinsopp, Isaiah 1–39; AB 19 (New York: Doubleday, 2000), 433–434.

17 *Ibid.*

18 Oswalt suggests that the imagery in verse 15 speaks only of abundance. Given a similar reference in Isaiah 29:17 and what follows in verse 19 where the forest imagery reappears and is said to disappear completely, I argue otherwise and suggest that the imagery has a double intent (see Oswalt, *Isaiah 1–39*, 588). Brueggemann notes the enigmatic tone of the verse and offers a variety of other suggestions (see Brueggemann, *Isaiah 1–39*, 258).

now be happy and will sow beside every stream, with ox and donkey roaming freely (v. 20). The sowing imagery in v 20 speaks of renewal and new life which can only happen when the old is cleared away, symbolized by the disappearing forest and the city to be laid low.

In summary, the poems present a different vision of leadership and serve as a reminder that only when leadership exercises justice and righteousness can peace be established, and only when the old way of life—symbolized by the forest and the city—comes to an end can room be made for that which is new which will coincide with and be the fruit of the new governance (vv. 1–8). The transformation will occur when the divine spirit is poured out (v 15). Finally, because change is difficult and involves a letting go process, lamentation is the appropriate response to the transformative changes that will take place to the people and to the land (vv 9–15). This sentiment of sadness will eventually give way to joy, peace, and freedom for all (vv 16–20).

5 Leadership and the Book of the Twelve

5.1 Micah 5:2–5 [Heb 5:1–4]

Within the Book of the Twelve, the past image of the king gives way to the vision of a new type of leader who will come forth from Bethlehem-Ephrathah (Mic 5:2). This new leader will be like a shepherd (Mic 5:4) and not like Israel's other kings, many of whom used their position of authority and power to oppress people. With a new type of governance will come security. This new leader will be the one of "peace" (v 5; see also Isa 9:6–7).

Several points come to the fore in these verses. First, Mic 5:2 [Heb] with its reference to a woman in childbirth harkens back to Mic 4:10 and could be an allusion to the Immanuel Proclamation in Isa 7:14. There the child is thought to be one in the line of David. Julia O'Brien argues that

> The promise of victory over the Assyrians in 5:4 [5:3 MT] likely is an allusion to Isa 7:17, which also mentions the Assyrian threat; if so, Micah shifts the meaning of Isaiah's proclamation. In Isaiah, God advises the Judeans not to fear the anti-Assyrian coalition besieging the city; the real threat they face is Assyria itself, whom God will use as the 'rod of my anger' (Isa 10:5) to punish Judah's sins. In Micah, these words are those of promise; a postponed threat in Isaiah becomes a lasting promise in Micah.[19]

---

19 Julia M. O'Brien, *Micah*; Wisdom Commentary 37 (Collegeville: Liturgical Press, 2015), 58.

The anticipated king is to be one like David.

Second, interpreters argue that the focus on Bethlehem is an anti-Jerusalem stance. For example, John Rogerson makes the claim that Bethlehem suggests "a radical rejection of Jerusalem and the existing Davidic dynasty and a completely new start from Bethlehem."[20]A. J. Parotta argues that the use of Bethlehem challenges both Jerusalem and monarchal succession, that "it is also an affirmation that God can once again work through humble means, as [God] did with David, and is not dependent on the royal city and household, which has so deteriorated."[21] I suggest that the use of Bethlehem is not necessarily a rejection of Jerusalem. Bethlehem seems to be more of a source of salvation. Just as David, a shepherd, was once anointed to lead the people, so now God will anoint/appoint a new David to finish gathering the exiles (5:1 [Eng 5:2]) and rule the people in a new land and in a new time. This hope for the return of the Davidic monarchy also appears in Amos 9:11 and Zechariah 3–4. To be noted, the issue at stake here, however, is the perpetuation of patriarchy as a social system. A male deity continues to anoint males to political power and roles of political leadership, moral authority, and social privilege.

With respect to further comment on Bethlehem, Viola Raheb, a Palestinian Christian, makes clear that "Bethlehem is a Palestinian city; since 1995 it has been formally under Palestinian Authority rule but in practical terms since 1967 it has remained under Israeli occupation. For Palestinians today the name 'Ephrathah' is integrally linked to the Israeli settlement south-west on Bethlehem named 'Ephrathah,' which is built on confiscated Palestinian land and on which seven thousand Israeli settlers live."[22] She continues to note that "for Palestinian Christians today to understand the prophetic voice of Micah, it is essential for us to remember that Micah was not predicting the future but rather explaining the past."[23] Thus, Raheb sees Micah taking a clear stand on naming injustice and its perpetrators and giving voice to the silent ones in the community. This interpretation brings hope to Christian Palestinians today if we hear the Micah text as more than a promise.

Third, this poem enjoys a rich early Christian interpretation whereby the envisioned new leader is thought to be pointing to Christ. Some early Christian interpreters see the "hidden Christ" in this passage. Contrary to such interpretations,

---

20 John Rogerson, "Micah," in *Eerdmans Commentary on the Bible*, ed. J. D. G. Dunn and John Rogerson (Grand Rapids, MI: Eerdmans, 2003), 5.

21 A. J. Petrotta, "A Closer Look at Matt 2:6 and Its Old Testament Sources," *JETS* 28 (1985): 50.

22 See Viola Raheb, "Reading Micah 5 in Modern Bethlehem," in Julia M. O'Brien, *Micah*, 65–66.

23 *Ibid.*, 66.

I suggest that a more plausible understanding is that the envisioned leader is a literary construct much like the servant in Isaiah 52:13–53:12.[24]

5.2 Zechariah 9:9–10

The image of the king returns in Zech 9:9–10. The king is not riding in a typical chariot; rather, he rides on a donkey, on a colt, the foal of a donkey (v 9c). This king will be righteous which is a quality of the deity (Deut 32:4; Pss 11:7; 116:5; 119:137; 129:4; Isa 45:21), and unlike other kings, this king not will not enter into battle to defend the people or the land. This king will put an end to war and will be completely different than the ones Israel experienced in the past. This king will command peace to all nations. The dominion of this king will be expansive. These images of peace recall images from Isa 2:1–5, Mic 4:1–5, and Isa 65:17–25.

Despite the change in imagery of the king riding on a donkey and not on a horse or in a horse-drawn chariot, the poem continues to perpetuate monarchal and kyriarchal leadership. Additionally, the poem feminizes a city: Daughter Zion. Daughter Zion has to give a command performance because her king is coming to her. The notion of the king coming to Daughter Zion instead of Daughter Zion going to the king (v 9a) is a gesture of profound humility on the part of the king, but the metaphor "Daughter Zion" fails to put Zion on equal footing with the king. She is "daughter," not "queen" or even "wife." Julia O'Brien points out that

> In contrast to the other females, [Daughter Zion] will be rescued by YHWH, himself depicted as a very masculine warrior king: he cuts off chariots, extends dominion to the ends of the earth, wields people as a bow and arrow, marches to tread down enemies, and makes them drink their own blood—all in protection of his people.[25]

Thus, Daughter Zion will become "indebted" to the King. Hierarchy, patriarchy, kyriarchy and power prevail; Daughter Zion remains subservient to a donkey-riding king.[26]

---

24 See Carol J. Dempsey, *Isaiah: God's Poet of Light* (St. Louis: Chalice Press, 2010), 146–48.
25 Julia M. O'Brien, "Zechariah" in *Women's Bible Commentary: Revised and Updated;* Twentieth-Anniversary Edition; eds. Carol A. Newsom, Sharon H. Ringe, and Jacqueline E. Lapsley (Louisville: John Knox Westminster, 2012), 348.
26 For further discussion on this poem and the metaphorical language of Daughter Zion, see Beate Schmidtgen, "Haggai and Zechariah" in *Feminist Biblical Interpretation*; eds. Luisa Schottroff and Marie-Theres Wacker (Grand Rapids: Eerdmans, 2012), 468–471.

Thus, through a collection of well-crafted poems in the book of Isaiah and the Twelve, a new kind of leader comes into view whose mission is to bring forth a new teaching and a new way of life achieved not through violence but through patience, gentleness, persistence, faithfulness, and measured strength. To be noted, however, is the fact that even though these poems offer a new vision of leadership, the one in the position of leadership is still a male. Additionally, the shepherd imagery relegates people to sheep who are incapable of leading themselves. Androcentrism, male power, and male hierarchy remain constant even though images shift.

6 Conclusion: Returning Home and Knowing the Place for the First Time

The poet T. S. Eliot once wrote:

> We shall not cease from exploration
> And the end of all our exploring
> Will be to arrive where we started
> And to know the place for the first time.

This essay was an exploration, a journey back into the "old country" of the biblical world while pushing ahead into the glorious present one of the twenty-first century, fraught with problems yet pregnant with possibilities.

Central to the journey has been the exploration of select texts on divine and human kingship in the books of Isaiah and the Twelve, and how various images of kings, both divine and human, intersect and even conflict with each other across texts and across time and space. Nothing exists in a vacuum, and nothing is objective. Everything is culturally, historically, socially, politically, religiously, and theologically conditioned, from kings who once ruled in biblical times to present day leaders whose strategies, goals, mindsets, attitudes, and ways of governing seem, at times, to be as archaic and ineffective as some of their ancient ancestors. This mixed portrait of divine and human kingship that we see in Isaiah and the Twelve has profound social, cultural, political, and theological implications for people today in the twenty-first century whose nations are being governed by leaders not so different from the kings depicted in the book of the Prophets.

If today's global communities continue to choose and allow to remain in power those leaders who resemble the kyriarchal God and kings of old, then our world will be forever changed into a pit of violence that will eventually engulf and destroy everything and everyone. If we choose to shift from power over to power with and recognize and acknowledge an alternative vision of leadership different from Isaiah and the Twelve, and one that goes beyond the androcentric confines of the biblical world, then our world can be transformed. Like the biblical characters who stood at a crossroads, we too stand at a crossroads as many people struggle to understand the Divine, their lives, and world experiences amid empires of power whose many leaders are oppressive and unjust. Which road will we choose? Will we remain in the "old country" or will we set sail to a new world whose morning light beckons us forward?

Bibliography

Blenkinsopp, Joseph, *Isaiah 1–39*, AB 19 (New York: Doubleday, 2000).

Bobo, Kim, "To Claim God's Vision of a New Earth," in *Prayers for the New Social Awakening*, eds. Christian Iosso and Elizabeth Hinson-Hasty (Louisville, KY: Westminster John Knox Press, 2008).

Brueggemann, Walter, *Isaiah 1–39*, Westminster Bible Companion (Louisville, KY: Westminster John Knox Press, 1998).

Cameron, Michael, *Christ Meets Me Everywhere: Augustine's Early Figurative Exegesis* (New York: Oxford University Press, 2012).

Dempsey, Carol J., *Isaiah: God's Poet of Light* (St. Louis: Chalice Press, 2010).

Ferrell, James L., *The Hidden Christ: Beneath the Surface of the Old Testament* (Salt Lake City: Deseret Book, 2012).

Guthrie, Nancy, *The Word of the Lord: Seeing Jesus in the Prophets* (Wheaton, IL: Crossway, 2014).

Leclerc, Thomas L., *Yahweh is Exalted in Justice: Solidarity and Conflict in Israel* (Minneapolis: Augsburg Fortress, 2001).

Lozano, Gilbert, "Words of Hope for Contemporary Exiles in South and Central America," in *Global Perspectives on the Bible*, eds. Mark Roncace and Joseph Weaver (New York: Pearson, 2014).

Mahon, Tom, "The Spirit in Technology," in *The Hand of God: Thoughts and Images Reflecting the Spirit of the Universe*, ed. Michael Regan (Philadelphia: Templeton Foundation Press, 1999).

O'Brien, Julia M., *Micah*, Wisdom Commentary 37 (Collegeville, MN: Liturgical Press, 2015).

O'Brien, Julia M., "Zechariah," in *Women's Bible Commentary*, 3rd edn, eds. Carol A. Newsom, Sharon H. Ringe, and Jacqueline E. Lapsley (Louisville, KY: Westminster John Knox Press, 2012).

Oswalt, John N., *Isaiah 1–39*, NICOT (Grand Rapids, MI: Eerdmans, 1986).

Paul, Shalom M., *Isaiah 40–66* (Grand Rapids, MI: Eerdmans, 2012).

Petrotta, A. J., "A Closer Look at Matt 2:6 and Its Old Testament Sources," *JETS* 28 (1985).

Raheb, Viola, "Reading Micah 5 in Modern Bethlehem," in Julia M. O'Brien, *Micah,* 65–66.

Rogerson, John, "Micah," in *Eerdmans Commentary on the Bible*, eds. J. D. G. Dunn and John Rogerson (Grand Rapids, MI: Eerdmans, 2003).

Schmidtgen, Beate, "Haggai and Zechariah," in *Feminist Biblical Interpretation*, eds. Luisa Schottroff and Marie-Theres Wacker (Grand Rapids, MI: Eerdmans, 2012), 468–471.

Scholz, Susanne, *Sacred Witness: Rape in the Hebrew Bible* (Minneapolis: Fortress, 2014).

Schreiter, Robert J., C.PP.S., "The Bible and Culture," in *The Collegeville Pastoral Dictionary of Biblical Theology* (Collegeville, MN: Liturgical Press), xlvii.

Silow-Carroll, Andrew, "Who is King Cyrus, and Why did Netanyahu Compare Him to Trump?" *Times of Israel* (8 March 2018), <https://www.timesofisrael.com/who-is-king-cyrus-and-why-is-netanyahu-comparing-him-to-trump/> [cited 1 August 2019].

Stewart, Katherine, "Why Trump Reigns as King Cyrus," *New York Times* (31 December 2018), <https://www.nytimes.com/2018/12/31/opinion/trump-evangelicals-cyrus-king.html> [cited 1 August 2019].

Vox, Lisa, "Why Don't Christian Conservatives Worry About Climate Change? God." *Washington Post* (2 June 2017), <https://www.washingtonpost.com/posteverything/wp/2017/06/02/why-dont-christian-conservatives-worry-about-climate-change-god/?utm_term=.d28b6bb31e3d > [cited 1 August 2019].

Archibald L. H. M. van Wieringen
The *Oracles Against the Nations* in Isaiah, Amos and Zephaniah. A Text-Immanent Reader's Perspective

Introduction

The "Oracles[1] Against the Nations" are considered to be a specific genre within prophetic literature. There are indeed texts concerning the nations, which are listed and then negatively portrayed. I would like to examine these prophetic texts in the books of Isaiah, Amos and Zephaniah from the perspective of the text-internal reader in order to gain insight into the similarities and differences between Isaiah, Amos and Zephaniah for the text-immanent reader.

1 The delineations of the pericopes

I would first like to give attention to the delineation of these texts. Due to the fact that I make my analysis based on the final text, the so-called *Endtext*, I prefer to delineate the pericopes concerned making use of the textual data instead of the genre-indication created by the word "nations."

For the book of Isaiah, I consider chapters 13–23 to be the text that can be indicated as "Oracles Against the Nations." In my view, the headings in the text of the book of Isaiah are the main markers leading the text-immanent reader through the structure of the text. Based upon these headings, chapters 13–23 form a demarcated unit within the book of Isaiah. The subsequent headings list the nations involved.[2]

This implies, for example, that I do not leave out chapter 20, which deals with Jerusalem, although some exegetes consider chapter 20 as not belonging to

---

1 I agree with T. K. Cheyne, *The Prophecies of Isaiah* (London: Kegan Paul, 1886), 81–82, in not translating the word מַשָּׂא with *burden*, but with *utterance* (or *statement*). In my view, the usual term *oracle* too often evokes the Ancient World, for example the Greek sanctuary in Delphi. I will nevertheless use the term *Oracles Against the Nations* because it is an established expression in Old Testament exegesis.
2 See also: Archibald L. H. M. van Wieringen, *The Reader-Oriented Unity of the Book Isaiah*, ACEBT.S 6 (Vught: Skandalon, 2006), 36–44.

https://doi.org/10.1515/9783110705799-011

the so-called "Oracles Against the Nations," because Jerusalem is not one of the nations.[3] In other words: it is not the indication "Oracles Against the Nations" that determines the delineation of the texts involved, but the textual markers, in this case the textual markers of the headings.

For the book of Amos, I consider 1:3–3:2 to be a unit.[4] The verses 3:1–2 form the discursive foreground to 1:3–2:16 due to the imperative in 3:1a and the vocative in 3:1b. Again, I do not limit the text to 1:3–2:3 because after 2:3 no nations are mentioned but rather only Judah and Israel. The Amos-text uses two different main patterns for the prophetic texts against the nations. The first pattern is used for Damascus, Gaza, Ammon and Moab; the second pattern for Tyre and Edom, however also for Judah and Israel.

For the book of Zephaniah, I consider 2:4–3:20 to be a unit.[5] This unit consists of two sub-units: 2:4–15 and 3:1–20. Both sub-units start asyndetically: in 2:4 with an emphatic כִּי, which I prefer to translate with *yes* instead of *because*, and in 3:1 with הוֹי *woe*. Although there is a clear *cesura* between 2:4–15 and 3:1–20, there are many links between these two sub-units. Both sub-units have a similar structure. While 2:10–11 functions as a kind of conclusion, in which the text-immanent author uses only the third person, dividing 2:4–15 into two blocks, 2:4–11 and 2:12–15, 3:13 functions as a kind of conclusion as well, in which the text-immanent author also uses only the third person, dividing 3:1–20 into two blocks, 3:1–13 and 3:14–20.

The text-syntactical markers כִּי in 2:4 for 2:4–16 and הוֹי in 3:1 for 3:1–20 are used in the two sub-units. An emphatic כִּי such as that used in 2:4 can also be found in 3:9, while the asyndetic particle הוֹי in 3:1 also occurs in 2:5.

---

3 *Pace* among others: Ulrich Berges and Willem A. M. Beuken, *Das Buch Jesaja: Eine Einführung*, UTB 4647 (Göttingen: Vandenhoeck & Ruprecht, 2016), 84–93. Although different, see also: Marvin A. Sweeney, *Isaiah 1–39*, FOTL 16 (Grand Rapids, MI: Eerdmans, 1996), 212.
4 See for more details: Archibald L. H. M. van Wieringen, "The Prophecies Against the Nations in Amos 1:2–3:15," *EstBib* 71 (2013): 7–19.
5 Cf.: Tchavdar S. Hadjiev, "Zephaniah and the 'Book of the Twelve' Hypothesis," in *Prophecy and the Prophets in Ancient Israel: Proceedings of the Oxford Old Testament Seminar*, ed. John Day, LHB/OTS 531 (London: T&T Clark, 2010): 323–338 (331). *Pace*: Hubert Irsigler, *Zefanja*, HThKAT (Freiburg: Herder, 2002), especially 42, who does not focus enough on syntactical aspects in dividing the texts into main units. Different: Daniel H. Ryou, *Zephaniah's Oracles against the Nations* (Amsterdam: VU University Press, 1994), especially 77–81. Cf. Paul R. House, *Zephaniah: A Prophetic Drama*, JSOT.S 69 (Sheffield: Almond, 1989), especially 56–61.

2 The toponyms in the pericopes and their order

The most obvious element which could be decisive for the text-immanent reader's position seems to be the names of the nations mentioned in the three texts. The three texts only have one single name of a foreign nation in common, as can be seen in the scheme below: Moab is mentioned in Isaiah, in Amos as well as in Zephaniah. Besides Moab, Jerusalem is also present in each of the three texts.

The following scheme lists the various toponyms. If, under a heading with a toponym, other toponyms are also mentioned, these toponyms are given in square brackets. The toponyms of Moab and Jerusalem, which are common to all three texts, are rendered in italics.[6]

Tab. 1

Isaiah	Amos	Zephaniah
Babel	Damascus	Gaza
[Assur]	Gaza	Ashkelon
Moab	[Ashdod]	Ashdod
Damascus	[Ashkelon]	Ekron
Egypt	[Ekron]	Seacoast
[*Jerusalem*]	Tyre	Cherethites
[Egypt]	Edom	Canaan = Land of the Philistines
[Cush]	[Teman]	Seacoast
Babel	[Bozrah]	Ashkelon
Dumah (= Edom)	Ammon	*Moab*
Arab	[Rabbah]	Ammon
the Valley of the Vision (= *Jerusalem*)	*Moab*	*Moab*
Tyre	Judah	Cushites
	[*Jerusalem*]	Assur
	Israel	Nineveh
		Jerusalem/Israel
		Cush
		Zion/Israel/*Jerusalem*

If we compare Isaiah with Amos and Zephaniah separately or if we compare Amos and Zephaniah, there are more toponyms in common, but still a minority of four to six different names, each time. The three following schemes show the parallel names.

---

6 See also: Patricia K. Tull, *Isaiah 1–39*, Smyth & Helwys Bible Commentary (Macon GA: Smyth & Helwys Publishing, 2010), 256.

Cush is the area south of Egypt, known as Nubia. If we consider Cush and Egypt as a couple (*confer*: Isa 11:11; 20:3–5), indicating the powerful nation to the south of the ancient Near East, the common toponym Cush in Isaiah and Zephaniah is intensified.

More important than the various names that are listed in the three texts, is the order in which they are mentioned.

Based upon the headings, we see two movements in Isa 13–23, both starting with Babel and ending with Jerusalem.[7] These two movements can be outlined as follows:

Tab. 2

	distant East	nearby East	distant West	final destination
first movement	Isa 13–14: Babel	Isa 15–16: Moab Isa 17–18: Damascus	Isa 19: Egypt	[Isa 20: Jerusalem]
second movement	Isa 21:1–10: Babel	Isa 21:11: Dumah (Edom) Isa 21:12–16: Arab		Isa 22: Jerusalem
transitional text			Isa 23: Tyre	

Both movements start in the distant East, i. e. Babel, and reach the final destination, Jerusalem, via the nearby East. Although mentioned in chapter 14, Assur does not form a separate unit due to the fact that Assur does not have its own heading. Assur is dealt with under the heading concerning Babel. The qatal-form (נִשְׁבַּע יְהוָה) *(the* LORD*) had sworn* in Isa 14:24 indicates that what is happening to Babel, previously happened to Assur.[8]

---

7 See for more details: van Wieringen, *Reader-Oriented Unity*, 86–87; Archibald L. H. M. van Wieringen, "Isaiah 13–23 and Its Text-Immanent Reader," in *Prophecy and Foreign Nations*, ed. Uwe Becker, Hannes Bezzel and Matthijs de Jong, FAT (Tübingen: Mohr Siebeck, 2019) (forthcoming). See also: Berges and Beuken, *Jesaja*, 84.
8 Archibald L. H. M. van Wieringen, "Assur and Babel against Jerusalem: The Reader-Oriented Position of Babel and Assur within the Framework of Isaiah 1–39," in *'Enlarge the Site of Your Tent': The City as Unifying Theme in Isaiah: The Isaiah Workshop: De Jesaja Werkplaats*, ed. Archibald L. H. M. van Wieringen and Annemarieke van der Woude, OTS 58 (Leiden: Brill, 2011): 49–62 (60).

After mentioning the East, the distant West receives its place in the first movement through the mentioning of Egypt. The couple East-West, with Jerusalem in the middle, suggests that foreign nations are surrounding the capital city of Jerusalem. However, such a West is absent in the second movement.

Jerusalem forms the final destination of both movements. The first one is completed in chapter 20. Although chapter 20 does not have a heading mentioning Jerusalem, parallel to the other headings in the chapters 13–23, it forms a separate unit due to the fact that it is the only narrative text amid all the discursive texts in Isa 13–23. The absence of a heading for chapter 20 also indicates that the first movement, although having reached Jerusalem, is still open-ended. The final destination is גֵּיא חִזָּיוֹן *the Valley of the Vision*, i. e. Jerusalem, in chapter 22.

This means that, for the text-immanent reader, the two geographical poles of Babel and Jerusalem are in focus. Because of the double movement and because of the nearby East, the tension between these two geographical poles is intensified.

Assur is absent with regard to the headings, but is nevertheless present in the text. From a topographical point of view, Egypt is not part of a movement from Babel to Jerusalem, but is nevertheless present in the text, even with a separate Egypt-heading. For the text-immanent reader, this implies that Assur and Egypt must have something to do with the main movement from Babel to Jerusalem.

The order in which the nations are listed is different in Amos. Based upon the introductory formula, eight nations are dealt with. Besides the eight nations, some other toponyms also occur in the text.

In the first oracle concerning Damascus in 1:3–5, בִּקְעַת־אָוֶן Bikat-Awen and בֵּית עֶדֶן Bet-Eden are mentioned (v. 5). However, these indications are generally considered as not being real toponyms, but symbolic names, synonymously used for Aram's capital Damascus. Their respective translation is: *Valley of Guile* and *House of Lust*.[9]

In the second oracle concerning Gaza in 1:6–8, the Philistine cities Ashdod, Ashkelon and Ekron are also mentioned (v. 8). They are used *pars pro toto* for the entire area of the Philistines, as the expression שְׁאֵרִית פְּלִשְׁתִּים *the rest of the Philistines* indicates.

In the fourth oracle concerning Edom in 1:11–12, the Edomite cities of Teman (in the south) and Bozrah (in the north) are mentioned (v. 12). These two main cities function as a hendiadys indicating the entire area of Edom.

---

9 R. Reed Lessing, *Amos*, Concordia Commentary (St. Louis MO: Concordia, 2009), 111–112.

In the fifth oracle concerning Ammon in 1:13–15, the capital Rabbah is mentioned (v. 14). This capital is used *pars pro toto* for the entire area.[10]

Tab. 3

Northwest
(3) Tyre

Northeast
(1) Damascus

(8) Israel

Southeast
(4) Edom
(5) Ammon

Southwest
(2) Gaza

(7) Judah

(6) Moab

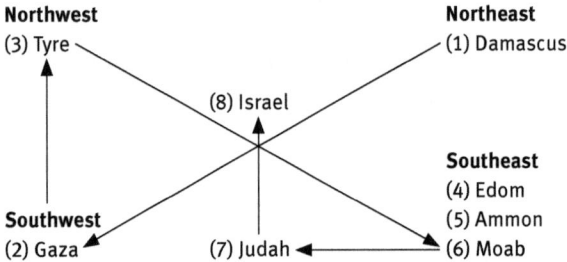

The eight nations are used in such a way that, in the process of reading, the text-immanent reader flies from one side to the other with Israel in the centre, as is shown in the scheme above. From Damascus in the Northeast (first oracle), he goes to Gaza in the Southwest (second oracle) and Tyre in the Northwest (third oracle). Then he goes from Tyre in the Northwest to Edom, Ammon and Moab in the Southeast (fourth, fifth and sixth oracle). After having mentioned all the different directions, he goes to Judah (seventh oracle) and finally to Israel in the centre (eighth oracle).

In Isaiah, the enumeration of the nations clearly consists of two parts according to the two movements from Babel to Jerusalem. In a way, the enumeration in Amos can be considered as consisting of two parts as well. Between all the oracles, concatenating word-repetitions occur, except between Edom and Ammon. Due to this, it seems that a kind of delaying stop is made with Edom. The first part runs from Damascus to Edom, the second starts with Ammon.

For the text-immanent reader, the order in which the foreign nations are mentioned in Amos expresses the idea that Israel is surrounded from all sides by various foreign nations. Israel is literally enclosed.

The order in which the nations are mentioned in Zephaniah differs from Isaiah and Amos. Just as in Isaiah, Zephaniah also plays with nearby and distant toponyms, while, just as in Amos, all four points of the compass are involved through jumping from one side to the other, but without mentioning Jerusalem in the centre. The following scheme shows the order of the nations.

---

10 See also: Lessing, *Amos*, 99–102.

Tab. 4

	nearby West	nearby East	transitional text	distant West	distant East	Jerusalem	transitional text	Zion/Israel/Jerusalem
first part	2:4–7 [Jerusalem]	2:8–10 [Israel]	2:10–11	2:12	2:13–15			
second part						3:1–12 [distant West]	3:13	3:14–20

The first part 2:4–15 zooms out from nearby, small nations to distant, powerful nations. I use the indication "distant West," because I consider Cush as being a magnification of the nearby West. *Mutatis mutandis*, I consider Assur with its capital Nineveh as a magnification of the nearby East, indicating the "distant East."[11]

In the second part, no nations are mentioned, except Cush, i. e. a distant West, in 3:10. However, there is no distant East (or some other foreign nation) present in the second part after the transitional text.

For the text-immanent reader, the order of nations in Zephaniah focusses on a movement that zooms out in the first part, whereas, in the second part, a movement is barely present.

3 The temporal aspects in the pericopes

The pericopes of the Oracles Against the Nations do not only influence the text-immanent reader through the toponyms and their order, but also through the temporal aspects in the text.

The temporal elements concerning Isaiah that I wish to discuss can be found in the scheme below.[12]

---

11 Cf. Ryou, *Zephaniah's Oracles*, 242, who uses the terms "north" and "south."
12 For more details see also: van Wieringen, *Isaiah 13–23* (forthcoming).

Tab. 5

	end of Babel/now-moment	end of Assur	Hezekiah	end of Ahaz	end of Syro-Ephraimite War	now-moment	end of Syro-Ephraimite War	open
first movement	13:1–14:23	14:24–27	20:1–6	14:28–32	15:1–16:12	16:13–14	17:1–18:7 19:1–25 as well?	
second movement	21:1–10		22:1–25			21:11–12 21:13–17		
transitional text								23:1–18

In my view, Isa 13–23 can be read as a journey back in time. Of course, the formal headings already suggest a past perspective. The headings make it clear that the nations are listed as belonging to the past.

The start of the Oracles Against the Nations in Isaiah evokes a temporal tension for the text-immanent reader: whereas the heading in 13:1 creates a past perspective, a kind of a now-moment is present as from 13:2 onwards.

Without using any introductory formula, Isa 13:2 starts with a direct speech. Due to this, the moment in time of the direct speech is not marked. The text-immanent reader is confronted with an unknown moment in time, which suggests that time seems to start at the moment the direct speech begins.

Assur's decline is discussed in 14:24–27, using a *qatal*-form: (יְהוָה) נִשְׁבַּע *(the LORD) had sworn* (v. 24a). This makes clear that Assur's past decline is the proof of the imminent decline Babel has to face. What the Lord announced in the past concerning the future decline of Assur, which he indeed carried out, he will also do concerning Babel.

Next, 14:28–32 deals with the year of King Ahaz' death. The introductory formula contains a qatal-form again, indicating the past perspective: בִּשְׁנַת־מוֹת הַמֶּלֶךְ אָחָז הָיָה הַמַּשָּׂא הַזֶּה *in the year of the death of King Ahaz this oracle had come* (v. 28). This implies that the text-immanent reader has moved in time: from the decline of Assur to the end of the reign of King Ahaz. This also means that, although the text of 14:24–27 leaves open which concrete Assyrian threat the Lord is speaking about, the Assyrian crisis under King Hezekiah, who is the successor of King Ahaz, is the most reasonable one.

Isa 16:13–14 contains the next temporal indication. It forms the conclusion of the oracle against Moab. A double temporal indication is used: מֵאָז *in the past* in verse 13 and וְעַתָּה *now* in verse 14.[13] Before the year of the death of King Ahaz, we have the period of King Ahaz' reign, which implies that 15:1–16:12 is related to the Syro-Ephraimite War. Although neither King Ahaz nor the enemies of Rezin and Pekah are mentioned, the negative consequences of the crisis of the Syro-Ephraimite War become visible.

After the explicit moments of time in 16:13–14, the temporal indications are almost absent in chapters 17–19. Chapter 20 again opens with a concrete temporal indication: the year regarding the Assyrian King Sargon's military action (v. 1). This moment of time belongs to King Hezekiah's reign; however, he is not mentioned anywhere in the narration of chapter 20.[14]

---

13 See also: Willem A. M. Beuken, *Jesaja 13–27*, HThKAT (Freiburg: Herder, 2007), 140.

14 Surprisingly enough, the absence of King Hezekiah in chapter 20 is hardly noticed in the exegetical literature; see e. g.: Ulrich Berges, *Das Buch Jesaja: Komposition und Endgestalt*, HBS 16 (Freiburg: Herder, 1998), 146.

The second movement from Babel to Jerusalem forms a repetition of the text-immanent reader's journey back in time, but now in a short form. Temporal phrases are hardly used. Only the main moments are mentioned again. First, the starting point in time is repeated. The journey back in time restarts with the decline of Babel. Secondly, chapter 22 concerning Jerusalem forms the repetition of the time of King Hezekiah. Although Hezekiah is not mentioned anywhere in chapter 22, the names of his staff-members Shebna and Eliakim make his presence undeniable.

In Amos, the Oracles Against the Nations, including the oracles concerning Judah and Israel, are also rendered from a past perspective, but without any textual temporal development.

The past perspective of the oracles is marked by the introductory formula כֹּה אָמַר יְהוָה *thus the Lord has said* in 1:3a,6a,9a,11a,13a; 2:1a,4a,6a. The direct speech in 2:10–16, however, is not marked by an introductory formula, which suggests that the moment of the direct speech in 2:10–16 is not indicated in the text. However, because of the concluding formula נְאֻם־יְהוָה *utterance of the Lord* in verse 16b, the past perspective arises at the end of this text-passage. Due to this construction, the text-immanent reader has the impression of reading about the now-moment, which emphasises the importance of the content of the direct speech to the text-immanent reader.[15] The accusation of silencing the prophets, however, is not the now-moment, but the appeal to listen to the word of the Lord in 3:1–2 is, because the imperative שִׁמְעוּ *hear!* and the vocative בְּנֵי יִשְׂרָאֵל *oh sons of Israel* are the foreground-characteristics. Therefore, 3:1–2 form the foreground to 1:3–2:16.

Whereas the past perspective is the main temporal point of view in Isaiah and Amos, in Zephaniah the now-moment is dominant. No qatal-form is used in 2:4 but rather an X-yiqtol-form opens the Oracles Against the Nations. The nominal clauses זֹאת לָהֶם תַּחַת גְּאוֹנָם *this is to them due to their hubris* (v. 10a) and נוֹרָא יְהוָה עֲלֵיהֶם *fearful is the Lord against them* (v. 11a) in the descriptive text of 2:10–11 also suggest a textual present time. The use of the yiqtol-forms (לֹא־)יַעֲשׂוּ (שְׁאֵרִית יִשְׂרָאֵל) *(the rest of Israel) does (not)* (v. 13a), (וְלֹא־)יְדַבְּרוּ *(and) speaks (not)* (v. 13b), (וְלֹא־)יִמָּצֵא *(and) is (not) found* (v. 13c) and (הֵמָּה) יִרְעוּ *(they) feed* (v. 13d) is in line with this textual present time. From there onwards, the past is mentioned as an

---

explanation for what is happening now, e. g. in 2:10b–c, or the future is discussed, often indicated by a temporal phrase such as אָז *then* (3:9a) and בַּיּוֹם הַהוּא *on that day* (3:11a). The past perspective is only present in 3:20e אָמַר יְהוָה *the Lord has said*, to mark God's concluding direct speech in the verses 18a–20d. This means that the text-immanent reader moves through time along with the text.

4 The addressers and addressees in the pericopes

The text-immanent reader is led through the text not only by the textual structure, by the textual order of the toponyms and by the textual order of time, but also, and above all, by being involved in the communication between the addressers and addressees in the text. In all three texts, the text-immanent reader is more or less directly addressed, although this is achieved using different techniques.

In Isaiah, the text raises the question of what role Jerusalem actually plays. The role of Babel is clear, but that of Jerusalem is not. Twice, this question becomes important, in chapters 20 and 22.[16]

In chapter 20 a difficult situation is present. However, Jerusalem does not seem to realize this. Even when Isaiah acts out the danger of the threatening situation for three years, Jerusalem does not understand him. Isaiah plays the role of someone who is taken away to exile. This deals with Egypt and Cush; nevertheless, Jerusalem is involved as well. In the direct speech of the Lord, the inhabitants of הָאִי הַזֶּה *this coastland* declare the fate of everyone who trusts Assur (v. 6). Who are these inhabitants of the coastland? Jerusalem might think of Ashdod, but from an Assyrian perspective all the land west of the Jordan could be considered, therefore also including Jerusalem.

The inhabitants of the coastland use a first person plural in their direct speech. A first person plural can be used both exclusively and inclusively.[17] In the case of an inclusive use, the addressee, as well as the text-immanent reader, is also intended. It makes their question extremely exciting: וְאֵיךְ נִמָּלֵט אֲנָחְנוּ *how may we escape?* The text-immanent reader should be able to answer this question. The

---

16 See also: van Wieringen, *Isaiah 13–23* (forthcoming).
17 Theodor Lewandowski, *Linguistisches Wörterbuch*, UTB 1518 (Heidelberg: Quelle & Meyer, 1994), 790.

answer to not trust Egypt or Assur is not sufficiently correct. The answer must be: only by trusting the Lord.

In chapter 22, Jerusalem is again the textual decor. Chapter 22 does not deal with a siege of Ashdod, but with the siege of Jerusalem itself. Again, the King of Jerusalem is not mentioned in the text. Instead, internal conflicts within Jerusalem's leadership concerning Shebna and Eliakim, are discussed. This implies that the situation in Jerusalem has become even worse. The question at the end of chapter 20 receives its answer in chapter 22. How may we escape? The answer is: we will not! This answer is realized twice in chapter 22. First in verse 14, where it is stated that there will be no atonement עַד־תְּמֻתוּן *until you die.* Next in verse 25: every pin, however firmly fixed, will break off.

Questions and the answering of questions as an expression of self-criticism, present in the Jerusalem-chapters 20 and 22, is prepared by communication about questions in both the first and second movement. In the first movement, the text concerning Assur in 14:24–27, rendered as proof from the past for Babel's imminent decline, concludes with a couple of rhetorical questions in verse 27. The prophetic voice ascertains that the Lord of hosts has indeed made a decision and that his hand has indeed been extended. Two questions follow this statement: וּמִי יָפֵר *who may be able to annul?* and וּמִי יְשִׁיבֶנָּה *who may be able to turn her (= the Lord's hand) away?* The questions are not addressed to Assur or some other character in the text. This means that they are meant to be answered by the text-immanent reader. And the text-immanent reader should answer 'no', twice. However, if no one is able to change the Lord's decision to destroy and to thwart his destructive hand, then no one seems capable of doing so when it will be Jerusalem's turn instead of Assur's.

In the second movement, enquiring, by asking questions, is explicitly dealt with in 21:11–12.[18] These verses are very enigmatic. It is not quite clear how the clauses are connected. Neither the identification of the first person singular (v. 11) nor that of the second person plural (v. 12) is clear. It is clear, however, that asking questions is important. In verse 11, a question is asked of the שֹׁמֵר watchman, present as a vocative: מַה־מִלַּיְלָה *what from the night?* The question is asked twice, which emphasises the question asked. In verse 12, a direct speech of the watchman is rendered. The words אָמַר שֹׁמֵר *the watchman has said* introduce the direct speech. Because of the qatal-form אָמַר, the watchman's direct speech is chronologically first, but rendered after the question evoked through the watchman's words. If verses 12d–g אִם־תִּבְעָיוּן בְּעָיוּ *if you wish to enquire, enquire, return, come* belong to the watchman's direct speech, it is an invitation to ask the question

---

18 See also: Beuken, *Jesaja 13–27*, 232–234.

posed in verse 11. If verses 12d–g do not belong to the watchman's direct speech, it is the text-immanent author addressing the text-immanent reader, in order to prepare him for the investigation which is necessary in Jerusalem in chapter 22.

The Oracles Against the Nations in Isaiah, although dealing with various foreign nations, eventually focus on self-criticism. It is not the nations that form the real problem, but Jerusalem herself.

In Amos, the text-immanent reader is, so to say, present as the ninth nation in the list of nations in 1:3–3:2. This can be outlined as follows.

Tab. 6

1:3a–5d	utterance concerning Damascus
1:6a–8e	utterance concerning Gaza
1:9a–10b	utterance concerning Tyre
1:11a–12b	utterance concerning Edom
1:13a–15b	utterance concerning Ammon
2:1a–3c	utterance concerning Moab
2:4a–5b	utterance concerning Judah
2:6a–9e	utterance concerning Israel
2:10a–16b	addressee of the utterances concerning the nations

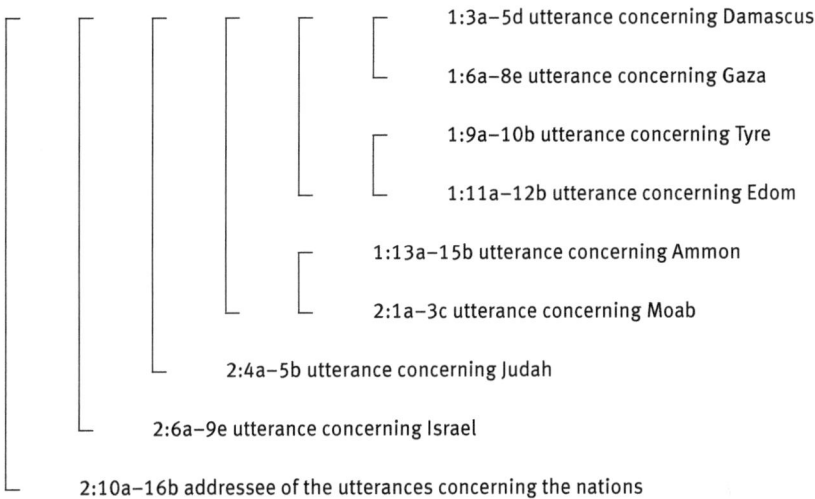

It is remarkable that the Lord does not address any of the nations. He does not speak to them, he only speaks about them. However, this situation changes in 2:10 because of the introduction of a second person plural, present in the suffix to the *nota objecti* אֶתְכֶם *you*.[19] This implies that the addressee of the Oracles Against the Nations is formulated as from 2:10. Because of the fact that the Lord's direct speech does not end before verse 16 and the second person plural remains present as from verse 10, 2:10–16 form a separate sub-unit within the Oracles Against the Nations.

---

19 Cf. also: Hellmuth Frey, *Das Buch des Ringens Gottes um seine Kirche: Der Prophet Amos*, BAT 23/1 (Stuttgart: Calwer, 1958), 62.

The big blow follows after the oracles against Damascus up to and including Moab. Surprisingly, it is not Assur (or Babel, the other great power at the time of the prophets), but Judah. To an audience in the northern Kingdom of Israel, this sounds attractive. The biggest surprise follows with the last nation mentioned: Israel, the northern Kingdom, itself. Criticism of nations is apparently nothing other than self-criticism.

This aspect is even magnified by a ninth "nation." Self-criticism is not limited to Judah or to Israel, but also concerns the text-immanent reader, even beyond the partition into a northern and southern Kingdom.

In Zephaniah, the order of the direct speeches in the first part (2:4–15) differs from that in the second part (3:1–16).

A vivid alternation of prophetic descriptive texts and direct speeches characterizes the first part. All these direct speeches are not marked clearly, due to which the text-immanent reader finds himself in a rapidly developing text. The text-immanent reader is a witness to these various direct speeches, which can be schematised as follows.

Tab. 7

	nearby West	nearby East	transitional text	distant West	distant East
first part	2:4–7	2:8–10	2:10–11	2:12	2:13–15
direct speech	embedded God → Philistines	embedded Moab → my people Ammonites → my people		God → Cushites	embedded Assur → Assur

The text-immanent reader hears God speaking to some of the foreign peoples and hears the senseless direct speeches of some of the nations.

Before the transitional text, a direct speech by God to the Philistines is given. The prophetic voice speaks to Canaan in verses 5b–d, using a second person plural in the statement דְּבַר־יְהוָה עֲלֵיכֶם *the word of the Lord is against you* and a double vocative כְּנַעַן *Canaan* and אֶרֶץ פְּלִשְׁתִּים *Land of the Philistines*. The continuation of this statement consists of a direct speech of the Lord, without any introductory formula, but recognisable by means of the first person singular in the verbal form וְהַאֲבַדְתִּיךְ *I will destroy you.*

After the transitional text, God speaks to the Cushites in verse 12. God, as the one who speaks, is recognisable due to the suffix first person singular in חַרְבִּי *my sword*. The addressee of the direct speech, present as a second person plural in the suffix to the *nota objecti* אֶתְכֶם *you*, is present by means of the vocative כּוּשִׁים *Cushites* as well.

Before the transitional text, speeches by Moab and the Ammonites are supposed by a divine direct speech. In it the Lord says that he has heard the insults and taunts of respectively Moab and the Ammonites, but the content of these speeches is not rendered. The insults and taunts, therefore, are inaccessible to the text-immanent reader, and not worth knowing. After the transitional text, a direct speech of Assur is given in verse 15. It is the only direct speech which is introduced in a normal way using the *verbum dicendi* אמר *to say*. However, Assur's communication is as senseless as the unmentioned speeches of Moab and the Ammonites. Assur is speaking to himself only; there is no addressee at all. Assur is also only speaking about himself; there is no one else. The direct speech אֲנִי וְאַפְסִי עוֹד *it is me and no one else*, therefore, is very sarcastic.[20]

In the second part, descriptive prophetic texts that alternate with direct speeches have as their focus the city of Zion. The foreign nations and peoples are no longer addressed. It is primarily the text-immanent reader who is a witness to these various alternating texts.

However, the text-immanent reader is not only a witness to the communications in the text but seems to be indirectly addressed as well. In both parts before the transitional text, a direct speech of the Lord is given but without mentioning to whom he speaks. Verses 8–9 contain a first person singular indicating the Lord. These verses, therefore, form a direct speech of the Lord. In this direct speech, the Lord discusses Moab and the Ammonites but he does not address them. There is no introduction to this direct speech, which mentions neither the addresser nor the addressee. In verse 9, however, the addresser is made explicit. The direct speech is an utterance of יְהוָה צְבָאוֹת *the Lord of hosts*, and even more, of the *God of Israel*. However, the addressee still remains unmentioned although the indication אֱלֹהֵי יִשְׂרָאֵל *the God of Israel* suggests that Israel might be the addressee. This openness gives the text-immanent reader access to the textual communication: he could understand himself as being addressed by the Lord, i. e. by the God of Israel, receiving the message of the destruction of the enemy and the salvation of Israel's remnant.

---

20 Instead of discussing the direct speech in 2:15 from the perspective of the rhetoric figure of 'sarcasm', Assur's words are generally explained from a theological perspective, i. e. that Assur is proud as it claims to be divine; e. g.: Irsigler, *Zefanja*, 310.

In a similar way, the direct speech in 3:6–13 functions towards the text-immanent reader. Whereas verse 5 mentions the Lord in third person singular, he is present as a first person singular from verse 6 onward. There is, however, no introductory formula to this direct speech indicating either the addresser or the addressee. The embedded direct speech of the Lord in verses 7b–d is introduced by אָמַרְתִּי *I said* (verse 7a). Once again, the addressee is not mentioned. The interjectional formula נְאֻם־יְהוָה *utterance of the Lord*, used in verse 8c, does not mention the addressee either. This direct speech leads to a positive message concerning Israel's remnant as well. The openness regarding the addressee gives the text-immanent reader the textual access to receive this message.

I will give just a short note on 2:12.[21] This verse is very complex because, on the one hand, a second person plural is used which is present in the personal pronoun אַתֶּם *you* and the vocative כּוּשִׁים *oh Cushites*, but on the other hand, a third person plural is used as well which is present in the personal pronoun הֵמָּה *they*. A possible interpretation of this verse is that the Lord, who speaks this direct speech, first addresses the Cushites and, next, shifts the direction and addresses someone else who is not identified in the text. Due to this anonymity, the text-immanent reader could consider himself as being addressed. If this is the case, the resumption of the oracles after the transitional text does not only focus on mentioning more nations but also on involving the text-immanent reader in these oracles against the nations.

Finally, the parallel הוֹי *woe* in 2:5 and 3:1 is also important for the text-immanent reader. The first הוֹי *woe* is related to the Philistine area; the second הוֹי *woe* is spoken regarding הָעִיר *the city*, which is portrayed as not listening to the divine voice and not trusting in the Lord. As a result, the leading elite consisting of שָׂרֶיהָ *top officials*, שֹׁפְטֶיהָ *judges*, נְבִיאֶיהָ *prophets* and כֹּהֲנֶיהָ *priests* do not act according to תּוֹרָה *the law/Torah* (verses 3–4). The name of this city is not mentioned, but it is easy to guess that the text deals with Jerusalem.

This means that the criticism of the nations is not only limited to the nations but also involves Jerusalem. It is true that the Lord acts against the nations in favour of Judah, mentioned in 2:7, and Israel, mentioned in 2:9, but Jerusalem, the capital, is not automatically something positive, i. e. a place which in God's eyes is sinless and well-functioning. In other words: the criticism of the nations could easily be applicable to God's people itself. In fact, the criticism of the nations is equal to self-criticism.

However, the Lord is different to the failing city. The elite in the city may fail but the Lord in its midst does not fail (v. 5): he stands up for it. The proper names

---

21 Cf. also: Rainer Edler, *Das Kerygma des Propheten Zefanja*, Freiburger theologische Studien (Freiburg: Herder, 1984), 240–242; Irsigler, *Zefanja*, 282–293.

צִיּוֹן *Zion* and יְרוּשָׁלַ͏ִם *Jerusalem* are absent in the criticism, but they are abundantly used in the future perspective of salvation.

The text-immanent reader, therefore, is not only involved in the criticism of the nations and the negative consequences for them, but he is also involved in the criticism of God's people. Negative consequences for God's people might be an option. The fact that these possible negative consequences are not realized is not due to any effort on the part of the elite but only due to God.

5 Concluding remarks

I would like to conclude my paper with a couple of summarizing remarks. Based upon my analysis above, I believe we can say that "Oracles Against the Nations" is a genre in the prophetic literature in the Bible.[22]

However, I also believe that the name "Oracles Against the Nations" is actually a slightly misleading term for this genre. The "nations" are very different in the various texts; too different to say that there are fixed nations belonging to this genre. The exception is Jerusalem/Zion, which is in fact a coherent part of these texts.[23] Jerusalem/Zion functions not only as a contrast to the nations, but the nations also function as a stepping stone to formulate the self-criticism concerning Jerusalem/Zion.[24]

This self-criticism is broadened by addressing the text-immanent reader more or less directly. The text-immanent reader's position is not a "safety zone," free of criticism concerning the nations and concerning Jerusalem/Zion. It is exactly this position of the text-immanent reader that Isaiah, Amos and Zephaniah have in common. In this way, Isaiah and the Twelve can be considered as being connected by using this "text-immanent reader-focussed" genre of "Oracles of Self-criticism Using the Nations and Jerusalem/Zion."[25]

---

22 Cf.: Pancratius C. Beentjes, "Oracles Against the Nations: A Central Issue in the "Latter Prophets"," *Bijdr* 50 (1989): 203–209. Cf. also: Christopher R. Seitz, *Isaiah 1–39*, Interpretation (Louisville, KY: John Knox, 1993), 117. See already: John H. Hays, "The Usage of Oracles Against the Foreign Nations in Ancient Israel," *JBL* 87 (1968): 81–92.
23 See also the criticism on the idea of a 'Book of the Twelve' by Hadjiev, "Zephaniah," 334–335.
24 Cf. also the biblical non-appropriation theology, e.g.: Archibald L. H. M. van Wieringen, "Psalm 65 as Non-Appropriation Theology," *Bib* 95 (2014): 179–197.
25 I am greatly indebted to Dr. Maurits J. Sinninghe Damsté (De Gordyk, Fryslân, the Netherlands/Breña Baja, San Miguel de la Palma, Spain) for his correction of the English text of this article.

Bibliography

Beentjes, Pancratius C., "Oracles Against the Nations: A Central Issue in the Latter Prophets", *Bijdr* 50 (1989), 203–209.
Berges, Ulrich, *Das Buch Jesaja: Komposition und Endgestalt*, HBS 16 (Freiburg: Herder, 1998).
Berges, Ulrich/Beuken, Willem A. M., *Das Buch Jesaja: Eine Einführung*, UTB 4647 (Göttingen: Vandenhoeck & Ruprecht, 2016).
Beuken, Willem A. M., *Jesaja 13–27*, HThKAT (Freiburg: Herder, 2007).
Cheyne, T.K, *The Prophecies of Isaiah* (London: Kegan Paul, 1886).
Edler, Rainer, *Das Kerygma des Propheten Zefanja*, Freiburger theologische Studien (Freiburg: Herder, 1984).
Frey, Hellmuth, *Das Buch des Ringens Gottes um seine Kirche: Der Prophet Amos*, BAT 23/1 (Stuttgart: Calwer, 1958).
Hadjiev, Tchavdar S., "Zephaniah and the 'Book of the Twelve' Hypothesis," in *Prophecy and the Prophets in Ancient Israel: Proceedings of the Oxford Old Testament Seminar*, ed. John Day, LHB/OTS 531 (London: T&T Clark, 2010), 323–338.
Hays, John H., "The Usage of Oracles Against the Foreign Nations in Ancient Israel," *JBL* 87 (1968), 81–92.
House, Paul R., *Zephaniah: A Prophetic Drama*, JSOT.S 69 (Sheffield: Almond, 1989).
Irsigler, Hubert, *Zefanja*, HThKAT (Freiburg: Herder, 2002).
Lessing, R. Reed, *Amos*, Concordia Commentary (St. Louis MO: Concordia, 2009).
Lewandowski, Theodor, *Linguistisches Wörterbuch*, UTB 1518 (Heidelberg: Quelle & Meyer, 1994).
Ryou, Daniel H., *Zephaniah's Oracles against the Nations* (Amsterdam: VU University Press, 1994).
Seitz, Christopher R., *Isaiah 1–39*, Interpretation (Louisville, KY: John Knox, 1993).
Sweeney, Marvin A., *Isaiah 1–39*, FOTL 16 (Grand Rapids, MI: Eerdmans, 1996).
Tull, Patricia K., *Isaiah 1–39*, Smyth & Helwys Bible Commentary (Macon GA: Smyth & Helwys Publishing, 2010).
van Wieringen, Archibald L. H. M., "Assur and Babel against Jerusalem: The Reader-Oriented Position of Babel and Assur within the Framework of Isaiah 1–39," in *'Enlarge the Site of Your Tent': The City as Unifying Theme in Isaiah: The Isaiah Workshop: De Jesaja Werkplaats*, ed. Archibald L. H. M. van Wieringen and Annemarieke van der Woude, OTS 58 (Leiden: Brill, 2011), 49–62.
van Wieringen, Archibald L. H. M., "Isaiah 13–23 and Its Text-Immanent Reader," in *Prophecy and Foreign Nations*, ed. Uwe Becker, Hannes Bezzel and Matthijs de Jong, FAT (Tübingen: Mohr Siebeck, 2019).
van Wieringen, Archibald L. H. M., "Psalm 65 as Non-Appropriation Theology," *Bib* 95 (2014), 179–197.
van Wieringen, Archibald L. H. M., "The Prophecies Against the Nations in Amos 1:2–3:15," *EstBib* 71 (2013), 7–19.
van Wieringen, Archibald L. H. M., "*The Reader-Oriented Unity of the Book Isaiah*," ACEBT.S 6 (Vught: Skandalon, 2006).
van Wieringen, Archibald L. H. M., "The Triple-Layered Communication in the Book of Amos and Its Message of Non-Appropriation Theology," in "*Multiple Teachers in Biblical Texts*," ed. Bart J. Koet and Archibald L. H. M. van Wieringen, CBET 88, 89–106.

Hugh G. M. Williamson

The Day of the Lord in the Book of Isaiah and the Book of the Twelve

The day of the Lord is mentioned in five verses in the book of Isaiah, namely in 2:12; 13:6 and 9; 22:5; and 34:8. Possibly related passages in the second half of the book may, perhaps, be left out of account for the time being: the wording in 61:3 of "the day of vengeance of our God" is hardly a "day of the Lord" reference as usually understood, though it was picked up and moved in that direction by 34:8, which I will consider later. As originally written, it serves as a parallel with "the year of the Lord's favour" in the first half of the line. There is a similar parallelism, albeit in reverse order, at 63:4. (58:5, of course, is not relevant at all, as the context there demonstrates.) Thus all the references to which we need pay attention here come in the first part of the book. They do not, however, all share the same date, and their use of the concept differs from one passage to another. Our first task, therefore, is to draw some careful distinctions between them.

It is simplest to start at the beginning. While Isa 2:9–22 was doubtless subject to some later expansion, especially towards the end of the chapter, there is widespread agreement that the basis of this poem reaches back to the prophet of the eighth century BCE. It introduces the day of the Lord in a slightly oblique manner, namely in the clause ... כי יום ליהוה צבאות על, "for the Lord of hosts has a day against ..." rather than the commoner use of the construct phrase יום יהוה, but there can be little doubt that the reference encompasses the same concept.

Despite those who have occasionally suggested that the term was first coined by Amos,[1] the way in which that prophet refers to it (cf. Amos 5:18) indicates that he is more probably interacting with something which he shares in common with his readers. Furthermore, his rhetoric indicates that he is reversing what it led them to expect; and since in his case it means darkness for his readers rather than light, we may deduce with reasonable confidence that in popular usage the day was thought to be one of light for Israel or Judah and darkness, therefore, for those who might oppress them.

Scholarly attention has focused primarily on the background and setting of this expression,[2] which is far from the most illuminating approach when it

---

1 E. g. Meir Weiss, "The Origin of the 'Day of the Lord' — Reconsidered," *HUCA* 37 (1966): 29–60.
2 For surveys of research, see Magne Saebø, *ThWAT* 3 (1982), 582–86; Richard H. Hiers and Kevin J. Cathcart, *ABD* 2 (1992): 82–85; and especially Hans Barstad, *The Religious Polemics of Amos: Studies in the Preaching of Am 2, 7B–8; 4, 1–13; 5, 1–27; 6, 4–7; 8, 14*, VTSup 34 (Leiden: Brill, 1984), 89–110.

https://doi.org/10.1515/9783110705799-012

comes to exegesis. Though he was not the first to do so, Mowinckel proposed in a manner which attracted considerable support that the phrase originated in the (hypothetical) annual cultic festival of the Lord's enthronement. From a present celebration of God's victory, this came over the course of time to be projected into the future; and, not least because of the use of the idea by the prophets, it was also detached from its cultic origins to become a more general eschatological expectation.[3]

In contrast, von Rad took note of the frequent association of the phrase with military language to argue that the day of the Lord was associated originally with the whole complex of material which he and others labelled the "holy war." It was the day on which God would march forth to conquer his (and hence Israel's) enemies. In origin, therefore, the concept went back to Israel's earliest days.[4] Although there had been some earlier adumbrations of this suggestion, and although it has attracted some significant criticism since, it is von Rad's view which has probably gained the widest following.[5]

Beside these two major views, note may also be taken of Weiss's observations that the day is most closely associated with biblical descriptions of a theophany,[6] of a small group of scholars who have attempted to relate the concept primarily with the covenant traditions, and in particular the execution of the treaty curses,[7] and of Barstad, who finds its setting in the public laments, thus positing a situation which combines a cultic milieu and a context of war.[8]

---

3 Cf. Sigmund Mowinckel, *Psalmenstudien* II (Kristiania: Dybwad, 1922); Sigmund Mowinckel, "Jahves dag," *NTT* 59 (1958): 1–56, 209–29; *He That Cometh*, trans. George W. Anderson (Oxford: Blackwell, 1956), esp. 126–33, 143–49.

4 Cf. Gerhard von Rad, "The Origin of the Concept of the Day of Yahweh," *JSS* 4 (1959): 97–108. For a survey of research on "holy war" both before and since von Rad's work, see Karl William Weyde, "Holy War, Divine War, YHWH War—and Ethics: On a Central Issue in Recent Research on the Hebrew Bible," in *Encountering Violence in the Bible*, ed. Markus Zehnder and Hallvard Hegelia (Sheffield: Sheffield Phoenix, 2013): 235–52.

5 For details, see Barstad, *Religious Polemics*, 91–93; Bob Becking, "Expectations about the End of Time in the Hebrew Bible: Do they Exist?" in *Apocalyptic in History and Tradition*, ed. Christopher Rowland and John Barton, JSPSup 43 (London: Sheffield Academic, 2002): 44–59.

6 Weiss, "Origin"; cf. Jörg Jeremias, *Theophanie: die Geschichte einer alttestamentlichen Gattung*, WMANT 10 (2d ed.; Neukirchen-Vluyn: Neukirchener Verlag, 1977), 97–100; Moshe Weinfeld, "The Day of the Lord: Aspirations for the Kingdom of God in the Bible and Jewish Liturgy," in *Studies in Bible*, ed. Sara Japhet, ScrH 31 (Jerusalem: Magnes, 1986): 341–72 (358–66).

7 Cf. F. J. Hélewa, "L'origine du concept prophétique du 'Jour de Yahvé'," *Ephemerides Carmeliticae* 15 (1964): 3–36; Cornelis van Leeuwen, "The Prophecy of the *YÔM YHWH* in Amos v 18–20," *OTS* 19 (1974): 113–34.

8 Barstad, *Religious Polemics*, 103–8. Barstad earlier criticized Mowinckel both because his theory of an annual enthronement festival remains hypothetical and because there is no textual

In my opinion, these disagreements stem from the problem of seeking to move from a single expression to a rigid and exclusive form-critical categorization. As others have observed,[9] there are elements of truth in several of these theories, and it seems inherently unlikely that so natural an expression should be limited to just one. Even if it was first coined in one setting rather than another, the evidence for knowing which is beyond our recall. By the time to which our extant sources bear witness, it is likely that the various matters discussed had become intermingled, at least in most people's thinking, and it is at this, rather than some narrowly technical, level that the prophets engage. The outward demonstration of the Lord's sovereignty or kingship would inevitably be accompanied by judgment on his enemies and by implication with victory for Israel, and this could only be described in the language of war. His advent in power to effect this was bound to be described in material drawn from the theophanic tradition, and we need not doubt that it was (as the Psalms suggest) prayed for and proleptically celebrated in public ceremonies at the sanctuary.

So far as Isaiah 2 is concerned, therefore, we may draw two conclusions. First, his use of the expression is probably working closely with its original sense in common parlance. Indeed, the distinctive designation here of God as "the Lord of Hosts" suggests that the warlike background we have noted is primary. He is Israel's champion who fights for and with his people. Second, however, he has turned the concept in an unusual but again distinctive direction. This day is not going to be against the enemies of Israel but rather "against all that is proud and high, and against all that is lifted up and lofty,"[10] a general designation which is then illustrated by a string of examples in the following few verses. This description is

---

evidence to support his understanding of the reference of "day" developing from a cultic feast to an eschatological idea where God destroys his enemies in battle (pp. 98–102). Similarly, he cites the influential article of Manfred Weippert, "'Heiliger Krieg' in Israel und Assyrien," *ZAW* 84 (1972): 460–93, in opposition to von Rad's view: all war in the ancient world was effectively "holy war," inasmuch as the gods were involved, and the manner in which the biblical texts describe this is by no means peculiar to Israel. In fact, it is now generally recognized that it is a mistake to talk of "holy war" as a formal institution; the material cited by von Rad relates rather to a literary convention for the description of warfare in which the protagonists believe that their God is fighting on their side.

9 See especially Frank M. Cross, *Canaanite Myth and Hebrew Epic: Essays in the History of the Religion of Israel* (Cambridge MA: Harvard University Press, 1973), 91–111; Weinfeld, "The Day of the Lord." This approach should not be confused, however, with that of Everson, who implausibly claims that the prophets referred to "a sequence of historical days of Yahweh"; cf. A. Joseph Everson, "The Days of Yahweh," *JBL* 93 (1974): 329–37.

10 For a full justification for the emendation of ושפל to וגבה and a suggestion to explain how the error may have arisen, see my commentary, *A Critical and Exegetical Commentary on Isaiah 1–27, 1: Isaiah 1–5*, ICC (London: T & T Clark, 2006), 198.

typical of Isaiah the prophet. Having started out with a vision of God whose throne is "high and lifted up" (6:1), he takes it as axiomatic that any person, natural phenomenon, or institution that arrogates such terminology to itself is automatically condemned because of its hubris. Nobody may usurp God's uniquely exalted status. This second conclusion is of importance, because it shows how a prophet can creatively take an expression in common usage and turn it to give expression to one of his own most fundamental theological convictions.

There need be little doubt that 22:5 should be closely associated with the usage in 2:12. The form of expression, which we saw already is unusual, is closely copied: כי יום ... לאדני יהוה צבאות. The addition of אדני, resulting in a divine designation that is identical with that found just a few verses later in 22:12, as well, more significantly, of three nouns to describe the day—מהומה ומבוסה ומבוכה, "panic and trampling and confusion"—makes it probable that this is an amplification of the same expression. The continuation in the immediately following words—בגיא חזיון, "in the valley of vision"—is similarly copied from the opening words of the passage in 22:1. Together with evidence drawn from the difficult v. 6, with its references to Elam and Kir, and with the mention of chariots and horsemen possibly drawn from v. 7 following, there is thus much to be said for the view that these two verses were added later to an Isaianic oracle in order to reapply them to the Babylonian destruction of Jerusalem in 587 BCE.[11] Though closely related to 2:12, therefore, the present verse shows that the day of the Lord could stay alive as a literary figure. Its precise application is not certain, but it may be that it reverts to its original sense of God's day being turned against Jerusalem's enemies.

More significant in terms of development are the two references in ch. 13. Here the day of the Lord is introduced twice (vv. 6 and 9), each at the start of a section of the poem. The poem as a whole has been repeatedly studied, arguably most helpfully and fully by Zapff. With some trepidation in the context of the present volume, therefore, I need to confess that I have elsewhere sought to take one of his major insights, with which I agree, and to develop it slightly in ways of direct relevance for our present concern.[12] I have time here for only a brief summary.

---

11 Jacques Vermeylen, *Du prophète Isaïe à l'apocalyptique: Isaïe, I–XXXV, miroir d'un demi-millénaire d'expérience religieuse en Israël*, vol. 1, EB (Paris: Gabalda, 1977), 337–38; Ronald E. Clements, *Isaiah 1–39*, NCBC (Grand Rapids: Eerdmans, and London: Marshall, Morgan & Scott, 1980), 182. Joseph Blenkinsopp, *Isaiah 1–39: A New Translation with Introduction and Commentary*, AB 19 (New York: Doubleday, 2000), 333, isolates just v. 5 as an "apocalyptic addendum." The strong use of assonance is certainly a factor in Blenkinsopp's favour; see, for instance, 24:16–17.
12 Hugh G. M. Williamson, "Decoding Isaiah 13," in *The History of Isaiah: The Making of the Book and its Presentation of the Past*, ed. Todd Hibbard and Jacob Stromberg, FAT (Tübingen: Mohr Siebeck, forthcoming).

In the present form of the text, the application of the poem comes in its concluding section, where God announces that he is raising up the Medes to destroy
Babylon. The implications for Judeans living in exile in Babylon towards the end
of the Neo-Babylonian period, when I date this material, are obvious.

The previous part of the chapter, vv. 2–16, offers a poetic description of the
day of the Lord on what at first sight looks like a much wider scale; indeed, some
parts may even be labeled cosmic. It is often treated as a literary unity, though
some have tried to find earlier and later material included within it.

Scholars have taken two approaches in relation to composition history. The
majority has argued that vv. 2–16 are chronologically prior and that this poem of
universal scope was then applied by the final author specifically to Babylon by
the addition of vv. 17–22.

The alternative approach sees things completely the other way round. While
it had sometimes been adumbrated previously,[13] it has become more popular following its fullest exposition by Zapff.[14] On this view, an original anti-Babylon
oracle in vv. 17–22 was later given a universal application by the addition of vv.
2–16. Given that elsewhere too there are examples of a "day of the Lord" passage
being developed in a universalizing direction (e. g. the use of the day of the Lord
in Joel 1–2 followed by 3–4), there seems to be an inherent attraction about this
alternative approach.

In taking up this approach, however, I have noted first that the inclusion of
עליהם in v. 17 suggests that something may have stood in front of it. More radically,
however, I have tried to demonstrate that two layers may be detected in vv. 2–16
and that they differ considerably in emphasis. For instance, vv. 2–3 and 4–5 seem
to sit uneasily alongside one another. In the former, God addresses a plural audience and speaks in the first person singular (v. 3). In vv. 4–5, by contrast, God is
referred to in the third person and the standpoint shifts to those whom the army is
approaching. It is therefore possible that we have two introductions to the oracle

---

13 See very briefly Karl Marti, *Das Buch Jesaja*, KHAT 19 (Tübingen: Mohr [Paul Siebeck], 1900),
128; Otto Eissfeldt, *Einleitung in das Alte Testament* (3d ed.; Tübingen: Mohr [Paul Siebeck], 1964),
429–30; Rudolf Kilian, *Jesaja II: 13–39*, Die Neue Echter Bibel 32 (Würzburg: Echter, 1994), 100–1;
John Barton, *Isaiah 1–39*, OTG (Sheffield: Sheffield Academic, 1995), 85.
14 Burkard M. Zapff, *Schriftgelehrte Prophetie—Jes 13 und die Komposition des Jesajabuches: ein
Beitrag zur Erforschung der Redaktionsgeschichte des Jesajabuches*, FB 74 (Würzburg: Echter,
1995), 220–39. See subsequently, for instance, Erich Bosshard-Nepustil, *Rezeptionen von Jesaia
1–39 im Zwölfprophetenbuch: Untersuchungen zur literarischen Verbindung von Prophetenbüchern
in babylonischer und persischer Zeit*, OBO 154 (Freiburg: Universitätsverlag, and Göttingen: Vandenhoeck & Ruprecht, 1997), 68–72; Ulrich Berges, *Das Buch Jesaja: Komposition und Endgestalt*,
Herders Biblische Studien 16 (Freiburg: Herder, 1998), 155–56; Konrad Schmid, *Jesaja*, vol. 1:
Jesaja 1–23, ZBK 19.1 (Zürich: Theologischer Verlag Zürich, 2011), 131.

about the mustering of the army. Second, as Bosshard-Nepustil has noted,[15] there is a sharp difference between vv. 9–13 and 14–16 in terms of the effects of the day of the Lord: the former is cosmic, the latter terrestrial; the former is selective in that it regards the day as punishment for the wicked and the proud (who v. 12 admittedly implies are the vast majority)[16] whereas the latter is all-embracing in terms of application and furthermore speaks only of their flight in terror, without any reference to judgment or punishment;[17] the former is marked off by a strong

---

15 Bosshard-Nepustil, *Rezeptionen von Jesaia 1–39*, 70–71, followed by Anja Klein, "Babylon Revisited: A New Look at Isa 13 and Its Literary Horizon," in *Imperial Visions: The Prophet and the Book of Isaiah in an Age of Empires*, ed. Reinhard G. Kratz and Joachim Schaper, FRLANT (Göttingen: Vandenhoeck & Ruprecht, forthcoming). It should be noted that Bosshard-Nepustil's own final analysis effects something of a median position between the two that I have summarized above: he thinks the earliest layer in the chapter comprised vv. 2–8 + 14–16, that vv. 1 and 17–22 were then added to it, and finally that vv. 9–13 were added subsequently. One of the reasons he drives a wedge between 17–22 and the immediately preceding verses is that he perceives a repetition of v. 16 in v. 18. This seems to me mistaken. Two of the words he lists are in the first clause, which on text-critical grounds that cannot be set out fully here was almost certainly not part of the text at all; anyway one of the two words (נעריﬡ) does not appear in v. 16, and it does not strengthen the case that he sets עלל alongside it. He also lists פרי בטן and בנים, but these both appear in v. 18 alone and so cannot count as evidence at all. Thus עין is the only word that the two verses share—hardly enough on which to build an argument.
16 The parallelism in v. 9b, however, shows that this is not incompatible with a universalistic understanding of "the earth" in this section, *contra* Charis Fischer, *Die Fremdvölkersprüche bei Amos und Jesaja: Studien zur Eigenart und Intention in Am 1,3–2,3.4f und Jes 13,1–16,14*, BBB 136 (Berlin: Philo, 2002), 73. This is the starting point for her analysis (pp. 69–99) which leads her to propose that there are three layers in this chapter, namely (in chronological order) (i) vv. 2–5, 7–8, 14–16 ("Das Gericht über die Völker"), (ii) vv. 1a, 17, 18b–22 ("Das Gericht über Babel," so giving historical application to the previously rather unspecific first layer), and (iii) vv. 6, 9–13 ("Der Tag Jahwes"). While there are some obvious points of comparison with alternative proposals (including my own), she seems to ignore the probability that we have parallel and hence separate introductions to the theme of the day of the Lord in vv. 6 and 9 as well as the difficulties explored above about treating vv. 2–5 as an original unity. Her argument that layers (i) and (iii) are distinguished by the fact that in the former God acts through his agents whereas in the latter he acts directly himself looks initially stronger, but in fact it is hardly true of 6–8. The nearest those verses come to supporting Fischer's case are the words "it will come like destruction from the Almighty" in v. 6b, but there we find only a simile descriptive of the day of the Lord (and one whose expression is clearly driven by the demands of word-play), not an actual description of God as actant, so that it remains unclear whether Fischer's distinction can fully support her proposed literary division at this point.
17 This tension was noted already by Bernard Gosse, *Isaïe 13,1–14,23 dans la tradition littéraire du livre d'Isaïe et dans la tradition des oracles contre les nations*, OBO 78 (Freiburg: Universitätsverlag, and Göttingen: Vandenhoeck & Ruprecht, 1988), 153, and by Peter Höffken, *Das Buch Jesaja: Kapitel 1–39*, Neuer Stuttgarter Kommentar—Altes Testament 18/1 (Stuttgart: Verlag Katholisches Bibelwerk, 1993), 130–31, albeit without any literary-critical consequences being drawn.

inclusio:[18] 9a and 13b both describe the day of the Lord (joined in construct in 9a, distributed over the two halves of the line in 13b) as characterized by עברה and חרון אף; the latter follows on very smoothly from v. 8: note especially the use of the איש אל idiom in both verses (repeated, in fact, in 14b), and so on. Finally, as already mentioned, there are two passages relating to the day of the Lord, each using relatively standard introductory phraseology at the start in vv. 6 and 9.[19]

Without going into further detail here, therefore, I have proposed that the reference to the Medes and to Babylon in vv. 17–22 belonged from the start with a good deal of what precedes it, namely vv. 2–3, 6–8 and 14–16. This whole block of material is related in wording quite closely with the diction of chs. 40–55 and some other parts of Isaiah and very strikingly is devoid of the kind of universalist outlook which has been the starting point for most scholars in making a separation between vv. 2–16 and 17–22. The much shorter passages which I regard as having been added later, namely vv. 4–5 and 9–13, lack the links with chs. 40–55 and elsewhere already mentioned but have instead a close association with chs. 24–27 (and 24 in particular). I cite as major examples the shared use of such major themes as the wholesale destruction of the earth for its wickedness by divine agents and the decimation of its population (13:12; 24:6[20]). On the other hand we

---

18 This was recognized already, and indeed strengthened, by the LXX; see Mirjam van der Vorm-Croughs, "LXX Isaiah and the Use of Rhetorical Figures," in *The Old Greek of Isaiah: Issues and Perspectives,* ed. Arie van der Kooij and Michaël van der Meer, CBET 55 (Leuven: Peeters, 2010): 173–88 (177–79).

19 There have been attempts to counter the possible implications of this duplication on the ground of common elements between the two sections so introduced, but the arguments are not convincing; see Jörg Jeremias, "Der 'Tag Jahwes' in Jes 13 und Joel 2," in *Schriftauslegung in der Schrift: Festschrift für Odil Hannes Steck zu seinem 65. Geburtstag,* ed. Reinhard G. Kratz, Thomas Krüger, and Konrad Schmid, BZAW 300 (Berlin: de Gruyter, 2000): 129–38 (133–34), closely followed by Judith Gärtner, "Die Völker und der Tag-JHWHs im Horizont des Jesaja- und des Zwölfprophetenbuches," in *The Books of the Twelve Prophets: Minor Prophets, Major Theologies,* ed. Heinz-Josef Fabry, BETL 295 (Leuven: Peeters, 2018): 131–56. Jeremias refers, for instance, to the use of פקד in vv. 4 and 11 without any mention of the fact that the word is used in completely different senses in the two verses; ארץ appears twice in v. 5 and also in 9 and 11, but this word is far too common to base anything on it; besides, all the occurrences come in what I regard as the later layer in any case, and it is noteworthy that the occurrence in v. 11 is distinctive by being parallel with חבל; אף in v. 3 should be distinguished from its occurrences in vv. 9 and 13 because in the latter it is part of the fixed expression חרון אף; and so on. The fact that one can read v. 9 as a development over v. 6 (e. g. בא > יבוא) does not determine whether they are part of the same original composition or whether a later author has built upon a former.

20 Note the use of the relatively uncommon word אנוש in each verse, though this is also found in 13:7, which belongs to the earlier version in my analysis.

should also note such specific points of contact as תבל as a qualifier for ארץ in 13:11 and 24:4, 26:9,18, and 27:6; the shaking (רעש) of the world by violent earthquake in 13:13 and 24:18; the genuinely cosmic scope of the description, with reference to the sun and moon, in 13:10,13 and 24:21–23;[21] the application to the whole of humanity of the vocabulary for wickedness, sin and guilt in 13:9,11 and 24:5–6 and 26:10; the description of divine action as "punishment" (פקד על) in 13:11 and 24:21; the use of עריץ in 13:11 and three times in 25:3–5;[22] and the use of שׁמּה to describe the resultant desolation (13:9; 24:12). While of course one or other of these elements may be put down to coincidence, their accumulation is impressive, and we should note in addition that this list of parallels covers the announcement, course, and consequences of the day of the Lord. I therefore propose that this material will have been added so as to introduce the collection of oracles against the nations in a way that closely parallels the larger universal application of them in the so-called Isaiah Apocalypse. Chronologically, it gives us a date for the continuation of the "day of the Lord" ideology until the latest major layer in the book of Isaiah as a whole.

This leaves only the reference in ch. 34 to consider, and that need not detain us long. As Vermeylen, among others, has well observed, ch. 34 has parallels throughout its full extent with ch. 13.[23] Given that the list of animals at the end gives particularly strong evidence that ch. 34 is based on and so later than ch. 13, we may conclude that its reference in v. 8 to the day of the Lord was also triggered from the same. The way it is formulated, however, is closer to 2:12 and 22:5: כי יום נקם ליהוה, so that we may assume the author was writing in conscious continuity with the wider book. In my opinion, the shift in focus from Babylon to Edom, echoed also in the reprise of this theme in ch. 63, suggests an introduction and conclusion to the main Babylonian section of the book as a whole by reference to a later archetypical enemy of the people of God as a hermeneutical key not to

---

21 The force of this particular feature will be strengthened by the observation of John J. Collins that descriptions of cosmic destruction are extremely rare elsewhere (though he does not apply this in our particular case because of his different, and I believe mistaken, narrowing of the application in 13:10–13); see "The Beginning of the End of the World in the Hebrew Bible," in *Thus Says the Lord: Essays on the Former and Latter Prophets in Honor of Robert R. Wilson*, ed. John J. Ahn and Stephen L. Cook, LHBOTS 512 (London: T & T Clark, 2009): 137–55.

22 Cf. David S. Vanderhooft, *The Neo-Babylonian Empire and Babylon in the Latter Prophets*, HSM 59 (Atlanta: Scholars, 1999), 125.

23 Vermeylen, *Du prophète Isaïe à l'apocalyptique*, 440–41. For a broader and more reflective analysis, see Claire R. Matthews, *Defending Zion: Edom's Desolation and Jacob's Restoration (Isaiah 34–35) in Context*, BZAW 236 (Berlin: de Gruyter, 1995), esp. ch. 4.

interpret Babylon as the historical nation alone but to invite a reading of it as paradigmatic of deliverance from all forms of oppression.[24]

I conclude this quick survey of the day of the Lord in Isaiah by noting that it is used in three main ways and that we can readily understand how they developed over time. First was the sense of God's attack on pride and hubris by way of reversal of the early popular notion that God would fight for his people against their enemies. Second, near the end of the exilic period, it was turned in a way which was not historically fulfilled at the time to predict the overwhelming defeat and destruction of Babylon. And third, in the much later post-exilic period, an interpretation was invited which elevated the whole image on to a universal and even cosmic scale, so encouraging a hermeneutic which enabled readers to take the Babylonian references not only in chs. 13–14 but also in 40–48 as paradigmatic of God's deliverance from any form of unjustified oppression.[25] The author of ch. 34 and the opening part of 63 moved in a similar direction by his references to the archetypical enemy of Israel, namely Edom, while the editor responsible for the equally late 22:5 seems likewise to be influenced by the form of wording in ch. 2 and to allow that the day can be turned against Israel's enemies. There are thus at least three distinctive ways in which the expression is used in Isaiah. Chronologically, they develop in a fully intelligible manner over time and were certainly not all known in the eighth century. The older ideas held on as well, however, so that this is not a development in the concept in a narrow sense so much as a widening of the ways in which it could be applied.

The question to which I now turn, therefore, is to explore the extent to which this pattern can also be mapped on the uses of the expression in the Book of the Twelve.[26] As Beck has noted in his major study of this subject, of the 16 occur-

---

24 See my *The Book Called Isaiah: Deutero-Isaiah's Role in Composition and Redaction* (Oxford: Clarendon, 1994), 217.

25 In an important study, John Barton, "The Day of Yahweh in the Minor Prophets," in *Biblical and Near Eastern Essays: Studies in Honour of Kevin J. Cathcart*, ed. Carmel McCarthy and John F. Healey, JSOTSup 375 (London: T & T Clark International, 2004), 68–79, argues that this is fundamentally what Amos's audience presupposed. In my opinion there remains a distinction of degree. I agree that Amos's saying implies the presupposition that Yahweh's power and authority extended beyond Israel in a way that may be broadly dubbed universalist. But within a broad common framework that does not mean that no development in the concept can be detected. The scale of God's intervention in the final layer of Isaiah 13 surely exceeds by far anything that Amos's audience or first readers would have imagined.

26 I am aware, of course, that there are also links of some of the relevant material in Isaiah 13 with Jeremiah (e.g. v. 14b and Jer 50:16b, and vv. 19–22 and Jer 50:39–40). They have to be excluded from the present specifically defined subject, however, but should be analysed in my forthcoming commentary on Isaiah 13–27. I am also aware that there may well be references to

rences of יום יהוה without any modification or variation in the Hebrew Bible, thirteen come in the Twelve.[27]

It is unnecessary to delay any longer over Amos 5:18–20. While any form of direct literary influence on the part of Isaiah 2 is unlikely,[28] there seems to be little doubt that, as noted above, conceptually the two passages presuppose a shared understanding of the day of the Lord, the then standard and popular application of which they have reversed as part of their rhetorical polemic. This gives us a secure starting point for our comparison.

Moving to Zephaniah,[29] the announcement of the day of the Lord in both 1:7 and 14 uses more or less stereotypical phraseology: כי קרוב יום יהוה; see Isa 13:6; Ezek 30:3 (7:7 is comparable); Joel 1:15; 2:1; 4:14; Obad 15. Questions of literary dependence are therefore inappropriate.[30] Conceptually it has some close parallels with Amos, not least that the day will be one of "darkness and gloom"

---

the day of the Lord which do not use our precise expression; see James D. Nogalski, "The Day(s) of YHWH in the Book of the Twelve," in *Thematic Threads in the Book of the Twelve*, ed. Paul L. Redditt and Aaron Schart, BZAW 325 (Berlin: de Gruyter, 2003): 192–213 (with references also to earlier literature). As I can make my case on the basis of the explicit references alone, however, I limit myself to them here for reasons of space and clarity.

27 Martin Beck, *Der "Tag YHWHs" im Dodekapropheton: Studien im Spannungsfeld von Traditions- und Redaktionsgeschichte*, BZAW 356 (Berlin: de Gruyter, 2005), 24, 43. For other studies of this topic, see Rolf Rendtorff, "How to Read the Book of the Twelve as a Theological Unity," in *Reading and Hearing the Book of the Twelve*, ed. James D. Nogalski and Marvin A. Sweeney, SBLSS 15 (Atlanta: Scholars Press, 2000): 75–87; Rolf Rendtorff., "Alas for the Day! The 'Day of the Lord' in the Book of the Twelve," in *God in the Fray: A Tribute to Walter Brueggemann*, ed. Tod Linafelt and Timothy K. Beal (Minneapolis: Fortress, 1998): 186–97; Barton, "The Day of Yahweh" (effectively, Joel and Amos only); Paul-Gerhard Schwesig, *Die Rolle der Tag-JHWHs-Dichtungen im Dodekapropheton*, BZAW 366 (Berlin; de Gruyter, 2006). It goes without saying that Beck and Schwesig include many more bibliographical data on the relevant passages than I am able to include here.

28 See Reinhard Fey, *Amos und Jesaja: Abhängigkeit und Eigenständigkeit des Jesaja*, WMANT 12 (Neukirchen-Vluyn: Neukirchener Verlag, 1963), 77–83; the possibility is not even considered in Jan Kreuch, *Das Amos- und Jesajabuch: eine exegetische Studie zur Neubestimmung ihres Verhältnisses*, BThS 149 (Neukirchen-Vluyn: Neukirchener Verlag, 2014).

29 For other connections between Zephaniah and Isaiah with a conscious aim to go "beyond the 'Day of Yahweh' and other tripartite markers in the book of Zephaniah," see John Ahn, "Zephaniah, a Disciple of Isaiah?" in *Thus Says the Lord: Essays on the Former and Latter Prophets in Honor of Robert R. Wilson*, ed. John J. Ahn and Stephen L. Cook, LHB/OTS 502 (New York: T & T Clark, 2009): 292–307.

30 Nonetheless Hubert Irsigler, *Gottesgericht und Jahwetag: die Komposition Zef 1,1–2,3, untersucht auf der Grundlage der Literarkritik des Zefanjabuches*, ATSAT 3 (St. Ottilien: EOS Verlag, 1977), 319–22, with earlier literature, observes that the use in Zephaniah is the earliest dateable occurrence.

(1:15), both words occurring in Amos 5:20, though not paired as they are here. The fact that the day is here turned against Judah is also closely comparable with Amos's innovative use of the concept. In addition, just as in Amos the expression is followed immediately by a harshly critical rejection of Israel's cultic worship, including sacrifices, so here Zephaniah twists a possible expectation that the day will be celebrated in the cult by sinisterly labeling it the day of the Lord's sacrifice, a dramatic reversal of expectation. Such points of connection suggest that in the broadest sense of the expression we are in the same ideological world as Amos[31] with only a slighter similarity with Isaiah 2.

Looking chronologically in the other direction for possible influence by Zephaniah on others, we are first struck forcibly, of course, by the fact that the last two clauses of 1:15 are identical with Joel 2:2. It is true that most of the components of these clauses can find separate parallels in theophanic descriptions, but the concentration that we have here occurs nowhere else. Given that the book of Joel makes quite frequent use of citations from other prophetic books (see below), the same is presumably the case here, and indeed that conclusion is only strengthened by the fact that in the preceding verse, 2:1, Joel may be further drawing from other elements in Zephaniah 1 such as the reference to the *shophar* in v. 16.

It is probable in addition, however, that there has been influence on Isaiah 13, albeit by way of echo of discrete elements rather than a full citation. Note, for instance, the imperative הילילו in view of the day at Isa 13:6 and Zeph 1:11, and the designation of the day as a day of God's wrath (עברה) at Isa 13:9, 13, and Zeph 1:15, along with a number of other such shared elements as listed by Beck.[32] Since this includes the latest layer in Isaiah 13 its dependence on Zephaniah rather than the reverse seems certain. Equally the nature of the borrowed elements is not such as would lead us to conclude that there is anything in these verses in Zephaniah which is indicative of the distinctively late features in Isaiah.

I conclude, therefore, that although there are some links with later texts by way of citation and allusion to Zephaniah, his own treatment of the day of the Lord fits easily within the earliest usage we have already identified: a turning of the usually positive expectations of the day against those who in standard and popular thought considered that they would be beneficiaries.[33]

---

31 My wording here is deliberate; Beck, *Der "Tag YHWHs" im Dodekapropheton*, 106–7, doubts that there was direct literary dependence, but that does not contradict the conclusion that they inhabit a similar ideological world that was at odds with majority opinion.

32 Beck, *Der "Tag YHWHs" im Dodekapropheton*, 108.

33 For a far more detailed analysis than has been possible here, including close attention to the relationship of Zephaniah's day of the Lord references with other prophetic passages, see Irsigler, *Gottesgericht und Jahwetag*, 319–90.

The book of Joel is, of course, the one which has a greater concentration of material relating to the day of the Lord than any other.[34] It also has some close links with Isaiah 13. In the first place we find that there is an extensive citation one way or the other between Joel 1:15 and Isa 13:6 (see too Ezek 30:2–3). Regardless of theories about the chronology of composition I agree with the majority (though not unanimous) opinion that it is Joel which has cited from Isaiah. This derives mainly from the opinion which I formulated many years ago, in close dependence on the even earlier work of Gray,[35] that the many links between Joel and the other prophets should be taken together as citations in Joel rather than the reverse. (i) At 3:5 (ET, 2:32) Joel's parallel with Obad 17 is followed by the words כאשר אמר יהוה, indicative of a quotation of some sort. (ii) In some cases such as 2:27 and 4:17 (ET, 3:17) (see Ezek 36:11 and frequently) the wording is characteristic of Ezekiel rather than of Joel, indicating dependence by the latter. (iii) Several of the citations (e. g. 2:2/Zeph 1:14–15 and 2:6/Nah 2:10) "seem better suited to the wider context of the passages in the other prophets than in Joel."[36] (iv) "Sometimes Joel combines phrases from two or more other passages ...; to reverse the dependence in these cases would be much more unlikely"; see 1:15 (Isa 13:6; Ezek 30:2–3; Zeph 1:7); 2:3 (Isa 51:3; Ezek 36:35); 2:27 (Ezek 36:11; Isa 45:5–6, 18); 4:16 (ET, 3:16/Isa 13:13; Amos 1:2). (v) Finally, in two cases, at 2:3 and 4:10 (ET, 3:10), Joel reverses sayings elsewhere (Isa 51:3 and Isa 2:4/Mic 4:3 respectively). This is more probably the feature of a single writer than the result of coincidence in two other independent ones.[37]

---

34 Rendtorff, "Alas for the Day!" has famously grouped the whole of his study of the day of the Lord in the Book of the Twelve around the varied uses in Joel. He recognizes the differences but seeks to read the book as a canonical whole. It seems to me that this is a form of reading that may legitimately be undertaken alongside, but not perforce instead of, a more diachronic approach to the growth of the book through time.

35 G. Buchanan Gray, "The Parallel Passages in Joel and their Bearing on the Question of Date," *Expositor* 8 (1893), 208–25.

36 Note also how Anna Karena Müller, *Gottes Zukunft: die Möglichkeit der Rettung am Tag JHWHs nach dem Joelbuch*, WMANT 119 (Neukirchen-Vluyn: Neukirchener Verlag, 2008), 79, uses this as an argument with particular reference to 1:15 as a citation of Isa 13:6.

37 See my "Joel," in *The International Standard Bible Encyclopedia*, vol. 2, ed. Geoffrey W. Bromiley *et al.* (Grand Rapids: Eerdmans, 1982), 1076–80 (1078–79). Studies since have done nothing to change this; for instance, reservations are expressed about some details, but the basic conclusion not questioned, in John Barton, *Joel and Obadiah: A Commentary*, OTL (Louisville: Westminster John Knox, 2001), 22–27. For some further considerations, see Beck, *Der "Tag YHWHs" im Dodekapropheton*, 156–57, including also the negative argument that there is no evidence for influence from either Zephaniah or Obadiah.

While it is questionable to what extent authors in antiquity took account of the wider context when citing an earlier work, it is noteworthy that in this case the citation is from what I have argued is the primary layer of Isaiah 13 and that it comes in what is agreed by all to be the primary layer of Joel which treats a natural phenomenon as a harbinger of the day of the Lord very much within the regular historical continuum. In terms of comparison, this therefore presents no problem whatsoever in terms either of date of composition or of understanding of the day of the Lord in broad terms. It fits well with what I suggested was the second use of the topic in Isaiah, the main difference being, of course, that Joel adheres to the notion that the day was turned against his own people, not some foreign oppressor.

Second there is contact of a looser kind between parts of Joel 2 and Isaiah 13.[38] This is not so much by way of citation proper as of a cluster of terms that both passages share in common. Commentators generally start by comparing 2:10 with Isa 13:13 because of the common reference to an earthquake and its counterpart in the sky (though interestingly Joel applies the two verbs in question to the other entity: רגז and רעש). They then move on to such other verbal associations as גבורים (v. 7; Isa 13:2), the twofold קול in v. 5 and Isa 13:4, הרים (2:2 and 5; Isa 13:4), עם רב (2:2 and Isa 13:4) יחילו(ן) (2:6 and Isa 13:8, though in the latter the verb is used purely as part of a simile by way of the motif of a woman in labour), פנים (2:6 and Isa 13:8). Beyond such common terminology, which I regard as completely trivial evidence, attention is drawn to such common themes as the devastation of the earth (2:3 and Isa 13:9—but by fire in Joel, which does not occur in Isaiah 13; the only approximate verbal link is that in Isaiah the earth becomes a שמה where in Joel the desert becomes a שממה), the impact on the sun, moon, and stars in 2:10 and Isa 13:10 (this links with the initial comparison with v. 13 noted already above), and the despoiling of houses in 2:9 and Isa 13:16 (though very differently handled).[39]

It is difficult to mount a case for direct and immediate influence on Joel from Isaiah 13 on the basis of this material. The vocabulary links are of common words

---

38 Though connections within the Twelve are not my main concern here, it is interesting to observe the additional close connection of 2:2 with Zeph 1:14–16. For what it is worth, this serves as another indication of the fact that use of the earliest form of the day of the Lord (reaching back at least to Amos) continued alongside widening understandings into the later period.

39 This list is based on Hans Walter Wolff, *Dodekapropheton 2: Joel und Amos*, BKAT xiv/2 (Neukirchen-Vluyn: Neukirchener Verlag, 1969), 55–56; for similar comparisons, albeit with some variations which add little to the essence of the argument, see Siegfried Bergler, *Joel als Schriftinterpret*, BEATAJ 16 (Frankfurt am Main: Peter Lang, 1988), 132–53; Bosshard-Nepustil, *Rezeptionen von Jesaia 1–39 im Zwölfprophetenbuch*, 292; Müller, *Gottes Zukunft*, 59–98; Jeremias, "Der 'Tag Jahwes' in Jes 13 und Joel 2," 130–31; Beck, *Der "Tag YHWHs" im Dodekapropheton*, 171–72.

which do not appear in the same order or sometimes even with the same referents in each passage, while the common themes are not unique to these two passages but are more symptomatic of descriptions of theophany more widely.[40] Joel 2 can still fit well within the parameters of chapter 1, and, as Barton has well shown, the references to the heavenly bodies may easily be explained as portents such as were often thought in antiquity to accompany natural events within a historical framework rather than necessarily indicating some form of apocalyptic or ultimate eschatological event. The description of the day of the Lord in Joel 2 is thus closer to the primary layer in Isaiah 13 than might otherwise be supposed. The additional material in that chapter moves the description in a far more universal direction than is envisaged here. What takes that material away from the scenario in Joel 2 is the fact that the day of the Lord is one when whole kingdoms and nations are mobilized and when it is the whole earth rather than just Israel or Judah which is threatened (see especially vv. 4–5 and 11).

When we turn to the second half of the book of Joel, however, we find ourselves in a completely different world (and this quite without regard to the narrower question of authorship). As has been argued with variations of detail for well over a century,[41] there are both literary and thematic distinctions to be drawn between the two main parts of the book. At the literary level, chapters 1 and 2 are well structured and coherent overall, whereas chapters 3 and 4 present a more miscellaneous collection. Nogalski in particular has made a fine attempt to demonstrate the careful redactional coherence of Joel 4.[42] Nevertheless he accepts that the redactor (responsible especially for vv. 1–3) has ordered what in some cases was pre-existing material into its present coherent literary shape and that the chapter presupposes knowledge of much of the rest of the book of Joel, so that in principle he explicitly does not deny that it may have been composed in its present form at a date later than chapters 1–2. Thematically, there is a shift from a focus on a specific event that afflicted Judah and which was interpreted in terms of the day of the Lord to an eschatological, end time application of the day as a time of judgment for all nations. Thus the scope, the timing, and the identification of those affected are all different.

---

40 Of course, the two traditions of theophany and of the day of the Lord are in any case closely associated, so that there is a danger of falling into a "chicken and egg" snare. Nevertheless, that does not detract from my point that we are dealing in these passages with use of shared tradition rather than of literary influence. For the vocabulary and motifs of theophany as well as of its close association with the day of the Lord, see still Jeremias, *Theophanie*.

41 See the survey of opinions with analysis in Barton, *Joel and Obadiah*, 5–14.

42 James Nogalski, *Redactional Processes in the Book of the Twelve*, BZAW 218 (Berlin: de Gruyter, 1993), 26–57.

Although once again we do not have any examples of full citation from Isaiah 13 we thus certainly find here the kind of universal emphasis which is characteristic of Isa 13:4–5 and 9–13, and incidentally one may devise similar perfectly acceptable strategies for reading the final form of the text. And I would emphasize that it was this cosmic element which was so important in drawing a distinction between the two parts of Isaiah 13 and in linking the later part with Isaiah 24–27. The application of the specific fate of individual nations to the global community of the nations seems to mark the development in ideology in the two distinguishable parts of both Isaiah and Joel.

The remaining references to the day of the Lord in the Book of the Twelve may be dealt with more briefly. In Obad 15 we read that "the day of the Lord is near against all the nations." Using stereotypical language at the start of the verse, this seems to apply the specific indictment of Edom in all that precedes to a more universal dimension, which is continued in the verses following. Whereas in the first half of the book "the nations (גוים)" are the agents of God's judgment on Edom (see vv. 1, 2), now they are its object. It is true that the second half of the book also includes further references to Esau (though not Edom as such) and other named regions, but the general parallel of overall structure with Joel is striking. Furthermore there are other close associations between the second half of each book, such as the reference to those who escape being found on Mount Zion (בהר ציון תהיה פליטה, Obad 17; Joel 3:5) as a possible citation one way or the other, very probably by Joel rather than the reverse. For our present purposes, therefore, there is little to be added to what has already been said about Joel.

Zech 14:1 begins with a uniquely worded reference to the day of the Lord: הנה יום בא ליהוה. With an unprecedented word order, this seems to combine the יום ליהוה of Isa 2:12 (and Ezek 30:3, where it is described as קרוב) with the verb בוא "come," as used stereotypically, for instance, in Isa 13:9; Joel 2:1; 3:4; Mal 3:23. While there are a number of places where יום and יהוה are separated by another noun in the construct state, this is the only example of a verbal form coming in this position. Theoretically it makes the sense uncertain: could it be rendered "a day is coming for the Lord"? Given the use of formulaic language, however, this seems unlikely. I prefer to label the usage "baroque," indicative of a late combination of familiar elements. And that same characterization suits what immediately follows, for we find in v. 2 that the day refers to an attack by foreign nations on Jerusalem succeeded immediately in v. 3 by God then turning against those same enemies. Both uses of the day are attested elsewhere, as we have seen, but their stark juxtaposition here is again baroque. The whole is thus decidedly indicative of a late stage in the development of the use of the image, and that impression is confirmed by what then follows (whether compositionally or only redactionally is disputed) with its highly portentous combination of a theophanic description of God standing on the Mount of Olives and then the mountain being split and the parts on the move. Were we to go on further to include the several "on that day" sections of both chs. 12–13 and the remainder of ch. 14, as many commentators wish to do,[43] the same point could be easily extended. I conclude, therefore, that this example shows dependence on many earlier uses of the day of the Lord, putting it firmly at the end of the development we have traced.[44]

The final direct reference to the day of the Lord is in the closing saying of the book of Malachi, in 3:23 (ET, 4:5), where we have the unparalleled promise that God "will send you the prophet Elijah before the great and terrible day of the Lord comes." This looks like a fully eschatologized understanding of the day, and its formulation—לפני בוא יום יהוה הגדול והנורא—is identical with what we find in Joel 3:4 (and this may derive in turn from the distributed form of the phrase over the two halves of the last line of Joel 2:11). Given that the last three verses of the book of Malachi may presuppose a more or less completed "law and prophets," this may be a single example where we have a citation *from* rather than *in* Joel.[45] At all events, with due allowance for the significantly distinctive feature of Mal 3:23, it clearly fits with what I have previously labeled the third category of "day of the Lord" references in the prophets.

To attempt to draw the results of this rapid survey together, I should like to make the methodologically rather unpopular suggestion that in both the book of Isaiah and in the Book of the Twelve we find the outlines of a broadly parallel development in the understanding of the day of the Lord. In the earliest form to which we have access, an apparently already popular notion, possibly celebrated in the cult, that it would be a day when God intervened on Israel's behalf to guarantee whatever form of deliverance might be categorized as light would be turned against Israel to punish her for her sin. We find this first attested in Amos, but also in the second half of Isaiah 2 as well as in Zephaniah. In Amos, the setting of the day of the Lord saying implies that social sin is the main problem, whereas it is

43 See, for instance, the relatively recent commentaries of David L. Petersen, *Zechariah 9–14 and Malachi: A Commentary*, OTL (London: SCM, 1995), 137–39, and Mark J. Boda, *The Book of Zechariah*, NICOT (Grand Rapids: Eerdmans, 2016), 686–89.
44 For a maximalist presentation of earlier passages on which Zech 14 may be drawing (including prominently Isa 13), see Konrad R. Schaeffer, "Zechariah 14: A Study in Allusion," *CBQ* 57 (1995): 66–91; more narrowly, see Douglas A. Witt, "The Houses Plundered, The Women Raped: The Use of Isaiah 13 in Zechariah 14:1–11," *PEGLMBS* 11 (1991): 66–74. For possible links specifically with other day of the Lord passages, see Schwesig, *Die Rolle der Tag-JHWHs-Dichtungen im Dodekapropheton*, 199–230.
45 See Petersen, *Zechariah 9–14 and Malachi*, 231; Schwesig, *Die Rolle der Tag-JHWHs-Dichtungen im Dodekapropheton*, 273. For some others who share this standard view, see Beck, *Der "Tag YHWHs" im Dodekapropheton*, 306 n. 227.

pride and human hubris in Isaiah, both characteristic of the two prophets' ideologies. In Zephaniah, it is less easy to define, but the sin in the first chapter seems to be more religiously orientated, and it is noteworthy that correspondingly the day of the Lord is likened to a day of sacrifice. It is true that this whole theology presupposes a measure of universal divine sovereignty and also that natural phenomena can serve as portents,[46] but I should still want to distinguish that from the third phase as described below.

Second, we find a comparable use of the day of the Lord as an anticipated historical event but turned now to announce the defeat of a foreign oppressor. This is what we find in the primary layer in Isaiah 13 as well as more briefly in 22:5. This therefore marks something of a return to the presupposed earliest use of the concept. While we found several points of connection between this material and Joel 1–2, the difference is that there the day is still seen as directed against Judah. Thus while chronologically the two passages may be said to derive from the same general time period, they serve as an important reminder that our authors were not enslaved to contemporary practice but could borrow and adapt from earlier uses as well. The development I am tracing is cumulative rather than exclusive.

The final stage takes a decisive step in both the chronology and the interpretation of the day of the Lord. It is cast into the more remote, if not eschatological, future and it is seen now to encompass all the world's nations. It is possible that the cosmic phenomena are still to be taken merely as portents, but there are occasions when even that element seems to move towards what would popularly be regarded as apocalyptic. This final stage is found in the additional material in Isaiah 13, with its close parallels in Isaiah 24 as well as a briefer reference in 34:8. This significant development seems also to be shared in Joel 3–4, and also to have echoes in Obad 15, Zech 14, and perhaps Mal 3:23.

Hermeneutically it is usually the final layer or redaction which influences the way that we read and interpret everything earlier. In the present instance, the time-bound and historically sometimes obscure applications of the day of the Lord are reapplied by way of paradigm or adumbration to the day of the Lord in a more universal future theophanic in-breaking of the divine on the affairs of this world. To give just one striking example we have seen both how Obadiah interprets God's day against Edom as portending his day against all the nations with a remnant that will escape in Zion and how in the book of Isaiah in 34:8 and its parallel in 63:1–6 Edom is turned into an archetypical oppressor of Israel, so inviting a reading of the Babylonian material which comes in between as indicative of freedom from all manner of oppression as suffered by later readers. I forebear here

---

46 Barton, "The Day of Yahweh."

to take this forward into New Testament applications, wholly legitimate though I regard those to be, and so conclude with the observation that, as so often, the tracing of the development of a major Old Testament concept through time paradoxically draws it nearer to informed modern appropriation. Critical method does not divorce Scripture from the modern community but enlivens it in unexpected ways.

Bibliography

Ahn, John, "Zephaniah, a Disciple of Isaiah?" in *Thus Says the Lord: Essays on the Former and Latter Prophets in Honor of Robert R. Wilson*, ed. John J. Ahn and Stephen L. Cook, LHB/OTS 502 (New York: T & T Clark, 2009), 292–307.

Barstad, Hans, *The Religious Polemics of Amos: Studies in the Preaching of Am 2, 7B–8; 4, 1–13; 5, 1–27; 6, 4–7; 8, 14*, VTSup 34 (Leiden: Brill, 1984).

Barton, John, *Isaiah 1–39*, OTG (Sheffield: Sheffield Academic, 1995).

Barton, John, *Joel and Obadiah: A Commentary*, OTL (Louisville: Westminster John Knox, 2001).

Barton, John, "The Day of Yahweh in the Minor Prophets," in *Biblical and Near Eastern Essays: Studies in Honour of Kevin J. Cathcart*, ed. Carmel McCarthy and John F. Healey, JSOTSup 375 (London: T & T Clark International, 2004), 68–79.

Beck, Martin, *Der "Tag YHWHs" im Dodekapropheton: Studien im Spannungsfeld von Traditions- und Redaktionsgeschichte*, BZAW 356 (Berlin: de Gruyter, 2005).

Becking, Bob, "Expectations about the End of Time in the Hebrew Bible: Do they Exist?" in *Apocalyptic in History and Tradition*, ed. Christopher Rowland and John Barton, JSPSup 43 (London: Sheffield Academic, 2002), 44–59.

Berges, Ulrich, *Das Buch Jesaja: Komposition und Endgestalt*, Herders Biblische Studien 16 (Freiburg: Herder, 1998).

Bergler, Siegfried, *Joel als Schriftinterpret*, BEATAJ 16 (Frankfurt am Main: Peter Lang, 1988).

Blenkinsopp, Joseph, *Isaiah 1–39: A New Translation with Introduction and Commentary*, AB 19 (New York: Doubleday, 2000).

Boda, Mark J., *The Book of Zechariah*, NICOT (Grand Rapids: Eerdmans, 2016).

Bosshard-Nepustil, Erich, *Rezeptionen von Jesaia 1–39 im Zwölfprophetenbuch: Untersuchungen zur literarischen Verbindung von Prophetenbüchern in babylonischer und persischer Zeit*, OBO 154 (Freiburg: Universitätsverlag, and Göttingen: Vandenhoeck & Ruprecht, 1997).

Clements, Ronald E., *Isaiah 1–39*, NCBC (Grand Rapids: Eerdmans, and London: Marshall, Morgan & Scott, 1980).

Collins, John J., "The Beginning of the End of the World in the Hebrew Bible," in *Thus Says the Lord: Essays on the Former and Latter Prophets in Honor of Robert R. Wilson*, ed. John J. Ahn and Stephen L. Cook, LHB/OTS 502 (London: T & T Clark, 2009), 137–155.

Cross, Frank M., *Canaanite Myth and Hebrew Epic: Essays in the History of the Religion of Israel* (Cambridge MA: Harvard University Press, 1973).

Eissfeldt, Otto, *Einleitung in das Alte Testament* (3d ed.; Tübingen: Mohr [Paul Siebeck], 1964).

Everson, A. Joseph, "The Days of Yahweh," *JBL* 93 (1974), 329–37.

Fey, Reinhard, *Amos und Jesaja: Abhängigkeit und Eigenständigkeit des Jesaja*, WMANT 12 (Neukirchen-Vluyn: Neukirchener Verlag, 1963).

Fischer, Charis, *Die Fremdvölkersprüche bei Amos und Jesaja: Studien zur Eigenart und Intention in Am 1,3–2,3.4 f und Jes 13,1–16,14*, BBB 136 (Berlin: Philo, 2002).

Gärtner, Judith, "Die Völker und der Tag-JHWHs im Horizont des Jesaja- und des Zwölfprophetenbuches," in *The Books of the Twelve Prophets: Minor Prophets, Major Theologies*, ed. Heinz-Josef Fabry, BETL 295 (Leuven: Peeters, 2018), 131–156.

Gosse, Bernard, *Isaïe 13,1–14,23 dans la tradition littéraire du livre d'Isaïe et dans la tradition des oracles contre les nations*, OBO 78 (Freiburg: Universitätsverlag, and Göttingen: Vandenhoeck & Ruprecht, 1988).

Gray, G. Buchanan, "The Parallel Passages in Joel and their Bearing on the Question of Date," *Expositor* 8 (1893), 208–25.

Hélewa, F. J., "L'origine du concept prophétique du 'Jour de Yahvé'," *Ephemerides Carmeliticae* 15 (1964), 3–36.

Hiers, Richard H./Cathcart, Kevin J., *ABD* 2 (1992), 82–85.

Höffken, Peter, *Das Buch Jesaja: Kapitel 1–39*, Neuer Stuttgarter Kommentar—Altes Testament 18/1 (Stuttgart: Verlag Katholisches Bibelwerk, 1993).

Irsigler, Hubert, *Gottesgericht und Jahwetag: die Komposition Zef 1,1–2,3, untersucht auf der Grundlage der Literarkritik des Zefanjabuches*, ATSAT 3 (St. Ottilien: EOS Verlag, 1977).

Jeremias, Jörg, "Der 'Tag Jahwes' in Jes 13 und Joel 2," in *Schriftauslegung in der Schrift: Festschrift für Odil Hannes Steck zu seinem 65. Geburtstag*, ed. Reinhard G. Kratz, Thomas Krüger, and Konrad Schmid, BZAW 300 (Berlin: de Gruyter, 2000), 129–138.

Jeremias, Jörg, *Theophanie: die Geschichte einer alttestamentlichen Gattung*, WMANT 10 (2d ed.; Neukirchen-Vluyn: Neukirchener Verlag, 1977).

Kilian, Rudolf, *Jesaja II: 13–39*, Die Neue Echter Bibel 32 (Würzburg: Echter, 1994).

Klein, Anja, "Babylon Revisited: A New Look at Isa 13 and Its Literary Horizon," in *Imperial Visions: The Prophet and the Book of Isaiah in an Age of Empires*, ed. Reinhard G. Kratz and Joachim Schaper, FRLANT (Göttingen: Vandenhoeck & Ruprecht, forthcoming).

Kreuch, Jan, *Das Amos- und Jesajabuch: eine exegetische Studie zur Neubestimmung ihres Verhältnisses*, BThS 149 (Neukirchen-Vluyn: Neukirchener Verlag, 2014).

Marti, Karl, *Das Buch Jesaja*, KHAT 19 (Tübingen: Mohr [Paul Siebeck], 1900).

Matthews, Claire R., *Defending Zion: Edom's Desolation and Jacob's Restoration (Isaiah 34–35) in Context*, BZAW 236 (Berlin: de Gruyter, 1995).

Mowinckel, Sigmund, *He That Cometh*, trans. George W. Anderson (Oxford: Blackwell, 1956).

Mowinckel, Sigmund, "Jahves dag," *NTT* 59 (1958), 1–56, 209–29.

Mowinckel, Sigmund, *Psalmenstudien* II (Kristiania: Dybwad, 1922).

Müller, Anna Karena, *Gottes Zukunft: die Möglichkeit der Rettung am Tag JHWHs nach dem Joelbuch*, WMANT 119 (Neukirchen-Vluyn: Neukirchener Verlag, 2008).

Nogalski, James, *Redactional Processes in the Book of the Twelve*, BZAW 218 (Berlin: de Gruyter, 1993).

Nogalski, James, "The Day(s) of YHWH in the Book of the Twelve," in *Thematic Threads in the Book of the Twelve*, ed. Paul L. Redditt and Aaron Schart, BZAW 325 (Berlin: de Gruyter, 2003), 192–213.

Petersen, David L., *Zechariah 9–14 and Malachi: A Commentary*, OTL (London: SCM, 1995).

Rendtorff, Rolf, "Alas for the Day! The 'Day of the Lord' in the Book of the Twelve," in *God in the Fray: A Tribute to Walter Brueggemann*, ed. Tod Linafelt and Timothy K. Beal (Minneapolis: Fortress, 1998), 186–97.

Rendtorff, Rolf, "How to Read the Book of the Twelve as a Theological Unity," in *Reading and Hearing the Book of the Twelve*, ed. James D. Nogalski and Marvin A. Sweeney, SBLSS 15 (Atlanta: Scholars Press, 2000), 75–87.

Saebø, Magne, *ThWAT* 3 (1982), 582–586.

Schaeffer, Konrad R., "Zechariah 14: A Study in Allusion," *CBQ* 57 (1995), 66–91.

Schmid, Konrad, *Jesaja,* vol. 1: *Jesaja 1–23*, ZBK 19.1 (Zürich: Theologischer Verlag Zürich, 2011).

Schwesig, Paul-Gerhard, *Die Rolle der Tag-JHWHs-Dichtungen im Dodekapropheton*, BZAW 366 (Berlin: de Gruyter, 2006).

Vanderhooft, David S., *The Neo-Babylonian Empire and Babylon in the Latter Prophets*, HSM 59 (Atlanta: Scholars, 1999).

van der Vorm-Croughs, Mirjam, "LXX Isaiah and the Use of Rhetorical Figures," in *The Old Greek of Isaiah: Issues and Perspectives,* ed. Arie van der Kooij and Michaël van der Meer, CBET 55 (Leuven: Peeters, 2010), 173–188.

van Leeuwen, Cornelis, "The Prophecy of the *YÔM YHWH* in Amos v 18–20," *OTS* 19 (1974), 113–134.

Vermeylen, Jacques, *Du prophète Isaïe à l'apocalyptique: Isaïe, I–XXXV, miroir d'un demi-millénaire d'expérience religieuse en Israël*, vol. 1, EB (Paris: Gabalda, 1977).

von Rad, Gerhard, "The Origin of the Concept of the Day of Yahweh," *JSS* 4 (1959), 97–108.

Weinfeld, Moshe, "The Day of the Lord: Aspirations for the Kingdom of God in the Bible and Jewish Liturgy," in *Studies in Bible*, ed. Sara Japhet, ScrH 31 (Jerusalem: Magnes, 1986), 341–372.

Weippert, Manfred, "'Heiliger Krieg' in Israel und Assyrien," *ZAW* 84 (1972), 460–93.

Weiss, Meir, "The Origin of the 'Day of the Lord' — Reconsidered," *HUCA* 37 (1966), 29–60.

Weyde, Karl William, "Holy War, Divine War, YHWH War—and Ethics: On a Central Issue in Recent Research on the Hebrew Bible," in *Encountering Violence in the Bible*, ed. Markus Zehnder and Hallvard Hegelia (Sheffield: Sheffield Phoenix, 2013), 235–252.

Williamson, Hugh G. M., *A Critical and Exegetical Commentary on Isaiah 1–27*, 1: *Isaiah 1–5*, ICC (London: T & T Clark, 2006).

Williamson, Hugh G. M., "Decoding Isaiah 13," in *The History of Isaiah: The Making of the Book and its Presentation of the Past*, ed. Todd Hibbard and Jacob Stromberg, FAT (Tübingen: Mohr Siebeck, forthcoming).

Williamson, Hugh G. M., "Joel," in *The International Standard Bible Encyclopedia*, vol. 2, ed. Geoffrey W. Bromiley *et al.* (Grand Rapids: Eerdmans, 1982), 1076–80.

Williamson, Hugh G. M., *The Book Called Isaiah: Deutero-Isaiah's Role in Composition and Redaction* (Oxford: Clarendon, 1994).

Witt, Douglas A., "The Houses Plundered, The Women Raped: The Use of Isaiah 13 in Zechariah 14:1–11," *PEGLMBS* 11 (1991), 66–74.

Wolff, Hans Walter, *Dodekapropheton 2: Joel und Amos*, BKAT xiv/2 (Neukirchen-Vluyn: Neukirchener Verlag, 1969).

Zapff, Burkard M., *Schriftgelehrte Prophetie—Jes 13 und die Komposition des Jesajabuches: ein Beitrag zur Erforschung der Redaktionsgeschichte des Jesajabuches*, FB 74 (Würzburg: Echter, 1995).

IV *Festvortrag*: Exegesis of the Prophets from the Perspective of Systematic Theology

Rudolf Voderholzer

Welche Exegese braucht die Kirche?

Zur Bedeutung der Schriftauslegung für
christliche Lebensentwürfe am Beispiel von Prophetie
und Prophetenexegese

Meine sehr verehrten Damen und Herren!

Ich danke Ihnen sehr für die Einladung heute Abend und für die freundliche Begrüßung. Es ist mir eine große Ehre, anlässlich Ihres Symposiums den Festvortrag halten zu dürfen. Ich bedaure außerordentlich, dass meine Amtspflichten als Bischof es mir nicht erlauben, selbst die Vorträge des Symposiums „Jesaja und die Zwölf" mitzuverfolgen. Ich hätte sicherlich viel lernen können. So werden nun aber meine Ausführungen unabhängig von dem sein, was schon gesprochen wurde und noch gesagt werden wird – was ja aber auch von Vorteil sein kann.

Sie erbitten sich von mir als Bischof eine Antwort auf die Frage: „Welche Exegese braucht die Kirche?" Und Sie stellen die Frage in den Kontext der Prophetenexegese und der Bedeutung der Schriftauslegung für christliche Lebensentwürfe. Was liegt da näher, als mit einem Blick auf die frühkirchliche Missionspredigt zu beginnen, wie sie uns in der Apostelgeschichte des Neuen Testaments überliefert ist.

I Biblische Besinnung im Blick auf das lukanische Geschichtswerk

1 „Verstehst Du auch, was Du liest?" (Apg 8,30)[1]

Der Evangelist Lukas überliefert uns im 8. Kapitel seiner Apostelgeschichte ein bemerkenswertes Stück frühchristlicher Katechese, in deren Zentrum die Ausle-

---

1 Vgl. Pesch, Rudolf, *Die Apostelgeschichte I* (= EKK V/I) (Zürich, Einsiedeln: Neukirchner Theologie, Patmos, 1986): 295: „Die Frage des Philippus (...) ist die Grundfrage biblischer Hermeneutik. Bedingung des Verstehens der Bibel ist nicht schon das Lesenkönnen; private Schriftlektüre ist noch keine hinreichende Bedingung dafür, daß dem Leser auch der Sinn der Schrift aufgeht. Die Schrift ist das Zeugnis eines ‚Weges', der Geschichte Gottes mit seinem Volk; und es bedarf zu ihrem Verständnis eines des Weges Kundigen, der ihren Sinn aufschließt. Daß der Prophet nicht

https://doi.org/10.1515/9783110705799-013

gung des Propheten Jesaja steht. Der Geist, so erfahren wir, führt den Philippus, einen der Träger des Sieben-Männer-Amtes, dem Kämmerer der äthiopischen Königin Kandake über den Weg, der sich gerade aufgemacht hat, den weiten Weg nach Hause anzutreten. Es handelt sich offenbar um einen sogenannten Gottesfürchtigen, einen Heiden also, der sich für den Glauben Israels interessiert und dafür sogar den Weg bis nach Jerusalem auf sich genommen hatte, um dort zu beten, zu opfern und (vielleicht) das Paschafest mitzufeiern. Auf seinem Wagen sitzend liest er, der antiken Gepflogenheit gemäß, laut – und deswegen auch für andere vernehmlich – aus einer Jesaja-Rolle vor sich hin. „Verstehst Du auch, was Du liest?" fragt ihn nun der Missionar Philippus; und er stellt damit die Grundfrage, worauf alle hermeneutischen und exegetischen Bemühungen abzielen. „Verstehst Du auch, was Du liest?" Die Antwort des Kämmerers ist erschütternd: „Wie könnte ich es, wenn mich niemand anleitet? Und er bat den Philippus, einzusteigen und neben ihm Platz zu nehmen." Und dann erschließt ihm Philippus ausgehend vom Buch des Propheten Jesaja, näherhin von den Gottesknechtstexten aus dem Deuterojesaja, das Evangelium von Jesus dem Christus (Apg 8,35).

Für den Äthiopier ist damit zugleich die entscheidende Lebenswende eingeleitet. Er fragt nämlich, was seiner Taufe noch im Wege steht, nachdem ja sogar ein Bach am Wegesrand das dafür nötige Wasser bereithält. Die Kirche in Äthiopien, eine der ältesten Kirchen überhaupt, führt sich bis auf den heutigen Tag auch auf diese Taufe zurück. Ich werde in wenigen Tagen mit Missio-München zu einer Reise nach Äthiopien, dem Gastland des diesjährigen Weltmissionssonntags, aufbrechen und rechne damit, dieser Überlieferung dort auch zu begegnen.

Für unser Thema bleibt festzuhalten: Für die Kirche der ersten Generationen ist das Buch des Propheten Jesaja das bevorzugte Medium der Verkündigung der Christus-Botschaft. Das aus dieser Verkündigung hervorgehende Neue Testament ist wesentlich die auf Christus hin gedeutete Schrift Israels. Vor diesem Hintergrund gewinnt die Aussage des heiligen Hieronymus noch einmal einen besonderen Klang: „Ignoratio enim Scripturarum ignoratio Christi est" „Die Schrift nicht kennen, heißt Christus nicht kennen", in Artikel 25 von „Dei Verbum" zitiert.[2] Diese Formulierung steht bekanntlich im Prolog zum Jesaja-Kommentar des Kirchenvaters, und damit lässt sich präzisierend sagen: „Das Buch Jesaja nicht kennen, heißt Christus nicht kennen." Hieronymus war freilich seinerseits davon

---

von sich selbst oder einem anderen seiner Zeit sprach, wie der Kämmerer zunächst meinte, läßt sich nicht durch schriftgelehrte Diskussion – heute nicht durch historisch-kritische Exegese – entscheiden, sondern nur aus der Ein-Sicht in die Geschichte Jesu von Nazareth als der Aufgipfelung der Geschichte Gottes mit seinem Volk."

2 Hieronymus, In Is. prol. (PL 24,17).

überzeugt: Christus nicht anerkennen, nicht an Christus glauben und die prophetische Botschaft nicht in sein Licht stellen, heißt das Buch Jesaja nicht in seiner ganzen Tiefe verstehen.

2 Der Herr „erschließt (διερμήνευσεν)" (Lk 24,27) den Sinn der Schrift

Die Stelle in der Apostelgeschichte hat innerhalb des lukanischen Geschichtswerkes eine vorausgehende Parallele in Lk 24, wo davon die Rede ist, dass der auferstandene Herr den Emmausjüngern den Sinn der Schrift erschließt. Lukas verwendet dabei zwei unterschiedliche Kanonformeln. Während es in Vers 24, 27 noch heißt, „Jesus legte ihnen dar, ausgehend von Mose und allen Propheten, was in der gesamten Schrift über ihn geschrieben steht", wird es einige Verse weiter, wenn der Auferstandene dann dem größeren Kreis der Jünger in Jerusalem erscheint, lauten: „Alles muss in Erfüllung gehen, was im Gesetz des Mose, bei den Propheten und in den Psalmen über mich geschrieben steht" (Lk 24,44).

Die Erweiterung des Kanons durch die Psalmen, die hier wohl stellvertretend für die Weisheitsschriften, die „Ch^etubim", als dritte Schriftengruppe des „TeNaCh" stehen, zeigt, dass der Kanonisierungsprozess zur Zeit der Abfassung des Neuen Testaments durchaus noch nicht abgeschlossen war. Kanonbildung, auch das lässt sich darin schon zumindest angedeutet sehen, war also nicht ein sich selbst vollziehender Prozess, sondern letztlich ein Akt der Kirche. Angesichts der Nicht-Abgeschlossenheit des Alttestamentlichen Kanons im späten ersten Jahrhundert, zumindest hinsichtlich der Zugehörigkeit der über Gesetz und Propheten hinausgehenden Schriftengruppen und hinsichtlich der Reihenfolge, besonders der Platzierung der Propheten, konnte Hartmut Gese zugespitzt sagen, dass das Alte Testament jünger sei als das Neue.[3]

Die Aussage, dass Jesus selbst den Sinn der Schrift erschließt (διερμήνευσεν), der nichts und niemand anderes ist als ER selbst, kommentiert Hans Hübner mit den Worten: „*Jesu erste Tätigkeit als Auferstandener* ist demnach das *alttestamentliche Kolleg über sich selbst.*"[4] Schon Paul Claudel hatte im Zusammenhang mit Lk

3 Vgl. Hartmut Gese, „Erwägungen zur Einheit der biblischen Theologie", in: Ders., *Vom Sinai zum Zion. Alttestamentliche Beiträge zur biblischen Theologie* (München: Chr. Kaiser, 1974): 11–30, hier 14.
4 Hans Hübner, *Hebräerbrief, Evangelien und Offenbarung.* Epilegomena (= Biblische Theologie des Neuen Testaments, Bd. III) (Göttingen: Vandenhoeck & Ruprecht, 1995), 142 (Hervorhebung im Original).

24 davon gesprochen, die Predigten des Origenes und seiner Schüler seien nichts anderes gewesen als die „Auswortung der Lektion" von Emmaus[5].

Lk 24 und Apg 8 zeigen strukturell bemerkenswerte Parallelen auf, und die Verkündigung des Philippus erweist sich als die in die Kirchengeschichte hinein fortgeführte, am Beispiel Jesu Christi selbst Maß nehmende, christologische Deutung des Alten Testaments. Mit dieser christologischen Deutung des gesamten Alten Testaments auf Christus hin ist freilich nicht nur ein (sogar maßgebliches) Modell für die Exegese, ein Beispiel, wie man es machen kann oder soll, gegeben. Diese Auslegung ist vielmehr identisch mit dem Ursprung des Neuen Testaments und somit in gewisser Weise auch identisch mit dem Gründungsgeschehen der Kirche selbst. Die universale Heilsbedeutung seines Kreuzestodes ist vermutlich Jesus selbst im Licht des Gottesknechtes deutlich geworden und uns vom Neuen Testament nicht anders denn als die Erfüllung der geheimnisvollen Worte des Propheten Jesaja überliefert. Dasselbe gilt für weitere zentrale Themen des Glaubens. Die Frage: „Welche Exegese braucht die Kirche?", schärft also den Blick dafür, als welche Form der Exegese die Kirche sozusagen selbst vom Ursprung her existiert. Soweit geht die Verknüpfung von Altem und Neuem Testament. Vor dem Hintergrund dieser Einsicht in die grundlegende Bedeutung dieser Exegese für die Fundierung der Apostolischen Kirche gewinnt der Titel dieses Symposiums „Jesaja und die Zwölf" noch einmal eine ganz neue Bedeutung. „Zwölf" ist dann nicht im Sinne des Dodeka-Prophetons, sondern im Sinne der „Zwölf" Apostel zu verstehen.

Sowohl in der Apostelgeschichte wie auch in der ihr vorausgehenden Emmausperikope führt die Sinnerschließung die zum Glauben Gekommenen schließlich zugleich und folgerichtig in ein neues, liturgisch vollzogenes und ratifiziertes, Existenzverhältnis: Der Kämmerer bittet um die Taufe und kehrt dann voller Freude in seine Heimat zurück. Die Emmausjünger, denen sich der Herr erst vollständig beim Brotbrechen, d. h. in der sakramentalen Selbstvergegenwärtigung in der Eucharistie erschließt, kehren buchstäblich um und werden zu österlichen Kündern der Botschaft von der Auferstehung Jesu Christi.

---

5 „Je veux parler de l'Écriture Sainte. C'est en elle que nous trouvons la surabondance du père, et quant à son rugissement, qui domine tous les bruits de la terre, c'est le verbe de la grande mer elle-même que le plus humble caillou suffit à rendre vocale. Cette ferveur vivifiante et profonde dont elle a le secret, c'est celle qui pénétrait sur le chemin d'Emmaüs Cléophas et son compagnon, tandis que le Seigneur lui-même, nous dit l'Évangile de saint Luc, leur ouvrait le texte sacré. (...) Des foules immenses se pressaient autour d'Origène et de ses émules dont les homélies ne sont qu'une paraphrase de la leçon d'Emmaüs." Paul Claudel, „L'Écriture Sainte. Allocutions aux étudiants des Sciences Politiques", in: *La Vie Intellectuelle* (Mai 1948): 6–14, hier: 6 f.; dt. in: *Ich liebe das Wort*, (Recklinghausen: Paulus, 1955): 53 f.

3 Der Logos als „Exeget" des Vaters (ἐξεγήσατο, Joh 1,18)

Von diesem Jesus Christus bezeugt das Johannesevangelium, dass der Logos, der am Herzen des Vaters geruht hat, Fleisch geworden ist und in seinem gesamten Wirken Kunde vom Vater gebracht hat, d. h. wörtlich: der Exeget des Vaters geworden ist (ἐξεγήσατο). Das gesamte begriffliche Instrumentarium von „Hermeneutik" und „Exegese" und auch die damit verbundene Sache ist somit im Neuen Testament selbst grundgelegt und eindeutig christologisch bestimmt. Zugleich ist der Horizont jeder christlichen Hermeneutik und Exegese aufgespannt. Es wäre jetzt hier auch noch auf die Fachtermini „Allegorie" (bezeugt in Gal 4,24) und auf das ganze Wortfeld „typos", „typicos", „antitypos" hinzuweisen, mit denen die vom Heiligen Geist getragene christologische Auslegung der Schrift ihre konkrete Methodik fand. Dies würde hier zu weit führen.[6]

Wenden wir uns nach diesem biblischen Auftakt nun der kirchlichen Antwort auf die Fragen nach einer sachgemäßen Exegese zu. Welche Exegese braucht die Kirche?

II Die Weisungen des Zweiten Vatikanischen Konzils

Die Frage nach einer sachgemäßen Exegese wird in der kirchlichen Lehrverkündigung erstmals umfassend beantwortet in der Offenbarungskonstitution „Dei Verbum" des Zweiten Vatikanischen Konzils.

1 Von den Bibelenzykliken zur Offenbarungskonstitution

In ihr kam eine Entwicklung zum Abschluss, die mit der Enzyklika „Providentissimus Deus" (1893) ihren Anfang genommen hatte. Alle lehramtlichen Texte bis herauf zum Zweiten Vatikanischen Konzil waren dabei von einer apologetischen Tendenz geprägt. Diese Apologetik war bedingt durch die Herausforderung vonseiten der historisch-kritischen Exegese, worauf das von einer ungeschichtlichen Systematischen Theologie dominierte Lehramt nur unzureichend vorbereitet war.

---

6 Ich verweise auf die von mir übersetzten einschlägigen Beiträge aus Henri de Lubacs Exégèse médiévale, im Deutschen: *Typologie. Allegorie. Geistiger Sinn. Studien zur Geschichte der christlichen Bibelhermeneutik* (= Sammlung Theologia Romanica) (Freiburg: Johannesverlag 2007, ³2014).

Providentissimus Deus (1893)

Im Vordergrund der ersten Bibelenzyklika *Providentissimus Deus (1893)* steht die Frage nach dem rechten Verständnis von Inspiration und Irrtumslosigkeit, die sich aus einem scheinbar unumgänglichen Konflikt zwischen den modernen Naturwissenschaften und dem biblischen Schöpfungsbericht ergab. Um eine richtige und angemessene Kritik von einer übertriebenen und falschen unterscheiden zu können, müssen die katholischen Exegeten, so fordert es die Enzyklika, bestens geschult werden. Der dritte Teil behandelt die Autorität und Glaubwürdigkeit der Bibel. Christoph Dohmen sieht die Bedeutung der Enzyklika letztlich darin, dass mit ihr eine Entwicklung eingeleitet wurde, die die Heilige Schrift wieder ins Zentrum des theologischen Forschens rückte. Das Bildwort vom Schriftstudium als „anima theologiae" wird denn auch von „Providentissimus Deus" ausgehend über „Divino afflante Spiritu" in die Offenbarungskonstitution des Zweiten Vatikanischen Konzils eingehen.

Spiritus Paraclitus (1920)

Ich übergehe die rein defensiven Responsa der Bibelkommission und nenne als nächste Etappe die so genannte Hieronymus-Enzyklika „Spiritus Paraclitus" von 1920, dem 1500. Todesjahr des „Biblikers" unter den abendländischen Kirchenlehrern. In ihr geht das kirchliche Lehramt einen kleinen Schritt weiter auf dem Weg zur Anerkennung des wahrhaft menschlichen Beitrags des Hagiographen. Es wird, neben der herkömmlichen Rede von einer instrumentellen Arbeitsgemeinschaft, auch von einer „echten Arbeitsgemeinschaft" zwischen der Autorschaft des Heiligen Geistes und des Hagiographen gesprochen.

Divino afflante Spiritu (1943)

Nach allgemeinem Urteil brachte die Enzyklika Papst Pius XII. *Divino afflante Spiritu* von 1943 der historischen Exegese in der katholischen Kirche den entscheidenden Durchbruch. Diese bis dahin bedeutendste Stellungnahme des kirchlichen Lehramtes in Fragen der Schriftauslegung und des Schriftverständnisses ist bezeichnenderweise nicht gegen die historisch-kritische Exegese gerichtet, sondern gegen die Schmähung der historischen Arbeit durch den italienischen Priester Dolindo Ruotolo.

In beachtlicher Schärfe wird der Mystizismus Ruotolos, der sich mit einer überaus unsachlichen Verwerfung der vermeintlich ungeistlichen historischen

Kritik gepaart hatte, zurückgewiesen und der mit dem historischen Fundament korrespondierende Literalsinn und seine Erforschung als Hauptaufgabe katholischer Exegeten bezeichnet: Die Schrifterklärer mögen sich gegenwärtig halten, „daß es ihre erste und angelegentlichste Sorge sein muß, klar zu erkennen und zu bestimmen, welches der Literalsinn der biblischen Worte ist" (Pius XII., Divino afflante Spiritu[7]). Auch die volle menschliche Beteiligung des menschlichen Autors wird anerkannt, wenn im Blick auf die Schriftdeutung die Anwendung derselben Methoden empfohlen wird, die auch bei der Profanliteratur zur Anwendung kommen. Als der größte Fortschritt wurde von exegetischer Seite die positive Bewertung der Gattungskritik empfunden. Weil die Inspiration die persönlichen Fähigkeiten und Eigenarten des menschlichen Schriftstellers nicht aufhebt oder ersetzt, sondern im Gegenteil trägt und zur Blüte bringt, wird man sich, so Pius XII. nicht wundern, dass „den Heiligen Büchern keine jener Redeformen fremd" ist, „deren sich die menschliche Sprache bei den Alten, besonders im Orient, zum Ausdruck der Gedanken zu bedienen pflegte, allerdings unter der Bedingung, daß die angewandte Redegattung in keiner Weise der Heiligkeit und Wahrhaftigkeit Gottes widerspricht" (Pius XII., Divino afflante Spiritu[8]). Die Enzyklika lässt die Mahnungen an die Exegeten ausmünden mit dem Hinweis auf ihre apologetische Aufgabe, durch die Berücksichtigung der literarischen Gattungen und den klugen Gebrauch der historischen Hilfsmittel die „Irrtumslosigkeit", die „Wahrhaftigkeit" und „geschichtliche Treue" der Schrift gegenüber allen Vorwürfen zu erweisen, die diese bezweifelten. Damit war die Enzyklika auf die berechtigten Wünsche der historisch arbeitenden Exegeten eingegangen und sowohl im Ton als auch sachlich von den überaus restriktiven Responsa der Bibelkommission abgerückt. Wie bereits die vorangehenden lehramtlichen Dokumente stößt aber auch „Divino afflante Spiritu" noch nicht zu einer umfassenden Reflexion auf das Wesen der Offenbarung vor. Es wird nur vorausgesetzt, dass die Heiligen Schriften die Offenbarung enthalten, wie einleitend mit einem Zitat aus „Dei Filius" bekräftigt wird[9],

---

7 „Quo in opere exsequendo ante oculos habeant interpretes sibi illud omnium maximum curandum esse, ut clare dispiciant ac definiant, quis sit verborum biblicorum sensus, quem *litteralem* vocant." (DH 3826, Hervorhebung im Original).

8 DH 3829 f.

9 *Über die zeitgemäße Förderung der biblischen Studien.* Rundschreiben Pius XII. Divino afflante Spiritu vom 30. September 1943, hg. vom katholischen Bibelwerk (Stuttgart: Katholisches Bibelwerk, 1962): 3 und 6. Zuvor freilich hatte es in der von Kardinal Faulhaber vorbereiteten Enzyklika Papst Pius XI. „Mit brennender Sorge" geheißen, in Jesus Christus sei „die Fülle der göttlichen Offenbarung erschienen"; vgl. zur Entstehung und zu unmittelbaren Reaktionen: Heinz-Albert Raem, *Pius XI. und der Nationalsozialismus. Die Enzyklika „Mit brennender Sorge" vom 14. März 1937* (Paderborn: Schöningh, 1979). Die Vorlage zur Enzyklika war im Januar 1937 vom damaligen

und die Schrift selbst als „Quelle der Offenbarung" bezeichnet. Die positiven Aussagen zur historischen Exegese konnten vor diesem Hintergrund nicht wirklich positiv rezipiert werden. Dies geschah erst im Zuge des Zweiten Vatikanischen Konzils.

2 Die Prinzipien der Schriftauslegung vor dem Hintergrund eines geschichtlichen Offenbarungsverständnisses

Die dogmatische Konstitution über die göttliche Offenbarung[10] „Dei Verbum", verabschiedet am 18. November 1965, ist hervorgegangen aus dem Schema „De fontibus revelationis". Der Fortschritt im konziliaren Diskurs bestand darin, nicht mehr Schrift und Tradition als Offenbarungsquellen zu bezeichnen, sondern „die Offenbarung selbst" (*de ipsa revelatione*) als geschichtliches Ereignis zu beschreiben und eine Besinnung darauf dem Thema Schrift und Tradition voranzustellen. Das Konzil spricht dabei übrigens, und zwar historisch exakt und in Einklang mit den historisch-kritischen Einsichten bewusst zuerst von Tradition und dann von Schrift, geht doch der Schrift die mündliche Überlieferung in einem umfassenden Sinn (Liturgie, Katechese, gläubiges Leben) voraus. Tradition und Schrift aber nun sind nicht „Quellen der Offenbarung", sondern als Weisen der Vermittlung (*modi transmissionis*) dieser in der Geschichte Gottes mit seinem Volk Israel beginnenden und im Christusereignis und der eschatologischen Sendung des Heiligen Geistes zu ihrem Höhepunkt gelangenden Offenbarung selbst zu qualifizieren. Christus in der Einheit von Tat und Wort (*gestis verbisque*: DV 2) ist Höhepunkt und Erfüllung der gesamten Offenbarung. In seiner Antrittsenzyklika *ecclesiam suam* (1964) hatte Papst Paul VI. praktisch zeitgleich ein dialogisches Offenbarungsverständnis entwickelt, worin er die Offenbarung und die Glaubensantwort der Kirche in Beziehung miteinander setzt.

Diese Verhältnisbestimmung von Offenbarung, Tradition und Schrift erlaubt es dann auch, die Anwendung der historischen Methoden zur Deutung der Schrift nicht nur als legitim – nolens volens –, sondern als notwendig zu betrachten (vgl. DV 12,2). Erst wo deutlich erkannt ist, dass die Offenbarung nicht in der Mitteilung

---

Münchener Erzbischof Michael von Faulhaber erbeten worden. Eine Synopse des Faulhaber-Entwurfes und des endgültigen Textes in: Dieter Albrecht (Bearb.), *Der Notenwechsel zwischen dem Heiligen Stuhl und der deutschen Reichsregierung*, Bd. I, Von der Ratifizierung des Reichskonkordats bis zur Enzyklika „Mit brennender Sorge" (= Veröffentlichungen der Kommission für Zeitgeschichte, Reihe A: Quellen, Bd. 1) (Mainz: Schöningh, 1965), 402–443.

10 Unter den Kommentaren ragt nach wie vor heraus: Henri de Lubac, *Die göttliche Offenbarung* (Freiburg: Johannesverlag, 2001).

ewiger Wahrheiten und auch nicht in der Überlassung eines Buches, sondern in dem geschichtlichen Ereignis des Bundes Gottes mit seinem Volk Israel und dann, zu ihrem Höhepunkt kommend, im Leben, Sterben und Auferstehen Jesu Christi besteht, kann die (seriöse) Anwendung historischer Methoden nicht irreführend sein, sondern sie wird es erlauben, dem Geheimnis näher zu kommen.

Einer der Väter des Zweiten Vatikanischen Konzils, Henri de Lubac, hatte bereits in seinem epochalen Werk „Catholicisme" von 1938 geschrieben – und damit die Basis für eine sachgerechte Verhältnisbestimmung von Offenbarung und Exegese benannt:

„Gott handelt in der Geschichte, offenbart sich durch die Geschichte, noch mehr: er geht selbst ein in die Geschichte und gibt ihr so jene ‚tiefere Weihe', die uns dazu verpflichtet, sie im letzten Sinne ernst zu nehmen."[11]

Der Weg zur Anerkennung der historischen Exegese fand somit nach der epochalen Enzyklika *Divino afflante Spiritu* (1943) in der Offenbarungskonstitution des Zweiten Vatikanischen Konzils nicht nur ihren definitiven Abschluss, sondern vor allem – fundamentaltheologisch gesprochen – die Überwindung der ihr immer noch zugrundeliegenden Blockadesituation. Erst die Formulierung eines geschichtlich-personalen Offenbarungsbegriffes, der auch miteinschließt, dass die Annahme und Weitergabe der Offenbarung geschichtlichen Charakter tragen muss, welcher wiederum einer geschichtlichen Forschung prinzipiell offen steht, ließ die zunächst nur zögernd eingeräumte Erlaubnis der historischen Forschung sich wandeln in eine dringende Empfehlung in DV 12 und in die Rede ihrer theologischen Unverzichtbarkeit. Es genügt, wenn ich darauf hinweise, dass *Dei Verbum* von den Hagiographen als „veri auctores" spricht, die möglichst exakte Erfassung des Literalsinnes zu erforschen fordert und das Thema Inspiration und Irrtumslosigkeit der Schrift positiv einbettet in die Formulierung, „dass alles, was die inspirierten Verfasser aussagen, als vom Heiligen Geist ausgesagt zu gelten" habe und deshalb „von den Schriften zu bekennen sei, dass sie sicher, getreu und ohne Irrtum die Wahrheit lehren, die Gott um unseres Heiles willen in den heiligen Schriften aufgezeichnet haben wollte" (DV 11).

Für viele überraschend schließt das Konzil im zweiten Absatz von DV 12 dann aber auch den Hinweis auf die Unverzichtbarkeit der klassischen Auslegungsregeln an (Stichworte: Einheit der Schrift, „analogia fidei", Tradition und Auslegungsgeschichte, usw.):

„Da die Heilige Schrift in dem Geist gelesen und ausgelegt werden muß, in dem sie geschrieben wurde [...], erfordert die rechte Ermittlung des Sinnes der hei-

---

11 Henri de Lubac, *Glauben aus der Liebe. Catholicisme [1938]* (Einsiedeln: Johannesverlag, ²1970), 145.

ligen Texte, daß man mit nicht geringerer Sorgfalt auf den Inhalt und die Einheit der ganzen Schrift achtet, unter Berücksichtigung der lebendigen Überlieferung der Gesamtkirche und der Analogie des Glaubens. Aufgabe der Exegeten ist es, nach diesen Regeln auf eine tiefere Erfassung und Auslegung des Sinnes der Heiligen Schrift hinzuarbeiten, damit so gleichsam auf Grund wissenschaftlicher Vorarbeit das Urteil der Kirche reift. Alles, was die Art der Schrifterklärung betrifft, untersteht letztlich dem Urteil der Kirche, deren gottergebener Auftrag und Dienst es ist, das Wort Gottes zu bewahren und auszulegen [...]. (DV 12,2.)

Das vermeintliche Zusammenspannen von uneingeschränkt positiv beurteilter historischer Exegese einerseits und traditioneller Schriftauslegung andererseits mochte in der Perspektive der 1960-er Jahre für manche als ein („fauler") Kompromiss erscheinen. Es erweist sich heute aber als Auftrag, eine sehr wohl mögliche Synthese zu vollziehen, und es ist gerade die Avantgarde der Bibelwissenschaft, die das erkannt hat. Joseph Ratzinger freilich hatte dies schon 1968 gesehen, wenn er in seinem DV-Kommentar im Ergänzungsband des LThK² mit der Kompromiss-Text-These ringt und schließlich resümiert: „Der Text [...] trägt natürlich die Spuren seiner mühsamen Geschichte, er ist ein Ausdruck vielfältiger Kompromisse. Aber der grundlegende Kompromiss, der ihn trägt, ist doch mehr als ein Kompromiss, er ist eine Synthese von großer Bedeutung: Der Text verbindet die Treue zur kirchlichen Überlieferung mit dem Ja zur kritischen Wissenschaft und eröffnet damit neu dem Glauben den Weg ins Heute"[12].

Das Ringen um die Offenbarungskonstitution und in ihr um die Anerkennung der historisch-kritischen Exegese fiel in eine Zeit nochmaliger Verhärtung und der Polemik. Erinnert sei an den sogenannten „Bibelstreit" um die Legitimität der historisch-kritischen Exegese, der in einer öffentlichen Debatte zwischen dem Alttestamentler Alonso Schökel und Antonino Romeo von der Lateranuniversität 1960 seinen Ausgang nahm und in der zwischenzeitlichen Zensurierung der Exegeten Zerwick und Lyonnet (jeweils von 1962 bis 1964) vom Bibelinstitut ein letztes Aufbäumen einer uneinsichtigen und geistlosen Exegese-Kritik mit sich brachte. Henri de Lubac stellte mit Recht fest, dass das Projekt einer Offenbarungskonstitution schon zu scheitern drohte, noch ehe sie überhaupt entworfen war.[13] So gesehen grenzt es fast an ein Wunder, dass den Konzilsvätern ein so abgerundetes Dokument gelang mit sachlichem und ausgewogenem Ton. Die Fixierung auf die Anerkennung der historisch-kritischen Exegese auch in der katholischen Kirche

---

12 Joseph Ratzinger, „Kommentar zur Einleitung und zu den Kapiteln I und II der Offenbarungskonstitution ‚Dei Verbum'", in: LThK² Erg.-Band II, 498–528, hier: 502 f., neu in: JRGS 7, 715–775, hier: 729.

13 Henri de Lubac, *Die göttliche Offenbarung*, 245.

ließ freilich leicht den wahren Fortschritt übersehen, der sich mit „Dei Verbum" auf der Ebene der Fundamentaltheologie vollzog. Dieser Fortschritt wird nicht zuletzt darin sichtbar, dass die wichtigen Grundsätze der Bibelhermeneutik und der Exegese gerade nicht in einer „Bibel-Konstitution", sondern eben in einer Offenbarungs-Konstitution grundgelegt sind. Die Grundlagen einer sachgemäßen Exegese lassen sich nur formulieren auf der Basis der allem vorausliegenden Bestimmung von Offenbarung als geschichtlichem und dialogischem Ereignis. Um auch dies mitwahrzunehmen, war die Zeit unmittelbar nach dem Konzil offenbar nicht reif. Dies änderte sich dann aber mit den kommenden Jahrzehnten und mit dem Nachrücken einer Exegeten-Generation, die sich die Legitimität der historisch-kritischen Exegese nicht mehr hatte erkämpfen müssen sondern sie wie selbstverständlich in Forschung und Lehre vermittelt bekommen hatte und sie entsprechend auch praktizierte. Auf diesen Generationenwechsel und den damit einhergehenden auch theologischen Mentalitätswandel hat vor kurzem erst im Kontext auch der Nachrufe auf Joachim Gnilka (1928–2018), seinen Vorgänger auf dem Lehrstuhl für neutestamentliche Exegese in München und im Übrigen auch meinen Lehrer im NT, Knut Backhaus hingewiesen.[14]

Ein wichtiger, auch quasi-lehramtlicher Schritt zur „Einholung" traditioneller, nicht un-kritischer aber eben doch den bloß historisch-kritischen Zugang überschreitender Zugangsweisen, oder sagen wir besser, die Einbettung der historischen Kritik in ein Gesamtverständnis der Schriftdeutung brachte das Schreiben der Bibelkommission mit dem Titel „Die Interpretation der Bibel in der Kirche" 100 Jahre nach der ersten Bibelenzyklika, 1993 mit einer Wiederanerkennung der Mehrdimensionalität des Schriftsinns.

3 Wiederanerkennung der Mehrdimensionalität des Schriftsinnes: „Die Interpretation der Bibel in der Kirche" (1993)

Das Schreiben erinnert unter anderem an neuere philosophische Hermeneutiken (genannt werden Rudolf Bultmann, Hans-Georg Gadamer und Paul Ricœur), die den Blick wieder geschärft hätten für den Zusammenhang von Text, Intention des Autors sowie Vollendung des Textes im Rezeptionsvorgang, ohne dass einer dieser Ansätze einfach unbesehen in eine biblische Hermeneutik übernommen werden könnte. Der Wert der hermeneutischen Reflexion wird aber vor allem darin gesehen, gegen einen historischen Positivismus wieder deutlich gemacht

---

14 Vgl. „Aufgegeben? Historische Kritik als Kapitulation und Kapital von Theologie" in: Zeitschrift für Theologie und Kirche 114 (2017): 260–288.

zu haben, dass bei der Deutung der biblischen Texte nicht objektive Kriterien im Sinne der Naturwissenschaften angewandt werden können, sondern dass es um ein Interpretieren von Geschehnissen und um Verstehen von Texten geht. Als ein erstes wichtiges Ergebnis, das sich aus der Auseinandersetzung mit der modernen Sprachwissenschaft und den philosophischen Hermeneutiken ergibt, wird die Mehrdimensionalität der Schriftsinne genannt: „Als Reaktion auf die Theorie des vielfachen Schriftsinnes hat die historisch-kritische Exegese mehr oder weniger offen die These eines einzigen Sinnes vertreten, derzufolge ein Text nicht gleichzeitig mehrere Bedeutungen haben kann. Das ganze Bemühen der historisch-kritischen Exegese geht dahin, *den* genauen Wort-Sinn dieses oder jenes biblischen Textes in der Situation seiner Entstehung zu bestimmen."[15] Dies lasse sich so nicht mehr halten.

Mittlerweile hat sich nach den Worten von Ludger Schwienhorst-Schönberger vor diesem Hintergrund ein Paradigmenwechsel in der alttestamentlichen Theologie vollzogen. Die traditionellen Methoden der Exegese wie typologische Schriftauslegung und christologische relecture werden nicht mehr als sachfremde Überformung abgetan, sondern als der Dynamik der Schriftwerdung der Schrift als Zeugnis der Glaubensgemeinschaft Israels und der Kirche angemessene Hermeneutik betrachtet.[16] Historisch-kritisch fragend wird man in einen Prozess des permanenten Wiederlesens hineingenommen bis hin zu einer *final form,* die letztlich nur als Ausdruck einer Glaubensgemeinschaft richtig verstanden werden kann. Georg Steins schließlich spricht von einer erheblich veränderten „hermeneutischen Großwetterlage"[17] aufgrund neuerer Literaturwissenschaftlicher Einsichten (Offenheit des Textes, Unabschließbarkeit der Lektüre, Rezeptionsästhetik). Vor diesem Hintergrund ist die Aktualität der in den traditionellen Worten[18] von DV 12 eher unbeholfen ausgedrückten Vision der gegenseitigen Ergänzung und Bereicherung von moderner Exegese und traditionell theologischer Schriftauslegung ganz neu in den Blick geraten. Steins spricht nicht nur davon, dass die Forderung nach Integration der spezifisch kirchlichen Auslegung mittlerweile

---

15 Bibelkommission, *Die Interpretation der Bibel,* (Citta del Vaticano: 1993): 68. Vgl. dazu Rudolf Voderholzer, *Die Einheit der Schrift und ihr geistiger Sinn* (Freiburg: Johannesverlag, 1998): 154 f.
16 Ludger Schwienhorst-Schönberger, „Einheit statt Eindeutigkeit. Paradigmenwechsel in der Bibelwissenschaft", in: HerKorr 57 (2003): 412–417.
17 Georg Steins, „Bibel im Gespräch. Die verkannte Offenbarungskonstitution Dei Verbum", in: HerKorr Spezial (Oktober 2005): 17–21, 19. Vgl. auch Helmut Hoping, „Wahrnehmung der Diachronie. Die Option des Konzils für die Geschichtswissenschaft, historisch-kritische Exegese und Glaubenshermeneutik", in: Hünermann/Hilberath, Herders Theologischer Kommentar (s. Anm. 2), Bd. 5 (Freiburg: Herder, 2009): 424–429.
18 Vgl. Steins, „Bibel im Gespräch".

durchaus „nicht mehr wissenschaftsfremd" wirke, sondern dass Schrift, Tradition und Kirche sich niemals trennen lassen, ja „eigentlich nur verschiedene Aspekte ein und desselben Phänomens der göttlichen Selbstmitteilung"[19] seien.

Mit alldem ist, wie mir scheint, nicht zuletzt über den Umweg profaner Literaturwissenschaft, ein wesentlicher Schritt zur Neuentdeckung auch der Lehre vom Vierfachen Schriftsinn getan. Bemerkenswerter Weise empfiehlt denn auch der 1993, im selben Jahr wie das Schreiben der Bibelkommission, in deutscher Sprache veröffentlichte Katechismus der Katholischen Kirche, für viele damals überraschend, in den Nummern 115 bis 119 diese klassische Theorie als umfassende Methode der Schriftauslegung.

III Die Lehre vom Vierfachen Schriftsinn als synthetische Theorie: Integration von Wissenschaft, Glaube und Mystik

Was besagt diese Lehre, die im Anschluss an den Apostel Paulus schon in der Frühen Kirche entwickelt, im Mittelalter systematisiert, von Martin Luther vehement abgelehnt und neuerdings als hochaktuell wiederentdeckt wurde?

Vorausgesetzt ist, dass die Bibel, ganz so, wie es *Dei Verbum* wieder formulierte, nicht als solche Offenbarung (und das Christentum deshalb auch keine Buchreligion) ist. Die Bibel ist vielmehr (vom Heiligen Geist inspiriertes) menschliches, genauer gesagt kirchliches *Zeugnis* der Offenbarung, die sich als Geschichte Gottes mit seinem Volk ereignet. Unüberbietbarer Höhepunkt dieser Geschichte ist das Christusereignis, das das Leben und Wirken, die Lehre, vor allem aber das Leiden, den Tod und die Auferstehung Jesu Christi umfasst. Die hebräische Bibel, für die Christen das Alte Testament, ist Christus-Zeugnis im Modus der Verheißung und Vorausverkündigung. Der auferstandene Herr selbst erschließt auf dem Weg nach Emmaus den Jüngern den Sinn der Schrift, indem er ihnen zeigt, dass Gesetz, Propheten und Psalmen von ihm reden (Lk 24,27.44). Im Anschluss an den Apostel Paulus (vgl. Gal 4,24) nennt man diesen christologischen Sinn des Alten Testaments auch den „allegorischen" Sinn. Weil ihn der Heilige Geist erkennen lässt, spricht man auch – wiederum mit Paulus (2 Kor 3,4–18) – vom „geistigen Sinn". In dieser *Zwei*heit von buchstäblichem (oder historischen) Sinn und (von Christus als Fülle der Offenbarung her erkennbaren) geistigem Sinn liegt

---

19 *Ibid.*

die Keimzelle von der Lehre vom *Vier*fachen Schriftsinn. Der vierfache Schriftsinn ist die Entfaltung des zweifachen Schriftsinns von historischem (oder buchstäblichem) und allegorischem (geistigem) Schriftsinn.

Dass historische Texte grundsätzlich deutungsoffen sind und vom Rezipienten in je neuen Kontexten neu und auch tiefer verstanden werden können, ist eine uralte Einsicht der Literaturwissenschaft. Dass ein (späterer) Leser in früheren Texten Gehalte entdecken kann, die die Intention des Autors übersteigen, ist für die Literaturwissenschaft keine Überraschung. Diese Einsicht findet in den letzten Jahrzehnten auch in der Theologie wieder neu Beachtung. Angewandt auf die Heilige Schrift bedeutet dies, dass erst mit der definitiven Neukontextualisierung der Schriften im Christusereignis deren Sinn vollends aufleuchtet, ohne dass der geschichtliche Anweg deswegen entwertet wäre. In der Exegese hat sich für diesen Sachverhalt der Terminus „relecture" eingebürgert: Im Neu- und Wiederlesen alter Texte enthüllt sich angesichts neuer Gotteserfahrung schon innerhalb der Geschichte Israels, besonders aber angesichts des eschatologischen Ereignisses von Tod und Auferstehung Jesu Christi, ein tieferer Sinn.

Jetzt aber direkt zur Lehre vom „vierfachen" Schriftsinn: Um sich die klassische Lehre leicht einprägen zu können, wurde sie im Mittelalter in einen rhythmischen Merkvers gegossen:

Littera gesta docet, quid credas allegoria.
Moralis quid agas; quo tendas anagogia.
(Der Buchstabe lehrt die Ereignisse; was du zu glauben hast, die Allegorie;
der moralische Sinn, was du zu tun hast; wohin du streben sollst, die Anagogie.)

1 Geschichte als Basis: Littera gesta docet

Schon ein erster Blick auf diesen vierteiligen Merkvers zeigt, dass es nicht um eine willkürliche Aneinanderreihung beliebiger Aspekte geht, sondern dass darin eine Struktur erkennbar wird, die den gesamten Glaubensvollzug umfasst: Die Schrift bezeugt ein Geschehen. Dieses Zeugnis (des Buchstabens) will im Leser und Hörer den *Glauben* wecken, der nun in der *Liebe* wirksam wird und in der *Hoffnung* auf die ewige Gemeinschaft mit Gott seinen letzten Ziel- und Orientierungspunkt hat.

Im Einzelnen: *Der Buchstabe lehrt die Ereignisse.* Dies besagt, dass die Heilige Schrift Alten und Neuen Testaments prinzipiell zu verstehen ist als Zeugnis einer geschichtlichen Offenbarung. Die Bibel ist Offenbarungszeugnis, insofern menschliche Autoren, vom Heiligen Geist inspiriert, in menschlichen Worten Ereignisse bezeugen, in denen sich Gott selbst kundtut: „Gottes Wort in Menschenwort" (1 Thess, 2,13). Die traditionelle Schriftauslegung ordnet dieser ersten Ebene den buchstäblichen Sinn zu.

Die Entwicklung der modernen Exegese bereichert die traditionelle Rede vom buchstäblichen Sinn um wichtige Einsichten: Nicht jeder biblische Text hat ein geschichtliches Ereignis im Blick. Es gehört schon zu den weitgehend einstimmig anerkannten Einsichten der Kirchenväter, dass die ersten und die letzten Seiten der Bibel, heute würde man sagen: die protologischen und die apokalyptischen Passagen, keinen wörtlich zu nehmenden historischen Sinn haben. Hinter diese Einsicht fallen leider fundamentalistische Kreise bis heute immer zurück und bringen damit oft die gesamte christliche Schriftdeutung in Verruf.

Man weiß heute aufgrund der Arbeiten der Gattungskritik darüber hinaus zu unterscheiden zwischen verschiedenen literarischen Formen, die jede Auslegung beachten muss. Wahr bleibt, dass christlicher Glaube sich nicht auf allzeit gültige philosophische Aussagen oder auf in Mythen und Märchen gekleidete menschliche Weisheiten stützt, sondern auf der Selbstoffenbarung Gottes in der Geschichte beruht. Dies wird in hohem Maße relevant bei der Deutung der Zentralgestalt christlicher Offenbarung, nämlich Jesu von Nazareth selbst.

2 Logos vor Ethos: quid credas allegoria

In seiner vielbeachteten Rede in den Vereinigten Staaten hat Kardinal Ratzinger dies 1988 unterstrichen und, mit Karl Barth,[20] eine Selbstkritik der Historisch-Kritischen eingefordert:

Der Exeget darf, wenn er seine Methode verantwortungsvoll handhabt, „nicht mit einer fertigen Philosophie an die Auslegung des Textes herantreten, nicht mit dem Diktat eines sogenannten modernen oder ‚naturwissenschaftlichen‘ Weltbildes, welches festlegt, was es geben und was es nicht geben darf. Er darf nicht a priori ausschließen, dass Gott in Menschenworten als er selbst in der Welt sprechen könne; er darf nicht ausschließen, dass Gott als er selbst in der Geschichte wirken und in sie eintreten könne, so unwahrscheinlich ihm dies auch erscheinen mag."[21] Viele vermeintliche Missverständnisse zwischen Exegese und Dogmatik dürften darauf zurückzuführen sein, dass manche Exegeten getarnt durch die Anwendung vermeintlich seriöser, historischer Methoden deistische, religionskritische Einsichten, damit aber eben ihre eigene Philosophie, für die Auslegung der Texte bestimmend sein ließen. Grundsätzlich bleibt festzuhalten, dass die Anwendung historischer Methoden zur Sinnerschließung nicht nur legitim ist,

---

20 Karl Barth, „Kritischer müssten mir die Historisch-Kritischen sein!", in *idem, Der Römerbrief* (Zürich: Theologischer Verlag Zürich, ²1922), Vorwort.
21 Joseph Ratzinger, *Schriftauslegung im Widerstreit* (Freiburg: Herder, 1989): 36, neu in: JRGS 9, 793–819, hier 811.

sondern theologisch gefordert. Der verschiedentlich zu beobachtende Relevanz-verlust der historischen Exegese heute, beginnend vielleicht schon mit der Kritik Eugen Drewermanns macht mir Sorgen.[22] Es darf keinen prinzipiellen Vorbehalt gegenüber der historischen Exegese geben, sie ist vielmehr ein notwendiger Schritt zur Sinnerschließung.

Was du zu glauben hast, die Allegorie: In einem zweiten Schritt, der seit dem Apostel Paulus mit „allegoria" bezeichnet wird, geht es um die theologische Deutung des geschichtlichen Ereignisses. Unter Allegorie versteht die Tradition der Schriftauslegung mit Paulus den theologischen Zugang zur Schrift, der auf dem historischen Fundament aufbaut und das geschichtliche Zeugnis auf die sich darin bekundende Selbstmitteilung Gottes befragt. „Die Allegorie baut den Glauben auf", wird Gregor der Große (gest. 604) sagen.

Seit Thomas von Aquin ist unstrittig, dass eine verbindliche Lehre in der Kirche nur von einer im Literalsinn bezeugten biblischen Grundlage her zu for-mulieren ist. Die Anwendung des geistigen Schriftsinnes beim Psalmenbeten (vgl. die Ober- und Untertitel in der aktuellen Ausgabe des Stundenbuches) oder – vorwiegend in Gestalt typologischer In-Beziehung-Setzung von alt- und neutes-tamentlichen Wirklichkeiten – in der liturgischen Gebetspraxis der Kirche (z. B. das Taufwasser-Gebet) ist durch den immer als notwendig erachteten Rückbezug auf die „Regula fidei" und den Einklang mit dem Credo der Kirche vor abwegiger Willkür geschützt.

Der in der Lehre vom Vierfachen Schriftsinn festgehaltene Primat des Glau-bens vor der Moral bewahrt den christlichen Glauben vor der Versuchung des Moralismus und der Werkgerechtigkeit, gibt andererseits der christlichen Moral-theologie und Sozialethik eine tragfähige und belastbare Basis im Glauben.

3 Geistlicher Tiefgang und eschatologische Perspektive: moralis quid agas, quo tendas anagogia

Denn mit der Erhebung des auf Gottes Heilshandeln antwortenden Glaubens ist für den Christen das Ziel der Schriftbegegnung noch nicht erreicht. Der über den buchstäblichen Sinn hinausgehende, „Allegorie" genannte Schriftsinn hat zwei weitere Aspekte in sich, die nicht einfach noch daraufgesetzt werden, sondern ein inneres Moment darstellen.

---

22 Aus der Fülle der Literatur zur Drewermann-Debatte nenne ich hier nur: Albert Görres, Wal-ter Kasper (Hg.), *Tiefenpsychologische Deutung des Glaubens? Anfragen an Eugen Drewermann* (= Quaestiones disputatae, Bd. 113) (Freiburg: Herder, ²1988).

Der moralische Sinn, was du zu tun hast: In der Schrift als ganzer und somit – zumindest grundsätzlich – auch in jedem Abschnitt ist auch Weisung zum rechten Leben enthalten. Die Schrift zielt auf die Verwandlung des Christen in einen liebenden Menschen ab. Der Glaube verwirklicht sich in der Liebe, sagt der Apostel Paulus (vgl. Gal 5,6).

Seinen Zielpunkt hat die Lehre vom Vierfachen Schriftsinn in der Eschatologie.

Wohin du streben sollst, die Anagogie: Anagogie, von griech. „ana" = „hinauf" und „agein" = „führen" ist eine Wortneuschöpfung und bezeichnet die letzte Dimension, in die sich das biblische Zeugnis erstreckt. Das in der Schrift bezeugte Wort Gottes baut nicht nur den Glauben auf und entfacht nicht nur die Liebe des Christen, sondern führt seinen gläubigen Blick immer auch hin zu den verheißenen und erhofften Gütern. Diese Abfolge der verschiedenen Dimensionen (Geschichte – Glaube – Handeln – Hoffen) dürfte über viele Jahrhunderte hinweg auch die Regel für eine christliche Predigt abgegeben haben auf der Basis der genannten Einsichten. Auch heute ist es nicht schlecht, diese zu beachten.

Weil es keinen Glauben ohne Hoffnung und ohne Liebe geben kann, bewegt der geistige Sinn der Schrift den Leser und Betrachter immer schon hin zu einem Leben in Glaube, Hoffnung und Liebe. Somit umfassen die drei über den buchstäblichen Sinn hinausgehenden Glieder insgesamt den „geistigen" Schriftsinn.

Zur Veranschaulichung der Lehre eignet sich das Beispiel „Jerusalem", das Johannes Cassian bereits im 5. Jh. zur Illustration des Vierfachen Schriftsinns herangezogen hat.[23]

Das vierfache Jerusalem

Es umgreift durch seine Weite irgendwie alle anderen möglichen Beispiele. Die Stadt Jerusalem kann nacheinander in einem vierfachen Sinn verstanden werden: 1. Jerusalem als historische Stadt ist der Schauplatz der Passion Jesu und damit Ort der Heilsgeschichte. 2. Im allegorischen Sinn kann Jerusalem als Sinnbild für die in Christus erneuerte Stadt Gottes (Civitas Dei) gelten. 3. Im moralischen Sinn bezeichnet sie die christliche Seele, in die der Herr Einzug halten will wie seinerzeit in das historische Jerusalem. Und schließlich 4. kennt schon die Apokalypse, und vorausgehend Jesaja, das Bild vom himmlischen Jerusalem als der Stadt der Vollendung.

---

23 Dieses Beispiel greift neuerdings auch auf: Christoph Böttigheimer, *Die eine Bibel und die vielen Kirchen. Die Heilige Schrift im ökumenischen Verständnis* (Freiburg: Herder, 2016): 318.

Nicht in jedem Wort oder jeder Perikope müssen alle vier Dimensionen enthalten sein. Entscheidend ist die Grundeinsicht und die aus ihr sich ergebende Dynamik: von der Geschichte zum Glauben, der sich in der Liebe verwirklicht und von der Hoffnung getragen ist.

Der Alttestamentler Norbert Lohfink hat schon in einer sehr frühen Publikation 1966 die Bedeutung der Lehre vom Vierfachen Schriftsinn mit folgenden Worten beschrieben: „Die uns heute so fremdartig anmutende Hermeneutik des Vierfachen Schriftsinns war nichts als ein genialer und durch viele Jahrhunderte hindurch praktizierter Versuch, jeden einzelnen Text immer vom Ganzen der Bibel her und auf das Ganze hin zu lesen und dabei nicht loszulassen, bis der Text so durchsichtig geworden war, dass er seine Bedeutung für die eigene Glaubensexistenz aufleuchten ließ."[24]

Und wenn Sie vielleicht gegenüber dem Urteil eines Jesuiten noch Vorbehalte haben, dann kann ich noch einen evangelischen Exegeten positiv ins Feld führen, nämlich Hans Hübner:

„Hätte mich jemand vor einigen Jahrzehnten gefragt, ob ich etwas Positives zur mittelalterlichen Lehre vom vierfachen Schriftsinn sagen könnte, ich hätte überlegen lächelnd, vielleicht sogar ein wenig von oben nach unten herab gesagt: ‚Fragen Sie doch einmal meinen Kollegen, vielleicht tut's der!' Vielleicht hätte ich als lutherischer Theologe auf Dr. Martin Luther, dessen frühe Bibelauslegung immerhin Thema meiner Dissertation war, verwiesen und hätte voller Stolz darauf aufmerksam gemacht, daß Luther auf dem Wege von seiner ersten Psalmenvorlesung (1513/15) zur Römervorlesung (1515/16) den vierfachen Schriftsinn, der doch Einfallstor für alle möglichen Auslegungssubjektivismen und Willkür sei, überwunden habe. Heute freilich schaue ich nicht mehr so despektierlich auf die sog. allegorische Schriftauslegung eines Philon von Alexandrien oder eines Origenes. Und heute scheint mir der bekannte mittelalterliche Zweizeiler über den vierfachen Schriftsinn gar nicht mehr als der Inbegriff aller Torheit (...). Natürlich, als Exeget einer theologischen Fakultät z. Z. des ausgehenden 20. Jahrhunderts lasse ich mich nicht mehr in das Prokrustesbett der mittelalterlichen Methodik hineinzwängen. Ich frage mich jedoch, ob sich nicht hinter all den Willkürlichkeiten, die unbezweifelbar durch die Praxis des mehrfachen Schriftsinnes produziert wurden, eine Wahrheit verbirgt, die zu bedenken uns unbedingt aufgegeben ist."[25]

24 Norbert Lohfink, *Bibelauslegung im Wandel. Ein Exeget ortet seine Wissenschaft* (Frankfurt a. M.: Knecht, ²1967): 23.
25 Hans Hübner, *Biblische Theologie als Hermeneutik. Gesammelte Aufsätze* (Göttingen: Vandenhoeck & Ruprecht, 1995): 286.

Die vier aufeinander bezogenen Sinndimensionen integrieren seriöse und unverzichtbare historische Wissenschaft und einen historisch-verantwortbaren Umgang mit den Texten mit dem im Glauben ernst zu nehmenden Anspruch der Texte selbst, in der Textendgestalt Ausdruck göttlicher Offenbarung zu sein, Gotteswort im Menschenwort.

Und diese Lehre integriert die gerade angesichts der oft beklagten geistlichen Fruchtlosigkeit einer bloß historisch-kritischen Zugangsweise die für christliche Schriftdeutung unverzichtbaren Dimensionen von Glaube, Spiritualität und Mystik.[26]

Welche Exegese braucht die Kirche? Wenn Sie mich fragen: Es müsste – nicht in sklavischer Wiederholung, aber doch von der wahren Intention geleitet – in diese vom vierfachen Schriftsinn abgesteckte Richtung gehen!

Bibliographie

Albrecht, Dieter (Bearb.), *Der Notenwechsel zwischen dem Heiligen Stuhl und der deutschen Reichsregierung, Bd. I, Von der Ratifizierung des Reichskonkordats bis zur Enzyklika „Mit brennender Sorge"* (= Veröffentlichungen der Kommission für Zeitgeschichte, Reihe A: Quellen, Bd. 1) (Mainz: Schöningh, 1965).

Backhaus, Knut, „Aufgegeben? Historische Kritik als Kapitulation und Kapital von Theologie" in: Zeitschrift für Theologie und Kirche 114 (2017), 260–288.

Barth, Karl, *Der Römerbrief*, (Zürich: Theologischer Verlag, ²1922).

Bibelkommission, Die Interpretation der Bibel (Città del Vaticano: 1993).

Böttigheimer, Christoph, *Die eine Bibel und die vielen Kirchen. Die Heilige Schrift im ökumenischen Verständnis* (Freiburg: Herder, 2016).

Claudel, Paul, „L'Écriture Sainte. Allocutions aux étudiants des Sciences Politiques" in: *La Vie Intellectuelle*, (Mai 1948): 6–14 (dt. in: Paul Claudel, *Ich liebe das Wort* (Recklinghausen: Paulus, 1955).

de Lubac, Henri, *Die göttliche Offenbarung* (Freiburg: Johannesverlag 2001).

de Lubac, Henri, *Glauben aus der Liebe. Catholicisme [1938]* (Einsiedeln: Johannesverlag ²1970).

---

26 Zur vertiefenden Befassung mit dem Thema verweise ich auf meine Dissertation *Die Einheit der Schrift und ihr geistiger Sinn* (Freiburg: Johannesverlag, 1998) und auf den Aufsatzband *Offenbarung, Tradition und Schriftauslegung. Bausteine zu einer christlichen Bibelhermeneutik*, (Regensburg: Verlag Friedrich Pustet, 2013). Vgl. auch Thomas Söding, „Kanonische Inspirationen. Fünf Antithesen, vom Neuen Testament aus entwickelt" in: Josef Rist (Hg.), *Wort Gottes. Die Offenbarungsreligionen und ihr Schriftverständnis* (= Theologie im Kontakt. Neue Folge, hg. v. Josef Rist in Verbindung mit Christof Breitsameter, Bd. 1) (Münster: Aschendorff, 2013): 53–63.

de Lubac, Henri, *Typologie. Allegorie. Geistiger Sinn. Studien zur Geschichte der christlichen Bibelhermeneutik* (= Sammlung Theologia Romanica) (Freiburg: Johannesverlag 2007, ³2014).

Gese, Hartmut, „Erwägungen zur Einheit der biblischen Theologie" in: Ders., *Vom Sinai zum Zion. Alttestamentliche Beiträge zur biblischen Theologie*, München: Chr. Kaiser, 1974): 11–30.

Görres, Albert/Kasper, Walter (Hg.), *Tiefenpsychologische Deutung des Glaubens? Anfragen an Eugen Drewermann* (= Quaestiones disputatae, Bd. 113) (Freiburg: Herder, ²1988).

Hieronymus, In Is. prol. (PL 24,17).

Hoping, Helmut, „Wahrnehmung der Diachronie. Die Option des Konzils für die Geschichtswissenschaft, historisch-kritische Exegese und Glaubenshermeneutik" in: Hünermann/ Hilberath, *Herders Theologischer Kommentar*, Bd. 5 (Freiburg: Herder, 2009), 424–429.

Hübner, Hans, *Biblische Theologie als Hermeneutik. Gesammelte Aufsätze* (Göttingen: Vandenhoeck & Ruprecht, 1995).

Hübner, Hans, *Hebräerbrief, Evangelien und Offenbarung*. Epilegomena (= Biblische Theologie des Neuen Testaments, Bd. III) (Göttingen: Vandenhoeck & Ruprecht, 1995).

Lohfink, Norbert, *Bibelauslegung im Wandel. Ein Exeget ortet seine Wissenschaft* (Frankfurt a. M.: Knecht ²1967).

Pesch, Rudolf, *Die Apostelgeschichte I* (= EKK V/I) (Zürich, Einsiedeln: Neukirchner Theologie, Patmos, 1986).

Pius XII., *Rundschreiben Divino afflante Spiritu vom 30. September 1943*, hg. vom katholischen Bibelwerk (Stuttgart: Katholisches Bibelwerk, 1962).

Raem, Heinz-Albert, *Pius XI. und der Nationalsozialismus*. Die Enzyklika „Mit brennender Sorge" vom 14. März 1937 (Paderborn: Schöningh, 1979).

Ratzinger, Joseph, „Kommentar zur Einleitung und zu den Kapiteln I und II der Offenbarungskonstitution ‚Dei Verbum'" in: LThK² Erg.-Band II, 498–528, neu in: JRGS 7, 715–775.

Ratzinger, Joseph, *Schriftauslegung im Widerstreit* (Freiburg: Herder, 1989), neu in: JRGS 9, 793–819.

Schwienhorst-Schönberger, Ludger, „Einheit statt Eindeutigkeit. Paradigmenwechsel in der Bibelwissenschaft" in: HerKorr 57 (2003), 412–417.

Söding, Thomas, „Kanonische Inspirationen. Fünf Antithesen, vom Neuen Testament aus entwickelt" in: Josef Rist (Hg.), *Wort Gottes. Die Offenbarungsreligionen und ihr Schriftverständnis* (= Theologie im Kontakt. Neue Folge, hg. v. Josef Rist in Verbindung mit Christof Breitsameter, Bd. 1) (Münster: Aschendorff, 2013).

Steins, Georg, „Bibel im Gespräch. Die verkannte Offenbarungskonstitution Dei Verbum", in: HerKorr Spezial (Oktober 2005): 17–21.

Voderholzer, Rudolf, *Die Einheit der Schrift und ihr geistiger Sinn* (Freiburg: Johannesverlag, 1998).

Voderholzer, Rudolf, *Offenbarung, Tradition und Schriftauslegung. Bausteine zu einer christlichen Bibelhermeneutik* (Regensburg: Verlag Friedrich Pustet, 2013).

V Synthesis

Joachim Eck

Converging and Diverging Lines in the Relationships between Isaiah and the Twelve

What can this volume teach us about Isaiah and the Twelve, and the exegesis of prophetic texts? Six of its contributions, those by F. Sedlmeier, U. Becker, J. Nogalski, R. J. Bautch, J. T. Hibbard and Chr. Hays, studied aspects or parts of the book of Isaiah and their relations to one prophet of the Twelve. B. M. Zapff treated Isa 40–55 and its relationship to the Twelve. Four articles, those by J. Eck, C. Dempsey, A. L. H. M. van Wieringen and H. G. M. Williamson, dealt each with variations of one specific theme occurring both in Isaiah and the Twelve. As a counterpoint to the scholarly work on specific problems within Isaiah and the Twelve, the *Festvortrag* by R. Voderholzer contributed fundamental thoughts on the role of exegesis, in particular of biblical prophets, for Christian faith.

While the individual results of these studies differ in accordance with the scope of their questions, methodological emphases and material analysed, an overall picture of certain tendencies can also be discerned. It is striking that F. Sedlmeier, U. Becker, J. Nogalski, B. M. Zapff and J. T. Hibbard agree in one important point. As far as similarities between Isaiah and the Twelve can be observed, they all come to the conclusion that these can hardly be explained by a personal relationship or encounter between the historic prophets whose names these prophetic books bear, or otherwise by mutual knowledge of their messages. Instead, those passages in Isaiah and the Twelve which show the clearest and most conspicuous agreements with each other were created in the course of the complex redactional processes which resulted in the final forms of the prophetic books concerned. In other words, quotations, references, echoes, shared terminology and other similarities are in most cases the outcome of an ongoing development comprising prophetic reading, transformative appropriation and scribal activity. Those who transmitted texts from one generation to the next, each time after revising it, gradually progressed to an increasingly unified interpretation of the prophetic messages. Although the surface of the traditional prophetic material they inherited would vary considerably, their own prophetic understanding of the theological depths of these messages, and their analyses of the courses of history in the light of faith, would allow them to discover a deep unity behind the manifold endeavours of earlier prophets, a unity, which they expressed by integrating their own prophetic words into older traditions.

https://doi.org/10.1515/9783110705799-014

Maybe the most obvious example of this tendency toward a unified reading of prophetic messages are the prophetic books' superscriptions, which are discussed in several articles of this volume. Such superscriptions are found in Isa 1:1 (as well as 2:1; 13:1), in Eze 1:2–3; Jer 1:1–3, and at the beginning of each prophetic book of the Twelve. While the oldest form of book headings may have comprised only a construct chain of two nouns (cf. above U. Becker) like e. g. Obd 1a, recent research has shown there are two main types of superscription,[1] the first of which uses the verbal phrase חזה על "to see against" [+ *a location*] in a relative clause following a varying title predicate (e. g. משׂא, דברי, חזון, etc.) in order to present the prophet as an actively perceiving subject of divine revelation (Isa 1:1; 2:1; 13:1; Am 1:1aα.b; Mi 1:1b; Hab 1:1), whereas the second main type uses the formula היה דבר יהוה אל "the word of YHWH happened to" [+ *a name of a prophet*] in order to underline that the word of the Lord is the active subject approaching a prophet for the purpose of revelation. The two traditions of book superscriptions are based on opposed concepts of what constitutes the essence of prophecy. The first, "visionary" type emphasizes the prophet's perception of divine matters and thus the importance of the prophet himself as a specially gifted human person, whereas the second, *dbr YHWH* type attributes all activity to the word of the Lord, which takes possession of and works through a human person exposed to divine power. Although the two types of superscription establish close connections between Isaiah, Amos, Habakkuk, on the one hand, and Jeremiah, Ezekiel, Hosea, Joel, Zephaniah, Jonah, Haggai and Zechariah, on the other hand, the opposition between these two groups was originally quite sharp. Now, the above considerations by F. Sedlmeier, U. Becker, and B. M. Zapff show from various perspectives that the final forms of the superscriptions in Isaiah and the Twelve do not only mirror the growth of the subsequent books (cf. U. Becker) but also and especially try to bridge gaps between the individual prophetic books (cf. F. Sedlmeier and B. M. Zapff). In this context, the chronological data noted in Isa 1:1; Hos 1:1; Am 1:1; Mi 1:1 and Zeph 1:1,[2] which have been identified as the result of late redactional activity, as well as the superscription Mi 1:1, which in its final form combines the two opposed types of superscriptions, are of particular importance as they mitigate the former opposition between the tradition emphasizing the prophet's visionary charism and the tradition interested in the active power of the word of the Lord. Thus, it is noteworthy that Hosea 1:1, as a superscription of the *dbr YHWH* type, is connected with Isa 1:1 and Am 1:1, which belong to the *visionary* type, by means

---

1 See the typological analysis of all prophetic book superscriptions by Eck, *Jesaja 1 – Eine Exegese der Eröffnung des Jesaja-Buches*, 28–61.
2 See also Jer 1,2–3; Eze 1,2.

of the names of the kings who reign in Judah/Israel during the prophets' ministry. The effect is that, in spite of differing concepts of prophetic mission, Hosea, Isaiah and Amos stand together and form a group of prophets who guarantee the authentic proclamation of YHWH's will under the Judean and Israelite kings of the 8th century BC. This unity is enhanced by Micah 1:1, which unifies the two opposed concepts in one superscription and, by its reference to Jotham, Ahaz and Hezekiah, presents Micah as a prophet of the younger generation after Amos, and as one who accompanies the ministries of Isaiah and Hosea. This group of prophets is succeeded by Zephaniah (and Jeremiah), to whom *the word of YHWH happened in the days of Josiah* (cf. Zeph 1:1; Jer 1:2). Although Zephaniah is thus *prima facie* a representative of the group who consider YHWH's word as the powerful subject of prophecy revealing itself through a human person, whereas Isaiah is presented in Isa 1:1 as *the* great visionary prophet, the contributions by J. Nogalski and Chr. Hays in this volume show, each one with his own focus and method, that there are nonetheless manifold intersections between these two prophets. While the text of Zephaniah is close to Isaiah, whose prophecies find a rich echo in Zephaniah, it seems that the superscription in Zeph 1:1 aligns this book as a whole to Hosea so that it can function as a bridge between the latter and Isaiah.

This and other examples in this volume show that Isaiah and the book of the Twelve are neither two disconnected texts detailing their own prophetic messages independently, nor just two books expressing the same messages in two different rhetoric styles. On the one hand, all present articles observe important differences throughout. On the other hand, it is interesting that these differences, which can often be assigned to earlier stages in the development of the prophetic books, were brought into communication with each other by means of certain bridges and connections. These could in part be consciously elaborated and developed by redactional activities, but they might also result from the dynamics of ongoing conversations and debates on the basis of shared traditions among prophetic groups. Prophetic debates could lead to the integration of topoi authored by earlier prophets into a largely oral process of reflection and discussion. In this process, those topoi could undergo a gradual and sometimes even unconscious transformation. It is remarkable that contrasts between different prophetic messages were not just wiped out but integrated into a lively dialogue. Evidence of these dynamics can be found not only in the various stages of textual growth within each prophetic book, but it is also and particularly documented by cross-references, common concepts and intertextual allusions between different prophetic books, as the present studies of Isaiah and the Twelve illustrate in many ways.

An example how a deliberate redactional reshaping of one prophetic book under the influence of another one might look like is given by Becker, who assumes that so-called social-critical texts in the book of Isaiah are not primarily the work of Isaiah himself but mainly later redactional compositions created under the influence of the tradition of Amos. In a comparable approach, Sedlmeier explains for Isaiah and Hosea that the two historic prophets' messages had only few similarities, among which the most prominent one is a theological turn from salvation to judgement, but certain links between the Isaianic and Hoseanic traditions were created by the redactions of the two prophetic books. A different pattern to explain similarities is proposed by Hays. He proves that Isa 24–27 and Zephaniah share an astonishingly broad field of vocabulary. Yet, only few shared ideas or phrases are so closely interconnected that it would be possible to make a case for direct dependency. Nonetheless, the amount and types of shared elements are so significant that they call for explanation. Therefore, he proposes the two literary works could be created by circles of early prophetic scribes who lived in the same period and drew on the same prophetic sources. This evaluation of the relationship between Isa 24–27 and Zephaniah has something in common with the conclusion which J. T. Hibbard draws from his analysis of the relationship between Zechariah 14 and the end of the book of Isaiah. On the one hand, he agrees with Steck, Bosshard, Gärtner, and Nogalski that Zechariah 14 shares a number of themes with the concluding part of Isaiah, which might therefore have influenced Zechariah. But, after comparing relevant statements on the inclusion of the nations into Israel's worship, the glorification of Jerusalem, YHWH's retribution on his enemies, and YHWH's kingship, he finds the roles which these shared themes play in the prophetic discourses are so different that Isaiah's influence on Zech 14 should be considered as minimal.

As these and other examples illustrate, it is a crucial feature of references to earlier tradition that they tend to be dynamic in nature. It is quite uncommon to repeat earlier messages merely in their original form.[3] Rather, they tend to be re-formulated, re-edited and/or re-contexualized. Zapff notes in his conclusion (point 5 no. 6) that statements or quotations from Deutero-Isaiah, when adopted in the Book of the Twelve, are isolated from their original context and re-contextualized to speak to a changed theological and political situation. This is not only true for Deutero-Isaiah but can, for example, also be observed in the reception of Isaiah's Vineyard Song (Isa 5:1–7) in Isa 7:23–25; 27:2–6 and Mi 7 as discussed by J. Eck. While the reference to this famous Isaianic word of judgement in Isa 7:23–25 serves as a redactional means of highlighting a first step in the fulfillment of this prophecy, Isaiah 27:2–6 endeavours to reverse the fatal verdict, and the concluding chapter of Micah marks the complete fulfillment of the prophecy of doom so that it can now be turned against the enemy who destroyed the female

---

3 Isa 2:2–5//Mi 4:1–5 are an exception, and even here, the differences are significant.

speaker (often identified with Zion). Both the announcement of the fulfillment of the prophecy of Isa 5:1–7 and its recontextualization give evidence of the long-lasting performative power which was attributed to a prophet's word. Since the negative consequences of a prophecy of doom could endure even for centuries after its proclamation, it was necessary to transform its power by announcing its fulfillment and turning its disastrous impact against enemies. Similar dynamics of an ongoing transformative dialogue can be noted in J. Nogalski's contribution on the role of Lady Zion in Zeph 3:11–20 and Isaiah 40–66. The two texts share the personification of Jerusalem as Lady Zion, they announce divine salvation and exhort her to rejoice, and they refer, albeit with different nuances, to YHWH as divine warrior. Nogalski affirms these shared motifs suggest the authors involved had at least some awareness of each other, but above all he underlines there are considerable differences in the way that these motifs are integrated and develop in each text. While Isaiah's personification of Zion integrates aspects of the city into the image of Zion as YHWH's bride and mother of children, Zephaniah's Lady Zion lacks these relational qualities. In Zeph 3:11–20, she is neither bride nor mother, but YHWH returns to her as a triumphant warrior king in order to gather a humbled people.

Another approach to describing relationships between different prophetic traditions and discourses was applied by R. Bautch in his article on intertextual backgrounds to Zechariah 11. Although the existing phraseological links between Zech 11:1–3,4–17, on the one hand, and Isa 10:16–19,33–34, on the other hand, are not so substantial as to support a hypothesis proposing direct dependency, it is notable that a reading of Zechariah's chapter which takes into account the situations and meanings of certain shared phrases occurring in Isa 10:16–19,33–34, as well as in Neh 10 and Jer 11:1–17, succeeds in deciphering some enigmatic traits of the text and comprehending the two prophecies in Zech 11:1–3 and 11:4–17, which at first glance might seem unrelated to each other, as a profound unity.

The above reflection on results emerging from the contributions to this volume shows that two or several prophetic texts may sometimes even communicate in a certain way with each other by means of shared phrases or other linguistic elements although they deal with quite different themes. Another, no less frequent pattern is that the prophetic discourses in Isaiah and the Twelve may circle around recurring themes which undergo a dynamic development across various prophetic scriptures in a process of adaptation and variation. The interpretation of both phenomena is a rewarding exegetical task.

The articles by J. Eck (see already above), A. L. H. M. van Wieringen and H. G. M. Williamson dedicated themselves particularly to the second one of the above-mentioned tasks and examined recurring themes functioning as pivot points of prophetic communication. Van Wieringen studied the oracles against the nations in Isaiah, Amos and Zephaniah from a text-immanent reader's perspective and came to the conclusion that, although the nations criticized and the contents of each prophet's critique vary considerably, the ultimate focal point of this genre of oracles is a critique of Jerusalem/Zion. Thus, the prophecies of doom against the nations, which at first glance appear to be favourable to Israel because the condemned ones are their enemies, assume a quite different meaning in the light of the words spoken against Jerusalem/Zion. When all three series of oracles against the nations underline at their end that Jerusalem/Zion is guilty of at least as grave iniquities as the nations, the latters' crimes are turned into a spiritual mirror visualizing the burden of Jerusalem's own sins and thus inviting the text-immanent reader to self-criticism. A comparable turn in the meaning of a concept was observed by H. G. M. Williamson in the course of his diachronic study of those prophecies in Isaiah and the Twelve which relate to the Day of YHWH. Here, a transformation of the original significance of this concept stands at the very beginning of its prophetic use. The reference by Amos (5:18) to the Day of YHWH presupposes an already well-known concept originally implying light to Israel and darkness to its oppressors. Reversing the idea, Amos proclaimed it would come as an event of divine judgement against Israel. Similarly, according to Isaiah (2:12,11b,17b) the Day of YHWH brings down what is proud and high in Judah so that the Lord alone shall be exalted. Zephaniah's use of the concept (1:7,14) shares this basic meaning, albeit with an emphasis on Judah's cultic sins. A transformation of the motif which reorients it to its original understanding is found in the primary layer of Isa 13 (vv. 2–3, 6–8, 14–16, 17–22), where YHWH's day of judgement is turned against the arrogance of Babylon (cf. the similar role of Edom in Isa 34; 63,1–6). Although Joel 1–2 dates more or less from the same period, this text retains the idea of a day of judgement against Judah. In the later, universalist layer of Isa 13, as well as in Joel 3–4, the Day of YHWH becomes an event of cosmic judgement against all the nations, a proto-eschatological expectation which is also echoed in Obad 15; Zech 14 and possibly Mal 3:23. An important insight conveyed by Williamson's study is that literary dependence does not necessarily coincide with identity of concepts. Unique phraseology taken over from young texts may qualify a prophecy as even younger but, at the same time, it may have retained or restored an older concept (see e. g. the discussion of Joel). In theological terms, this means the hope that YHWH will reveal his sovereignty by liberating his faithful ones from oppressors is a kind of *basso continuo* accompanying the prophetic objection that this hope must transmute into an expectation of judgement as soon as faith is perverted into a hubris which is typical of YHWH's enemies. With this belief becoming more and more detached from transitory political hopes associated with human powers, a universal and eschatological perspective gains weight and proves itself as the ultimate truth of faith in YHWH.

This eschatological dimension of some prophetic messages represents an orientation towards the future which, in a way, is also adopted by certain hermeneutical approaches to biblical interpretation. Such approaches mostly do not content themselves with researching the meaning which prophecies had in their original historical contexts but emphasize the question of what they imply for the solution of problems of the present and future. The hope that the study of biblical texts is able to contribute to the solution of current problems will, in many cases, have its deepest roots in the biblical belief that the reign of God is about to come, a belief which finds one of its most pregnant expressions in proto-eschatological prophecies. A hermeneutical approach of this kind is applied in the present volume by C. Dempsey in her contribution on divine and human kingships in Isaiah and the Twelve. By analysing both historic implications and present uses of prophecies concerning kingship, the article pursues to unmask oppressive applications and highlight liberating aspects of biblical texts on kingship for readers now and then, and deals with the question of how such biblical visions may help to inform and transform our present global world. In this context, the prophetic ideal of a divine kingship in justice and righteousness is a timeless hope of biblical faith. However, Dempsey also identifies some aspects in the applied imagery which may be subject to abuse and thus inhibit the advent of this hope.

The experience that texts can be abused by way of inadequate interpretation raises the issue of an adequate hermeneutical framework guiding interpreters to a both enriching and intellectually sound comprehension of prophetic texts. While the scholarly disciplines of biblical studies are subject to binding guidelines which intend to ensure that the academic work is compliant with human reason and intellect, theological disciplines such as biblical exegesis and related fields do not only address questions of general scholarly interest but also and particularly questions which are relevant to communities of faith. This is not a limitation but an advantage for the authentic interpretation of biblical texts since these were written for communities of faith from their very beginning. In spite of deep cultural differences and historical changes by which present communities of faith are distinguished from those of biblical times, the attitude of faith in the biblical God has an existential quality which is timeless, and for this reason, the essence of many of the questions posed then and now also remains at least similar. It was therefore of common interest to the interdenominational conference on Isaiah and the Twelve to listen to the scholarly view of a Christian minister who had specialized in questions of biblical hermeneutics before being ordained a Catholic bishop. In his *Festvortrag* on the question of what kind of exegesis may correspond to the needs of the church, R. Voderholzer exemplified the relevance of biblical prophets for Christian faith from its very beginnings. In order to be aware, understand, describe the multiple aspects and dynamics of communication between biblical witnesses, writers and addressees, Voderholzer recommends to reconsider the classical doctrine of the fourfold sense of scripture as a synthetic theory which integrates science, faith and mysticism. In this scheme, the literal sense is the domain to be researched by reason and thus constitutes the main field of historio-critical study. The allegorical sense is a hermeneutical approach on the basis of faith. Since faith is a response to the proclamation of the gospel of salvation, an interpretation of biblical texts exploring the allegoric dimension has intrinsic affinities with reader-(or hearer-)response criticism. In line with the biblical principle that ethics are an answer to faith, and cannot grow out of a moralizing attitude alone, the third domain of the fourfold sense includes those aspects which provide ethical guidance to the faithful. This domain corresponds to a whole set of current hermeneutical approaches to biblical studies which have a particular focus on ethical issues in the ancient text. The fourth domain called anagogic comprises hope for the future on the basis of divine promises, including the eschatological perspective. When reflecting on this last dimension of meaning, it appears to be not particularly associated with specific methodological approaches but an attitude of confidence founded on the testimony of God's faithfulness to his promises. It will result in a reading sensitive to and emphasizing the manifold aspects of hope in the biblical text.

Regarding the subject of this volume, the classical doctrine of the fourfold sense of scripture describes in a systematized way certain types of interpretive approaches already present in the relectures of prophetic words or themes which are typical of the relationship between Isaiah and the Twelve. Complementary to Voderholzer's presentation of a Christ-centered interpretation of Jerusalem by J. Cassianus, the role of Zion in the two corpora gives an example of how the four dimensions of sense unfold in the process of interpretation and re-interpretation. The name of Zion is used in a literal sense where it designates the mountain of God's dwelling, e. g. in Isa 8:18. A similar literal use is attested in Mi 4:7, where the mountain of Zion is the seat of YHWH's kingship. In other texts, e. g. Isa 1:27, Zion occurs as a *pars pro toto* for the city of Jerusalem. This use forms the basis for the allegoric role of Zion as a personified female character in Isa 40–55. Zion is here depicted as YHWH's wife and mother of many children, to whom YHWH personally promises salvation (see Nogalski above). This representation of Lady Zion is an allegory based on Israel's belief that God will neither forsake the place where he resides nor, by extension, the faithful ones who trust him. Developing a perspective of hope out of the relationship between JHWH and Zion, it intends to strengthen faith in YHWH. When Nogalski observes that Zephaniah, although sharing with Isaiah the personification of Zion as a woman, does not attribute to her the same relational qualities, this appears to serve the intention of reducing the weight of this allegory to the benefit of the aspect of ethical purification

(Zeph 3:11–13) and the image of YHWH approaching as a royal warrior in order to save Zion (Zeph 3:15–17). The combination of the allegory of Lady Zion with an announcement of ethical purification thus prepares a second allegory emphasizing the anagogic perspective of final salvation.

While acknowledging that academic interpretation does make its own, specifically intellectual contribution to illuminating the multiple dimensions of sense in the Bible, it should not be forgotten that some aspects are better served by the creative and performative approaches of the arts and liturgy. As the present studies in Isaiah and the Twelve illustrate, the liveliness of the ongoing dialogues among prophetic circles which have resulted in these books, their richness in interpretative approaches to prophetic traditions, and their productive creativity in the proclamation of the divine word can be an intellectual fountain and a spiritual encouragement for choosing to advance on a way inspired by the bibilical scriptures. Ultimately, their deepest and most universal sense needs to be lived, and to this kind of fulfilment, biblical studies can be no more, but no less either, than a preparatory exercise.

List of Contributors

Richard J. Bautch
Prof. of Humanities
St. Edward's University
Austin
Texas

Uwe Becker
Prof. für Altes Testament
Friedrich-Schiller-Universität
Jena

Carol J. Demsey, OP
Prof. of Biblical Studies
University of Portland
Oregon

Joachim Eck
Dr., Akad. Rat. am Lehrstuhl für Altes
Testament
Katholische Universität Eichstätt-Ingolstadt
Eichstätt

Christopher B. Hays
Associate Prof. of Ancient Near Eastern
Studies
Fuller Theological Seminary
Pasadena
California

J.Todd Hibbard
Associate Prof. of Religious Studies
University of Detroit Mercy
Detroit
Michigan

James Nogalski
Director of Graduate Studies
Prof. of Hebrew Bible/Old Testament
Baylor University
Waco
Texas

Franz Sedlmeier
Prof. für Alttestamentliche Wissenschaft,
Universität Augsburg
Augsburg

Rudolph Voderholzer
Prof. für Dogmatik
Bischof von Regensburg
Regensburg

Archibald L. H. M. van Wieringen
Prof.
Department of Biblical Sciences and Church
History
Tilburg School of Catholic Theology
Tilburg

Hugh G. M. Williamson
Emeritus Regius Prof. of Hebrew
Christ Church
Oxford

Burkard M. Zapff
Prof. für Alttestamentliche Wissenschaft
Katholische Universität Eichstätt-Ingolstadt
Eichstätt

Index